D0148650

The Growth of the Liberal Soul

The
Growth
of the
Liberal
Soul

David Walsh

UNIVERSITY OF MISSOURI PRESS
COLUMBIA AND LONDON

Copyright © 1997 by
The Curators of the University of Missouri
University of Missouri Press, Columbia, Missouri 65201
Printed and bound in the United States of America
All rights reserved
5 4 3 2 1   01 00 99 98 97

Library of Congress Cataloging-in-Publication Data

Walsh, David, 1950–
    The growth of the liberal soul / David Walsh.
        p.   cm.
    Includes bibliographical references (p.   ) and index.
    ISBN 0-8262-1082-1 (alk. paper)
    1. Liberalism.   I. Title.
JC574.W37   1997
320.51'3—dc21   96-48462
                                                    CIP

∞™ This paper meets the requirements of the
American National Standard for Permanence of Paper
for Printed Library Materials, Z39.48, 1984.

Designer: Mindy Shouse
Typesetter: BOOKCOMP
Printer and Binder: Thomson-Shore, Inc.
Typefaces: Galliard and Imago

Publication has been generously supported by the Earhart Foundation.

To Katie, Brendan, and Patrick

Contents

Acknowledgments

It is almost a sufficient incentive to publish a book to be given the opportunity to thank all those whose support made the work possible. My students and colleagues at Catholic University were the first and most tolerant recipients of my efforts to develop the ideas contained herein. The hospitality provided by various other institutions and organizations provided an opportunity to road test the approach. In particular I would like to single out the annual summer institutes at Rose Hill College in South Carolina, under the indomitable leadership of Owen Jones. The manuscript itself received a careful reading from Brendan Purcell at an early stage of its development and, subsequently, an insightful review from the readers selected by the Press, Barry Cooper and Josh Mitchell. To all three I am deeply grateful. I am sincerely appreciative of the warm welcome the work received from Clair Willcox, acquisitions editor at the University of Missouri Press, and for the skillful copyediting provided by Annette Wenda. Compilation of the index was graciously undertaken by Linda Raeder. I wish to thank *Modern Age* for permission to reprint "Truth and the Problem of a Liberal Tradition." Financial support to undertake the project was generously provided by the Bradley Foundation and the Earhart Foundation, as well as through a sabbatical leave from Catholic University. As always, I thank the unfailing support of my wife, Gail, and dedicate this book to our three children.

The Growth of the Liberal Soul

Introduction

The most striking feature of the liberal political order is that it is still not understood. This is so despite the historic success of the liberal tradition that has now become global, in the disappearance of all rival models of political legitimacy. With the collapse of communism, the last competitor with any moral or intellectual credibility, there is now no challenge to the liberal definition of what is politically right. There continue to be numerous political challengers to the liberal conception of politics, but their naked exercise of power cannot stand before the glare of public scrutiny. Lacking an ideology, power invariably reveals its instability and is succeeded by equally precarious claimants to its exercise. Liberal politics has emerged as the undisputed touchstone of the good in politics.

Yet the liberal tradition, at this moment of its most universal triumph, seems to be afflicted with a confusion more profound and more pervasive than at any time in its history. This is the case despite the number and talent of contemporary thinkers, across the political spectrum, who have lavished their attention on the nature of the liberal construction in recent years. We are further than ever in the long historical tradition from a consensus on the meaning and character of liberal political order, and this theoretical confusion is mirrored by the ever widening cleavages within liberal democratic society and politics. Assaulted by a cacophony of rights claims and a bewildering profusion of political visions, we are left without any reliable means of deciding between them or even determining the outcomes toward which they are likely to lead. The sense of being cast adrift without a rudder to steer or a direction to follow has become pervasive. This impression has, of course, much to do with the disappearance of an enemy against whom the "free" world could measure itself, but its roots lie deeper still within the nature of the liberal tradition itself.

1

Suspicions about its vacuity cannot but be reinforced when one contemplates the strange inability of virtually all exponents to identify the sustaining strength of the liberal democratic tradition. To follow the analyses of contemporary commentators on liberal politics, both critics and defenders, one could conclude only that the liberal political tradition is of such an insubstantial nature that its demise is either long overdue or imminently likely. The view of its critics, of an impossibly precarious house of cards, seems to be confirmed in the incoherent foundations adduced by its defenders. No one could reasonably bet on the survival of liberal political order, and it is even something of a mystery that it does not instantly fly apart under its centrifugal tendencies. One misses any realistic sense of what it is that accounts for the solidity, durability, and resilience of liberal democratic regimes that are, after all, still with us and that are now without prospect of any alternative on the horizon. By focusing on the failings we miss what has constituted the success of liberal politics and, as a consequence, have deprived ourselves of the most realistic means available for dealing with the same undeniable failings.

It is this disconnection from the capacity of liberal formulations to evoke, even today and even in the midst of the manifest difficulties, a responsive concrete assent that is the source of the unreality in most contemporary academic discussions. Whether it is the espousal of neutrality as a sufficient ground of support for the liberal paradigm or the pragmatist retreat from the search for all sources of justification, the distance from actual political practice is the most remarkable feature of the debates. What they fail to recognize is that there would be no political order at all, liberal or any other, unless it were experienced by those who support and sustain it as legitimate and worthy of their participation. No variation on the theme of self-interest can explain what it is that compels human beings to support an order that depends on such support precisely when it is in conflict with the satisfaction of interest. The inability of liberal theorists to explain what holds liberal political regimes together is a long-standing difficulty, but the challenge has been intensified by the narrowing of the debate to rarefied philosophical articulations of the possible justifications. That line of reflection has ended, predictably, in a progressive narrowing to the point of extinction of all possible reasons.

But a parallel disconnection seems to occur when the problems are approached from outside the liberal tradition, from a critical vantage point rooted in earlier religious or philosophical traditions. Recognizing the distorting tendencies within the liberal promotion of rights at the expense of duties, the inclination of theorists has been to propose a return to the more robust emphasis on individual and civic virtue as the means of reinvigorating a moribund liberal politics. The call for a return to traditional values has become a staple of political rhetoric. A new emphasis on the education of virtue and a recognition of individual responsibility represents an important political factor on the contemporary scene. The individual is depicted no longer solely as a rights claimant but as a member of a concrete community to which and from which certain relationships of obligation are binding. This is often associated with a "conservative" orientation within politics, but the appeal of communal virtues is by no means absent from left-wing inclinations. The partisan affiliations are, however, quite secondary to the central problem of the unreality of the announced prescriptions.

Proposed correctives consist of exhortations to virtue that are utterly innocent of the means of achieving it. The objection that the rhetoric of virtues and values is simply rhetoric arises because the appeal is made without reference to the concrete social world in which we live. Virtue cannot be created through exhortation, no more than through governmental fiat. Calls for a return to the communal sense and setting of yesteryear betray, by their utopian nostalgia, the absence of any connection with the world in which we now live. Such cries are bound to remain ineffectual until we begin to understand why traditional worlds were left behind, what it is that constitutes the focus of moral authority within the contemporary liberal evocation, and how the sources of dissatisfaction within it might be used as a means of enlarging the constricted moral horizons of our day. Simply haranguing the deficiencies of contemporary liberal politics in the name of abstract virtues is only a way of demonstrating one's irrelevance.

In the case of neither the increasingly attenuated philosophical discussions of justification nor the shrill irrelevance of the appeals for traditional and communal values does one have a sense of the substantial amplitude of actual liberal practice. The mystery is that liberal politics works at all given, in the view of so many commentators, either its superficiality or its bankruptcy. Nowhere in these voluminous debates is there the slightest hint of the genius of the liberal arrangement that has limited and refined its moral appeal as the means of evoking the widest and least-contested responsiveness, or that it is this dual strategy of refinement that has been the secret of its evident strength and durability. Liberal political order, whatever its limitations, is a remarkable political achievement functioning, as it does, as the only publicly authoritative moral language on the world scene today. This is the core of the liberal phenomenon, and any adequate attempt to come to grips with it must recognize this inner moral appeal. Only in that way can we understand the secret of liberal political success, the durability and resilience that have enabled it to defy all the historical odds in conflicts with numerous competitors from monarchy to communism. It is in order to take stock of this formidable strength of the liberal tradition in the hope of gaining some insight into the means of extending it that the present study is undertaken.

The expansive nature of the subject matter itself dictates the utilization of the term *liberal*, with all the multiplicity of attendant meanings, to identify the core of the issue to be investigated. It is a necessity because the liberal tradition is not a fixed quantity, and the proliferation of definitions accurately reflects the changeable nature of the political reality itself. At the same time, one should recognize that the term *liberal* is not simply equivocal. Its various meanings can be more or less intelligibly related on a spectrum of interpretations. These meanings coalesce around the core emphasis on individual liberty as the beginning and the end of political order and vary in their assessments of the impediments to the full exercise of that liberty and the correlative means of removing or ameliorating such obstacles. At every stage the source of the moral appeal remains the promotion of self-determination as the route to the growth of the person. In this sense, the liberal tradition is not a self-contained persuasion but is in continuity with the discovery of the soul through philosophy and its transcendent fulfillment through revelation. Specification of the movement toward transcendence as a political form and language is, however, a distinctly modern achievement.

The term *liberal* as a political self-designation is of relatively recent vintage, its first prominent usage occurring with the Spanish party of Liberales in 1812. As it became the name for political movements and parties throughout the nineteenth century, liberalism became more self-consciously recognizable as a tradition whose sources lay very far back in history indeed. The most evident line of transmission was the Whig political tradition that was decisively shaped by the Glorious Revolution of 1688 and that in turn had roots back through the common-law tradition, medieval constitutional forms, and the republican foundations of the ancient world. The nineteenth-century liberal thinkers of course saw themselves as doing something different, in the context of the movement toward mass participation in government and society, than those engaged in the seventeenth- and eighteenth-century struggles against royal absolutism. The twentieth century has in turn modified the meaning of *liberal* to invoke the necessity of government intervention to promote and protect individual liberty—especially liberty of opportunity. As a result, the term *liberal* must support varying and often conflicting interpretations, such that conservatives often claim they are the true liberals and their opponents counter that to be truly liberal requires the departure from earlier conceptions. The shifting interpretations of *liberal,* in other words, are not simply semantic; they are of the essence of the political conflicts themselves. What is most noteworthy in the whole process is the degree to which there continues to be a consensus on the goal by which such political divergences are to be measured. In a curious way the continuing disagreements over the meaning of *liberal* attest the continuity of the underlying tradition that, in the absence of an alternative, we too are compelled to identify as the *liberal tradition*.

The difficulty in obtaining an exact designation arises from the diffuse nature of a movement that began in the sixteenth century and reaches all the way to the present, while drawing into itself the essential residue of the millennial Western conjunction of Greek philosophy with Judaism and Christianity. The need for a self-designation was clearly a later development when this movement became conscious of its opposition to other alternatives, as in the situation that arose with the ideological movements beginning in the nineteenth century. It is at that point that the liberal tradition became designated as one of the "isms." We are therefore inevitably compelled to use the singularly ugly denomination *liberalism* because it arises within the intellectual and political debates. But we must always do so with the recognition that the liberal construction is not really one of the closed ideological systems that have competed for dominance in the last two centuries. The tradition's more extensive historical lineage and its broader political appeal testify to its difference from the narrowly ideological passions now thankfully on the wane. But this still does not solve the problem of the most adequate conceptual definition, since such other alternatives as the "constitutional tradition" or "the rights tradition" are too narrow, while the utilization of "modernity" or the "modern political tradition" are too broad. We are left with the only overarching self-designation, *liberal,* which is used to describe the sense of what is so self-evidently right that an exact definition is deemed unnecessary.

It is this ubiquity, the inescapability of the measure of liberty, that is the most powerful testament to the strength of the liberal construction. Even when the disputes draw on the broader perspectives of virtue or of law, the extent to which the argument turns on the liberal conception of the enhancement or the contraction of human dignity is remarkable. The disagreements emerge, not so much in opposition to liberal formulations, as disagreements within or about the meaning of the liberal determinations. This does not mean that all the older spiritual and intellectual traditions now must submit before the bar of liberal judgment. Rather, the apparent superiority is a natural outgrowth of the degree to which liberal philosophy has itself arisen as a differentiation of the subjective or interior dimension of the earlier traditions. Freedom, dignity, and self-determination become pivotal within a context in which they are the crucial preconditions for growth in virtue and obedience to the divine law. The liberal specifications, far from constituting a break with the earlier traditions, may more properly be viewed as a differentiation within philosophy and Christianity.

The character of a differentiation explains why, as I will try to show, liberal convictions can operate so well as a practice without a coherent theoretical formulation. The nature of the liberal political tradition, as primarily a pragmatic and relatively unreflective enterprise, has long been observed, and I will draw on the most profound contemporary recognition of it in the work of Michael Oakeshott. Where I go beyond this practical understanding of liberal politics is in extrapolating the underlying dynamic. Instead of treating the acknowledgment of the practical characterization of liberal order as the limit of theoretical penetration, I regard it as the starting point for an expansive illumination of the inner meaning that sustains and supports it. In this way

I hope to show how the theoretically incomplete formulations, which the liberal construction self-confessedly is, can nevertheless unfold into an order of reality that seems to exist without ostensible foundations. The gulf that theory bridges between practice and ends can also be bridged by a practice that recurrently and successively brings the ends into view. Liberal practice, we shall see, entails an understanding of human action and human nature as a reality that is constituted through the process of self-actualization but that can neither explain nor unfold itself apart from the struggle to follow the intimations of goodness already contained within.

Such an understanding is recognizable to anyone familiar with classical ethics or Christian conversion, but it is the specific genius of the liberal construction to have isolated the structure of spiritual growth in itself. The structure is, of course, meaningless apart from the transcendent reality by which the process of growth is ordered, and this is the source of the suspicion of the hollowness of the liberal formulations. Yet the structure by itself can carry all the resonances of that expansive movement of the spirit within a context fractured by divergent conceptions of its fulfillment. The liberal articulation can be a means of preserving the philosophic-Christian consensus within a context in which its actual explication is no longer possible. The liberal outlook presupposes and invites a growth of the soul that it can no longer bring about.

The secret of the tradition's success is that the elaboration of the process alone contains enough of the intimations of its direction to evoke a responsive unfolding. Once the movement of moral enlargement occurs, the process begins to sustain itself as the existential illumination of the good draws the soul ever more profoundly toward itself. The theoretical objections that had previously posed such insuperable problems begin, at that point, to fade away. Their significance shrinks in comparison to the more eminent moral reality disclosed through the movement of greater participation within it, and the difficulties recede in seriousness even if they are never and perhaps can never be resolved in principle. In a sense theory is no longer needed, as the practical elaboration of meaning works out what had previously been attempted at the level of discourse. Reality has been illumined from within the perspective of participation through the growth of the soul that changes the reality involved. Like all successful symbolisms, the liberal tradition has been able to evoke the responsive growth of the soul that when it occurs, renders the theoretical objections to its realization moot. Its specific genius is to have learned, in the greater absence of theoretical defenses, to rely more than most on an opening toward the fulfillment inchoately present within it.

This characterization helps to explain how the liberal political tradition, despite its innumerable philosophical deficiencies, has been able to beat the oddsmakers to become the most authoritatively durable modern political form. One can hardly attribute all the tradition's success to the happy accident of circumstances, and the triumph clearly does not derive from its compelling intellectual justification. Only the power of its existential appeal, or something similar, can account for its avowed historical reach. It is an impressive moral hegemony that limits even our capacity to visualize an alternative that is not itself a development of the liberal impulse. That condition defines the present study as well, for it is a reflection within the liberal tradition that envisages its improvement and not its supersession.

I am sanguine enough to believe this analysis may be of some assistance to the liberal tradition because, unlike so many, it attempts to understand the source of the formidable liberal strength. By doing justice to the residual authority that still attaches to the liberal construction, even in the face of the virtual disappearance of all coherent articulations of its foundation, we can make sense of the substantive ethos that for all its deficiencies still characterizes liberal politics. We are not mystified by the persistence of liberal regimes that, from the perspective of our theories, have no right to exist. It is possible for liberal political arrangements to function without visible means of support. But the process of foundational withdrawal has very definite limits, and it is the principal contribution of this existential analysis of liberal politics to provide a more accurate means of identifying them. Only an analysis that focuses on the level of the inner resonances can identify the point at which an order begins to come apart. For it is not the absence of foundations that per se is the source of danger, it is when such absence becomes symptomatic of an alienation from the moral and political structures that remain.

The correlative of greater accuracy in diagnosis is moreover a greater cogency in the proposed direction of therapy. A clearer sense of what has sustained a liberal order, including an identification of the points of greatest strain, permits a more effective illumination of the only means we have for restoring and repairing the damage. The only resources available within the liberal crisis are those that remain within that tradition; they are the only ones that can evoke a response, rather than invoking a revolutionary overthrow in favor of something utterly different. The revolutionary direction always carries a high index of improbability and destruction. Much more likely to effect improvement is an appeal that builds on the remaining residue of moral authority, working to expand its foothold into a full-fledged recognition of its obligatory force in individual and political existence. This is a task not primarily for discursive argument, although rational elaboration has a definite place within it, but for a return to the moving existential forces that have always been there, before even the questions of order and disorder arise. Evocative moral sources constitute the ultimate background below which we cannot penetrate. The work is therefore an exercise in the therapeutic expansion of the sources of liberal order that continue to be the only living impulses from which a renewal of its order might be possible.

It goes without saying, although I am aware that no amount of saying will protect me from the accusations of naive liberal optimism, that the picture of liberal order presented in the course of these reflections is an attempt to convey the best possibilities contained within it. I hope to also give sufficient indication of the depravity and deterioration to which I believe liberal politics is prone. Indeed, the existential depth I seek out in the meditation is required by the profundity of the crisis at which I am convinced the liberal tradition has arrived. All that distinguishes me from the vast majority of critics of the liberal construction is that I am not yet prepared to throw up my hands in despair at its incorrigibility. This is because, in the first place, the invisibility of the liberal substance perennially belies the inner reserves that always remain and that no one can count out without a much more extensive trial of resuscitation. Second, we have no foreseeable alternative to the liberal arrangement as a publicly authoritative form of order. It is the failure to recognize this position that reveals the utopian character of the most hard-bitten critics of the liberal impulse. The expansive vision of liberal order, the growth of the liberal soul toward which the book points, is not by any means a rosy idealization of the liberal possibilities. It is a genuine articulation of spiritual and moral growth that can only be achieved by confronting the abyss within the liberal impulse and, in the struggle against it, finding the inner strength and resolve to overcome it. The result is a morally confident and reinvigorated liberal order that is a genuine growth of the best within its tradition.

Access to this inner liberal order is provided, as it is for any order, by those who are its most articulate exponents, the philosophers. Existential order is what constitutes the social and political reality, but our only avenue into it must be through those who have been able to render it intellectually trans-parent. For this reason, the examination of the strata of crisis within liberal politics in the first part of the book follows the attempts of contemporary theorists to grapple with the meaning of liberal democracy. Their inability to render it coherent exemplifies and illuminates, although it clearly does not cause, the broader sense of social and political crisis. It is simply that the social and political upheaval is at root a moral and spiritual disintegration that can only be understood through the reflections of those who have sought to articulate its dimensions most profoundly. From that reflection, the second part follows the path of historical diagnosis to uncover the sources of the contemporary crisis and to assess the resources that remain within the liberal tradition for its resolution. This extensive reexamination of the historical sources of liberal philosophy is the most crucial because it reveals the depth and richness of a tradition that, from the contemporary perspective, is all too often dismissed with one-dimensional epithets of "individualism" and "self-interest." The result is that the capacity for resuscitation and reinvigoration is completely overlooked. Thus, the meditation on the growth of the liberal soul, pursued in the third part, is completely incomprehensible. It is in this part that I suggest ways in which this existential understanding of liberal order can provide a means, not only of confronting the conflicts endemic to our politics but also of utilizing them in the process of struggle that is itself the means of drawing forth the best that lies within us.

We have all suffered enough of the endless discussions of the failures of the liberal project and witnessed a sufficiency of inconclusive debates about the intellectual and political schemes to remedy the situation. It is surely time to begin to approach the subject from a different perspective and to make the effort to think it through from a different vantage point. I am aware that the existential reexamination proposed in the present study has few practitioners on the contemporary scene, and I am even more painfully aware of the difficulty of suggesting a new approach within an arena that is already overcrowded with speakers. There is first of all the difficulty of being heard at all. But the deeper difficulty is that the proposal of a growth of the liberal soul as the means of overcoming the moral and intellectual conflicts that bedevil our politics is bound to appear impossibly vague and downright strange. My only defense is the book itself, which attempts to build the meditative path by which such a process can be undertaken within the liberal tradition. The only demonstration consists in undertaking the journey, which, I am convinced, ends in the realization that the conflicts that assail us are not so insuperable in light of the transcendent good toward which the liberal order continues to point. The reader who is prepared to accompany me thus far will discover that Nietzsche's depiction of liberal democracy as the offspring of philosophy and Christianity was indeed correct. The only difference is that now we are prepared to acknowledge the positive sense of a relationship that to him was overshadowed by its negative connotation.

Part I

Dimensions of the Problem

1

Crisis of Liberal Politics

In one sense liberal theory and politics have always been in a state of crisis. Even in its earliest appearance in the reflections of John Locke and his contemporaries, in their uneasiness with the Glorious Revolution of 1688, there was hesitation about the foundations. The American framers at Philadelphia and afterward frequently sounded their uncertainties as to whether their historical experiment in self-government was destined to survive. The advent of mass democracy in the nineteenth century, when "liberalism" became both a movement and a creed, provoked the most profound misgivings in such leading theorists as Tocqueville and Mill. And our own century has witnessed the global confrontation with totalitarianism that has made it the century of the fall and rise of the liberal tradition. So what is different about the present crisis? In what way is liberal democracy, that most defyingly durable of all modern political forms, particularly in danger today?

Perhaps there is nothing more to the alarms than the outbreak of one more of the perennial bouts of liberal self-doubt. True, there are well-recognized social, political, and economic problems. Rates of family breakdown in the advanced liberal democracies have reached catastrophic proportions, especially for the millions of children who are deprived financially and impoverished emotionally as a consequence. The epidemic of indulgence and escape, whatever the choice of narcotics, testifies to a society that is deeply unhappy and with few resources for dealing with the vicissitudes of the human condition. A new callousness toward human life is everywhere in evidence, from the explosion in violent crime to the unthinking cruelty to which human beings are exposed at every stage from conception to death. The collapse of civility is widely deplored in everything from the coarseness of popular culture to the aggressiveness of interpersonal relations in everyday life.

Within this social maelstrom the ministrations of political figures appear particularly ineffectual. Liberal politicians of course share the moral

13

disorientation of the social world from which they come. They are, moreover, used to operating within a fairly narrow range of instrumental policy choices. Nothing in their experience prepares them for confronting the advanced process of spiritual disintegration they witness at work in their societies. At best they can help at the margins by enforcing the law and targeting programs of assistance for those who can be helped; they can neither compel nor transform the majority whose creature they ultimately remain. At worst they accelerate the process of disintegration through the recurrent competition for votes that can only be obtained by overpromising what can be achieved. The resulting disillusionment and cynicism ends by fueling the very process they sought to arrest.

Along with these self-made cycles of destruction has been the additional layer of autonomous economic cycles with all of their wrenching readjustments in human terms. Central to liberal political philosophy has always been the philosophy of economic growth in one form or another. It is no secret that the relative quietude of liberal societies is purchased in considerable measure through a growing economy. Political conflicts over wealth can be less divisive when the fund available is an expanding one, rather than one that is static or contracting. But growth always includes decline and instability, which translates into real human dislocation and suffering. The difficulty is that governments have neither mastered the self-discipline nor risen to the challenge of educating their citizens concerning the principles of action required to confront economic uncertainty. Such powerlessness is exacerbated when the global economic interdependence makes evident the limits of their control.

Yet a few problems do not make a crisis. Taken individually the difficulties faced by the liberal democracies are no greater than the historic challenges they have overcome, such as the totalitarian confrontation or the upheavals of the industrial and social revolutions. They are difficulties that could be overcome through the application of a determined common sense. If politics has raised exaggerated expectations, lower them; if economic adjustments have to be made, make them as rationally and as compassionately as possible; if family breakdown is a problem, legislate in ways that encourage the formation and stability of family life. Such steps would not, of course, eliminate the problems nor would they be free of costs, but they would clearly be a movement in the required direction. No insuperable obstacles lie in the way of the appropriate action, if we will to undertake it.

Therein lies the difficulty. We find ourselves lacking the necessary resoluteness of will that would enable us to overcome the problems before us. It is not that the solutions are unavailable, but that we are unable to avail of them. A peculiar ambivalence, a conflict of inclinations grips us, and we are unable to shake free of the desuetude that overwhelms us. We cannot take action because we are not yet willing to undergo the painful reorientation. Like

Saint Augustine's "Lord, make me pure, but not just yet," or the alcoholic who is ready to quit after "one more drink," we are not yet serious about the changes we need to make. Deep down we are still attached to the problems that plague us, and we have not yet felt that we really need to change.

Anatomy of the Crisis

Liberal society does not yet realize the depth of the crisis within it. In popular lingo, we are still "in denial." Yet the marks of the crisis are widely in evidence, from the incapacity to take effective action in the public policy arena to the profound moral conflicts that rend the liberal soul. A paralysis of action everywhere arises from the "interminable" and "incommensurable" disputes that cleave liberal society into a multiplicity of hostile camps.[1] Common sense is decreasingly in evidence because we share less and less of a common understanding of things with one another. With the decline in what is common, there is less of a community between human beings. *Pluralism, multiculturalism,* and *difference* are the watchwords. Liberal politics does come to resemble Alasdair MacIntyre's notorious description of it: "civil war carried on by other means" (*After Virtue,* 253).

This disappearance of a shared social and political world means ultimately the disappearance of the liberal ethos itself. That is the first leg of the crisis. The common self-understanding constitutive of liberal democracy is itself in danger of extinction to the extent that a multiplicity of private viewpoints overshadows it. A profound crisis of confidence, the equal of any that it has historically faced, is now shaking liberal order to its foundations. Unsure of what it believes and uncertain of the grounds for what it holds, liberal democracy is vulnerable to the centrifugal forces that it has for so long held within itself. Without a liberal center "things fall apart and mere anarchy is loosed upon the world."

What makes the crisis determinative is that the corrective centripetal forces have all but disappeared. It is not the pressures to disintegrate that are the core of any social or political crisis, for such forces are always present. It is the absence of any countervailing forces of union, a shared conception of the common good, that enables the destructive powers to appear so strong. This is the case today because liberal principles no longer seem to possess a core of their own; it has been lost in the process by which the present crisis of pluralism unfolded. There is little possibility of a reassertion of unifying dogma, because it has been the inexorable logic of the liberal orientation itself that has led to the present disintegration. Liberal pluralism cannot stand apart to impose coherence on the very incoherence it has brought forth.

The collapse of the liberal center has been the work of liberal principles themselves. That is the crucial second leg of the crisis. Not only is there a hollowness at the heart of the public order, but it is a vacuum that has been largely self-created. The ethos of neutrality so studiously cultivated by liberal theory and liberal practice is what has evacuated the soul of its politics. By extending the principle of neutrality far enough, liberal conviction has finally been unable to resist the last step. It has become neutral regarding itself. There can be no dogma that all must accept, because that would be an illiberal imposition contrary to the freedom of choice that the liberal construction is intended to promote. The only foundation to liberal political order must be the aggregation of the private valuations of the individuals who compose it. There can be nothing approaching a shared worldview, because being liberal means precisely that we do not have to share a worldview.

Such is the "strange death of liberal" society that seems to loom before us.[2] Gone is the confidence that a community of free and equal individuals is a sufficient condition for the emergence of a good political order. We are no longer convinced that there is a universal human nature that can be relied upon to draw the vast majority in a common direction, toward their common good. In the absence of a shared nature there seems to be less justification for treating one another as equal—equal in what?—or for regarding rights as anything more than a social convention. Like Justice Holmes, we are inclined to believe that there is nothing more to the rights of man than what men will fight for, in much the same way that "a dog will fight for a bone."[3] Finally, having lost the sense of a human core that will form the basis of agreement and constitute the basis for the acknowledgment of fundamental rights between human beings, we lose the liberal faith in reason. We can no longer indulge the expectation that the historical trend of politics is progressive. Nothing justifies our sanguinity that the future will be better than the past.

The central ideas of the liberal creed have taken a beating, and without them it is doubtful that liberal politics can be sustained. That is the situation in which we find ourselves, and the problem that the present study is a modest attempt to address. Without the liberal faith in a common human rationality, however vaguely defined, can we continue to enjoy political institutions that presuppose it? The protection of a sphere of individual liberty that cannot be invaded by others, public or private, is based on the assumption that this is the best way for human beings to flourish. But if human flourishing has itself become an empty concept, of what value is the liberty that protects it? If we take happiness or satisfaction as the overriding political goal then the line between public and private may be redrawn quite differently. Constitutional limitations become much less significant if we are aiming at a society of "contented slaves."

Nor is there any compelling reason that we should endure the cumbersome and untidy exercise of political liberty. Self-government is only of value if human beings must attempt to govern themselves in order to reach their full human stature. If there is no common growth in self-responsibility to be attained, then there is little purpose in the inefficiency of participatory politics. Public order can be obtained in a less costly manner. There might even be methods of checking the abuse of power by public officials. Why is it necessary for the people to be consulted? Only if we believe that it is somehow essential to being human is it necessary to encourage the free-flowing chaos of self-government. Unless humans are essentially self-governing beings, there can be no case for self-governing societies.

With the disappearance of the view of humans as rational beings there dissolves also the liberal faith in the progress of reason. However variously formulated, liberals have always held to some form of belief in the capacity of men to improve collectively and individually. It is bound up with the notion of reason itself, that we can learn from our mistakes and that in history advances do occur. The amplitude of meliorism, from utopian expectations of a change in human nature to more sober assessments of the incorrigibleness of humanity, was united around a core confidence in the ability of reason to guide human existence and at least to build incremental improvements in the political realm. Without a faith in the human capacity for self-improvement it seems unlikely that the experiment in self-government can be sustained. The inevitable failures and disappointments will eventually engulf it.

All the major elements of the liberal worldview appear to have lost their footing. The value of private liberty has been put in doubt, the need for self-government appears less compelling, and the likelihood that reason can guide political agreements seems ever more unlikely. In place of the confident self-evidence of liberal principles is a gnawing sense that the dissolving process has occurred from within. There can be no solution because it has been the extension of the liberal impulse itself that has undermined the foundations. The very success of a liberal order is ironically what encouraged the peeling of successive layers, only to end by discovering after the last layer had been pulled back that the onion itself had disappeared. No one step or layer appeared indispensable, but the cumulative effect was conclusive. Nothing could survive the withering skepticism of analysis.

If the test was that one cannot be compelled to accept any principle whose truth cannot be conclusively demonstrated to everyone, then one could not be compelled to accept much. Yet that has been the logic of the liberal starting point. In the slow but inexorable march toward a neutrality beyond all objections, the very heart of the liberal impulse itself has been lost. For it turns out that even the most expansive expressions of tolerance harbor a residue of cruelty, in the forms of behavior they exclude. We are pushed to go one step further in the application of our liberal principles of choice. We must acknowledge that there are no limits on what consent can authorize. We must accept even intolerance in the name of tolerance. It is at that point that liberal politics has stepped over the abyss from which it cannot easily recover, because the principles that guide it have been the very ones that have pushed it over the edge.

The quest for an impregnable foundation to justify and guide the exercise of liberal authority has proved illusory. Every principle adduced has become in turn a petitio principii, itself in need of justification and ever vulnerable to the corrosive "Why?" Even when that question is answered there still remains the problem of the application of any standard in social and political practice. The disputes that may have been settled at the level of abstraction begin all over again. We discover that the consensus we appeared to have reached did not extend beyond appearance. The meaning of the standard to guide the application of liberty in concrete is itself replete with the same uncertainty and conflict that prevailed in the philosophical debate. The confusion of philosophy has merely been transferred to politics.

It is this utter failure of any formulation of liberty to shape a concrete consensus of interpretation that has crystallized the crisis of the liberal tradition. The crisis has become self-conscious. That is the third leg, added to the collapse of the center and the self-induced nature. Now all three elements are present in the awareness that the more liberal we have tried to be, the more incoherent we have become both intellectually and politically. The crisis has arisen, not from a failure to apply liberal principles but from a too consistent application. The ever more rigorous search for a neutral foundation has evacuated all foundations; the injunction against cruelty has progressively removed even the barriers that define cruelty itself; the ever widening demand for popular participation increases the sense of alienation from a process over which the individual has no control. The unfolding of events and reflections has now made the crisis transparent. We recognize that it is specifically a crisis of liberal order itself, not attributable to any extraneous factors.

That recognition is the outer limit of our present awareness politically and intellectually. It is what is behind the more pragmatic political mood that has prevailed in the liberal democracies. The search for new political paradigms, the experimentation with new labels, *neoliberals* or *neoconservatives*, testifies to nothing so much as the defunctness of the old orientations. There may not be a clearly formulated direction to take their place, but there can be no further implementation of the outmoded conceptions of the past. The extension of liberal principles into welfare-state liberalism, as it occurred in this century, has reached its limits.[4] Having successfully responded to the most pressing social needs, the continued expansion of such efforts has begun to threaten the exercise of liberty itself. The welfare state ceases to serve the welfare of its beneficiaries when it has transformed them into its wards and can no longer recognize the harm it has done. An order of liberty presupposes some limits that lie beyond even benevolent control.

The parallel intellectual straining of the limits of liberal principles has reached an equivalent transparency, collapsing in the recognition that the quest for foundations impregnable to skeptical critique is an impossible enterprise. There are no foundations beyond foundation. Some of the most impressive contemporary liberal theorists have both reached and exemplified this recognition in their own writings. A revival of liberal theoretical reflection that reached a high point in John Rawls's *A Theory of Justice* has reached a dead end. A line of reflection that seemed to be full of promise, both theoretically and politically, has suddenly ended in the desert. Moreover, it is a landscape that bears striking resemblance to the desert of nihilism against which the liberal tradition has attempted to define itself.[5] The conclusion toward which both the practical and the theoretical extensions of the liberal impulse point is that very vacuity of purpose it all along sought to avoid.

Irony of Liberal Nihilism

The irony is that it was precisely the confrontation with totalitarian nihilism that provoked the contemporary rejuvenation of liberal convictions. We have difficulty remembering the extent to which the liberal ethos died in the period between the two world wars. The Great War had discredited the nineteenth-century brand of liberal politics that had seemed so helpless to avoid the conflagration. Social and economic upheavals that reached a crescendo in the Great Depression seemed to have sealed the fate of liberal economics. Even the historically stable democracies of the West appeared to be in a prerevolutionary state. Communist and fascist movements were not exclusively a German or Italian or Slavic phenomenon. Ideological mass movements were to be found in most of the countries of Europe and the Americas.

The realization of the destructiveness of such movements if they were to attain power was the shock that jolted liberal democracies back to life. Suddenly, liberals discovered that they were unarmed, militarily and spiritually, against far more vigorous opponents. Faced with movements that inspired fanatical commitment, with members that were willing to kill and be killed for the cause they overwhelmingly believed in, liberal democracies discovered the depth of their own ambivalence. Having drifted along as the danger mounted before it, liberal societies and liberal intellectuals suddenly awoke to the realization that history was about to pass them by. Without any apparent deep, sustaining convictions they were no longer a match for the more vital revolutionary forces of the day.

Something of the shock that stirred the liberal democracies into life on the eve of the Second World War can be sensed in T. S. Eliot's lecture "The Idea of a Christian Society." The craven capitulation of the Western powers before the demands of Hitler at Munich was the event that brought home the depth of the problem. It made clear the severity of the liberal crisis to "the many persons who, like myself, were deeply shaken by the events of September

1938, in a way from which one does not recover; perhaps to whom that month brought a profounder realization of a general plight." More than a political crisis, he understood in the events of Munich the eruption of a spiritual crisis, for they had cast "a doubt about the validity of a civilization."

> We could not match conviction with conviction, we had no ideas with which we could meet or oppose the ideas opposed to us. Was our society, which had always been so assured of its superiority and rectitude, so confident of its unexamined premises, assembled around anything more permanent than a congeries of banks, insurance companies and industries, and had it any beliefs more essential than a belief in compound interest and the maintenance of dividends?[6]

The crisis revealed failures beyond any errors in government and called for a response beyond the purely political. Betrayal and humiliation could be surmounted only by contrition and repentance. Eliot called in his lecture for the revival of the idea of a Christian society as the only adequate spiritual support for the superstructure of a liberal political order. This is a call that was to be echoed by many thinkers in the postwar period. The confrontation with totalitarianism had convinced them that liberal democracy needed, if not a religious foundation, something approaching a political creed if it was to have the inner strength to withstand its implacable ideological opponents.[7]

More broadly, an effort at energetic rearticulation was undertaken, largely inspired by the impression that liberal principles had never been adequately defended. The suspicion that liberal order had declined because it had never been elaborated with sufficient force or consistency gave rise to an impressive succession of liberal retheorizations. Some of them, such as Karl Popper's 1945 *The Open Society and Its Enemies,* were not the most felicitous in the judgments hurled across the centuries of the history of philosophy, but there was no denying the depth of commitment to the defense of the "open society"—however ill defined. A similar predilection for conviction over logic characterizes Isaiah Berlin's famous distinction between positive and negative freedom. He makes it clear that the dangers of the misuse of positive freedom to justify all manner of totalitarian abuse, invoking Rousseau's unfortunate dictum of "forcing men to be free," are so great that he would prefer to yield the intellectual defense rather than surrender the defense of principle. Berlin quotes approvingly Schumpeter's nostrum: "To realize the relative validity of one's convictions and yet stand for them unflinchingly is what distinguishes a civilized man from a barbarian."[8]

Even more impressive is the great restatement of classical liberal principles that we find in Friedrich Hayek's *The Constitution of Liberty.* Hayek, too, had begun with the critique of the ideological alternatives to the liberal tradition. His *Road to Serfdom* was one of the earliest and most trenchant warnings of the inevitably totalitarian nature of socialism. *The Constitution of Liberty* was likewise a pioneering defense of liberal political philosophy and one of the first to demonstrate the intellectual and moral credibility of that tradition. Hayek anchored his account in the notion of the rule of law that applies equally to all, thereby guaranteeing the equal enjoyment of liberty by all. "The conception of freedom under law that is the chief concern of this book rests on the contention that when we obey laws, in the sense of general abstract rules laid down irrespective of their application to us, we are not subject to another man's will and are therefore free" (153). Anything else is merely the discretionary activity of authority that, by definition, is arbitrary and unlimited by any rule. He shows how this principle can provide the connecting thread that weaves together all the major elements of the liberal worldview: economic, social, political, and historical. It is again powerful testament to the vitality of the liberal faith that inspires it, although it stops short of a more philosophic articulation of the sources of that faith itself. We must after all be convinced that we ought to follow the rule of law and that the liberal values are themselves worth defending.

The following generation took up this challenge of a more philosophical defense of liberal ideas. For the past twenty years we have witnessed a proliferation of increasingly sophisticated approaches to the justification of liberal principles. Dominating the conversation has been John Rawls's *A Theory of Justice,* which probably deserves most of the accolades heaped upon it for the simple reason that it is the only work that outlines a comprehensive philosophy of liberal order. Most of the others focus on more specific problems within the whole, but Rawls is the one who defines the whole and thereby identifies what the problems are. Within contemporary Anglophone philosophy where all of the emphasis has been on discrete technical analyses of problems—in the expectation that somehow, somewhere, someday all of the solutions will accumulate into a whole—Rawls provides an invigorating rediscovery of the power of theory. Analytic liberal philosophers were not condemned to deal with ever more fragmented aspects of problems. They could now envision what a liberal theory might look like, even if Rawls was not right on many of the specifics of obligation, contract, natural justice, and so on. The need for additional nuance and refinements did not obviate the success in constructing a whole. Almost for the first time since Mill and perhaps even longer, the liberal tradition acquired intellectual credibility. Its principles had not simply been cobbled together by history and common sense; now they cohered.

The success of Rawls naturally inspired emulation. While there have been few grand theorists, there has certainly been a much higher, more serious, and less purely technical level of debate in the past two decades. Works such as Robert Nozick's *Anarchy, State and Utopia* attracted well-deserved attention as expositions of what a minimal, libertarian justification of liberal principles might look like. Alan Gewirth, in *Reason and Morality,* provided a persuasive account of the way in which a revised Kantianism could provide the noncontroversial foundation long sought for liberal morality and politics. Ronald Dworkin, in *Taking Rights Seriously* and *Law's Empire*, carried forth Rawls's emphasis on the primacy of rights—especially "equal concern and respect"—to show how it constitutes the guiding principle of the liberal legal order.

With the many other examples that could also have been cited, it is evident that we have been living through one of the great periods of liberal theorizing.[9] To the formidable array of liberal talent must also be added the even more extensive range of individuals who sought the renewal of liberal democracy from other sources. Dissatisfied with the atomistic individualism inherent in liberal thought, the communitarian perspective has been effectively articulated by such thinkers as Charles Taylor and Michael Sandel. Jacques Maritain and the natural-law theorists, who have included such impressive recent representatives as Alasdair MacIntyre and John Finnis, have continued to mine the Thomist tradition for a more substantive foundation. Eric Voegelin, Leo Strauss, Hans Gadamer, and (somewhat more idiosyncratically) Hannah Arendt sought in the encounter with classical political philosophy the reorientation that would ultimately rejuvenate liberal democracy. The revival of an intellectually powerful conservatism, as in Michael Oakeshott and others, has been clearly directed toward the reconceptualization of liberal ideas and practice. And perhaps just as significant has been the steady stream of returnees from the social left, bearing every conceivable banner from socialism to postmodernism, who regard a reformed liberal ethos as the best practical hope of realizing their ideals.

Yet despite the formidable range and depth of efforts reaching back more than half a century, we are still no closer to a consensus on the meaning and justification of a liberal order. Indeed, we seem to have slipped further away from it. The crisis of the liberal tradition has mounted. While repairs and rejuvenations have occurred, the secular movement has continued down toward disintegration. This is all the more disheartening in light of the resilience and fortitude that liberal societies have demonstrated in the struggles they have endured. It is surely one of the supreme ironies of history that, having won the third great war of the century, the Cold War, the liberal democracies now suffer from a growing crisis of confidence in their own values. Contrary to the briefly famous fantasies of the "end of history," our situation more resembles the repeat of history in the slow decline of Rome after the defeat of Carthage.[10]

Liberal philosophy has, of course, always been prone to becoming a victim of its own success. Its self-understanding has from the start been defined by the opponent to which it is opposed. First it was feudalism and aristocratic privilege, then it was absolutism and arbitrary rule, and in our own time the forces of totalitarian democracy. Deprived of a foe, it seems perennially inclined to relax its discipline and unwind toward a state approaching chaos;

faced with an enemy, it initially appears weaker than it is and is perpetually inclined to tempt aggression. The inability to maintain anything like an equilibrium, in other words, is a problem that lies deep within the nature of the liberal ethos. The failure of the enormous range of efforts, theoretical and practical, that we have surveyed is not surprising. The propensity of the liberal tradition for crisis cannot be resolved through argument. Its roots lie deeper still.

Neither the periodic reinvigorations of liberal society nor the continuing struggle to find an intellectually compelling justification have been sufficient to stop the endemic unraveling tendencies of liberalism. The instability is not purely institutional or conceptual. As a consequence, the remedy cannot lie simply in institutional, social, or political reforms or in the development of arguments of impenetrable brilliance. Liberals typically have behaved as if such steps were indeed all that was needed to bring about utopian perfection or something very close to it. But it is not enough to have a clear and compelling argument, for that will not lead irresistibly toward the transformation of politics. Nor will the reform of laws and institutions lead willy-nilly to political improvement, unless they are accompanied by an underlying improvement of the spirit of those who operate them. The most crucial dimension of any order, Montesquieu recognized, was the "spirit of the laws."

It is the neglect of this spiritual or moral dimension that is the source of the liberal instability. Alternating between license and discipline, coherence and incoherence, it has suggested to many critics that liberal politics is bereft of any existential core. Such a judgment hardly stands up to the formidable resilience we have just acknowledged. But it does point at least to the right level of analysis. It is not that liberal order lacks a moral or existential foundation in the lived experience of both masses and elites. Indeed, it is one of the principal objects of this study to demonstrate the presence and significance of such a living consensus as the only foundation upon which we can rely. The problem more specifically is that liberal theory and practice studiously avoid attending to their own existential roots. It is almost as if the neglect is willful; more in the manner of a flight from reality, it is uncomfortable with contemplating. That, of course, is an existential and not simply an intellectual error, as the most perceptive critics of the liberal orientation have long understood.

The question is whether the flight from the spirit so characteristic of the liberal ethos can be reversed. Is there a possibility of an existential turning around that would reorder the nature of liberal politics? Or is the unraveling process that we have seen proceed apace, despite the periodic reversals, destined to reach its denouement? The question ultimately is an attempt to probe the condition of the contemporary liberal soul. What is the state of its resources? Having endured so much, does it now have within itself the capacity to rise again from the ashes of its own dissolution? Or is it to suffer the final irony of its history that, having defeated the totalitarian emperor, it now finds that it too is without clothes?

Liberalism without Clothes

Enemies, like friends, come to resemble one another. The difficulty is that their long-standing enmity prevents them from recognizing the extent to which they have become alike. A first step in any attempt to understand the nature of contemporary liberal order is to break free of the received patterns of thought. Any political science worthy of the name cannot afford to take the categories of ideological conflict for granted. While the world has been divided into ideological blocs for much of the twentieth century, this does not mean that we have been living in the rhetorically different "worlds." Totalitarianism has not been a phenomenon in one corner. We have not lived through a gnostic war of good and evil, light and dark. Rather it has been a struggle against a common enemy—the evil of totalitarianism—that has infected different parts to different extents. The less seriously infected have mercifully been able to rally the forces of resistance that seem eventually to have exhausted the disease, but no segment can claim immunity from its effects. Western liberal democracy has demonstrated its moral superiority to the totalitarian ideologies, but that must not be allowed to conceal the degree of Western responsibility for the horror. Besides the efforts of heroic resistance there have also been the shameful episodes of collaboration with all the butchers of the twentieth century.[11] The moral darkness of totalitarianism has also made itself felt not infrequently in the liberal West.

Viewed in this context, the suspicion of nihilism as the truth of the liberal tradition comes as no surprise. It is only shocking to liberals themselves who had always assumed that they stood for something more. In this sense, the crisis of liberal politics that has culminated in the recognition of its own nakedness is a blessing in disguise. It enables liberal intellectuals and societies to come to grips with their identity with a clarity unique in their history. They must now confront not just the nihilism of their opponents, but the beam of darkness that has lain hidden in their own souls. Perhaps they might even begin to reflect on the degree of their own collusion in the evil of the century we are leaving behind. Instead of triumphalism, we might begin to revise our understanding to see our own role in the events as that of accomplices, as much in need of repentance as those whom we opposed. Finally, we might begin to understand the modern civilization itself from which both of us have sprung and recognize that the fatality of power without purpose has been the common darkness from which we have all suffered.[12] The possibility of breaking free from its influence begins with such an understanding of its appeal.

Like the rest of the modern world, the liberal tradition can only overcome its own nihilism by going through and beyond it. This is the prescription of Nietzsche who called himself "the first perfect nihilist of Europe who, however, has even now lived through the whole of nihilism, to the end, leaving it behind, outside himself" (*The Will to Power*, 3). It was this willingness to confront the problems at their deepest level, in the soul of modern man, that enabled the most clear-sighted, such as Dostoyevsky and Nietzsche, to foresee the disasters that lay in the future.[13] At the height of the liberal nineteenth century, Nietzsche understood the extent to which " 'moral man' is dressed up, how he is veiled behind moral formulas and concepts of decency" because he cannot bear to appear naked (*The Gay Science*, 295). But the truth was that the clothes of his morality had completely worn out. Nothing was more insubstantial than "the most threadbare and despised ideas [of liberalism]: equal rights and universal suffrage" (*Will to Power*, 396).

Nietzsche seems to harbor a particular scorn for the very unreflective capacity of the liberal tradition that enables it to soldier on when the whole world seems to be crumbling around it. This was best exemplified for him in the "English twaddle *(niaiserie anglaise)*" of John Stuart Mill and his compatriots. Mill's conception of liberty, "Do not unto others what you would not have them do unto you," struck Nietzsche as the height of vulgarity, of the herd mentality. It bore no resemblance to the real world where a Corsican's honor would demand a vendetta, and the probability of getting shot would not deter his efforts at revenge in the slightest (*Will to Power*, 488). The liberal guarantees of equal freedom would work only among a people that no longer believed in honor. They could be controlled by manipulating the small pleasures and pains of their petty existence.

The picture of this oppressive liberal apocalypse was brilliantly captured in Nietzsche's portrait of "the last man." When Zarathustra has failed in all his efforts to rouse his listeners to the new life he proclaims to them, he finally tries to insult their pride by portraying their future as the "most contemptible" of men. They are men who are no longer men, having turned away from struggle with the great questions. All that they can do is blink mindlessly. They do not want to know "What is love? What is creation? What is longing? What is a star?" More like an ineradicable swarm of flea beetles, they have turned away from all that is challenging and difficult.

> Becoming sick and harboring suspicion are sinful to them: one proceeds carefully. A fool, whoever still stumbles over stones or human beings! A little poison now and then: that makes for agreeable dreams. And much poison in the end, for an agreeable death.
> One still works, for work is a form of entertainment. But one is careful lest the entertainment be too harrowing. One no longer becomes poor or rich: both require too much exertion. Who still wants to rule? Who obey? Both require too much exertion.

> No shepherd and one herd! Everybody wants the same, everybody is the same: whoever feels different goes voluntarily into a madhouse.
>
> "Formerly, all the world was mad," say the most refined, and they blink.
>
> One is clever and knows everything that has ever happened: so there is no end of derision. One still quarrels, but one is soon reconciled—else it might spoil the digestion.
>
> One has one's little pleasure for the day and one's little pleasure for the night: but one has a regard for health.
>
> "We have invented happiness," say the last men and they blink. (*Thus Spoke Zarathustra*, 18)

The portrait is chillingly close to the kind of cocooned existence that has become the unquestioned goal of liberal democratic societies today. Insulated from all the risks and pains of human existence we become satisfied with our measured quality of life, until we are prepared to go all too "gently into that good night." We know the seductive appeal of comfort and, most telling of all, are not shocked by the response Zarathustra receives. "Give us this last man, O Zarathustra," they shouted.

The truth, of course, is that this is not a mere aberration of liberal aspirations. It is a logical outgrowth of the modest range of virtues that a liberal ethos promotes. In place of the old ideals of heroism, self-sacrifice, and honor, there are the more moderate practices of restraint, consideration, and caution. The difficulty is that the contraction of the virtues to those of the liberal gentleman was a process of shrinkage likely to continue, until all that was admirable in human character had shriveled up. In the absence of the supererogatory ideals, of the hero and the saint, there was no counterbalancing pull against the seductive enervations of materialism.

This was a problem noted by many of the leading nineteenth-century liberal theorists, including, it should be noted, John Stuart Mill. Alexis de Tocqueville comes closest to Nietzsche's contempt for the impoverished range of aspirations in the newly populous bourgeoisie. What they most needed was not humility but pride, a more enlarged idea of themselves. "I would willingly exchange several of our small virtues for this one vice" (*Democracy in America*, 2:262). Tocqueville too contemplates the depressing prospect of a society of petty hedonists. In a passage that sounds remarkably like Nietzsche's castigations against the soul-destroying effect of equality, he concludes with an unforgettable metaphor of the process.

> The reproach I address to the principle of equality is not that it leads men away in the pursuit of forbidden enjoyments, but that it absorbs them wholly in quest of those which are allowed. By these means a kind of virtuous (*honnête*) materialism may ultimately be established in the world, which would not corrupt, but enervate, the soul and noiselessly unbend its springs of action (*ressorts*). (141)

The problems were, as Tocqueville suspected, and as Nietzsche made searingly clear, deeper than the influence of equality. The disappearance of the great overarching virtues of the Western moral tradition was itself only a symptom of the much deeper crisis of the spirit engulfing the modern world. The very foundations of morality had collapsed. This was the news that Nietzsche's prophet proclaims and valiantly struggles to overcome, even though he is greeted with incomprehension. Like the madman who bursts into the marketplace in search of God, he encounters only derision from the passersby. They do not understand the enormity of the moment or of their own responsibility within it. Even though they are themselves the murderers of God, they have not yet asked themselves: "What did we do when we unchained this earth from its sun? Whither is it moving now? Whither are we moving now? Away from all suns? Are we not plunging continually? . . . Are we not straying as through an infinite nothing? . . . What was holiest and most powerful of all that the world has yet owned has bled to death under our weapons. Who will wipe this blood off?" We are not yet ready to contemplate the question that the murder of God forces upon us: "Must not we ourselves become gods simply to seem worthy of it?" (*Gay Science*, 181–82).

Nietzsche understood the enormity of the modern secular experiment, the creation of a human order in which the question of God had become obsolete, because he realized the degree to which our whole moral tradition had depended on divine authorization. In contrast to the glibness with which the idea of a rational moral order was endorsed by liberal intellectuals, he was among the very few who foresaw the crisis of morality that would unfold. The death of God meant the advent of nihilism. All of Nietzsche's efforts were directed to awakening his contemporaries to this realization and struggling courageously, if tragically, to find a means of confronting it.

He understood that the abandonment of faith in God would put all the greater pressure on morality. But it would soon collapse. "Every purely moral value system (that of Buddhism, for example) ends in nihilism: this is to be expected in Europe. One still hopes to get along with a moralism without religious background: but that necessarily leads to nihilism.—In religion the constraint is lacking to consider *ourselves* as value-positing" (*Will to Power*, 16). Now we are constrained by the realization of our own responsibility for positing values. There can be no grounding or authorization beyond the discretionary impositions of our own will. Opposing what he considered the typically English assertion of George Eliot—that morality can survive unaffected by the loss of God—Nietzsche insisted on the wholeness of Christian morality. When they continue to insist that good and evil remain intuitively self-evident to them, "we merely witness the *effects* of the dominion of the Christian value judgments and an expression of the strength and depth of this dominion: such that the origin of English morality has been forgotten, such that the very conditional character of its right to existence is no longer felt. For the English, morality is not yet a problem" (*Twilight of the Idols*, 516).

Should we add that in our day morality has become a problem? Its effect is making itself felt in the crisis of self-confidence shaking the liberal institutions erected upon it. Nietzsche was under no illusion about the extent to which the core liberal conception of individual rights was derived from this doomed Christian morality. It was the Christian idea of the soul whose origin and destiny is transcendent that first made it possible for the individual to stand over against society and the world, as a reality that can never simply be contained by them. This was the source of individual rights. To this, Christianity added the related idea of the equality of all souls before God. "This concept furnishes the prototype of all theories of equal rights: mankind was first taught to stammer the proposition of equality in a religious context, and only later was it made into morality: no wonder that man ended by taking it seriously, taking it practically!—that is to say, politically, democratically, socialistically, in the spirit of the pessimism of indignation" (*Will to Power*, 401). Now all of that magnificent superstructure has had its supports kicked from under it, for "man has lost the faith in his own value when no infinitely valuable whole works through him" (12).

What remains is nihilism, a nihilism that liberal formulations are unable to conceal as their own truth. That realization was what made Nietzsche one of the intrepids of our history, launching out on a path of exploration for a passage beyond nihilism. He sought, in a resolute acceptance of the situation in which "nothing is true, everything is permitted," the strength that would enable him to live without positing a meaning to life. By unreservedly embracing the will to power as the force in all reality, he sought to find a way beyond all *ressentiment* or bitterness toward the futility of our condition. He would finally, he hoped, become like the overman *(Übermensch)* he visualized, capable of affirming even the eternal return of everything meaningless, including the "last man." Through this love of his fate *(amor fati)* he sought to avoid the wallowing despair of nihilism. "It wants rather to cross over to the opposite of this—to a Dionysian affirmation of the world as it is, without subtraction, exception, or selection—it wants the eternal circulation" (*Will to Power*, 536).

But the path was not there. Nietzsche could not find in the indomitable defiance of his fate the means that would overcome the realization of the futility of his own achievement. Of what use is the triumph of the will over nihilism? Is not it too futile? Too brilliant to be deceived by errors and too honest to construct illusions, every page of Nietzsche testifies to the ache he endured in his soul. He had not reached the *Übermensch,* nor attained the "joyful science" *(fröliche Wissenschaft).* He was still "the most pious of all those who do not believe in God" (*Thus Spoke Zarathustra,* 260), and he knew the extent to which "we godless antimetaphysicians still take our fire, too, from the flame lit by a faith that is thousands of years old, that Christian faith that was also the faith of Plato, that truth is divine" (*Gay Science,* 283).

For all the talk about "extending grace to himself," Nietzsche knew that it was impossible.

Like many of Dostoyevsky's heroes, he could not live in a world without God. He experienced the abyss opened by the loss of God with a depth unknown to liberal self-assurance. He longed for a god that would fill the absence of the God who had died. Yet Nietzsche could not find his way to divinity because, at a controlling level, he willed the absence of God. There is a play of masks and levels in Nietzsche, where we are asked to admire the heroic defiance of absurdity but nowhere permitted to ask if the absurdity is not after all willed. Is there not a pride of megalomaniacal proportions at work in this assertion of the human spirit triumphing over all? A superiority for which the absence of God is somehow essential? The tragedy of Nietzsche is that on the one hand he experienced the loss of God yet refused to follow the intimations that would lead to the rediscovery of the transcendent. It was, as the last now unemployed Pope explained to Zarathustra, "your piety itself that no longer lets you believe in God" (*Thus Spoke Zarathustra*, 262). The crisis of nihilism is rooted in Christianity itself. "The end of Christianity— at the hands of its own morality (which cannot be replaced), which turns against the Christian God (the sense of truthfulness, developed highly by Christianity, is nauseated by the falseness and mendaciousness of all Christian interpretations of the world and of history . . ." (*Will to Power*, 7). What is there to prevent an unfolding of this Christian inspiration toward a deeper realization of its meaning?

The crisis of the Christian world (which is, after all, what the crisis of the modern world is about) could just as easily lead to a deeper rediscovery of the Christian truth. That is the path uncovered by Nietzsche's great contemporary explorer of the spirit. At the same time that Nietzsche was struggling with these issues in Germany, Dostoyevsky was undertaking a parallel spiritual journey with very different results. "Nihilism" had already been invented in Russia (by Turgenev in *Fathers and Sons*) by the time Nietzsche came to write about it, and Dostoyevsky had lived among the circles of atheistic revolutionaries that had gone beyond the boundary of good and evil into terrorism. He had contemplated the abyss and understood "the magic of the extreme" (*Will to Power*, 396). Dostoyevsky had peered over the edge and recognized himself in it. Reflecting on the notorious Russian terrorist Nechaiev, he concludes "probably I could never have become a Nechaiev, but a Nechaievetz—for this I wouldn't vouch, but maybe I could have become one . . . in the days of my youth" (*The Diary of a Writer*, 147).

Instead, he was saved by the encounter with grace, an utterly free gift of himself by another that pierced Dostoyevsky to the core. Through his recollection of the experience of wholly gratuitous kindness, an episode unremarkably ordinary in the life of a human being, he came to see this as the deepest measure of reality.[14] Beyond the will to power is the transformative power of love. This is the great insight that Dostoyevsky struggled to unfold in all his novels, particularly the last five great ones. In them he explored the inner world of the Napoleonic criminal types who lived beyond good and evil, beyond all boundaries, in whom Nietzsche recognized his own free creators of values, the highest men. But he carried the meditation further into the awareness of demonic self-closure that also troubled Nietzsche. The overman or higher man, for all his titanic striving, does not step outside the human condition. All he is left with is his defiance, which can neither provide a meaning nor create an order. He ends with a nihilism even darker than the one with which he began because now it is self-imposed. Dostoyevsky had discovered the secret of the will to power as a will to closure against any truth beyond the self.

It is precisely the refusal against all that does not derive from the self that is the essence of his will. But that does not mean that now man extends grace to himself. The project remains futile. How can he extend what he does not have? From where shall it come? Man has already resolved to close himself off against the appeal of all that is beyond himself. All that is accomplished then is the confinement of the self within a demonically self-constructed prison, an imprisonment that can be successful only if it is extended to include all others who might call forth a response. The spirit of indomitability ultimately merges with the spirit of domination. Yet the imprisonment is never quite complete. An inchoate glimmer of awareness of an order of reality beyond the self remains. Stavrogin, the formidable hero of *The Possessed,* once he has finally taken the last step of denying all difference between good and evil, declares that he knew he would be free of convention "but that if I ever attained that freedom I'd be lost." His suicide mirrors his spiritual self-destruction. "What was I supposed to *apply* my strength to? That I could never see and I still don't see it to this day" (426, 690).

Dostoyevsky's focus is always on the moment of struggle within the personality before it has definitively decided. This is particularly the case with Ivan Karamazov whose soul is the battleground between God and the devil. Its culminating exposition is surely the celebrated "Legend of the Grand Inquisitor," which is so often misinterpreted when lifted from its context. The most important aspect is that the story is recounted by Ivan (not Dostoyevsky) and the personae, the Inquisitor and Christ, represent dimensions of his inner struggle. Ivan, by means of the tale, is testing the extent to which one form of existence can stand comparison against another. The Inquisitor represents the spirit of revolt against the injustice of the order of Creation, the Christian order in which men are given freedom without any firmly controlling hand to guide them. Left to their own devices they have irresponsibly churned up the ocean of misery that is human history. The Inquisitor is convinced, by contrast, that he possesses a superior knowledge of justice. Instead of abandoning the millions who misuse their freedom so that a few may be saved, he would save them all by abolishing the source of the trouble in freedom itself.

No one can deny that the Inquisitor's complaints have justification or that his motives are laudably humanitarian. However, as the conversation between the cardinal and Christ continues, it becomes apparent that the old man has not created a higher order of justice or that he knows what genuine love for mankind is. What he constructs is not a realm emancipated from all misery, but the greatest hell imaginable. It is a world in which men have lost their humanity, they have been stripped of the very thing that makes life itself worthwhile. Having stepped outside the "conventional" restraints on what is permissible toward human beings, he has not reached a fuller reality in which the welfare of all is fully protected. He has set forth on a sea of control that has no boundaries, because any possible boundaries would have to be built on the shifting sands of his own arbitrary will. He cannot care for man because there is no longer any means of knowing what it is that makes man worthy of care. Without the parameters of his nature, neither the ruler nor the ruled can know what counts as human.

Even the pride of Nietzsche's overman seems to depend on a notion of what a human being ought to be. In its absence can there even be overmen? The awareness of the inner contradiction of creating our own values in utter freedom is brilliantly exposed in the self-justifying protests of the Inquisitor. He is eager to have his love for humanity measured against that of Christ. The very lack of confidence in his own rightness is laid bare through the insistence that he is the one who is perfecting the work of the Savior. But the deceptiveness of his defense finally becomes transparent in the admission that "We are no longer working with Thee, but with *him* [the tempter]—that is our mystery" (*The Brothers Karamazov*, 305). It is not love of mankind that has sustained him, nor any desire to perfect the work of God, but the will to persist in the spirit of revolt that will hear no voice beyond its own.

Alyosha, Ivan's brother, is the one who declares that the ostensible purpose of the tale, to render a critique of Christ, has been reversed. "Your poem is in praise of Jesus, not in blame of Him—as you meant it to be" (309). Indeed, the silent unaccusing presence of Christ is widely conceded as the most effective presentation of Jesus in any literature other than the Gospels. Its significance here is that it establishes the most profound connection between Christ and the defense of human freedom. The relationship between liberty and Christianity is complex and will be explored further below, especially by means of a fuller reflection on the "Legend"; here it is sufficient to note the connection that is revealed when the defense of freedom is pushed to its limit. When the attack against it comes from the most radical perspective, the nihilistic overturning of all values, only the spiritual truth of Christ is sufficient to withstand the assault.

When the value of human freedom itself is put in question, liberal modes of argument are themselves badly exposed. Freedom is for liberals the starting point for argument, not a premise that stands in need of its own support. What can they say against an opponent that rejects the self-evidence of their foundations? What response can be made to the assertion that freedom is the root of human unhappiness? What can one say to someone who does not see that without freedom one cannot be humanly happy? Arguments are of no avail because the opponent has already crossed into a realm where "nothing is true, everything is permitted." What can one say when rational argument is no longer possible?

All that remains is the silent witness of existence. What cannot be demonstrated can still be lived, and the force of that living still contains the possibility of stirring to life the reality that lies dormant within the other. The witness of Christ is that he is the Suffering Servant who "will not crush a bruised reed or quench a flickering flame." Dostoyevsky understood, as no one before him had so clearly, that Jesus is not only the spiritual redeemer of mankind but also its political emancipator. Through the restraint in the manner of his communication with us, Jesus shows the importance of the free response of faith that he awaits. Through his willingness to suffer all the consequences of human freedom, including his own crucifixion, he makes unmistakably clear the value he places upon it. Through the unconditioned love of God for man, human freedom is made possible. Dostoyevsky powerfully conveys all this in the unspeaking forgiveness of Christ, made piercingly real to the Inquisitor in the kiss of Jesus at the end of their conversation.

Unconditional forgiveness is the reality that underpins human freedom. Without the readiness to forgive, freedom would have a limit or value that when exceeded would justify its elimination. A serious commitment to freedom can be sustained in the face of the most powerful opposition only if the power of love is even stronger. The integrity of the person, which is what the struggle over freedom is all about, depends upon a transcendent love nowhere evidenced so clearly in history as in Christ. That is the discovery yielded by a contemplation of the most devastating attack, theoretically and practically, that can be made against it. Those who have rediscovered human freedom on the far side of nihilism affirm its spiritual foundation. The question now is whether the liberal tradition itself can rise to the truth of liberty discovered outside of it. The examination must begin with the contemporary liberal thinkers who have sought a way out of the nihilism within and surrounding their own liberal convictions.

Tumbling Liberal Defense

An awareness of the depth of the critique ranged against liberal theory is what has inspired its late flowering in our own time. Viewed in a wider historical perspective, it is astonishing to see the revival of concepts and modes of thought that received opinion had long declaimed as outré. Even ideas that in liberal circles had not had much play since the eighteenth century, such as the social contract, began to assume a new prominence. A rediscovered pride in the liberal understanding of individual rights, especially by contrast with the dismal record of individual protection within any more expansive construction of rights, led to a new appreciation of the centrality of liberal political order. Protections for the individual *and* limitations on the power of government became the currency of political discussion. Even liberal political economy, so long disdained as laissez faire, acquired new respect and influence. The political counterpart is found in the universal embrace of liberal democracy as the only legitimate political model around the globe.

Yet there has been something enormously brittle about this liberal rejuvenation, a brittleness that ultimately is the source of the sense of crisis that has reached into public consciousness. The problems become visible in the work of the greatest liberal theorist of the generation, John Rawls. His *A Theory of Justice*, despite the deficiencies so frequently seized upon, did provide the theoretical justification of principles so long absent from liberal practice. This is the explanation of the impact of the work. He seemed to have squared the liberal circle. Rawls had overcome the two most bedeviling problems afflicting every attempt at a rational articulation of liberal convictions. The first was how to construct a public order that did not presuppose a level of virtue in the citizens that liberal politics itself did not produce and could not sustain. Liberal democracy could not presuppose virtue because it had no uncontested criterion for good and bad; it could hardly promote a particular form of the good without incurring the kind of controversy it sought to avoid. Rawls delineated the requirement with unprecedented clarity in his insistence that "the concept of right is prior to that of the good" (*A Theory of Justice*, 31). The liberal order can be founded on an understanding of what is right, apart from the competing and conflicting conceptions of the good that humans hold, and thereby established on a basis that no minimally rational individual can reject.

The second related challenge was to find a means of giving concrete content to the moral principles that defined the liberal order. All previous accounts of morality that had escaped the Scylla of contestable foundations, such as Kant's, had perished on the Charybdis of formalism without practical guidance. It was not enough to find a formulation of what is right that could not be rejected without self-contradiction: there must also be a substantial connection with the liberal political order it is intended to support. This lack of specific guidance infects, in Rawls's view, all the more substantive conceptions of morality, including the Aristotelian, the theological, and the utilitarian. Moral principles are themselves in need of a further set of principles to guide their application. If one wants to be virtuous or God-fearing one still has to know what is right in those terms.

These two interrelated problems seemed to have been solved in Rawls's conception of the original position in which human beings meet to formulate the principles that ought to govern their relations with one another. "The crucial thing," he observes, "is not to use principles that are contested" (585). This is accomplished through the thought experiment in which we meet behind a veil of ignorance, not knowing who we are, what our position will be relative to others, or how our particular conception of the good will be defined. Most important of all, he explains, "I have avoided attributing to the parties any ethical motivation. They decide solely on the basis of what seems best calculated to further their interests so far as they can ascertain them" (584). The considerations made in this egalitarian anteroom to politics, which is reminiscent of nothing so much as the egalitarian opening and conclusion of the *Republic* in the underworld, are all of a prudential nature that presuppose little more than a rational interest in furthering one's own interests.

It is not the individuals who meet that are just but the situation that defines their encounter. "The original position is defined in such a way that it is a status quo in which any agreements reached are fair" (120). There may be a generalized sense of justice that must be conceded to the moral pioneers, but nothing hinges on it. All that is necessary is that they be people who at least are concerned to further their own interests and aware that this will involve some degree of conflict with the self-fulfillment of others. The arrangements they work out will reflect their general sense of justice because the settlement will be "everyone's best reply, so to speak, to the corresponding demands of others" (119). For each one the decision will simply reflect the best arrangement of principles that will serve their individual self-interest.

Rawls has been much criticized by communitarians for deriving everything from such an ideal convention of "unencumbered" selves (516).[15] But he appears to be doing no more than projecting the self-understanding of liberalism back to its beginning. In that sense, we are "mutually disinterested" (129), without many strong ties of affection to one another or at least no such attachments can be assumed. We do have different and often conflicting conceptions of the good; this is the problem that has prompted the development of the liberal construction. It makes eminent sense to concentrate, as Rawls suggests, on the "primary goods"—rights and liberties, opportunities and powers, income and wealth—that together with a sense of self-worth constitute those things that everyone will desire irrespective of their ultimate goal. The agreement he maps out aims, therefore, at the just distribution of those instrumental goods.

Individuals, intent on whatever their own understanding of the good turns out to be and ignorant of their social position, would choose to be governed by principles that all would accept irrespective of their eventual status determination. Their interest would dictate that they endorse the most fundamental of all liberal principles. In its simplest formulation, the first principle is that "each person is to have an equal right to the most extensive basic liberty compatible with a similar liberty for others" (60). This is the first principle, Rawls insists, in the order of priority because it represents a distribution of the most significant primary good: the equal liberty to pursue all other goods. It is the basis for the self-esteem that is derived from "the publicly affirmed distribution of fundamental rights and liberties" (544), the only way of ensuring equal treatment.

The second principle, which has provoked far greater comment, is often taken as indicative of Rawls's fundamentally egalitarian leanings. His own personal politics aside, however, the second principle can just as easily be read as a more traditional liberal justification of social inequality. Again in its simplest formulation, the principle is that "social and economic inequalities are to be arranged so that they are both (a) reasonably expected to be to everyone's advantage, and (b) attached to positions and offices open to all" (60). Rawls later underlines the insistence that inequalities must be justified in terms of their benefits to the least-advantaged members of society. But this is no more than the resistance that liberal society has always felt was needed against an extension of its own first principle of equality in liberty. Friedrich Hayek makes essentially the same case, in very different tones, when he asserts that the advantages of a few do not injure but rather promote ultimately the welfare of all (*The Constitution of Liberty*, 88).

Taken together, the two principles provide a fair equality of opportunity that maximizes the well-being of all, not simply a majority, and can be presented as the scheme that is most likely to win the acceptance of all. The principles constitute, Rawls concludes, the best foundation for "constitutional democracy" whose major institutions and practices can be derived from them. "My aim has been to indicate not only that the principles of justice fit our considered judgments but also that they provide the strongest arguments for freedom" (243). The guarantees of individual liberties and the rights of political participation, as well as the rule of law, are all more securely grounded in the ordered principles of justice that all must acknowledge. Avoiding both a dogmatic assertion of ungrounded principles and a reductionist admission that all principles are mere preferences, Rawls's principles rely on "weak and widely held presumptions" that can be expected to win general acceptance. "Surely, our liberties are most firmly based when they are derived from principles that persons fairly situated with respect to one another can agree to if they can agree to anything at all" (244).

It is perhaps not unfair to detect in that "surely" the germ of self-doubt that disturbs the whole system. Even the weak stipulations that seem to have made the smooth emergence of agreement possible may turn out not to have been weak enough. Toward the end of the book Rawls reflects on the possibility of individuals who do not find acting from a sense of justice good for them, and concludes that "it is rational to authorize measures needed to maintain just institutions." To those who must be thus compelled "one can only say: their nature is their misfortune" (576). Agreement, it turns out, cannot be counted on to reach all or to form a seamless social whole. There will continue to be expressions of dissent, both with and without malice aforethought, and no amount of liberal thinning of the presuppositions can evoke harmony from the parts.

The problem of pluralism returns with renewed centrality to Rawls's later writings and effects the most profound critique of the achievement that had earlier seemed so secure. The fabled priority of the right over the good, the very cornerstone of *A Theory of Justice,* dissolves before the admission that liberal order is not based on the right that is compatible with every conceivable conception of the good. Some formulations of the good cannot be contained within liberal democracy, and the struggle to eject such representations can be won only at the cost of the liberal claim to universality. The suspicion is confirmed that liberal order has not escaped connection with a particular affirmation of the good. It was only that Rawls's skillful construction had temporarily obscured that realization.[16]

An awareness of the problem was certainly present in *A Theory of Justice.* He not only contemplated the possibility of individual perceptions of the good incompatible with the thinnest of liberal definitions but also recognized that even those who embraced the liberal order would have to do so in the realization that not all of their aspirations for the good could be satisfied. Not knowing what their conceptions of the good will be, their agreement commits them not to press their moral or religious convictions beyond what is compatible with a like liberty for all. "They cannot risk their freedom by authorizing a standard of value to define what is to be maximized by a teleological principle of justice" (328). The preservation of autonomous freedom, it seems, is the highest value, for which everything else may be risked but which itself must never be placed in jeopardy.

Nothing bespeaks the confidence of the liberal tradition so much as Rawls's inability to see that such an absolute vision of liberty could be open to question. And nothing announces so loudly the crisis of confidence that has overtaken it as the revision of Rawls's thoughts on this issue. He now recognizes that there is a very specific conception of the person and the human good that underpins the theory of justice. The conception is of the autonomous moral person characterized by the two powers of "a capacity for a sense of justice and a capacity for a conception of the good. A sense of justice is the capacity to understand, to apply, and to act from the public conception of justice which characterizes the fair terms of social cooperation. . . . The capacity for a conception of the good is the capacity to form, to revise, and rationally to pursue a conception of one's rational advantage or good" (*Political Liberalism*, 19). But if free rational autonomy is the highest goal, then the whole process of the original agreement has been stacked against any alternative human ideal. What then happens to the priority of the right over the good, the principle that had been the core of the liberal claim to public legitimacy? "The answer," William Galston shrewdly remarks, "is that the priority of the right is subtly reinterpreted as the priority of the public over the nonpublic" (*Liberal Purposes*, 148).

The question that is begged, of course, is why should I go along with an arrangement that may patently undermine my highest ideal, such as trust in God or faith in the truth? It is most significant that Rawls does not attempt to philosophically defend his *democratic perfectionism* (which is Galston's term). That is the project that has collapsed in the recognition that his defense serves after all a particular vision of the human good. All he can do is point to the "overlapping consensus" concerning respect for the autonomy and dignity of persons that has historically emerged in liberal democratic societies as the justification for his position. He then takes his own failure to find a rational justification as conclusive that no such attempts at a coherent articulation of the meaning of justice will be successful. "Philosophy as the search for truth about an independent metaphysical and moral order cannot, I believe, provide a workable and shared basis for a political conception of justice in a democratic society" ("Justice as Fairness," 230; *Political Liberalism*, 10).

Rawls revises his earlier theoretical account of justice as fairness to emphasize it "as a political conception that is practical and not metaphysical or epistemological." Now liberal democracy rests not on its claim to represent the truth about human nature or the human condition but simply on the fact that it has successfully enabled certain concrete societies to live with the not-insignificant philosophical differences that pervade them. Justice as fairness then "presents itself not as a conception of justice that is true, but one that can serve as a basis of informed and willing political agreement between citizens viewed as free and equal persons." There is something poignant and autumnal about Rawls's appeal that "we try, so far as we can, to avoid disputed philosophical, as well as disputed moral and religious, questions" ("Justice as Fairness," 230).[17]

The problem, as he himself acknowledges, is that there may well be certain issues or values whose importance outweighs the social and political agreement.[18] If there is no neutral state basing itself on the weak stipulations that all can accept, then it is inevitable that the public order will diverge from some of the profoundly held convictions of its members. The public order must tilt toward certain metaphysical or theological positions, causing the probability of conflict to become high. The discomfort is palpable in Rawls's response to those who compel us to articulate our own philosophical or religious premises. "This happens whenever someone insists, for example, that certain questions are so fundamental that to ensure their being rightly settled justifies civil strife . . . At this point we may have no alternative but to deny this, or to imply its denial and hence to maintain the kind of thing we had hoped to avoid" (*Political Liberalism,* 152).

Rawls's assurances, that the reason for bracketing such disputes about principles in order to avoid the imposition of political power, begin to ring hollow. Absent a rational resolution of differences, he admits, "the only alternative to a principal of toleration is the autocratic use of state power" ("Justice as Fairness," 230). The crux of the matter is, however, that it is precisely the protection of differences that has been the basis for toleration. What are we to do when that policy itself puts in jeopardy our fundamental principles? What can we say when toleration becomes intolerant? The argument that liberals have been trying to avoid the introduction of state power to settle the disputes is scant consolation when the liberal consensus itself is the instrument of repression. The yoke of tyranny is just as oppressive when imposed by a smiling liberalism as it is when inflicted by the brute force of autocracy.[19]

The fate of Rawls's justification of liberal principles is shared by the many other serious and impressive efforts of the past generation to find a noncontestable foundation to morality. The foundations turn out in the end to be noncontestable only within a liberal context. The arguments presuppose the conclusions they seek to prove. This circularity is transparent in the similarly Kantian construction of Alan Gewirth. He skillfully uncovers within the performative assumptions of all human action a "deontic" morality that cannot be denied without self-contradiction. Since all voluntary and purposive actions presuppose the value of voluntariness and purposiveness, as well as their supporting conditions, we are already committed to a morality of respect for the rights of all potentially voluntary and purposive agents. Gewirth believes he has escaped from the all-corrosive "why" because his Principle of Generic Consistency has been drawn forth from the agent's own purposive striving. Rejecting it would not only expose him to inconsistency but also reveal his indifference to his own good. "Consequently, the agent must care about being rational and avoiding self-contradiction if he is to engage in action, as against going through motions that he emits with no control exerted by him for purposes he regards as good" (*Reason and Morality,* 194–95). The elegance of the demonstration is undeniable, but can cogency alone suffice to keep us on the strenuous path of duty? We recall Socrates's argument that the tyrant is of all men the least powerful because he was unable to do anything to advance his own good, and all that he did made him worse (*Gorgias* 466). What of the many human beings today who cannot find a reason to be serious about their own good, who without being responsible toward themselves can hardly be responsible for others, and whose actions are driven by blind impulse from one self-destructive behavior to another? Gewirth's principle presupposes the rational purposiveness it seeks to demonstrate. His principle says nothing to those who are not yet convinced that they ought to be purposive and should respect the liberal institutions of rights that are its expression.

Gewirth is peripherally aware of the problem and wonders aloud about the possibility that democratic majorities may "fail to endorse the redistributive justice of the supportive state" to implement the full recognition of rights (*Reason and Morality*, 321). In extreme cases, such as starvation, we can bypass the democratic process entirely; in the ordinary course of events, the process of "moral education" will render such emergency measures unnecessary. But what if the educational efforts are less than successful? No answer is forthcoming to this disturbing possibility. Nor can much confidence be placed in the "deontic" principle that recognizes others as deserving of rights only to the "degree to which he approaches having the generic abilities constitutive of such agency" (142). This renders predictably the rights of the fetus minimal but more alarmingly establishes the Principle of Proportionality by which certain individuals could be virtually excluded from the class of prospective agents. The defense of liberal "reason and morality" turns out to be merely a rationalization of liberal agents for liberal agents by liberal agents.

The deontological eschewal of any foundation in nature or reality (*metaphysics* as it is derisively termed) condemns us to wandering within the artificial biosphere of liberalism. We have not yet been able to take a breath of fresh air. This is true of the other promising and brilliant rearticulation of liberal thought from the 1970s, Robert Nozick's *Anarchy, State and Utopia*. Nozick returned to the oldest of all liberal thought experiments, the state of nature, in order to find the structure that connected us all to the liberal state. In a condition of anarchy, human beings would inevitably begin to form and join mutual protection associations. They would recognize the benefits to be derived from having some reliable means of resolving disputes. Since such protective agencies cannot coexist, the dominant one would have to compensate individual and independent agencies for its monopoly over the enforcement of justice. In this way, a state comes into being that is fair because it at no point deprives anyone of the freedom enjoyed in the state of nature.

Much of the book is taken up with a response to Rawls and others who desire more than this minimal state. In a brilliant libertarian refutation of redistribution, Nozick argues that there is no justification for a more extensive state. Any efforts in the direction of "end-state" results could be obtained only at the cost of real invasions of rights "historically" acquired, and it would entail continuous political intervention in order to maintain the particular state of distribution desired. So the only state that can be justified without violating anyone's rights is the minimal state, although Nozick concedes that people may voluntarily agree to submit to a greater degree of government control for the sake of the benefits of living together. In principle, however, the minimal state is utopia because it is a stable association in which "each person receives his marginal contribution" (*Anarchy, State and Utopia*, 302). That is, the state receives more of a contribution from each than they are likely to take out of it, and each receives more in return than they could obtain in any other association to which they could imagine belonging. The result is a stable exchange.

It is also infuriatingly glib as a conclusion, as most tellingly indicated by Nozick's own subsequent abandonment of this style of argument. There was, of course, always more to his argument than its style, as we will see later, but its reach here did little more than restate the most elementary liberal self-understanding. The exchange or contract model of liberal society, while it may have served as a convenient metaphor for public order, did not really explain how a state comes into being and maintains itself over time. All the significant questions concerning fidelity and trust in agreements are simply begged. The social contract is not like an economic exchange, in that it is perpetual and irrevocable even when the terms have changed. Nozick's book is one more signpost that points to the inability of the liberal construct to explain itself in any neutral terms.

The collapse of the foundational project within liberal theory has become so commonplace that it virtually amounts to a consensus. Indeed it is the starting point for all further discussion within the liberal context. While surrendering any claim to the objective status of individual rights, liberal theorists and liberal societies continue to insist that rights must be taken with absolute seriousness. The approach is exemplified by Ronald Dworkin who flatly rejects any "ghostly metaphysical" basis for rights, yet insists that they do not rest simply on the conventions adumbrated by legal positivism. People do have rights other than those explicitly created by the legislative process, and these rights are not derived from any conception of human nature. By examining the actual practice of judicial interpretation of rights, Dworkin discovers that the assumption of some extralegal foundation plays no role. Judges are quite capable of taking rights seriously, expanding and applying them simply on the basis of a constructive interpretation of the legal tradition.

But what then is the source of the rights presupposed by the legal tradition? Dworkin's answer is that we cannot get back beyond that point. Rights continue to be natural in the sense that they are not merely the product of convention, but they are also not dependent on some incorrigibly shaky definition of what human nature is. The only reliable basis for rights is the recognition that they are the indispensable condition for all political agreements concerning what we owe to one another. Commenting on Rawls, Dworkin observes that "the right to equal respect is not, on his account, a product of the contract, but a condition of admission to the original position"

(*Taking Rights Seriously*, 181). His development of Rawls is the assertion that it is not the contract that establishes rights, but the rights that establish the conditions for contract. These are rights we possess "not by virtue of birth or characteristic or merit or excellence but simply as human beings with the capacity to make plans and give justice" (182).

Dworkin has gone on to clarify this precontractual priority of rights by distinguishing between internal and external skepticism. The internal skeptic questions the rightness of certain claims from within the perspective of a moral universe; the external skeptic raises metaphysical objections concerning the possibility of any moral truth. External skepticism neither adds nor subtracts anything to the struggle for the right moral or legal interpretation and can thus be safely neglected. All we need is the reassurance that our internal debates are in no way threatened by such metaphysical suspicions. "I hasten to add," Dworkin concludes, "that recognizing the crucial point I have been stressing—that the 'objective' beliefs most of us have are moral, not metaphysical, beliefs, that they only repeat and qualify other moral beliefs— in no way weakens these beliefs or makes them claim something less or even different from what they might be thought to claim. For we can assign them no sense, faithful to the role they actually play in our lives, that makes them not moral claims. If anything is made less important by that point, it is external skepticism, not our convictions" (*Law's Empire*, 83).

Once reassured of the reality of our convictions, we can accompany Dworkin in his overview of "law's empire." It is a sophisticated and inspiring conception of law as integrity, in which successive decisions are made on the principled basis that draws on the best interpretation of the whole tradition. Now that any appeal to an external natural law is out, the two plausible alternatives are conventionalism and pragmatism, a slavish attachment to strict construction and original intent or a risky invitation to all forms of judicial freethinking and arbitrariness. Dworkin avoids both of the pitfalls in his common-law model that retains the protected expectations of conventionalism and the flexibility of pragmatism by insisting that the resolution of conflicts must be on the basis of principles internal to the tradition of political morality as a whole.

The crux of the matter is, however, that we have not been able to avoid any appeal to what itself legitimizes the tradition. Moral and legal disputes have themselves proved so divisive that we have not been able to find a means of resolving them in the usual manner. We have not been able to begin with a set of rights that define the conditions for the conversation, because it is precisely the nature of those rights themselves that are in dispute. The common-law tradition historically rested on the natural-law tradition, and it has been the disappearance of the latter that has provoked the crisis of the former.[20] Dworkin's method of internal debate leaves us with no means of clarifying the very principles that constitute the tradition, so when a dispute arises there is no means of settling it through an expansion of the underlying principles. One cannot simply assert that the bedrock is the right to "equal concern and respect" when it is precisely the grounds for equal concern and respect that are at issue. How else are we to determine whose claim is to take priority when they come into conflict?

The nonfoundationalist approach represented by Dworkin and now widely practiced has the advantage of avoiding sterile philosophical debates that cannot reach a conclusion. By directing us back to the common-law tradition it reminds us that men do not have to explicate all of the grounds of their judgments before reaching well-founded conclusions. If we cannot resolve our theoretical differences we can return in the best liberal spirit to the development of a practical consensus. But it cannot paper over the crack of nihilism that has fissured the liberal tradition. Nor are we likely to be much reassured by Dworkin's aspiration that behind all the muddle of practical judicial interpretation in the empire of law stand the philosophers, "the seers and prophets" of law. "It falls to philosophers, if they are willing, to work out law's ambitions for itself, the purer form of law within and beyond the law we have" (*Law's Empire*, 407). They are the ones who weave together the tattered ends of law and reveal it in its pure integrity.

So far, of course, they have kept it pretty much to themselves, otherwise we would not have the kind of wrenching conflicts that have forced us to confront our own nakedness. On the other hand, if the philosophers themselves are just as much at a loss, then a nonfoundationalist approach will serve little better than any other. It will merely disguise the nihilism that lies deep within itself but that is brought to the surface in the palpably self-serving character of its justifications. Like the pattern of bioethical professionals on hospital staffs, the cumulative effect will be to allow people a cover for doing pretty much whatever they want to do anyway. At the end of the day, one suspects that the nonfoundational approach is one that really believes in very little. How, otherwise, could one reach the kind of conclusion advocated by Richard Flathman, that the right to an abortion includes the right "to demand an abortion from a medically competent individual who personally believes that abortion is morally wrong?"[21] If one can be compelled to commit what one regards as murder, then we have entered a realm that is, in Dworkin's chilling phrase, "beyond the law."

This even takes some of the jaunt out of that most impish of nonfoundationalists, Richard Rorty. The abyss of liberal coerciveness implied in the readiness to treat liberal principles as an invitation to creative interpretation is wickedly concealed in his playful rhetoric of irony. How can any interpretation be challenged if the principles do not really stand for something else? If their only basis is the fact of their historical emergence, what privileged status does any one formulation have over all the alternatives? Who is to say that the rights of one may not be sacrificed for the rights of another? What is the necessity even for maintaining a consistency of principle? Why should we be slaves of conventions historically inherited anyway? Rorty's term, *liberal ironist,* is intended to describe the kind of individual who can keep these kind of questions under his hat. More and more, however, it begins to sound like the brave whistling in the dark of a man who cannot repress the monsters of unanswered questions.

"Putting on a brave face" is a pathetic metaphor for the fate of the liberal tradition. No amount of rhetorical brilliance can disguise the note of pleading in Rorty's efforts to convince us and himself not to take the questions seriously. It is a scintillating piece of bravado that almost succeeds in "joshing" us out of our philosophical earnestness, were it not for the patent contradiction with the sense of solidarity he wishes to put in its place.[22] He is convinced, with Foucault, that the quest for truth has been at the source of the cruelty that human beings have inflicted on one another, and so he welcomes the ironist critique that undermines truth itself as a project. Solidarity must now be based, Rorty is convinced, on the feeling of sympathy with the sufferings and needs of others. But why should we give way to this feeling rather than any others, especially in the absence of any good reasons? What indeed will solidarity mean when we do not truly know what it is that is appropriate to all others?[23]

Rorty recognized the abyss of the centerless self in the example of Heidegger, for whom there was no contradiction between writing great books and betraying his colleagues (*Contingency, Irony, and Solidarity,* 111, n. 11). Or there is Rorty's recognition of Smith in *1984* as a plausible account of the kind of society "in which the intellectuals had accepted the fact that liberal hopes had no chance of realization" (183). But perhaps the most touching passage of all is where Rorty imagines what he would say when the secret police come to torture the innocent. He or we will not be able to say anything. We can only remember Sartre's remark on such an occasion, that then "fascism will be the truth of man." It is, Rorty admits, "a hard saying . . . that there is nothing deep down inside us except what we have put there ourselves, no criterion that we have not created in the course of creating a practice, no standard of rationality that is not an appeal to such a criterion, no rigorous argumentation that is not obedience to our own conventions" (*Consequences of Pragmatism,* xlii).[24] The question is whether there is anything at all that would make Rorty shout "No!"

That is the decisive question, for the collapse of the liberal efforts at theoretical self-articulation is of concern only to the extent that it presages a more profound inner collapse of conviction. It is one thing to not be able to justify what one believes, it is quite different if one no longer believes anything. The two are clearly connected and mutually reinforce one another. The whole arduous effort to develop a nonproblematic account of liberal order has been motivated by the concern that the underlying morality may be in danger of draining away. A gnawing anxiety that little of substance may remain lurks behind the urgency to plug the theoretical cracks. This accounts for the sense one often gets from liberal writers that if only they can make it all coherent then our political problems will be solved. Unfortunately, the problems lie deeper.

We cannot ignore the contingent relationship between theory and practice. Just as the disassembling of theory does not necessarily lead to the disappearance of liberal practice, so the reassembling of theory will not necessarily lead to the restoration of liberal practice. Their relationship is reciprocal and complex. Both must be taken into account if we are to get the full measure of the long liberal crisis that is upon us. We must be willing to confront at the deepest level the possibility contemplated by Nietzsche and Dostoyevsky: that nihilism had become not only the intellectual but also the existential truth of liberalism. What is it that keeps liberal democratic societies together if we cannot philosophically account for it? Or have we reached the point where liberal societies have awoken to their own incoherence and are already headed down the path of disintegration?

Many of the most perceptive liberal critics have concluded that the tradition is now bankrupt. "Liberalism as a doctrine implicitly presupposed," observes John Gray, "what contemporary cultural pluralism destroys or diminishes, a single cultural tradition as undergirding the institutions of civil society. Those who welcome cultural diversity (as I do) must be ready to confront the task of maintaining civil society without much help from the resources of the cultural tradition which gave it birth and sustained it to maturity" (*Liberalisms*, 214). Increasingly, in the view of Gray and many others, we cannot rely on any core liberal conviction to sustain a public order. We are thrown back upon the continuity of social conventions and the enclaves of traditional communities as the only solidities that remain. The universalism of liberalism as an ideology is abandoned, and we acknowledge the extent to which it has been tied to the peculiar historical conditions of its genesis and development. Philosophy is replaced by history.

Within such a setting the task of the theorist ceases to be that of searching for new evocative formulations of liberal principles. There are no noncircular justifications of the priority of liberty that do not presuppose the primacy they wish to establish. Nor is there any way of moving from abstract principles of liberty to political practice without presupposing the more concrete experiences of liberal politics. But most devastating of all is the vacuum that is revealed by this failure of explanations. There are no liberal convictions that can be articulated because there are no liberal convictions period. All that exist are the liberal practices themselves as a precious historical bequest, and it becomes the task of the theorist to bend all his efforts to the work of sustaining them. The liberal theorist becomes, according to Gray, a "political Pyrrhonist" who works to salvage what can be saved from liberal skepticism.

This may include the rendering of plausible accounts of liberal political morality, but it will not extend to "the vain project of constructing a liberal doctrine. Indeed, if his inquiries have a practical aim (and they need not), it will be to protect the historical inheritance of liberal practice from the excesses of an inordinate liberal ideology" (264).

There is an admirable modesty in this approach that focuses on repairing the habits and institutions that have constituted liberal politics. A tone of refreshing realism about politics has been sounded in the acknowledgment of the need for restraint, especially in regard to the abstractions that have defined the liberal ideals. It is true that the liberal order has been a victim of its own success and that any more success could destroy it altogether. But for all the laudable respect for historical traditions that we find voiced by writers across the political spectrum today, there is also a sense of weariness and resignation that feels uncomfortably like the last gasp of an exhausted political movement. No longer able to explain itself, liberalism reverts to taking care of the inheritance bequeathed to it by its ancestors.

One wonders how well liberalism will be able to take care of what it no longer understands. How long will it be able to sustain an order that does not arise from its own convictions? One cannot simply jettison "the myths of universal humanity and personhood"[25] without affecting the concrete institutions and practices that such general notions underpinned. The flight from theory, itself a perennial proclivity of liberals, cannot abolish the questions and conflicts to which theory had sought a response. Disputes about the meaning and application of liberal principles will return, except now they will not find even a partially coherent account to control them. The failure of the liberal philosophical enterprise to date does not mean that no philosophical account of liberal democracy is possible. It means only that the form in which the search was undertaken is unlikely to yield fruitful results. The demonstration of an alternative approach is the principal object of this book. But before we proceed we must first establish that a liberal ethos exists that can be theoretically explicated. We must respond to the deepest challenge that has been mounted against the liberal consensus: that it does not exist. Is nihilism the truth of the liberal soul?

2

Enduring Moral Authority

The death of liberal democracy has been, as Mark Twain quipped of his own demise, greatly exaggerated. Indeed, the story of the liberal tradition has been the story of its capacity to defy all expectations of its terminal condition. Opponents and defenders alike have recurrently been surprised at the powers of resuscitation that lie buried within the liberal impulse. The dogged durability of the liberal tradition testifies more powerfully than any arguments to the bedrock on which it rests, impervious to most of the critical assaults launched against it. Because it is not derived from discursive argument, this liberal core is substantially unaffected by the critique of the incoherence of its formulations. The inner liberal convictions are what the formulations seek to articulate. As sources they can survive the disappearance of particular conceptualizations and remain to inspire the emergence of new imperfect evocations of their deeply intuited truth.

This does not mean that the depth and symbolizations can be separated. The depth lives only through the struggle toward articulation, and the only access we have to the depth is through its self-expression. Nor does it mean that the liberal tradition is invincible against all the damaging consequences of the discrediting of its representations. The destruction of established forms and understandings is traumatic, and the effect of an accumulation of shocks can be critical. We live at a time when the crisis of confidence in liberal order has become self-conscious. But we must not make the mistake of so many critics and defenders who identify the collapse of theoretical liberalism with the disintegration of the liberal inspiration. One of the ironic consequences of the theoretical collapse is to make more dramatically visible the extent to which liberal society and politics rest on a level of experience prior to conceptual elaboration.

Nietzsche was only the first in a long line of underestimators of the liberal achievement, both friendly and hostile. Like him, they consistently failed to appreciate the genius of the construction, which has been its ability to conceal the sources of existential resonance that give it its strength. For this reason a liberal polity perennially appears weaker, more incoherent, less cohesive than it actually is. This has been a source of great problems both for liberal societies and for those opposed to them. Self-confidence has declined as liberal societies become more aware of their disconnection from substantive foundations, and this vulnerability has in turn tempted the aggressiveness of those who would take advantage of a weakness more apparent than real. The search for a means to address its indefensibility is the central problem confronting the liberal tradition today, and it forms the principal purpose of the present investigation in the chapters that follow. But first we must examine the extent to which an implicit liberal consensus survives the winnowing self-examination of the previous chapter. Is there an unspoken depth from which the liberal truth can be reborn?

Public Authority of Liberal Principles

The primary evidence for the continuing viability of liberal order is that, despite its deficiencies, it continues to function as the authoritative public symbolism. Politically this is evident in the remarkable stability of the liberal democracies. It is the one modern political form that has endured through the vicissitudes of history and the conflicts of competition. We have now reached the point where liberalism is the undisputed exemplar of political order throughout the world. This does not mean that all countries will become or remain liberal democracies but that no other form will exercise a comparably authoritative appeal. Legitimacy has largely come to be defined in liberal democratic terms. The remarkable implosion of the communist claims to legitimacy, the last real competitor in a universal moral sense, has confirmed the most progressivist expectations of the nineteenth-century liberals. Perhaps the unanticipated nature of this event could be thought even to excuse some of the excesses of the liberal cheering section.[1]

The enthusiasm is understandable in light of the global ascendancy of the liberal democratic model. As the whole world rushes, often rashly and incautiously, to embrace the economic and political institutions of the West, we realize that whatever the outcome it certainly represents a triumph of the liberal idea. Many countries may never be truly swept into membership in the liberal club (and the experiment may be largely unsuccessful), but they will not be able to escape the taint of falling short of the standard for a contemporary society. Thus, even when the liberal substance is absent, the pressure is enormous to cloak the shortcomings in its flattering imitation. This may be the highest compliment to liberal order, but it contains the seeds of the tragic failure of its success. The very rush toward the trappings of liberal democracy may precipitate the collapse into the anarchy or autocracy the newly liberal countries had sought to avoid.

The aspiration, however, is understandable. In a century in which we have seen state-sponsored murder on a scale unprecedented in history, it is only natural that—given the chance—societies will gravitate toward the political forms that have most successfully preserved and nourished the lives of their citizens. Compared to the rest of the world, the liberal democracies have been oases of tranquillity in a desert of misery. Securely at peace with one another and without expansionist designs on their neighbors, liberal democracies could concentrate on the economic prosperity and welfare of their people that has made them the envy of the rest of the world. The enjoyment of the highest standard of living has been the boast of all who have seriously pursued the liberal principles of economic freedom and political self-government. National wealth has been dramatically increased and has benefited a broader distribution of society than at any other time.[2] Only the seductive effects of prosperity itself have seemed to threaten liberal democracies, as they have failed to act promptly enough to counter some of the more ruthless opponents that have loomed against them.[3]

Yet even in the political struggle the liberal democracies do not have an undistinguished or ungenerous record. After the catastrophe of the First World War and the equally disastrous peace settlements, both of which would give serious cause for concern that liberal statesmen were capable of a rational pursuit of their own interests, there was the even more disturbing irrationality of their response to the rise of Hitler. But the realization of the magnitude of their mistake was the event that galvanized liberal thinking into a more clear-eyed assessment of the world and prompted the heroic effort of resistance that eventually proved sufficient to defeat the threats of Nazism and fascism. That awakening was what enabled the liberal democracies to recognize the dimensions of their next foe, totalitarian communism, and to marshal the determination needed to prevail in the third great conflict of the century, the Cold War. In many ways, this war was the greatest test for liberal societies because it called for endurance and flexibility for a much longer period of time. Apart from a few notable slips, the liberal states did succeed in saving many countries from the communist maw and, most surprising of all, managed to withstand the totalitarian opposition until it disintegrated under its own internal weaknesses.

From any perspective the liberal democracies' tenacity has been a notable achievement, made all the more remarkable by the collective effort of perseverance required to maintain attention on the goal. NATO has possibly been the most successful alliance in history, which reflects not only on the wisdom of the statesmen who conducted it but also on the maturity of the societies that through all the vicissitudes of their internal politics sustained an unbroken commitment to the organization's goals. A lion's share of the credit must of course go to the largest state, the United States, which was willing to shoulder the leadership burden that it alone was in a position to undertake. Without the initiative and sacrifice of the United States, proportionally much higher than the costs its allies were able or willing to bear, the effort would simply not have occurred. The historic role of the United States, as the country in which the idea of liberal democracy was rooted deepest, was reconfirmed in the liberal protectorate it has sought to extend in this century.

Curiously, citizens in the United States and other liberal democracies have, as they have become more preoccupied with their own problems, become less conscious of the significance of their "experiment in liberty" for the rest of the world.[4] We are only intermittently made aware of it when we confront the waves of immigrants knocking at the doors of the liberal democratic West. Or we are astonished at the hardships patiently borne by people in the newly democratizing states as they participate in their own free elections. But no more powerful witness to the authority of the liberal democratic ideal can be imagined than the voluntary movement of millions of human beings around the world toward its realization. In one way or another, they vote in the most basic manner of all: with their actions. The idea of a society that guarantees personal liberty and enables popular participation in its government exercises an irresistible hold on the imagination.

The power of the liberal ideal is perhaps best illustrated by the realization that we can conceive of no alternative that would better solve the problem of social and political order. For all the carping complaints that are hurled at liberal democracy, as in Churchill's remark that it is "the worst form of government except for all the rest," there is no serious quest for anything different. It is not only that we have no choice but to live with liberal democracy but also that it is the form that best reflects our sense of how we should order our lives together. The dangers, drawbacks, and defects are daily impressed upon us, yet they do not dislodge the conviction that, allowed to work as it should, liberal democracy is the most appropriate form of government for human beings.

The deepest level of its appeal is that this is the form of order that speaks to our human dignity as rational, self-governing beings. At some point the liberal construction ceases to be a mechanism for compromise between diverging cultural and philosophical positions and becomes a positive vision of the way in which free men and women should live their lives and determine their common good. All alternative approaches represent a retreat into some form of tutelary relationship, in which citizens are treated as wards of the state and not as fully mature human beings. Liberal democracy constitutes the limit toward which political development reaches, and all other forms of government are more or less to be tolerated to the extent that they more or less approach this ideal. Not only is liberal democracy the best realistic political form that is possible, but it is also the best that can be conceived as a political goal.

We cannot conceive of any other that could supplant its authority, because we cannot seriously contemplate any diminution of the prerogative of self-determination. Suggestions for alternatives—such as a public order enforcing natural or divine law, aristocracies of virtue or birth—are recognized even by their advocates as partial, private visions. The most that is to be expected is that such alternatives might moderate the spirit of liberal democracy, not reverse its direction.[5] No one anticipates the replacement of the liberal construction with something distinctly different. Even the most daring efforts to rethink the problem of order do not break the pattern of working for improvement at the margins within a framework that remains substantially liberal.[6] A radical restructuring of our politics is not to be anticipated except in the direction of something much worse.

Something much worse does of course occur when a liberal democratic order breaks down. It is also true that the worst totalitarian regimes of the century, the Bolshevik and Nazi revolutions, emerged from the collapse of poorly conceived liberal democracies. A similar experience occurred in the transition of many of the newly decolonized states from unstable democracies into anarchy and dictatorial military rule. Many of the reservations voiced about the present enthusiasm for global democracy arise from such concerns. We have surely had enough experience of the difficulties involved in forcing the growth of liberal democracy on soil whose conditions are not yet ready to support it. A healthy dose of caution is advised at the end of a century that began with the slogan "making the world safe for democracy." Even the so-called stable democracies are not immune to the strains and tensions of pluralist self-government, and that realization has become evident in the crisis of confidence we have seen overtake the liberal tradition.

The decisive aspect is, however, that whatever the shortcomings and risks of liberal democracy, most of which are abundantly visible, no coherent proposals are advanced in favor of an alternative political form. Liberal democracy is the political form of the modern world. Its defects must be treated within a framework that remains consistent with its own liberal and democratic principles. Reforms are suggested along the lines of supplements to the spirit that already animates the political structure. None contend that a radical substitution is required. This is especially true now that the extreme ideological opponents have either been co-opted into liberal forms or begun to assume liberal clothing. Today more than ever, we are all liberals. That very inescapability of the liberal conception is what makes the struggle with its defects all the more crucial.

Depth Unspoken

The principal evidence that the liberal ethos contains a depth from which the effort of self-renewal can emerge is in the struggle it has already undertaken to overcome its internal and external nemeses. We have already noted the struggle that the liberal alliance waged reluctantly and somewhat fitfully but eventually successfully against the totalitarian foe. In the preceding chapter we followed the serious if ultimately unsuccessful efforts to develop a coherent defense of liberal principles. Now we must view those endeavors in a different light. For even though they did not attain their intended objective, the struggles gave impressive evidence of the liberal convictions that animated them. Without that prediscursive faith there would be no elaborate intellectual quest, nor would the liberal convictions survive the demise of their theoretical formulations.[7]

Clearly, the inability to find a coherent liberal formulation that would command assent in the public arena is not an encouraging sign. Indeed, it suggests that the incoherence is more than intellectual, that the conceptual nihilism has grown to become existential nihilism as well. The very urgency of the quest for a compelling argument may mask the deeper insecurity that liberal intellectuals no longer believe the case they are attempting to make. One suspects that the search is itself tainted with illusion, for even the most persuasive demonstrations will not convert those who have already hardened their hearts against the conclusions. But the fact that the effort is undertaken at all, even in desperation, is an indication that the old faith has not died and that it still retains a flame that could be fanned back to light. There are few true nihilists among the liberals.

Liberal intellectuals are more in the manner of lost souls who carry within them the flickering sense of that for which they search. The darkness is not total because they continue to know what is right even though they can no longer give a fully satisfactory justification for it. Otherwise, there would be nothing to explain the willingness to stand by one's principles "unflinchingly" even in the full awareness of "the relative validity of one's convictions." Isaiah Berlin proceeds to reflect that this pluralism of values may only be "the late fruit of our declining capitalist civilization," yet he remains unshaken in his belief that the ability to do without metaphysical confirmation is a sign of human maturity. It is at this point that one suspects the liberal mind of making a transition it has not properly declared. What is at issue is not the "relative validity" of all values but the relativity of all except the liberal core itself. "Principles are not less sacred because their duration cannot be guaranteed" (*Four Essays on Liberty,* 172). The only language appropriate to what moves Berlin is the "metaphysical" language of the sacred. How else can he convey that this alone is both true and the measure?

It is astonishing how frequently remarks of this nature crop up in the writings of contemporary liberals. John Rawls's *A Theory of Justice* is replete with them. The opening page expresses the deeply held conviction that is the inspiration of the whole theoretical effort yet itself cannot be examined further or left open to question. "Each person possesses an inviolability founded on justice that even the welfare of society as a whole cannot override" (3). It is that strong sense of the transcendent value of each individual that is brought home over and over again as the certainty from which everything else unfolds. One feels it as the force that animates Rawls's stern strictures against utilitarianism, the great alternative foundation of justice in our pluralistic moral universe. Utilitarianism fails to respect the irreducible uniqueness of persons by aggregating their interests into the great beast of society, which is then free to sacrifice the well-being of the few for the benefit of the many. The whole extended exercise of the original position and the veil of ignorance are simply the means of allowing the perspective of transcendent justice to become clear in our lives.

The appeal of the idea of justice, Rawls concludes, is not that it is best calculated to further our interests but that it best expresses our nature as free and rational beings. Its appeal is the realization of our spiritual nature. "It is acting from the precedence [of justice] that expresses our freedom from happenstance and contingency" (574). When he finally asks why we should be just and accept the conditions of fairness in the original position, Rawls replies that they are conditions that we already accept in the depths of our nature. "Thus to see our place in society from the perspective of this position is to see it *sub specie aeternitatis:* it is to regard the human situation not only from all social but also from all temporal points of view." Having contemplated our human world from this eternal viewpoint, we possess the unseen measure that is the source of order. "Purity of heart, if one could attain it, would be to see clearly and to act with grace and self-command from this point of view" (587).

It is not only the language that evidences a metaphysical or religious inspiration, but the very structure of the argument is pervaded by the same realization as well. The "deontological" turn introduced by *A Theory of Justice* proclaims that the defense of the inviolable uniqueness of each person is too important to be left to the shifting vagaries of political and philosophical debate. Traditional foundations for human dignity in the ideas of creation or nature appear too uncertain, since they are more contestable than the rights they proposed to support. All varieties of teleological argument, in which we appeal to an ultimate end or reality that justifies all, cannot overcome the indeterminacy that infects all conceptions of the highest good. In practice, the dominant end collapses into some form of hedonism, some subjective qualities that merely mask the realization that we have no one highest good. Rawls concludes that the teleological approach is ineradicably subjective. The deontological alternative he proposes is to bracket all talk of final ends and focus on the concrete convictions of justice and right that already inform our reflections. Such preanalytic convictions inevitably underpin our quest for the good anyway.

We should not attempt to give form to our life by first looking to the good independently defined. It is not our aims that primarily reveal our nature but rather the principles that we would acknowledge to govern the background conditions under which these aims are to be formed and the manner in which they are to be pursued. For the self is prior to the ends which are affirmed by it; even a dominant end must be chosen from among numerous possibilities. There is no way to get beyond deliberative rationality. We should therefore reverse the relation between the right and the good proposed by teleological doctrines and view the right as prior. (560)

The later writings in which Rawls concedes the objections of his critics—that is, that his account of the right is itself a substantive conception of the good that permits and excludes certain other goods—does not alter the core. He merely accepts that the liberal conception of right cannot be demonstrated in any neutral fashion and continues to assert that it is, nevertheless, right. The accession of nonfoundationalist approaches among liberal theorists is perhaps the strongest evidence of the prerational source of their commitments.

Ronald Dworkin's sophisticated conventionalism is designed to insist that the dignity by which each of us is entitled to be treated "with equal concern and respect" is not itself derived from conventions or agreements. It is the irreducible condition for a liberal democratic order, itself incapable of demonstration. Richard Rorty has gone as far as to declare the quest for foundations off-limits, as too dangerous for liberal politics. "When the two come into conflict, democracy takes precedence over philosophy" ("The Priority of Democracy to Philosophy," 270). Few are as outrageous in acknowledging what has become commonplace, that the liberal order never really depended on the reasons adduced for it and cannot be endangered by the collapse of its rational surface. Even the basis suggested by Rawls, Rorty, and many others, of a Burkean respect for the liberal historical traditions whose fortunate beneficiaries we are, cannot quite capture the depth of reverence behind it. Ultimately, it is that they can conceive of no other way that is more right. Why should philosophical disagreements be allowed to jeopardize our common life together?

Rorty's efforts are quite deliberately directed at showing how we can create an order that does not derive from anything more than the solidaristic impulses scattered within us. His "fundamental premise" is that "a belief can still regulate action, can still be thought worth dying for, among people who are quite aware that this belief is caused by nothing deeper than contingent historical circumstance" (*Contingency, Irony, and Solidarity*, 189). Rorty is quite explicit that it is only the experiential level that can be relied upon to support liberal freedoms, not the philosophic defenses that are more dubious than the freedoms themselves. The solidarity that is required to treat all others with dignity and respect can be promoted only through the enlargement of our existing feelings of solidarity. "The wrong way is to think of it as urging us to *recognize* such a solidarity that exists antecedently to our recognition of it" (196). Rather than argument, he proposes the existential enlargement of our sympathy with the suffering of others as the means of securing a liberal order.

The same living consensus is what enables Jeffrey Stout to claim, in a development of Rorty's pragmatism, that we must not confuse the "relativity of justification with the relativity of truth" (*Ethics after Babel*, 94). His appropriately titled book shows how the fact of moral disagreement does not necessarily undermine the possibility of any common moral order. Stout argues that disagreement occurs against a background of agreement and presupposes it. We would not argue with one another at all if we were convinced that there was nothing in common and no possibility of reaching a convergence of minds on the controversies that beset us. The existence of disagreement has, Stout maintains, clouded our awareness of the large area of uncontroversial consensus that allows us to reach so many decisions routinely and without conflict. When seriously divisive issues do emerge they should not be permitted to expand beyond their respective purviews to call into question the very possibility of moral agreement in principle.

This is what Stout sees as the greatest danger of the prominence of such apparently irreconcilable conflicts as abortion or homosexuality. The relativity or perspectivism that attaches to these debates is quickly expanded to make the entire moral consensus appear problematic. In fact, the controversies are pursued seriously only because of the sense that the areas of agreement are large enough that we could expect that an evocative appeal should be capable of extending them into the areas of disagreement. It is because of the preexisting moral consensus that we take our opponents seriously. The difficulty is that we have sought to short-circuit the process, to eliminate the controversies through the construction of an incontestable neutral criterion to resolve them. When that effort fails, as it has in contemporary liberal politics, the collapse threatens the possibility of any common moral ground between us. The relativity of all the attempts at moral justification seems to suggest the relativity of moral truth.

Stout presents a forceful refutation of the conclusion and thereby makes explicit what is more often unspoken in Rorty, Rawls, and the "nonfoundationalists." That is, their acceptance of the contingency of their principles is not tantamount to conceding the arbitrariness of their convictions. Stout overcomes the apparent indefeasibility of this position by overturning the demand for a rational foundation. Any proposed foundation would itself be more uncertain than what it is intended to support. We must recognize the inescapability of moral starting points. Moral truth is given in immediacy with a conviction that cannot be improved and may even be threatened through the resort to demonstration. Pragmatism, with its deflection of foundational questions, can therefore be understood more properly as an assertion of the irreducibility of moral truth rather than of its radical contingency.

It is not clear whether Rorty accepts Stout's extrapolation of his liberal irony, but it does make plausible the reconciliation of the inner tensions. The reconciliation occurs on the level not of theory but of practice. Stout shows how the lack of theoretical coherence can be borne without misgiving, through the realization that it is the living moral convictions that constitute the irreducible presupposition of our converse. "A modest pragmatism, fully understood, would encourage us to view most of our first-order moral beliefs as more certain, and most of our dispositions as more worthy of confidence, than any of the pictures philosophers have introduced in hope of explaining and grounding them" (253). We simply know it is wrong to torture the innocent and, like Aristotle, must insist that only those who have this sense can talk intelligibly about ethics.[8]

This insistence on the priority of virtue, of a knowledge of good and evil, is what enables Stout to avoid the nihilism that Rorty seems to approach. Even though we may not have a language that can conclusively demonstrate the wrongness of fascism, that does not mean our opposition to it is based on a purely arbitrary whim. Reflecting on Rorty's confessed inarticulacy when the torturers come to seize their victims, Stout rejects the implication that the truth about man is made simply by such brutality. "Whatever Rorty means to suggest in this passage, I suggest that our inability to secure an ultimate language of rational commensuration shouldn't induce us to think of our decisions to invent or employ a vocabulary as ultimately unconstrained, as taking place, by necessity, outside of and epistemically prior to the adoption of any vocabulary" (263). We already live in a common world that is structured by the knowledge of the moral good and evil we possess.

Stout is, in other words, able to show more clearly than Rorty or Rawls that the deflection of metaphysical questions is really a way of making morality more secure. But how then does he propose to deal with the conflicting moral convictions that arise, especially if the resort to rational argument has already been set aside as unpromising? The answer is in part the traditional liberal response that we cannot expect agreement on all of the most serious issues. It is enough that "moral discourse in our society can itself be understood as held together by a relatively limited but nonetheless real and significant agreement on the good" (211–12). While recognizing that many things separate us, we can still build a public order on the basis of the real partial agreement that unites us. That is certainly preferable to the alternative of permitting our partial disagreements to undermine all possibility of resolution. "Even civil war carried on by other means is preferable to plain old civil war" (224).

The other more substantive part of the answer to the question of conflict is not fully developed by Stout, but it is worth noting since it will be explored more fully below. It begins with the recognition that knowledge of good is the fruit of moral growth and is not to be attained simply through ratiocination. "That is, you need to be formed into the kind of person who can see a certain sort of activity as unjust, the kind of person for whom moral reasons have motivating force. Becoming that sort of person is not distinct from acquiring a conception of the good" (*Ethics after Babel*, 52). Given that this is the way we acquire moral knowledge, we would expect that a somewhat similar process would play a role in the resolution of moral conflicts. Since the disagreements are themselves moral, they cannot be resolved through an intellectual formulation however sophisticated. A probably substantial part of the resolution of moral conflicts is to be attained through a process of moral growth by which we come to "see" things rightly. If morality is founded on the practice of morality, then its conflicts must be confronted through the medium of practice as well.

The pragmatists are not yet ready to confront all the implications of their existential turn, but they have begun to point to the resources available to liberal society to confront its own uncertainties. Such resources are largely within the living practice of liberal political institutions and traditions and are not to be sought in any more objective criteria beyond them. The authority of a liberal public order is most firmly grounded in the existential resonance of the men and women who live under it and not in the theoretical coherence of the arguments that are from time to time adduced to support it. Nothing is, of course, solved by that recognition, but some of the anxiety about liberalism as a halfway house to nihilism may perhaps be removed. Something of the earlier unquestioning self-confidence and self-assurance of the liberal tradition seems to have been recovered, only now it is on the other side of the abyss that the liberal impulse has contemplated as one of the darker possibilities contained within itself.

Nonfoundational Truth of Liberal Politics
MICHAEL OAKESHOTT

The man who has given most profound expression to this postmodern liberal philosophy is Michael Oakeshott. The full measure of his achievement in evoking what a nonfoundational liberal politics might look like has not yet been taken.[9] He is not even widely recognized as a liberal thinker. That is understandable because his intellectual reach is considerably beyond the range of arguments we have become accustomed to among analytic liberal philosophers. But Oakeshott's public contribution is most appropriately considered as a contribution to the self-understanding of liberal society. He has shown how a liberal political order can be sustained without a theoretical underpinning because it is, like all politics, primarily a practice that must be there prior to all reflection on it. Oakeshott has clarified this performative dimension of politics which thereby obviates the need for foundations. Theory comes later, as an "abridgement" to a practice that is more or less functioning successfully.

What makes Oakeshott's work a contribution to liberal reflection on politics is that the practice that most concerns him is that of his own society, England, and others like it. Liberal practice constitutes the subject matter for his ruminations. It is significant that Oakeshott does not attempt to construct any universal political theory, capable of applying to all men in all places and all times. He takes seriously his own injunctions against the independence of theory and more modestly undertakes the task of reflecting on the practice that is already in place. For this reason he is perhaps not even self-consciously a liberal political thinker, but simply a political thinker who happens to live in a liberal democratic tradition. His reflections on politics are then inescapably reflections on liberal democracy.

Yet he also remains a theorist, however closely he follows the contours of historical tradition. That means that Oakeshott never becomes captive to the concrete practice of politics from which his reflections begin. Unlike a mere defender of the status quo, he moves from the practical world to an understanding of its place in relation to the wider context of human life that is the goal of all genuine theory. The result might best be described, as so much else in Oakeshott, in terms of an Aristotelian sense of the practical as the starting point from which all theoretical reflection must begin. It is because Oakeshott reaches a philosophical understanding of politics that he no longer sounds like an exponent of liberal ideas. But because he does attain such a depth of insight, Oakeshott presents us with the theoretically most profound account of liberal political order currently available.

That qualitative difference becomes visible in his understanding of the historical moment in which our reflections must begin. Oakeshott has understood the crisis of the liberal tradition sufficiently to recognize fully its self-created nature. He never mouths the platitudes that even on the lips of "liberal ironists" never quite succeed in overcoming their flatness. The failure of the Enlightenment project of finding a rational demonstration of the principles of moral and political order does not carry the reverberations of anxiety that it does even for Rorty. Oakeshott knows that it is not simply a matter of recognizing that we now must get along without our "metaphysical" or "epistemological" props, in a world now seen to be based on nothing more substantial than our own contingent willingness to cooperate. His position is the even more profound response of recognizing that the idea of demonstrative foundations for order was a categorial mistake from the start. There is nothing to be missed since there never was anything there, even when we seemed to believe there was.

The moral life is based not on ideals or arguments but on a living practice. A habit of affections and behavior become established when certain ways of living become connected with our amour propre, our sense of our selves. Moral education has taken hold in a person "when the spring of his conduct is not an attachment to an ideal or a felt duty to obey a rule, but his self-esteem, and when to act wrongly is felt as a diminution of his self-esteem" (*Rationalism and Politics,* 470). Such a practice is, Oakeshott observes, "remarkably stable" because, not being based on a system, the disappearance or collapse of one part of it does not spread to affect any other parts. It has the living variability and durability of custom that is capable of changing and remaining at the same time. But when a major crisis does occur, something that shakes the self-confidence of customary morality, it has few resources to defend itself. Recovery is often sought by searching for an intellectual formulation of the truth that has been lost in the living practice.

The elaboration of morality, with its criteria and rules, comes to seem a more reliable avenue to the good than the customary practice of virtues. When the right course of action is no longer apparent in the confusion of prescriptions, there is a sense that clarity can be regained if we can only articulate the essential principles that apply everywhere. But the quest for moral ideals, Oakeshott maintains, has the unintended effect of drawing attention away from the habitual character of moral practice. Knowledge of abstract ideals often comes to be seen as the means of moral formation. This is to deny the fundamentally "poetic" nature of all human activity. Like the poet we do not know what we want to say or do first and then proceed with the operation. Rather we discover what is on our mind and what we intend through the very process of bringing it forth in the activity.

There are no moral ideals before the concrete moral practices and so the effort to move from ideals to realization reverses the relationship that exists between them. It fails to recognize that "the capital of moral ideals upon which a morality of the pursuit of moral ideals goes into business has always been accumulated by a morality of habitual behavior, and appears in the form of abstract ideas only because (for the purposes of subscription) it has been transformed by reflective thought into a currency of ideas" (*Rationalism and Politics,* 480). Nothing in these observations is intended, according to Oakeshott, to devalue the role of reflective thought in guiding moral life, but only to point out that the prescriptive principles are not the foundations for that life. The attempt to treat moral principles as if they were capable of such a transformative role can only be disastrous. "In the life of an individual this collapse need not necessarily be fatal; in the life of a society it is likely to be irretrievable. For a society is a common way of life; and not only is it true that a society may perish of a disease which is not necessarily fatal even to those of its members who suffer from it, but it is also true that what is corrupting in the society may not be corrupting in its members" (480).

That insight is what enables Oakeshott to make sense of the moral chaos and darkness that has overtaken much of our world. It explains how "in a world dizzy with moral ideals we know less and less about how to behave in public and in private than ever before" (481). The futility of the attempt to construct a moral Tower of Babel has become apparent in the failure to establish any of our ideals with incontrovertible certainty. But that inability is less significant than the failure of the reflective exercise in morality to advance the life of virtue one whit. Indeed, it very often has the opposite effect by promoting a sense of moral superiority through the self-conscious discussion of ideals, while neglecting the more concrete efforts required to make real moral improvements in the practical lives of human beings. Contemplation of the ideals becomes an irresponsible flight from reality. "For the remarkable thing about contemporary European morality is not merely that its form is dominated by the selfconscious pursuit of ideals, but that this form is generally thought to be better and higher than any other" (486).

That is the dangerous self-deception against which Oakeshott bends his efforts. His study *On Human Conduct* is a masterly account of the participatory character of order whose nature is disclosed primarily through its concrete enactment, and only secondarily through its summary self-identifications. More clearly than Dworkin or Rorty he can explain why morality is capable of standing without presuppositions. It is irreducible to any further reality because its reality is that of a practice. All discussion of foundations is at a remove from that concreteness and adds nothing that is not already present in the practice. There is no superior viewpoint than the engagement in morality and politics itself, and the most satisfactory theoretical account is one that arises through the meditative explication of the practice.

All talk of a teleological or metaphysical foundation to action misses, according to Oakeshott, the fundamental nature of human conduct. That is that it is intelligent and not merely intelligible activity. It is the outcome not of causes that impinge objectively on the agent, but of reasons that have been consciously adduced in the action. One falls into a "categorial mistake," failing to grasp the most elementary feature of the reality one is talking about, if one pursues the methods of psychology or sociology in studying human conduct. These disciplines seek an explanation in terms of so-called objective factors beyond the subject. In their willingness to consider the causative influences of everything from diet to toilet-training, from genetics to demographics, they exhibit an empirical obscurantism that is willing to consider every explanation but what people themselves say. In contrast, Oakeshott insists that "a belief is what it means to the believer" (*On Human Conduct*, 23).

Human action is not like the movements of a clock or the growth of a plant. It is a conscious activity whose existence depends on the consciously chosen course of action, and whose nature is defined by what the agent understands or misunderstands it to be. Unlike a mere feeling, our reason for acting is open to question and examination. We may be mistaken in our understanding of the situation to which we respond and our response may be wholly inappropriate to the situation, but the relationship is neither blind nor determined. It is constituted by our understanding and therefore open to free reflective examination. Even our likes and dislikes, Oakeshott emphasizes, "are not 'merely subjective'; they are exhibitions of intelligence capable of being investigated" (52). Our actions are not autonomic but the products of intelligence and therefore free.

Will is, Oakeshott emphasizes, "nothing but intelligence in doing" (39). Freedom is the reflective consciousness in action that is not determined to anything but what it has apprehended as a reason for acting. That is why human agency always contains the possibility of acting differently because the reasons adduced may be considered anew and revised. We are not irrevocably confined within our own skins, compelled always to act out of our self-interest. We can consider the interests of others and that can become a reason that supersedes the preference of self. From beginning to end the process is one of reflective self-determination that is open to revision and reconsideration just because it is a process of reasoning. It does not matter that the self-understanding of the agent may be small for "his powers of self-determination may be modest, he may be easily imposed upon, he may be duped into acting, but he is what he understands himself to be, his contingent situations are what he understands them to be and the actions and utterances in which he responds to them are self-disclosures and self-enactments" (41).

This means that there is no nature that already structures his behavior before he comes to act. "He has a 'history', but no 'nature'; he is what in conduct he becomes. This 'history' is not an evolutionary or teleological process. It is what he enacts for himself in a diurnal engagement, the unceasing articulation of understood responses to endlessly emergent understood situations which continues until he quits the diurnal scene" (41). I do not understand Oakeshott to suggest that man creates himself, with all of the schemes of unlimited possibilities that such visions usually imply. It is possible to maintain that our nature is a project rather than a product without maintaining that we thereby create ourselves. Human nature is incomplete in the sense, not that everything is possible, but that its possibilities are not known in advance and are unfolded through the intelligent self-enactment of our daily lives. The determination of our nature is a process in which we cooperate through our reflective freedom.

The good in this context is not something objective at the end of the process, but the manner that defines how we go about the actions that disclose and enact who we are. Nor is the good some universal quality, like pleasure or happiness, to which the specific activities we engage in can be reduced. All actions are concretely chosen responses to concrete situations and "cannot be understood as a means to the achievement of an end not implicit in itself" (53). Good is neither prior to nor separable from the particular purposes we pursue in the concrete settings in which we find ourselves. "I cannot *want* happiness," Oakeshott observes, "what I want is to idle in Avignon or to hear Caruso sing" (53). This recognition of the concrete diversity of goods and their untranslatability into a common medium sounds remarkably like Rawls's assertion of the radical heterogeneity of goods. The difference is that Oakeshott does not feel compelled to abandon the idea of the good as a defining dimension of all our endeavors.

He understands his position to be closest to Aristotle who also did not regard the good life as a substantive end, but the formal context that permeated all our actions. "He appears to have thought that *eudaimonia* was difficult if not impossible of attainment in the absence of certain substantive conditions (e.g. good health and adequate material means) but it is not itself a substantive condition of things. It is an agent continuously disclosing and enacting himself in his own chosen actions while subscribing adequately to considerations of moral propriety or worth" (118–19). While this is not necessarily the way Aristotle puts it, there is no doubt that Oakeshott understands himself to be within the Aristotelian framework here. Human excellence or good is not a substantive purpose to be pursued in preference to some others, but the practice within which all other purposes are pursued. It is best described as the most inclusive of all practices, as morality.

Without extrinsic purposes of its own, morality defines the conditions of propriety that must be observed in the quest for substantive goods. The echoes of deontological liberal theory are particularly strong in this formal understanding of morality. Where Oakeshott differs is in the nonchalance of his acceptance that there are no rules of morality, or none that are particularly useful in concrete applications. For it is the nature of morality to extend to the full diverse range of human activities and therefore not to be reducible to a few principles, any more than the endless variety of our interests and situations can be reduced to a unity. There may of course be general moral guidelines, but these do not turn out to be of much use because the crucial thing to know is how and when and to what extent they are to be applied. Morality is, like all else that is practical, a practice to be learned only by doing. The measure of what is right in any given situation is, according to a passage of Aristotle that Oakeshott might well have quoted, what the man of practical wisdom or mature man would do under the circumstances.[10] No more specific criterion is possible.

Yet the absence of a conclusive yardstick does not inevitably lead to "interminable and incommensurable" moral disputes. The fact that the criterion remains personal does not entail that it is only subjective. Most moral questions continue to be settled routinely through the more or less stable consensus of meaning that constitutes moral practice. What unites us is not the set of rules, which are themselves episodic "abridgments" of an underlying coherence, but the living practice itself. It does not entail, Oakeshott emphasizes, any commitment to substantive goods because moral practice is the set of conditions within which all substantive goods must be pursued. Morality is the recognition of the proprieties that must be observed as we follow our particular interests and desires. It exists, not through its capacity to deliver certain benefits or to demonstrate its own necessity, but solely and simply through the recognition of its authority in relation to us. This noninstrumental understanding of morality is the key to Oakeshott's conception of civil association.

When the practice of the recognition of rules that ought to govern our substantive purposes acquires institutional expression, we have the essence of a civil association. Oakeshott emphasizes the degree to which this development rests not on a prior approval of the rules themselves or of the institutional representatives who are to enforce them, but simply on the recognition of their authoritative application to us. He introduces the delightfully British example of the process by which a private cricket club, the Marylebone Cricket Club, came to be recognized as the authoritative interpreter of the rules of the game. How is it possible for such public authority to be conferred on an essentially private entity, no different from many other such potential authorities? The answer is that it is simply a practice of recognition that has consolidated itself over a period of time and has come to be seen as the indispensable condition for the existence of a rule defined game.

This is the answer Oakeshott also gives to the question that has bedeviled liberal theorists since Hobbes and Locke. Why do individuals continue to feel obligated to support a public order when it may no longer serve their self-interest? Political order cannot be explained or justified in terms of benefits that, though real, would not exist at all if the citizens were first not willing to support it. "Thus, *respublica* cannot be authoritative on account of its providing shelter from some of the uncertainties of a human life. . . . this cannot be a reason (let alone the reason) for recognizing the authority of *respublica:* civil association can provide these blessings only on account of this recognition" (152). The relationship is strictly noninstrumental. It is neither defined nor measured by the benefits received. We are part of it, not through our choice of rules and institutions of which we approve or disapprove, but primarily through the recognition that it is something that obliges us. As in making a promise we place ourselves under rules; we do not choose the rules, we merely acknowledge them as our own.

Oakeshott distinguishes civil association from what he calls an *enterprise association.* The latter is characterized by the presence of a common purpose, to which the particular purposes of the individual members must be subordinated. In an enterprise association, such as a business, a church or a university, the members have agreed to pursue a particular purpose and by implication have already surrendered their freedom in a range of areas to the managers of the association. They have committed their resources to the common effort that unites them. It is quite otherwise in a civil association that is defined by the freedom of its members. Not having submitted to a common purpose, they cannot be compelled to subordinate themselves to the pursuit of any substantive goods. They remain free to pursue their own wide variety of interests because it is the essence of a civil association that it does not tell them what to do, but only constitutes the conditions in which their free choice may be exercised. A favorite analogy for Oakeshott is the practice of language. Nothing in the rules of language, which also cannot be fully specified, dictates what we are to say, all that it does is provide the ordered framework within which an endless diversity of communications may occur.

That is why Oakeshott can define civil freedom as constituted by the relationship of obligation and authority. What makes the freedom of enterprise associations possible is that they occur within a context of authoritatively recognized rules of civil association. The rules are not imposed. They cannot be imposed because it is their essence that they be recognized as rules, as obligatory, otherwise they would simply have no effect. Just as the rules of cricket have no effect unless they are freely recognized, so the rules of civil association, while they may be backed by more force than is available to the Marylebone Cricket Club, would hardly exist at all without their recognition as rules. A language exists through the free acknowledgment of its rules, civil association arises whenever it is apprehended as the set of conditions that make all other transactions possible.

The rules of civil association cannot function except through the intelligent acknowledgment of their obligatory force over us. It has long been a traditional liberal insight that a man cannot be obliged to anything except through his own voluntary agreement. Oakeshott, it seems to me, has carried this principle a step further by showing how it is connected with the rule observing nature of politics. Rules do not constitute a civitas, a political order, if they are not recognized as applying to us, as specifications of the practice in which we are engaged. There would be neither games nor polities if there were not the free acknowledgment of their authoritative role in relation to us. It is the essence of both that they are played by people who are free, for whom the framework of authority is understood to make possible the particular exercise of that freedom. A game in which one is coerced is not only not cricket, it is no longer a game.

Oakeshott draws a telling analogy between this situation and our relationship to divine law. Just as God does not compel our obedience to his law, but seeks the free response of our acknowledgment of his authority over us, so the state does not impose a purpose on us, but leaves us free to determine our purposes without interference even from the authority that makes that freedom possible. "There is, then, nothing in civil association to threaten the link between belief and conduct which constitutes 'free' agency, and in acknowledging civil authority *cives* have given no hostages to a future in which, their approvals and choices no longer being what they were, they can remain free only in an act of dissociation. Civil freedom is not tied to a choice to be and to remain associated in terms of a common purpose: it is neither more nor less than the absence of such a purpose or choice" (157). To be truly human our actions and purposes must be "self-chosen" or free. The state that recognizes that cannot itself demand subordination to its own purposes. It must acknowledge that its own reason for existence is to make self-direction possible and will understand that its own authority rests on just such a recognition of its role.

The basis of the state is the recognition of its authority as the indispensable dispenser of a system of law, defining "not satisfactions to be sought or actions to be performed, but moral conditions to be subscribed to in seeking self-chosen satisfactions and in performing self-chosen actions" (158). Unlike an enterprise association, Oakeshott emphasizes, the state does not award interests nor is it based on the approval of its members. In language that is strikingly different from that of liberal pluralism but which, on reflection, turns out to be a more profound formulation of the pluralistic ethos, he insists that the *respublica* is based on its recognition as a system of law. "Civil authority and civil obligation are the twin pillars of the civil condition" (149). It is association in terms of recognized rules that enables it to be an association of strangers, people who have different loves and lack moral allegiance to one another (129).

Most modern states have failed, Oakeshott complains, because they have failed to understand the difference between an enterprise and a civil association, between *universitas* and *societas*. As a consequence, the source of their authority has always been precarious as they vacillated unstably between realizing a common national purpose and impartially enforcing a system of law. They have confused authority with power, policy with legitimacy. A *societas*—like a state, friends, neighbors, speakers of a common language—is in a relationship that is not based on choice but on the recognition of rules that apply. The ruler is merely the custodian of the rules, not the manager of a common purpose. "His office is to keep the conversation going, not to determine what is said" (202–3). A corporation, a *universitas,* is the formation of a unity of persons to pursue a substantive purpose; by definition the majority is entitled to take whatever steps it sees fit. The history of the so-called nation-state, itself on Oakeshott's conception a contradiction in terms, has been the history of the confusion of these two fundamental modes of association. For it cannot remain a state if it subordinates all to the good of the nation.

The magnificent modern achievement of the nomocratic state is, in Oakeshott's view, threatened by the ever present possibility of the teleocratic state. Endangered is the sense of self-esteem that derives from taking responsibility for ourselves and directing our own lives, the mutual respect that is expressed in a certain fastidious reluctance to invade the autonomy of others even for their own good. It is no less than the recognition of *das Recht,* the concept in which Hegel gave clearest expression to what it means to be part of a ·community of persons. "To be associated in terms of *das Gesetz* [a system of non-instrumental rules of law] is to be related in terms of conditions which can be observed only in being understood, which can be subscribed to only in self-chosen actions and cannot themselves prescribe substantive conduct; which not only allow 'free' agency but postulate 'free' agents as their Subjects" (261). What is at stake is what it means to be a person, which is to be engaged in actions directed by intelligence and therefore following rules that can be observed only through our own intelligent recognition of them.

This self-transparency becomes clouded through the recurrent demands for a more energetic promotion of purpose. It may be military, economic, social or national but the effect is always the same. The apparatus of government is increased and the individual sinks to the unconsciousness of a cog in the machine. This is the other half of the modern experiment with its repeated efforts to turn the state into a cultural and religious *universitas,* mobilizing the vast resources that are capable of building national solidarity. But the demand for such substantive governance only arises from failed individuals unwilling or unable to support the burden of self-responsibility. They have been taken in by the illusion that they will remain free individuals when the government has secured all of the goods they desire. They do not see that such a state is an inherently compulsory association where all choice has been surrendered to the managers. "The 'freedom' inherent in such a state is the condition of being released from every care in the world save one; namely, the care not to be idle in fulfilling one's role in the enterprise, not to inhibit or prejudice that complete mobilization of resources which constitutes such a state. . . . The member of such a state enjoys the composure of the conscript assured of his dinner. His 'freedom' is warm, compensated servility" (317).

Continuing Resources of Liberal Tradition

Michael Oakeshott provides the clearest illustration of how a nonfoundational liberal order is still capable of identifying the dangers that tend to undermine it and finding the appropriate theoretical means to defend itself. It is not stuck irretrievably in the morass of historicist contingency. There is no need to helplessly observe the steady disintegration of the liberal order while we await the arrival of an incontrovertible demonstration of its truth. Nor are we condemned to surrender the contest in light of the failure of all existing theoretical formulations. Resistance can begin from the mode of knowledge that is already present in our practice. A meditative expansion of the conviction that animates our living is impervious to the criticism that it is in need of a foundation. The fact that the liberal intuition already guides our existence is the irrefragable proof that it arises from a bedrock of knowledge.

The liberal unfolding may not be derived from a very comprehensive or sophisticated knowledge of order, nor is it necessarily susceptible to a definitive formulation, but it is a mode of knowledge however halting and inarticulate. There is no getting behind this to a set of philosophical principles that explain why we happen to share these particular conceptions of how we should live. As Rorty, Stout, and the constructivist liberals recognize, the principles likely to be adduced are more questionable than the practical convictions they are supposed to support. That is where the certainty lies, as evidenced by their own acceptance of the historical contingency of their convictions rather than abandonment of the convictions themselves. They simply "know" it is wrong to torture the innocent.

Oakeshott has clarified the situation by explaining how morality is a mode of knowledge not deduced from principles. It is a practice whose knowledge is learned by taking part in the practice. He does not conclude that there are no principles to guide it and that it is therefore incurably subjective. Principles can be abstracted from the practice, but by themselves they provide no assistance in knowing how to apply them. In asserting that no rule of reason, principle of utility, or categorical imperative can establish the desirability of a particular course of action, Oakeshott insists that "this is not on account of any doubt there may be about a rational or divine cosmic order of unquestionable worth or because the moral prescriptions (for example) from which civil rules are said to be deduced are not self-evidently desirable, but because inference of this kind is impossible: no civil rule can be *deduced* from the Golden Rule or from the Kantian categorical imperative" (*On Human Conduct*, 174).

Impregnable formulations and demonstrative conclusions from principles may be impossible, but this does not mean that there is no such thing as knowledge of good and evil. Such knowledge is universally practical. No doubt this is a source of difficulty in that good action is vulnerable to the clever objector who demands to have its goodness demonstrated to him. But it is also a source of strength, as Oakeshott has suggested, since the actions will continue independent of the merits and defects of the surrounding intellectual skepticism. The source of the actions' strength lies not in discourse but in the sense of reality that may come more fully into consciousness through discourse yet is already there prior to the start of all our efforts to express it. We cannot get back beyond the preanalytic awareness of an order in which we participate through our practice of living.

There is no other guide but what has become available to us through the practice itself; anything else is either empty or useless. The historical contingency of our moral knowledge must be taken seriously, because it is only what has been discovered through the historical struggle for order that can point the way. There is no knowledge other than what has concretely emerged in the life of human beings over time. If it is transmitted to us then it forms the bulk of what we know, added to the meager store of insights that occur in our own experience. There is no need to bewail it as a mere "historical contingency" to the extent that the tradition speaks to our deepest intimations of what is right in human life. It is contingent only in its transmission to us, not in its truth that cannot be doubted, however imperfectly we may yet glimpse it.

This situation explains why Oakeshott is so strong an advocate of immersion in the tradition as the best moral and political formation.[11] It is through contact with that wider range of practical experience that our own limited sense of things is enlarged. Even when the tradition has broken down, as he recognizes it has for so many people today, the only resources of renewal are the elements of the tradition that still retain their vitality. A practice can be revived only from within, otherwise it is a mere artificial imposition whose hollowness will soon become evident as it collapses. The strengthening and reinvigoration of the liberal tradition, which has been the inspiration for the writers we have surveyed, would be best served by an effort to expand the core convictions that still exist even in fragmentary form. This is preferable to the attempt, now largely abandoned, to find a demonstrative formulation, or to the now more prevalent attempts to immunize liberal politics against theoretical questions.

The advice is similar to that which Solzhenitsyn once gave to his countrymen during a period of even greater moral confusion, when cruelty seemed to have all the force of ideological righteousness on its side. "Live not by lies," he advised, and in the process of resistance the truth will become plainer to us. It does not matter that everyone, like Pilate, has a different answer to the question "what is truth?" or that controversy swirls around the issues. "But the answer could not be simpler: decide *yourself*, as your conscience dictates . . . each person will have his own perception of the line where the public and state lie begins . . . And *there*, at the point where *you yourself* in all honesty see the borderline of the lie, is where you must refuse to submit to that lie. You must shun *that part* of the lie that is clear and obvious to you."[12] Growth in virtue does not have to await the resolution of the theoretical disputes nor, as we have seen, can the philosophical elaborations arrive at any coherence without relating them to concrete moral practice.

By following the fragments of the practice that are still viable, an effort of expansion and recovery can be undertaken that is itself a revitalization of the tradition from within. Oakeshott's work, I have argued, is such an expansion of the fragmentary liberal tradition within which we live. He exemplifies the process by which the meditative unfolding takes place through resistance against the tendencies that work to undermine it. In contemplating the forces that conspire to destroy the essence of the liberal understanding of human self-responsibility, Oakeshott brought forth an impressive evocation of the core liberal pride in the sense of living life in one's own way. We sense the tone of disdain for all who, like the conscript settling for his dinner rather than his liberty, have allowed the gruel of material security to draw them away from their birthright of intelligent independence.

Oakeshott perceives that it is this nobility of self-responsibility that is the core of the liberal appeal. It is evoked in the contemplation of the abyss opened up by the transformation of the state into an enterprise association, even when the enterprise consists in securing the substantive welfare of all its citizens. The paternal reach of all such schemes of universal care, quite apart from any practical questions of efficacy or cost, can only stifle the exercise of responsibility that is so central to the growth of a human being. Nor is there any possibility of retaining one without the other. The thought that one can progressively relieve individuals of the risks and burdens of living without also making them less self-reliant and less independent minded is an illusion that is scarcely indulged by the most utopian liberals today.

But the real danger, Oakeshott emphasizes, is political rather than psychological. It is not merely the will to act that may be sapped by paternalism, but the political liberty of action will disappear, too. Enterprise associations are "inherently compulsory." By definition, they must subordinate the purposes of the members to the attainment of the common purpose, for that is the justification of their existence. They are governed by the will of the majority that is free to make whatever decisions it chooses and is entitled to impose them on those who remain in the minority. The latter have agreed to abide by the majority will as the only effective means of procuring the purpose for which the association has been constituted. But what of those who do not wish to be a part of the enterprise? How will their liberty be preserved?

That is the provenance of the state whose function is to ensure that we are not coerced into enterprises against our will. The difficulty arises when the state itself has virtually become an enterprise association. There is then no barrier between the individual and the majority whose will happens to define the common task at hand and possesses the necessary means of compelling the cooperation of all in its attainment. It is no longer a state if it cannot provide the conditions in which human beings can pursue the good according to their own reason. Nor does it make possible a properly human life if individuals are not left free to follow the lights of their own intelligence. There must be the freedom to make mistakes, even with regard to our own welfare, if we are to be the kind of beings who determine our own lives. It is not enough that our actions be intelligible in relation to their goal; the actions must be intelligent as well. They must be chosen because we understand how they relate to our telos.

Such a realization, which is unfolded so elegantly by Oakeshott, does not arise from any freestanding principles or from any contestable premises. There is no necessity to posit an elaborate speculation on the beginning of society nor to assert the irreducibility of moral rights. His meditation flows from the practice of the liberal understanding of self-government and is rooted, as it is for all the other theorists surveyed, in the living conviction of what is right in their practical experience. Prior to all reflection is the sense of a right order that must be defended through its articulation. Without that preanalytic sense there would be neither a reason nor a direction for the unfolding of the moral reflection.

Just as the process does not have to await the attainment of an unquestionable first principle, since there is no beginning that is not itself also saturated with moral significance, so there is no privileged point at which the process of objectifying our convictions must begin. We cannot step outside the stream of existence in which we find ourselves in order to map the whole. Obligations emerge within our experience, and we are called to respond to them in all the whirling, buzzing confusion of ongoing life. Which ones are taken up first is unimportant. What matters is that we not turn our back on the problems that impose themselves on us, that we follow the intimations of goodness and resist the attractions of evil as they begin to disclose themselves in the small and large arenas of our lives. All this is admirably summed up in Oakeshott's conception of politics as a moral practice.

It is a mode that is increasingly, if not yet very coherently, being accepted by more conventional liberal thinkers. Robert Nozick reveals the effect that such a reorientation is likely to have in the approach to philosophizing. His later work has abandoned the brittle brilliance of analysis present in *Anarchy, State and Utopia* to recognize that the real issues are existential and that no chain of argument, however logically compelling, can effect the growth of the soul in which real moral knowledge takes place. "No longer, however, would we try to justify the good from within a largely neutral theory of reality; reality gets built upon truth, goodness, beauty, and holiness from the beginning." He has come to suspect that the project of finding a neutral ground for the good arises from an anxiety that goodness is not strong enough to draw us on its own.

> How would we view ethics if we *did* trust our inclinations? We then might see it as an amplification of our good inclinations, as enlarging, regularizing, and channeling them, as telling how to become light's vessel and transmitter. If the theoretical building of foundations for ethics is born of distrust of light's allure—that is, distrust of our configuration of desires—then the task is not to buttress that light by argument but to turn ourselves into beings who then can trust our inclinations. (*The Examined Life,* 215, 216)

It bespeaks the vitality of the liberal tradition that the deepest challenges confronting it are recognized as moral. All the implications of that insight may not yet have been realized, but the direction to be pursued has been strongly sensed. The regeneration of moral convictions must be the work not of conceptual clarification but of entering into the struggle to live out what we already sense to be our own best intimations. From the confrontation with injustice we are compelled to bring forth our understanding of what justice is. The resistance to dehumanization illumines our sense of what is constitutive of our humanity; the inchoate sense of what is precious expands into a more transparent awareness of what it is that cannot be lost without likewise losing what makes life itself worth living. Beneath the surface of liberal "abridgments" we discover a depth of moral conviction that is ultimately its sustaining source.

But that discovery is the fruit of the struggle with untruth. The insights gained by liberal theorists such as Rawls or Hayek or Rorty have themselves been won through such a confrontation with the dangers that were perceived to threaten the liberal achievement of order. None of the theorists succeeded in definitively articulating the truth that is glimpsed in the liberal tradition. But their reflections leave us in no doubt that there is such a moral inspiration behind it. This is transparent in the cases of Rawls and Rorty who admit that they can find no clearer way of articulating it than to confess that liberal order is rooted in their deepest nondiscursive sentiments. Struggle has in the same way been the means by which liberal polities have found within themselves the resources to withstand the more virulent revolutionary opponents. The same willingness to confront their own problems has been the indispensable means for liberal societies to regenerate, if only fitfully through periodic calls for reform, the moral convictions that remain to them.

Instead of turning away from the difficulties that confront them, liberal democracies can preserve themselves only if they are willing to take up the challenges that are pressed upon them. That requires taking the full measure of the historical situation in which the liberal tradition finds itself and acknowledging the true extent of its own limitations and failures. A self-study of this nature would entail the admission of what we have seen to be liberalism's own responsibility for much of the crisis of confidence that has overtaken it. Liberals must acknowledge that the corrosive effects of liberalism itself, with its ceaseless demands to expand the rights to liberty, has dissolved the sense of the limit that must be preserved through the protection of liberty.

Beyond even its own confusion, the liberal mind must begin to appreciate the depth of the moral crisis that has engulfed all of modern civilization. It is a crisis so extensive that many of the most perceptive observers, such as Alasdair MacIntyre, have concluded that the liberal tradition simply lacks the resources for dealing with it. I am both more sanguine about liberal practice and, I hope, more realistic in accepting Oakeshott's pronouncement that whatever can be done must arise from the remnants of the tradition that are still viable. For while the liberal construction is itself an element within modernity it is not simply a product of the spirit of domination that has preeminently defined our world. Liberal order has its roots in spiritual and moral traditions that are premodern and may be considered a public translation of them in the modern world. It is always an error to misapprehend the appearance of liberal politics for the spirit that gives it life.

Yet it must struggle with another spirit, the drive to control and dominate reality, which it has neither wholly rejected nor wholly embraced. The untangling of this ambivalent relationship is at the center of the crisis in which the liberal tradition finds itself. The outcome depends on the question of the extent to which liberal convictions of the inviolable dignity of the individual and the absolute necessity of respecting the exercise of intelligent self-responsibility will survive. The denigration of "freedom and dignity" as incurably outmoded notions was not simply a prejudice of the totalitarian ideological movements. It is an attitude more pervasively embedded in the drive for scientific and technological domination that has spread to every corner of the modern world. The temptation to accept "the abolition of man" in the name of the extension of his power is a danger from which none of us can claim immunity.[13]

It is perhaps the most deeply ingrained part of our modern outlook that we can through our concerted efforts overcome the vicissitudes of the human condition. The experience of conquering disease and of so successfully "relieving man's estate" inevitably encourages the expectation that nothing stands in the way of a final victory over our own finitude. All of our efforts to conquer disease and stave off suffering are bent toward this goal. Only the occasional setback, such as the AIDS epidemic, prevents the conclusion from becoming irresistible so that there are no limits to what can be accomplished. We do not take up the task in a spirit of fatalism, prepared to accept the inevitable encounter with a limit beyond which we cannot go. The path we have already traveled has demonstrated that the meek do not inherit the earth. Only those who have the temerity to prevail, to test their wills against a recalcitrant reality, can compel nature to yield the secrets by which we become its masters.[14]

Within that context all traditional talk of respect for limits sounds paltry and quaint. How can we allow outmoded scruples about what human beings should be permitted to do to one another or to themselves stand in the way of the great engine of science? We all know what happens to those who are foolish enough to stand in the way of engines thundering toward them. The premise of science and technology is that we cannot assume there are any preset limits to what is possible—otherwise, we would never have made such staggering progress. A strong consciousness of the uniqueness of modernity, in being the first civilization to discard all traditional limits, forms the self-understanding of our world. And it is difficult to dispute its accuracy, in light of the overwhelming success of modern technological science within its own frame of reference.

How can we assert that there are rights of a human being that can never be invaded? That is the quandary of contemporary liberal politics at its most perplexing level. Liberal self-understanding has already embraced the value of free rational inquiry and the benefits that devolve from it in the modern world. In addition, liberal thought has accepted, albeit ambivalently, the conception that the expansion of individual freedom is its own deepest justification. What, then, can be said to those who insist on using that freedom in order to abandon it? This is different from the earlier liberal reflections that it was contradictory to sell oneself into slavery since there would be no independent person left to receive the payment. Now we are asked to accept the possibility as a benefit to the person. All our reservations pale before the imperious rights of free consent.

The danger of voluntary and eventually involuntary dehumanization has become increasingly prominent as the control of nature has become more and more the control of human nature. What are the limits beyond which we should not go? Is there a human essence that we must struggle at all costs to preserve? How can such a human core be defined other than as the exercise of free consent? Is it necessary to preserve the possibility of future exercise of liberty as one of the restraints on liberty? Contemporary liberalism confronts its own incoherence in such questions. They painfully drive home to us the extent to which the respect for individual freedom and dignity rested on sandy ground. When put to the test our fundamental convictions seem to come tumbling down.

Do we believe in anything more substantial than is captured by that most dubious of all contemporary evocations, "quality of life"? Is our life then something whose value can be measured and therefore must carry with it a fixed quantity of rights? When that quantity is overstepped, a person's right to life has been exhausted and nothing stands in the way of his termination. Of course, all of this is expressed in the conventional liberal language of expanding the liberty of the individual, who should never be compelled to endure a quality of life that has become intolerable for him. The confusion of contemporary liberal reflection is best illustrated by its inability to recognize that in allowing an individual to set a value on his life we have also consented to the principle that his life is only of limited value. There is nothing to prevent the state or society from acting on the same assessment of his value and assigning a limit to the preservation of his rights. No publicly authoritative grounds remain for an objection, and certainly all claim to render an objection has been surrendered by the individual.

There is no use saying that the state is not entitled to invade the prerogative of the individual's exercise of liberty, that what may be allowed to the individual is never allowed to the state. Liberty means very little if there is no recognition of an unconditional right to life. How can the exercise of liberty be protected if we have not agreed that the being who possesses it must first be preserved? The value of liberty is itself infected with the same finiteness that has become attached to the value of life. How can liberty be accorded unlimited respect if its foundation in life has been rendered conditional? What is the value of the liberty of that which does not exist? It is a purely hypothetical value.

The same is true of the many efforts to preserve the quality of life from the unborn to the terminally ill. The confusion is best shown in our unthinking usage of this kind of language despite the fact that the contradictions are immediately visible. How can there be any quality if there is no life? It makes no sense to speak of the quality of life except in the context of accepting unconditionally the value of life. We cannot speak of therapeutic abortions as protecting the quality of life of the fetus, no more than active euthanasia can be justified in the name of preserving the quality of life of the patient. Neither can have any quality of life because they have no life. What is often not so subtly indicated is that their demise preserves the quality of life for the rest of us.

The distillation of such confusion, however, does not require the importation of a religious viewpoint or the appeal to an extraneous philosophical tradition. It can be undertaken from within the perspective of a liberal philosophy motivated and guided by a sense of the personal depth that is at stake. The deepest appeal of the liberal tradition, as we have seen, is that it evokes the most profound respect for what a human being is. Different from a computer or a cabbage or a cat, not only do we exhibit intelligible patterns of behavior but we are intelligent as well. We are capable of understanding what we do and doing it because we understand. To the extent that we are treated as subordinate to some particular characteristics or contributions of our existence, our intelligent self-direction is undermined and we become interchangeable with any other unintelligent elements. If the exercise of our free self-responsibility is denied, then no other benefits are possible.

By contemplating the prospect of this kind of inversion of our satisfactions to our liberties we begin to sense the reality that is in danger of being lost. There can be no real fulfillment if it can no longer be freely enjoyed by our own choice. All that is distinctive in human relationships, most of all the giving and receiving of love, is rendered nugatory if the person is deprived of his source in free personal decisions. Who wants to be loved through compulsion? Can we even call it human love? This is the danger that is courted as we begin to think of ourselves in wholly instrumental or functional terms, as having a defined course of development or contribution that must be implemented. Strictly speaking, a human being is not for any purpose, since we are the kinds of beings whose nature is to define their own purpose. It is a grave error to adopt the instrumental language of contemporary medical therapy. When we are exhorted to become functional human beings, we should always retort, "functional for what?" Or when we are advised to produce optimum babies, the reply should be, "optimum for what?"

In this way we might become aware that such instrumental language simply does not apply to human beings. It might alert us to the nature of the Faustian bargain that the most acute observers have long perceived at the heart of the modern world. We have not only vastly expanded the power available to the human race but also simultaneously eliminated the principles of goodness that are needed to guide its use. The two are intimately related. What has made possible the great extension of our power over nature is that we ceased to look on nature as something fixed; instead, we regarded nature as a field whose potentialities were open to exploitation by those who possessed the ingenuity and will to master it. The problem is that nature can then no longer guide its use, for we have long since ceased to treat the order of nature as sacrosanct.

The crisis comes to a head only when the extension of our control begins to include human nature. Without a stable notion of what constitutes "man's estate," what is there to guide the efforts designed for its relief? The vast expansion of power has been purchased at the price of what would make the power itself worth having. Without a conception of what a human being should be, the power, far from serving man, becomes his master. Nothing restrains its application, for in the absence of any criterion of whether it is well or ill used, we are forced to contemplate the prospect of our endless technological reconstruction. Even happiness cannot provide a goal, because what is to constitute happiness is susceptible of unlimited modification. What has evaporated is the idea of man as something fixed whose good is to be served.

Without an understanding of human nature as something given, however ill defined its parameters may be, there ceases to be anything substantive to benefit. It is not simply that we no longer have a consensus on what is good for human beings, but that there are no longer fixed human beings whose good is to be sought. What humanity is to be is itself something to be decided. In breaking free from the order of nature as something given we have learned to make nature our servant, but in cutting the link to the givenness of our own nature the master too has been overcome. By stepping beyond good and evil, as the prophets Nietzsche and Dostoyevsky understood, we have lost ourselves. Adrift without any sense of who we are or what we are to become, we enter the abyss of nihilism that is indeed the abolition of man.

We have already encountered this nightmare in the totalitarian horror of the twentieth century. The ideological systems provided the crucial justification for the reconstruction of human nature, by proclaiming the removal of all moral limitations on what may be done. As the product of historical contingency, human beings are simply so much malleable material to be remade at will. Now we recognize that the same inspiration prevails in the technological science that continues to define our modern world. Nothing is absolutely prohibited. There may be more caution and more reservations admitted along the way, but the path is just as inexorable. The trajectory of our interventions in shaping human beings through genetic and behavioral science does not encounter any absolute barriers. There is no limit whose boundaries we cannot contemplate transgressing.[15] Even the prospect that we are approaching an end point where the human being will be defined wholly in functional terms does not seem to raise the alarm that the entire enterprise will then have lost its own justification and purpose. Whose estate is to be relieved when man himself has been wholly absorbed into the instrumental chain?

The perfunctory character of liberal political language has been ill equipped to come to grips with the most profound issues. Comfortable with a surface evocation of rights where the depth remains unarticulated, liberal-opinion leaders have generally not gone much beyond the most elementary reflections on the necessity of informed consent. What the consent is for—and whether it is consistent with a scheme of growing self-responsibility in which the inviolable dignity of free intelligent beings is above all to be respected—is generally not broached. Yet this is not to say that inarticulate misgivings are not present. They are often strongly in evidence, but they cannot find the formulations that would render them coherent. Often they simply take the shape of silent relief when the burden of objection is taken up by the representatives of a religious viewpoint, such as the Catholics or evangelical Protestants.

The reason is not that the liberal tradition lacks a depth of conviction whose coherence can be brought forth. We have seen in this chapter that credible formulations are possible and that liberal principles continue to represent an authoritative public truth. Rather, the reason for the incoherence is that the liberal construction is almost constitutionally incapable of acknowledging its own depth. Occasionally the depth becomes visible as when Rawls observes that in the prospect of "a society in which no one had the slightest desire to act on these duties [of justice], we see that it would express an indifference if not disdain for human beings that would make a sense of our own worth impossible" (*A Theory of Justice*, 339). Instead of articulating the sense of revulsion at injustice, as Camus had done earlier in *The Rebel* (which had been the real reason for Rawls's rejection of such an order), Rawls returned to his reflections on the original position as the embodiment of our sense of fairness as a whole. His problem, then, is that the original position does nothing to explain the sense of fairness that is its own underpinning.

What needs to be explained, therefore, is the peculiar reticence of the liberal tradition in regard to its own depth. It is not, as we have seen, that it lacks depth, for the flimsy coherence of its evocations does not plausibly account for the authority that the liberal symbolism exercises on the public imagination throughout the contemporary world. Nor would it explain the surprising resilience of liberal democracies, especially in a century where they have defied the odds to triumph over all rivals. Nor does it account for the rich profusion of liberal theorizing that, despite the failure of any formulation to win uncontested preeminence, has made the latter half of the century one of the high-water marks of liberal philosophizing. No, there is an undeniable depth of liberal conviction that has all along been the secret of its strength. But now perhaps the very secret of its invulnerability, the unspoken depth of its appeal, has become a liability. When liberal thought can no longer avoid confronting the abyss of philosophical nihilism that has also grown within its bosom, then it can no longer avoid a full confession of the existential grounds of its own convictions. The process must begin with an acknowledgment of the utopian conceit that liberal society could dispense with an acknowledgment of any spiritual underpinnings.

3

Utopian Forgetfulness of Depth

Discussion of an existential depth to our discourse inevitably engenders a degree of methodological discomfort. This is particularly the case among theorists whose occupation is in dealing with the discursive level of argumentation. What cannot be detected through the medium of language can scarcely be detected at all, let alone rendered transparent through the methods of analysis. Without the theoretical equipment to examine experiences and symbols, most contemporary philosophers are content simply to follow Ludwig Wittgenstein's observation that "what we cannot talk about we must pass over in silence."[1] More recently, many have also abandoned even the notion that coherent discourse is possible because of the incommensurability of all starting points. Largely overlooked is the possibility that the starting point lies in the existential resonances that can be reconstructed on the basis of their discursive elaborations.

The neglect of the experiential becomes politically significant when it converges with the customary liberal silence concerning its own foundations. It has been deeply impressed upon the liberal mind frame that its particular construction is specifically designed to prevent the resurfacing of the question of foundations. Minimal liberal order was to guarantee public peace by avoiding the kind of divisiveness that arises when ultimate questions are posed. Contemporary liberal theorists are, as they acknowledge, not departing in the slightest from the practice of insisting that the public good is too important to be jeopardized by the injection of such uncertainty. The demand to bracket ultimate philosophical or religious questions is not only a methodological exigence but also in line with the long-standing inclinations of the liberal tradition.

A crisis arises, however, only when liberal society begins to believe its own rhetoric. Silence concerning its roots is mistaken for the absence of any underpinnings. The notion is indulged, contrary to the warning of

George Washington in his Farewell Address, that the moral and political order can be sustained without the benefit of any deeper spiritual impulses.[2] Gradually it becomes accepted that the state has no role even in encouraging the formation of virtues that are desirable or indispensable in its citizens and leaders. Eventually it becomes impossible even to discourage those tendencies that render the citizens and their leaders callous and cruel toward one another. When the crisis explodes publicly, it is greeted with shrill hectoring about values from public figures who have up to then displayed no sustained interest in the formation of virtue.

We have already examined the nature of the crisis of confidence in its theoretical and practical dimensions in Chapter 1. The inability to mount a coherent defense of liberal principles undermines any forceful attempt to instill them in social and political practice. The second chapter took issue with the all-too-ready characterization of this collapse of liberal formulations as spelling the outbreak of civil war carried on by political means. I tried to show that the disintegration of the theoretical enterprise was not equivalent to the disintegration of the liberal impulse and that the demise of some of its supporting virtues was not tantamount to the dissolution of liberal democratic order. The liberal construction continues to function, albeit less confidently and less consistently, because it embodies an authoritative moral truth that resonates with the deepest intimations of who we are. That existential resonance has always been the source of its appeal.

We must now examine what prevents a recognition of the experiential movement that is powerfully, if inarticulately, the indispensable basis for the liberal tradition. Why is it so difficult for liberals to acknowledge that they are drawn by a vision of the good? The discomfort is palpable in the many injunctions against "ontology" or against the raising of "metaphysical" questions, for there is more than an inability to find a satisfactory resolution of such difficulties. There is an abiding unwillingness within the liberal tradition to acknowledge the depth of the moral impulse from which it springs. This is evident in its reticence concerning its own historical antecedents but is more significant in the refusal to countenance its own dependence on virtues that it does not and cannot create.

What is it that prevents liberal theory and practice from returning to the experiential sources from which a renewal might emerge? Is there not something strange about a tradition that when pressed to defend itself is unwilling to acknowledge the roots of its own convictions? That is the deepest level of the crisis that has been building within the liberal ethos for at least a couple of generations. A crisis is characterized not so much by the breakdown of established patterns of order as by the failure of forces that ought to restore and renew it so that it may rise to the challenge of the time. Is it the case that the moral impulses behind liberal political order have ebbed to such a point that they cannot be rejuvenated? Or is there a peculiarity of the liberal tradition that restrains their open reassertion? Such are the questions that now impose themselves.

Liberal Invincible Rightness

Perhaps the first factor militating against a serious reflection on the liberal tradition's own existential depths has been the long-standing liberal coolness toward theory. Liberal democracy is a practical political symbolism developed by practical political individuals. Relying on their own intuitive sense of what is right, they were principally concerned with finding a means of translating their convictions into actual political life. They were successful because their construction resonated with the immediate sense of what is right in a great many other human beings. No one needed any elaborate defense because it never occurred to anyone to question the meaning of the truths they held to be "self-evident." The truths' self-evidence was sufficient.

For long stretches of liberal political history, that has continued to be the case. Without the germ of self-doubt, liberal tradition continued in the conviction of its own invincible rightness. It was impervious to the kind of skeptical subversion with which we are familiar because that kind of critique had never found an opening through which to insinuate itself in the liberal soul. It was not that liberal theory and society were unfamiliar with Marx or Bakunin or Nietzsche or the kind of radical perspective that their critique represented. It was simply that the genealogical analysis of its principles was not seriously admitted as a problem for the liberal understanding itself. Their questions had not yet managed to dislodge the self-assurance of the liberal mind.

The pattern is perhaps best exemplified in the most eminent liberal statesman of the twentieth century, Winston Churchill. It fell to him to mobilize the resistance to the totalitarian juggernaut of Nazism and to sustain a bastion of liberal freedom from which the victorious countermovement could eventually be launched. Yet despite this formidable effort, and most striking in a man of Churchill's undoubted literary and rhetorical capabilities, there was scarcely a word that explained why a liberal order is superior to a fascist one. What was it that made that heroic effort of resistance worthwhile? The question simply does not arise. Indeed, it can hardly arise because it is taken for granted as so obvious as not to deserve serious consideration. Only from the retrospect of our own fractured polity does it seem like a question to which we would like to hear a persuasive response.

So long as there was no hesitation about the self-justifying truth of liberal principles, an elaborate defense was not only superfluous but might even invite the germ of self-doubt it was intended to repulse. It is better not to engage in reflection that is bound to be less secure than the tangible common sense of practice. It might even be said that the more liberal a society became, the less it was given to reflection on the justification for its liberal convictions. The historic liberal democracies, such as Britain or the United States, have long been noted for their lack of interest in theoretical or philosophical concerns. Tocqueville observed the singularly practical bent of most U.S. citizens and the unlikelihood of original philosophical reflection emerging within such an environment. The liberal tradition as a whole has been so bereft of major theoretical exponents that almost a century separates John Stuart Mill and John Rawls without the appearance of a figure of comparable intellectual stature.

In this regard liberal democracies have been victims of their own practical success. Not requiring an extensive philosophical elaboration for their principles, they continued with remarkable stability and assurance until the day dawned when they would have to give an account of their convictions. That was the jolt of the encounter with the revolutionary movements. Pressed to defend the modest faith that had constituted liberal civilization, they found that they were indeed hard-pressed to articulate a coherent defense. It was not that they no longer had convictions but that, having taken them for granted for so long, liberal societies lacked the intellectual means to render them transparent. This realization has today rebounded on a liberal practice that is no longer as certain as it once was and correspondingly more prone to confusion in action.

Yet it is hard to blame liberal statesmen and liberal writers for this condition. How could it be otherwise? They are like the Romans whom they admire so greatly, incapable of apprehending the gap between their own constitutional order and the best regime. They do not have that Greek sense of the difference between the two that irrevocably sets philosophy in tension with politics. To the liberal mind, theory and practice are a seamless whole. The practice is the best exposition of the theory, and the theory adds little essential to the practice. There is a characteristic complacency about the liberal arrangement that has for so long basked in the assurance of its own rightness that it has become incapable of viewing itself with any critical distance. Without that element of reflexivity it lacked the perspective from which to understand the critiques posed against it and eventually the comprehension from which to develop a response to them.

Among even the most self-conscious liberal thinkers, such as the American Founders, one scarcely finds any extended reflection on why human beings ought to be accorded their inalienable rights or why consent of the governed is the fundamental principle of political rule. The reasons are taken as so self-evident that no one could seriously question them. From that surety of conviction there naturally arises the sense that liberal order rests on nothing more fundamental than itself, that it is a self-contained symbolism that represents the most elementary common sense of the human race.

Forgetful of its own particular historical sources, in a civilization formed by the conjunction of philosophy and revelation, liberal politics begins to assume that it rests entirely on its own immediate self-evidence.

The liberal order is not inclined to reflect on the extent to which it presupposes a particular understanding of the human being or of the order of reality within which it exists. Yet it is clear, as James Madison acknowledged, that liberal democracy or republican government, as he generally named it, rests on a quite specific understanding of the human condition. "As there is a degree of depravity in mankind which requires a certain degree of circumspection and distrust, so there are other qualities in human nature which justify a certain portion of esteem and confidence. Republican government presupposes the existence of these qualities in a higher degree than any other form" (*Federalist Papers,* no. 55). Madison does not elaborate on what those virtuous qualities are and whence they are derived nor what expectation we might have concerning the prospects of remediating the degree of depravity in the human race. All of that is simply taken for granted as the parameters that are well understood by the audience he addresses. In fact, they are presuppositions that are derived from the philosophic Christian understanding of an order of right by nature that is also in tension with an abiding proclivity to wrong in nature.

Neither Madisonian liberal republicanism nor any other brand rests on its own two feet. Beneath it lies a whole complex of assumptions about ourselves and the world in which we live. It is the degree of agreement about those assumptions that eliminates the need for explication, to the point that they are often forgotten in their invisibility. But they are there and become manifest when the geologic plates of consensus begin to shift. The result can then be as shattering as an earthquake when the fragility of our public order is suddenly exposed. More frequently, the slow imperceptible process of change works a transformation of the mores of society that only later registers in consciousness. One day we wake up to discover, perhaps in the reactions of our children, that we are living in a different world.

At that point we become aware of the extent to which our liberal order had depended on a larger worldview whose demise it could not easily survive. We begin to understand that the crisis is not so much a crisis of liberal politics as it is a crisis of the philosophical assumptions that had made its principles appear so self-evident. The liberal superstructure has fallen because the moral and spiritual convictions on which it had rested have been shaken. It is no longer possible to regard the liberal way as the invincibly right one for all mankind. Perhaps it is no longer even valid for us? Without the sense of an order beyond itself in terms of which its rightness can be seen, liberal democracy loses the landmarks that hold it fast. If it rests on nothing but itself, liberal order rests on nothing.

The Illusion of Progress

The factor that has prevented liberal self-understanding from recognizing the need to attend to its own foundations has been the illusion of progress. When the philosophic-Christian presuppositions had sunk below the level of articulate discourse, becoming bare, silent presuppositions, then it was possible for a variety of distorting influences to shape the context as well. One of the most potently seductive was the idea that the burden of moral struggle would gradually be relieved through the inexorable effect of progress. The attraction of this myth is perennial since the human condition imposes the necessity of struggle as the price of growth in every age. Inevitably, the painful nature of the requirement invites imaginations of its abolition. What renders such perennial musings so fatal in the modern period is that, in the absence of the rationality derived from philosophy and Christianity, they are not subjected to critical examination. Indeed, the fantasy of progressive self-perfection can even clothe itself in the residual appeal of salvation history.

The effect of such apocalyptic fantasies in the most militant branch of modernity, the ideological movements of revolution and totalitarianism, has been disastrous. When the construction of second realities gets underway, it becomes increasingly difficult to distinguish the first reality of the world we inhabit. Normal moral restraints cease to be effective as the second reality insulates the believer from the inhibitions that can usually be counted on to place a limit on the perpetration of evil. A boundary has been passed in which all things are possible and all possibilities are permitted. The practical effects are not only the inhuman cruelty countenanced on a grand scale but also the equally catastrophic inability to act on the basis of a rational grasp of cause and effect. Actions that are taken within the framework of an illusory second reality have a multitude of unintended consequences in the real world. All of this is familiar in the moral nightmare of totalitarianism and the peculiar practical obtuseness that gave such societies the air of a lunatic asylum.[3]

A more moderate form of the same disorder also manifested itself within the liberal horizon. While not as convulsive as the apocalyptic visions of revolutionary transformation, the idea of the progressive perfection of the human race had some of the same distorting effects. Pressure to sustain the moral struggle against evil and the sense of the contest as a perennial feature of the human condition were removed. It would now be enough to allow nature and history to do their beneficent work; it would no longer be necessary to legislate and govern on the basis of the idea that human nature would remain pretty much the same in the future. Instead, we could build on the less strenuous assumption that the inexorable moral improvement of the race would continue. The twentieth-century holocausts have been a shocking reminder of the depth of depravity of which we are still capable.

And the steady moral deterioration of liberal societies has finally begun to disabuse even the most complacent of liberal progressives.

On the pragmatic level, too, the experience of three global conflicts in the twentieth century as well as the endless proliferation of regional and civil wars has worn off most of the luster of progress. Compared to the colossal blunders of liberal statesmen after the two world wars, international relations are now more likely to be conducted in an atmosphere of sober realism. Gone are the comforting illusions that the human race has progressed to the point that unspeakable cruelties are no longer possible. We know that they are continuing even today and that the future is unlikely to be qualitatively different from the past. The best that can be expected is that a beneficent conjunction of forces might restrain the most inhumanly destructive tendencies within and between states. We are not moving toward any paradise within history.

Yet the dream of progress dies hard, and it is undeniable that a kind of progress does occur within history. The very notion of history suggests something progressive; otherwise, what is the point of remembering what is significant in the past? It is also not simply progress within the fairly narrow range of science and its technological applications. The most significant aspect of history is the history of the emergence of order, fragile and reversible as each advance is. Clearly, the eruption of the great spiritual movements, philosophy and the world religions, are of this type. Liberal order itself, I will argue, represents an advance within such a frame of reference; it is not simply a compromising response to the disintegration of the medieval Christian order. But liberalism, like the ideological movements it has opposed, extrapolated its own limited progress into an infinite future. It forgot that no historical advance escapes the fate of the history that brought it forth, in which nothing remains forever and no achievement overleaps the bounds of the human condition.

The difficulty in maintaining this balance, especially in the modern context that is virtually defined by the orientation toward a greater future, is well illustrated by the contemporary liberal disorientation. Only those thinkers who have taken the full measure of the totalitarian possibility of modernity, as it has been actualized in the twentieth century, have managed to slough off the last remnants of the myth of progress. There is not the slightest hint of an expectation of the moral improvement of humanity in the urbanely austere reflections of Michael Oakeshott. Even Friedrich Hayek, who wishes to preserve his self-identification as a classical liberal and is prepared to endorse a faith in the capacity of reason to effect an improved quality of life, never suggests that this might be part of an inexorably ascending movement of history. His faith in the creativity of freedom is tempered by his witness of the horrors of which it is capable, a nightmare he was among the first to denote as "the road to serfdom."

Other thinkers, generally those whose ruminations remain within the parameters of liberal democratic politics, still betray the lingering influence of the idea of progress. Again, Rawls provides a measure because he has been one of the very few with the theoretical range to make most of his presuppositions visible. By attempting a comprehensive theory of justice, rather than the more conventional small-scale work on "problems," he inevitably exposes more of the links that hold the liberal worldview together. Not surprisingly, one of the essential elements has been a certain uncritically accepted notion of the malleability of human nature. What human beings are, he insists, is not to be determined on the basis of our own social and political experience, because we would then be describing merely the kind of individuals who happen to arise from the institutional structures of our own time.

Instead, we should look to the possibility that some of the most intractable moral shortcomings, such as envy or domination, might not be so problematic under different social circumstances. Rawls builds into his thought experiment not only the weak assumption that most people will want more rather than less of the primary goods but also the assumption that individuals in the original position will be relatively disinterested in one another. That is, their own happiness will not be substantially affected by the happiness or unhappiness of others. Rawls refers to this as "the special assumption I make" that is necessary to make the decisions of each to maximize his or her access to primary goods fully rational. "The parties do not seek to confer benefits or to impose injuries on one another; they are not moved by affection or rancor. Nor do they try to gain relative to each other; they are not envious or vain" (*A Theory of Justice*, 144).

Rawls justifies this unusual assumption on the grounds that he is constructing an ideal theory. Once it is completed, he promises to return to the question of whether it will work under conditions where it is likely that human beings are envious and vain. But he does not even wait until the end of the book to dispose of that concern. He goes on to indicate that he does not believe that envy and vanity will be realistic problems under the conditions specified in the theory of justice. The principles of equal liberty and inequality benefiting all will, when they are put into practice, "lead to social arrangements in which envy and other destructive feelings are not likely to be strong. The conception of justice eliminates the conditions that give rise to disruptive attitudes. It is, therefore, inherently stable" (144).

Apart from the problem of how we move from the theoretical ideal to its application, a formidable challenge given the acknowledged incompatibility between the assumptions of the two of them, there is an even deeper difficulty. Rawls is asking us to accept the progressivist premise that human nature is susceptible to such institutional determination. Now the degree of moral progress to which human nature is amenable is itself an empirical question.

There is no need to erect any absolute limits. Even if we knew what they were, we would not know where to place them. What is required is a modest quantity of skepticism that insists, in the absence of any countervailing evidence, that we should not expect human behavior to markedly differ from the range of our ordinary experience. Are not envy and vanity and the desire to dominate more deeply rooted temptations than Rawlsian liberalism seems to suspect? Do we not sense them as possibilities that can perhaps infect even our most noble aspirations? It might indeed be nice if the darkness of our ulterior motives could so easily be dispelled.

But it is not so easily dismissed, and one is struck by the baldness of Rawls's assertion that "men's propensity to injustice is not a permanent aspect of community life; it is greater or less depending in large part on social institutions, and in particular on whether these are just or unjust" (245). This seems an extraordinarily rash assumption on which to base a moral and political order, and the unease it provokes is not relieved when he finally does address the translation to the actual world. After explaining that a perfectly just society is an ideal that rational beings would desire more than anything else, Rawls suggests that the obstacles to its stabilization in practice are all tractable. He still recognizes that instability of one kind, our ability to count on justice as a predictable dimension of our social relations, will be removed through the existence of a sovereign. But Rawls assumes the deeper instability of the human heart, what he calls our "sense of justice," will be remediated through the progressive movement of reality itself.

There is a quaintness to many of the passages in the last chapters of *A Theory of Justice* as Rawls reaches back to the old-time faith that had sustained liberals in the past. He invokes the shade of Mill to valorize the expectation that as society develops, individuals converge toward the recognition "that society between human beings is manifestly impossible on any other basis than that the interests of all are to be consulted." As with Mill, the hope expands into the eschatological vision of a perfected state that "leads the individual to desire for himself only those things in the benefits of which others are included." Searching around for confirmation of this aspiration, Rawls finds it again in another nineteenth-century faith, evolution. The progressive emergence of a sense of justice can finally be understood as part of the larger cosmic process by which order emerges from chaos. "The theory of evolution would suggest that it is the outcome of natural selection; the capacity for a sense of justice and the moral feelings is an adaptation of mankind to its place in nature" (501–3).

The temptation to extrapolate from the fragile island of order, imagining that it will be extended infinitely into the vast sea of disorder that surrounds it, is virtually irresistible to some of the leading liberal thinkers. Ronald Dworkin in the closing pages of *Law's Empire* similarly invokes the move toward "utopian theory" (408). Again it is defended on the grounds of theoretical completeness, necessary for the full unfolding of the picture of law as integrity, a principled means of reaching agreement between individuals who may disagree about a great deal. "This purified interpretation speaks, not to the distant duties of judges or legislators or any other political body or institution, but directly to the community personified. It declares how the community's practices must be reformed to serve more coherently and comprehensively a vision of social justice it has partly adopted, but it does not declare which officer has which office in the grand project" (407). Not indeed that there is anything untoward in such aspirational rhetoric within an author's vision, it is more what is omitted that is the chief source of the distortions. Dworkin, like Rawls and a long line of liberal forebears, seems to suggest that all that stands in the way of the realization of the dream of integrity is its rational elaboration. Once it is explained, its persuasive logic will be compelling.

There is little of the sense of caution that would temper the eschatological expectations. The possibility that human society may never actually aspire to, let alone achieve, the pure idea of law is simply not entertained. This is defended even at a time when its stunning unreality can scarcely be avoided. After a half century of expanding concern with social justice, involving a steady enlargement of the liberal guarantee of rights over an ever widening range of activities and individuals, we are further than ever from a stable moral consensus. This is not to deny that the expansion of civil rights, enforcing the liberties of groups who had not hitherto enjoyed the full protection of the laws, and the development of a network of welfare and security arrangements that sustain greater real individual liberty have been a positive benefit. They have, and that is precisely the point of their limitation.

The enlargement of liberal guarantees and opportunities does not constitute a step in the progressive emergence of the eschaton. It is simply one fairly tangible set of improvements that have been made in a concrete legal and institutional structure that may or may not be able to sustain them materially and morally. One of the most significant factors tending toward their degeneration has been just the sense of false assurance promoted by the progressivist dream itself. If the process of maturation and self-responsibility is part of the autonomic movement of history, then there is no necessity to undertake the arduous effort to inculcate and practice the virtues themselves. We can simply wait for history itself to perform the task. This is what makes the shock of the collision with reality all the more traumatic. Liberals are typically astonished to discover that the generation that has grown up under its less demanding tutelage is less responsible and caring than any prior generation.[4]

It is particularly incomprehensible that a generation that has grown up with less disadvantages than any previous one should exhibit patterns of behavior that can be regarded only as pathological. The epidemic of lethal violence coursing through our society can partly be explained by the easier availability of the means of violence. A very large part can only be accounted for by the increased callousness toward the suffering of others. As members of a liberal society we are appalled to discover that the cumulative solicitations for the rights and autonomy of individuals have only spawned greater indifference and irresponsibility. A mushrooming of out-of-wedlock births can surely not be blamed on a lack of information; it is more plausibly explained by a widespread disregard for the welfare of those for whom we are responsible. Nor can the surge in white-collar crime and socially condoned cheating of all types be attributed to a lack of material and psychic privileges. Examples can be multiplied indefinitely, apparently without plumbing the depths of liberal naïveté and also without gaining much more than a sense of superiority to it.

It is enough to note that liberal reflection appears particularly helpless when confronted by the contradiction between its expectation of progress and the reality of its history. The myth of progress has served to insulate it from the awareness of this divergence and has prevented liberal societies from taking the realistic steps required by the objectives it intends. Expanding individual liberty without the correlative moral discipline does not promote autonomy. In most human beings, it only encourages self-serving irresponsibility. Liberal philosophy has always harbored a weakness in lacking a vocabulary of virtue. But it is only the dream of progress that has allowed the liberal philosophy to overlook its own deficiency altogether by reassuring us that the evolution of humanity itself will take care of our moral improvement. The self-deception is palpable in that most transparent of contemporary liberals, Richard Rorty.

Much of his not inconsiderable rhetorical flair is employed in the demonstration that there is no noncircular defense of liberal principles of morality. He acknowledges that this means that the public consensus, on which our life together is based, depends on the presence of pervasive social feelings of solidarity. Yet these are feelings that we are not well able to promote. At bottom they arise from the hope that Rorty is right that there is a moral progress "in the direction of greater human solidarity" (*Contingency, Irony, and Solidarity*, 192). When pressed to explain how such a hope might be realized and to reflect on the means by which solidarity toward the sufferings of others might be engendered, he can provide no further illumination than that it happens. The identification with humanity he characterizes as "the self-doubt which has gradually, over the last few centuries, been inculcated into inhabitants of the democratic states—doubt about their own sensitivity to the pain and humiliation of others, doubt that present institutional arrangements are adequate to deal with this pain and humiliation, curiosity about possible alternatives" (198). It is a characterization that smacks of nothing so much as the concern of the comfortable for the distressed, more designed to relieve the conscience of the former than the suffering of the latter. Nothing suggests that the solidarity will become anything more than a salve. The ambivalence of the liberal abhorrence of cruelty cannot finally be eliminated.

Hollowness of Liberal Construction

It is this apparent hollowness of a liberal polity unable to acknowledge the depth of its own convictions that has caused so many of its critics to conclude that it is beyond remediation. The idea that a liberal order can be sustained in the absence of the virtues indispensable to its existence, is a conceit so incredible that it hardly deserves to be taken seriously. How can we expect that respect for the dignity and rights of one another can continue if there is no way of teaching that human beings are deserving of dignity and respect? Why would anyone accept the right of all to "equal concern and respect" if there is no way of explaining the source of such a conviction? Can we have any realistic hope that rights will be observed if we cannot make the reasons for them even minimally plausible? How can virtues be promoted if we can no longer teach them?

Virtue has long been the Achilles' heel of the liberal disposition. The awareness that a liberal public order depended on a fund of moral capital that it was not well-positioned to augment but could readily draw down, has been present as far back as we care to trace the beginning of the formulation. It has even given rise to an uneasy tension between two traditions within liberal reflection: pluralist self-interest and republican virtue. The latter, which goes back to the Florentine and English republicanism of the sixteenth and seventeenth centuries, has had a continuing influence through the American founders and the various strands of communitarian thought all the way up to the present. The former, pluralist individualist perspective, also has a long historical lineage from the rising commercial bourgeoisie of the seventeenth century up through the federalists, the progressives and the liberal pluralists of our own day. Quite often the split has been less between individuals than within individuals, as the pulls of self-interest and of virtue seem alternately more or less reliable foundation of order. Madison is a classic illustration of a thinker in whom both sides exist in uneasy alliance.[5] The decisive aspect is that the tension has never been fully confronted within the liberal tradition itself.

Without such a clarification in principle the result has been an inexorable drift toward the easier of the two poles, self-interest, with only fitful reminders that the liberal order is also sustained by a certain level of virtue. The reason is that without an incontrovertible defense of virtue its proponents have always been compelled to beat a tactical retreat before the more vocal claimants of the liberty of self-interest. It has been astoundingly difficult to make the case within liberal societies that one ought not press all of the rights to which one is entitled. The notion that there may be higher moral claims has not generally won the day. This is why liberal societies present that seemingly irrational configuration so noticeable to outsiders such as Solzhenitsyn.[6] They seem to be composed of individuals who share nothing except the impervious conviction that their rights must be served at any cost, no matter who else is affected or how the long-term welfare of all may be undermined.[7]

The identification of the morally right with the legally right should come as no surprise, although it does, to a society that sees it daily played out in the courts to which it looks as the final arbiters of human life. There is, of course, nothing final about the judgment of the courts, except in the practical sense that they have the power to settle disputes. In fact litigation is a very clumsy means of resolving the innumerable differences that arise between human beings who, long after the case is over, must continue to bear their responsibilities in relation to one another.[8] Litigation is quite incapable of capturing the depth, complexity and subtlety of human relationships and ought only to be a blunt instrument of last resort. The effect of turning to it as the first resort for all disputes has been to create the idea that all of our responsibilities can be reduced to legal ones. But what of the responsibility of parents to love their children? Or of friends to be loyal to one another? Or of each of us to help our neighbor?

None of the depth of moral life can be contained in the formality of the courtroom. Nor apparently can it be fostered readily by the institutions of liberal democracy. More than anything else it has been the inability of liberal societies to develop any institutional means of transmitting its own virtues that has precipitated the crisis. Few more pathetic pictures can be imagined than this image of liberal self-assertiveness utterly incapable of sustaining its own claim to authority. Small wonder that it gives the impression of being hopelessly inept, attempting the dizzyingly impossible task of maintaining itself in the air without any visible means of support. It would surely come crashing down more frequently than it does, were it not for the great many invisible bases of support that emerge to sustain it from a variety of conventional and traditional sources. But by itself liberal democracy seems hopelessly incapable of existence.

This is the aspect that has made it from the start such an easy target for its critics. None perhaps caricatured the liberal balancing act so wickedly as Jeremy Bentham in his scathing dismissal of the language of rights. "*Natural rights* is simple nonsense: natural and imprescriptible rights, rhetorical nonsense,—nonsense upon stilts."[9] Marx too could find nothing of substance in the liberal assertion of abstract rights. He regarded the invocation of rights as an instrument by which "the political community is degraded by the political emancipators to a mere means for the preservation of these so-called rights of man, the sphere in which man behaves as a communal being is degraded below the sphere in which man behaves as a partial being, finally that it is not man as a citizen but man as a bourgeois who is called the real and true man."[10] Burke is, of course, the one who diagnosed the revolutionary destructiveness that lay at the heart of the liberal impulse as he beheld its most potent manifestation in the French Revolution. He recognized it as the expression of the bare abstract assertion of rights.

> On the scheme of this barbarous philosophy, which is the offspring of cold hearts and muddy understandings, and which is as void of solid wisdom as it is destitute of all taste and elegance, laws are to be supported only by their own terrors and by the concern which each individual may find in them from his own private speculations or can spare to them from his own private interests. In the groves of *their* academy, at the end of every vista, you see nothing but the gallows.[11]

All of the critiques point toward the fundamental objection that Nietzsche was to express so powerfully. That is, that liberal politics had cut itself off from its own roots in philosophy and Christianity and had no comparable motivating appeal to put in their place. His prediction of its impending collapse has still not materialized but that does not negate the force of the warning that he has only been the most prominent in sounding.[12] Without the formative spiritual traditions that produced order in the soul, liberal democracy seemed only to provide the outer shell that concealed the hollowness within. The liberal construction had merely been a secularization of the philosophic-Christian understanding of the person, but once it cut itself off from those roots it cut itself off from its own means of support. That step had been taken when the liberal ethos came to regard itself as self-sufficient.[13]

The process by which this self-subversion took place was, of course, gradual. Eighteenth-century liberals were still aware of the innovation they were taking in de-emphasizing the dependence of the legal order on its transcendent authorization. "Is there a possibility," John Adams asks, "that the government of nations may fall in the hands of men who teach the most disconsolate of all creeds, that men are but fire flies, and this *all* is without a father? Is this the way to make man as man an object of respect? Or is it to make murder itself as indifferent as shooting plover, and the extermination of the Rohilla nation as innocent as the swallowing of mites on a morsel of cheese?" Even Robespierre is perhaps not disingenuous when he declares that a legislator cannot be an atheist since he depends on a "religious sentiment which impresses upon the soul the idea of a sanction given to the moral precepts by a power greater than man" (quoted in Arendt, *On Revolution*, 192). Such observations strike a particularly somber note when read, as Hannah Arendt suggests, from the perspective of our own "ample opportunity to watch political crime on an unprecedented scale, committed by people who had liberated themselves from all beliefs in 'future states' and had lost the age-old fear of an 'avenging God' " (192).

Yet it was not the intention of the liberal founders to lead us into the nihilistic wasteland. They were convinced, with considerable justification, that a public order could be erected on the basis of the human capacity for self-government, and that the experience of self-responsibility would be sufficient to promote the virtues that would be necessary to sustain it. A liberal public order would not have to depend on any overtly transcendent grounding, although it would certainly draw on the virtues that continued to be formed through the uninterrupted influence of the Christian churches. The virtues required in the public order could be derived from this indirect source and immediately from the practice of liberal politics itself. This is the genius, Arendt insists, of the American founding that recognized that "it was the authority which the act of foundation carried within itself, rather than the belief in an Immortal legislator, or the promises of reward and the threats of punishment in a 'future state,' or even the doubtful self-evidence of the truths enumerated in the preamble to the Declaration of Independence, that assured stability for the new republic" (200).

The act of foundation develops its own legitimacy. *Auctoritas* in its original meaning, Arendt explains, is to augment and preserve what is already there. She looks back to the Roman parallel in the convergence of authority, tradition and religion. *Religare* always meant to bind oneself back to the order that had already been there and in the process to augment and preserve it in the present. The authority is therefore derived from the practical reevocation of the tradition today. "From this it follows that it is futile to search for an absolute to break the vicious circle in which all beginning is inevitably caught, because this 'absolute' lies in the very act of beginning itself" (205). There is no beginning that does not itself derive from a beginning that is not already there, but in the taking of action both its beginning and its principle are rendered transparent. "What saves the act of beginning from its own arbitrariness is that it carries its own principle within itself, or, to be more precise, that beginning and principle, *principium* and principle, are not only related to each other, but are coeval" (214).

The American innovation, on this view, was the separation of power from sovereignty. It was no longer necessary to rely on a source of absolute sovereignty, with its transcendent valorization, as the only reliable locus of political power. For the Americans such absolute sovereignty was not even properly speaking power. It was no more than a paltry imitation that had usurped the only genuine power that is derived from the reciprocal and mutual agreement of individuals. The necessity for joint action had taught them that "power comes into being only if and when men join themselves together for the purposes of action . . . Hence binding and promising, combining and covenanting are the means by which power is kept in existence" (174). The division of power, far from weakening it, was the indispensable means by which it was strengthened through the necessary conjunction of wills in its exercise.

Yet despite the formidable force of this conviction in the foundation of the American regime, its clarity has generally not been sustained. With the exception of the Supreme Court, whose authority is derived from its continuity with the founding actions, itself "a kind of Constitutional Assembly in continuous session" (Woodrow Wilson, quoted 201), the public space for freedom of action has shrunk markedly in the American and all other modern states. In language strikingly similar to Oakeshott's strictures against the state as enterprise association, Arendt complains of the overwhelming of the political with the demands of the social. The latter represents the dominance of production and consumption, which arises when politics admits the exigencies of man's physical necessities as its primary concern. Such an invasion is invited through compassion, but it becomes virtually irresistible under the pressure of the modern technological reduction of all activities to their instrumental value.

The root failure she sees as the inability of the liberal revolution to ensure a continuing space for public action, once the revolutionary action itself had passed. There was no longer an arena in which the citizens could act in the same concerted manner as in the assertion of their political liberty. All had contracted to the preservation of civil liberty, the private pursuit of happiness. Arendt singles out the neglect of the townships, with their communal self-government, as pivotal to the loss of the public space within which free political action is possible. The pattern is repeated in all the modern revolutions where the spontaneous self-organization of society into councils or wards is quickly suppressed in the name of the efficiency of national or central order. This may have been an effective way of marshaling the resources of society toward the collective welfare, but becoming the blind instruments of the governing elite did nothing for the self-responsibility of the citizens. "Wherever knowing and doing have parted company, the space of freedom is lost" (268).

The astonishing aspect is the illusion that nevertheless a liberal political order can survive. Even the preservation of civil rights, the guarantee of being left alone without paternal interference in the running of our own lives, presupposes the recognition that human beings ought to be responsible for themselves. The possibility of sustaining the practice of political self-government can hardly survive the disappearance of all substantive opportunity for the exercise of common political action. If the people are no longer free, but only their representatives, then it can hardly take much time for the sense of self-responsibility itself to disappear. They cease to be individuals who are capable of making their own decisions and willing to participate in the deliberative pursuit of their common good. Instead they sink to the level of the mass man, an obstreperous bundle of impulses and passions, who can no longer be swayed by rational argument but must be manipulated by the techniques of behavioral control in the panoply of forms created by the twentieth century.

Without membership in a variety of self-governing intermediate institutions, the individual is reduced to the isolated atomistic membership in the mass. Nothing intervenes between this disconnected individual and the sovereign government at the top. Besides the radical lostness and loneliness of such individuals, whose identity is increasingly defined by their relationship to the abstract government above them, they are particularly disadvantaged by the lack of any experience in public action by which to measure the events around them. It is the state of utter disorientation that Arendt had earlier diagnosed as the fertile ground for totalitarianism. The experience is that of the individual who is not only politically isolated but also fundamentally lonely, without the contact with other men that would confirm his identity and their common sense of a common world. All that remains is the capacity for logical reasoning working away on the abstractions of ideology. "It is the inner coercion whose only content is the strict avoidance of contradictions that seems to confirm a man's identity outside all relationships with others" (*The Origins of Totalitarianism*, 478).

There is an eerie familiarity to Arendt's description of the superfluous individuals who, lacking membership in any tangible community, exhibit a "passionate inclination toward the most abstract notions as guides for life, and the general contempt for even the most obvious rules of common sense" (316). We recognize the disturbing echoes of our own mass democracies in which the anonymous television audience is manipulated by the media and political elite to generate an emotional activism about such grand national issues as the budget deficit or health care reform. The problem is not that the issues are not real, but that the citizens lack any meaningful frame of reference within which to judge them. Even when the issues are of a more concrete nature, as in the numerous moral failings of public figures, the public reaction is often so shrilly moralistic that it bears no relation to the common sense acceptance of an imperfect world. The important thing after all is whether a political representative is competent to fulfill the duties of his office. But without the experience of concrete participation in responsibility how can we expect voters to act on the basis of a realistic assessment of the circumstances?

Unsustainable without Tradition

The unsustainability of a liberal order is driven home in the baldness of the assertion that it is a tradition that is not a tradition. This gives rise to the improbable expectation that the unfolding of liberal democracy, which the originators considered to require a most fortunate blending of moral and political conditions, can be counted on to continue its autonomic progress indefinitely. It is the one practice that does not need to be sustained through the practice of it. Instead, it provides the overarching neutral framework within which competing traditions of the good must struggle toward realization, but the liberal state itself exists in splendid impregnability beyond the fray. That is because there is no liberal good toward which it strives and because there are no liberal virtues on which it depends. The liberal order itself is not threatened because it has become a wholly permeable medium.

The bursting of the bubble of liberal neutrality and independence is, as we saw in Chapter 1, the core of the crisis currently afflicting it. The increasing inability of liberal politics to sustain itself has made it painfully aware both of the degree to which it depends on a certain conception of the good and that it cannot survive if liberals no longer experience this orientation *as* good. Such compulsory self-examination does not, as we saw in the last chapter, mean that the liberal construction is evacuated of all moral authority. It still contains the residue of moral truth that has sustained it from the beginning, and it has shown itself through history to be capable of remarkable efforts of resuscitation. But now it is called to move beyond such ad hoc rejuvenations by articulating the existential depth from which it has always drawn its inspiration. The previous liberal strategy of remaining silent about the roots of its own conviction can no longer work because the erosion has now reached the point where skepticism about its convictions is rampant. Is there a liberal good?

In this chapter we have examined why contemporary liberals are not well placed to deal with this question. They have played the neutralist tune for so long that it is doubtful they have any other notes. Indeed, they have shown themselves captive to those very liberal tendencies that in the past have mitigated against any prolonged meditation on what inspired it. An unreflective sense of their own evident rightness and an inclination to believe in historical progress conspired to remove the urgency to attend to the existential underpinnings of liberal order. But now that such comforting illusions have begun to lose their hold, the question is whether liberals are up to the task of articulating an account of the good that has guided them. Can we expect an evocation of the liberal tradition of the good from thinkers who have never properly understood the nature of a tradition?

Alasdair MacIntyre is not sanguine about the possibility. Liberal theorizing began as the attempt to define a tradition-independent morality that would be universally compelling irrespective of circumstances. The result has been that "liberalism, which began as an appeal to alleged principles of shared rationality against what was felt to be the tyranny of tradition, has itself been transformed into a tradition whose continuities are partly defined by the interminability of the debate over such principles" (*Whose Justice? Which Rationality?* 335). It has become the tradition whose essence is its self-negation as a tradition. This is, as MacIntyre perceptively explains, the function of its emphasis on the heterogeneity of goods, on the individualism of the actor, of the indecisive making and unmaking of decisions, and of the continuous philosophical debate on principles that is always promising but never conclusive. All the features work to preserve the liberal tradition of autonomous self-determination but in such a way as to render its validity inherently unstable. What, after all, is the value of promoting self-responsibility if all of the justifications proffered seem to dissolve into incoherence?

Everything turns on the possibility of liberal society recognizing what it means to acknowledge its own dependence on a tradition. The liberal order would have to acknowledge that the liberal failure to elaborate a self-evident neutral ground is "by far the strongest reason that we can actually have for asserting that there is no such neutral ground" (346). Nothing can be established on the basis of its plausibility to individuals of every conceivable persuasion and none. Nor can we expect that the strenuous efforts required to sustain a liberal democratic order will be forthcoming if its appeal is only to the mixture of episodic altruism and recurrent self-interest that is the prevailing image of its citizens. Moral and political order does not exist in the bare skeleton of promises and contracts. It is rather the living conviction of the necessity of having and abiding by agreements that makes them possible and is the real source of their life. The explication of a liberal order consists in the thematization of the living tradition that underpins it.

The difficulty with this recognition is that its articulation will involve a transformation of the liberal self-understanding as a nontradition. It will necessitate the recognition that the liberal conception can be sustained only if it recognizes itself as a tradition that is willing to defend itself against the alternative traditions posed against it. The way to consolidate liberal convictions is not to abandon the conflict of positions as an irresolvable clash of perspectives but to engage in the dialogue as rationally and comprehensively as possible. MacIntyre clarifies the nature of a rational tradition as one that is willing to confront epistemological crises, acknowledge what is valid in its rivals' critiques, rearticulate its own principles in such a way as to take account of them, and then elaborate an account of order that demonstrates its superiority over its rivals. He concedes that the dialogue does not always extend so far, but he insists that the possibility of its rational resolution must be preserved.

The alternative is the perspectival claim that no tradition can vindicate its claim to truth. That recurrently liberal proclivity "fails to recognize how integral the conception of truth is to tradition-constituted forms of enquiry. It is this which leads perspectivists to suppose that one could temporarily adopt the standpoint of a tradition and then exchange it for another, as one might wear first one costume and then another, or as one might act one part in one play and then a quite different part in a quite different play" (367). That is the pathology of the "nomadic thinker," whose homelessness would prove fatal if it engulfed a whole society. What sustains a tradition is the conviction that it is true or right, and that cannot survive if the possibility of truth itself is abandoned. Truth must remain the measure, even if it is not fully attainable, if the seriousness of the quest is to be preserved.[14]

The great strength of MacIntyre's analysis is his insistence on the presupposition of truth as a necessary precondition for the viability of a tradition. "Only those whose tradition allows for the possibility of its hegemony being put in question can have rational warrant for asserting such a hegemony. And only those traditions whose adherents recognize the possibility of untranslatability into their own language-in-use are able to reckon adequately with that possibility" (388). If liberal order bases itself on the confession of the impossibility of truth, then its public hegemony is a hegemony of power and like all such assertions inherently unstable. It cannot rest its authority on the claim to truth but must perpetually guard against the raising of the question of its own legitimacy. Only a tradition that is willing to put its own hegemony to the test of truth can acquire the stability of rational self-confidence.[15] With traditions as with everything else, only those who are willing to lose their lives will save them.

The challenge is to admit that the testing of the truth of traditions opens us up to the testing of ourselves as well. It involves the more substantive risk of our own self-exposure in light of the truth disclosed by traditions. Not only do we test the traditions but the traditions in turn test us as well. That acknowledgment is crucial to the possibility of establishing their claim to authority. There is no neutral language into which all the rival claims to truth can be translated; the greater cogency of one calls into question the validity of another. There is no Archimedean skybox from which to view the debate. We are involved with the contest, and it is the coherence, rationality, and reality of our way of life that is at stake. The only means available to us for rendering a judgment about the truth or falsity of the various positions is through our own struggle toward truth. The only method available to us is the testing of the claims in the juxtaposition of what Dostoyevsky called the truth of "living life."

The notion that we are in possession of a means of evaluating truth that does not involve our own inchoate struggle toward it is one of the great distorting conceptions of our world. "This belief in its ability to understand everything from human culture and history, no matter how apparently alien, is itself one of the defining beliefs of the culture of modernity" (385). It is evident in the conceit that all the richness of traditional meaning can be captured through our meager placement of them in museums, lists of great books, or under the impoverished rubrics of aesthetics. The governing assumption is that all historical wisdom can be absorbed in ways that do not fundamentally challenge the shallowness of our own world. The culminating expression of this approach is reached in contemporary deconstructionism, which no longer even regards texts as wholes and permits us to interpret them freely without any controlling reference to historical context or authorial intention.[16]

Recognition of their untranslatability into contemporary language pulls us up sharply against the limitations of our modern worldview. It reminds us of the existential depth from which all symbolization arises and knocks the supports from the modern conceit that we can have a language that presupposes nothing. All constructions of meaning, even the minimal constitution of liberal neutrality, arise from the way of life through which liberal meaning is rendered transparent. Without reference to the practice of the tradition we can neither make sense of nor sustain the meaning subscribed. The hermeneutical challenge then becomes not finding a philosophical Esperanto in which the least common denominator can be expressed but testing that our own existential-symbolic horizon is rich enough to include all the types it seeks to interpret. If our own tradition of meaning is not up to the level of the texts we attempt to read then we face an impasse. It can be broken only if we permit the texts of our inquiry to expand our horizons sufficiently to include them.

At that point we will, in MacIntyre's conception, have taken seriously the nature of a tradition. We will have entered at least imaginatively into the way of life of a tradition and acquired the basis from which to understand the rationality that forms its coherence. Rather than going along with the typical liberal tactic of "reformulating quarrels and conflicts with liberalism, so that they appear to have become debates within liberalism" (392), we will have taken the first step of putting liberal conviction itself to the test and thereby evoke its own living foundations. That will be the indispensable means by which substance is restored or perhaps rediscovered in the hitherto hollow appearance of liberal principles. The way will then lie open to the recognition that liberal practice too is a tradition and that it is sustained principally through its capacity to evoke existential order within its adherents.

The story of the liberal persuasion has been the story of its progressive amnesia toward its own sources. The sequel of its recovery must follow the correlative path of an anamnestic rediscovery of its own inspiration. As Oakeshott and Arendt (and Rawls and Rorty in their own way) emphasize, liberal order is a practice that is sustained by the virtues endemic to the practice itself. More important than any principles or foundations beyond liberal order is the reality constituted through the engagement with individual and communal self-government. That is what forms the core of the liberal tradition, and its continuance depends on that recognition. Like every tradition, liberal order must insist that it can be understood only from within and refuse to concede the interpretation placed from the outside. Participation in it, also like other traditions, must be conditioned on the ability and willingness to enter into its way of life. The exercise of authority must be strictly limited to those who have clearly demonstrated their virtue in sustaining the tradition's order. Only in this way is it possible to preserve an order that, not being something that can be maintained indifferently by every human type, depends for its flourishing on the capacity to evoke those qualities in its citizens that are its living foundation.[17]

Insufficiency of Critique

The problem with the recommendation that liberal politics acknowledge its own dependence on a tradition is that MacIntyre does not seem to think it can be taken seriously. He does not appear to believe that liberal practice is capable of understanding its historical unfolding. The liberal mind-set is too unalterably opposed to the whole notion of a tradition, in his view, for it ever to acknowledge its own self-constitution in-depth. Instead, he looks to the liberal encounter with more substantive rational traditions to bring about first "an awareness of the specific character of their own incoherence and then accounting for the particular character of this incoherence by its metaphysical, moral, and political scheme of classification and explanation" (398). This is also the reason that he is somewhat vague about how this transformation of the liberal tradition into one of the earlier, more coherent traditions is possible. He allows as it is likely to come about only through a fundamental "conversion," since it will involve the detached liberal self becoming "something other than it now is, a self able to acknowledge by the way it expresses itself in language standards of rational enquiry as something other than expressions of will and preference" (396–97). How such a conversion might come about and how the process might be set in motion are considerations beyond the limits of MacIntyre's reflections.

In this regard he is representative of a very formidable movement of thought that has been gaining momentum since the beginning of the century. The discovery of the richness and depth of premodern philosophical traditions, such as the classical and the medieval, has convinced many thinkers that only the infusion of truth from these sources can save the liberal ethos. Left to itself, the tradition remains irretrievably bankrupt. This is particularly the conclusion of the generation of European émigrés, such as Leo Strauss and Eric Voegelin, who witnessed the corruption and disintegration of liberal democratic regimes before the onslaught of totalitarianism. Arendt, too, often sounds as if she is speaking from a Greek perspective, with her emphasis on the immortality of publicly effective action. The long-standing Catholic critique of liberalism from Leo XIII to John Paul II is similarly rooted in the conviction of the superiority of natural law and solidaristic perspectives over liberal atomistic individualism.

They are all friendly critics of liberal democracy in the sense that, unlike the now largely defunct revolutionary ideologies, they wish to see it improved rather than abolished. Like the Canadian critic George Parkin Grant, they concede that the liberal construction is "the only political language that can sound a convincing moral note in our public realms" (*English-Speaking Justice*, 5). But they cannot see any way that the moral residue of liberal order might be coherently expanded to secure it against its inherently centrifugal tendencies. Only one of the traditions with "more substantive presuppositions of truth" possesses the requisite durability to withstand the corrosive relativism of egalitarianism. A tradition requires the fortitude to be able to insist that not everything within it is equally accessible to everyone, if it is to preserve the conditions in which the substantive rationality of practice can be maintained. In most respects the liberal tradition struck its most serious friendly critics as a poor candidate for the position. It is simply too difficult for the emphasis on individual autonomy to be corralled by the authoritative requirements of a practice.

Yet despite the evident merit of this assessment, it is also difficult to avoid the suspicion that the evaluation too is tinged with a certain utopianism. True, the charges directed against the liberal construction are largely valid, and the greater cogency of premodern spiritual and philosophical traditions is indisputable, but is there not an element of escapism secreted in the very heightening of the contrast between such juxtapositions? A trenchant critique of liberal politics is an indispensable first step, but can the meditation afford to rest there? It is almost as if the critics have given up entirely on the effort to remediate the liberal framework from within and are now confined to recording its inexorable descent into the maelstrom. One is struck by the absence of much serious reflection on how liberal self-understanding might be modified to accommodate the critics' insights. An impression is conveyed of having already abandoned the effort at remediation.

This is a perpetually tempting possibility, especially for those who have reached a personal viewpoint of greater meaning and depth. The task then becomes to find a modus vivendi that will enable the life of reason to be carried on in a world that is pervaded by unreason; the challenge to do what one can to bring about a growth of the soul within that world is declined. The tendency to dismiss responsibility is increased by the very power of the critique of liberal hollowness, which strongly reinforces the sense of the critics' own superiority to contemporary vacuity. Whether reading MacIntyre, Strauss, Voegelin, or Arendt, one comes away with a very strong sense of the power of the Platonic or Thomist viewpoint on the world and of how paltry the confused gropings of modern liberal philosophy really are by comparison. There is little encouragement to consider the substantive achievements of liberal order or to think through the way it might be internally redirected to overcome its manifest defects. Even the realization that the liberal conception is the only option available to us for the foreseeable future is not often made.

Such blithe dispensation creates the air of unreality that Rorty has pilloried as "terminal wistfulness" in the various shades of communitarianism. Without

some concrete indication of how liberal democracy might be nudged toward
the transformation, it is difficult to resist the conclusion that the discussion
has been merely an exercise in longing for an irrevocably vanished past. After
all, what is the purpose of reflecting on the superiority of the premodern
traditions if it is not to draw them into this world as a source of order? If that
is the intention, then some attention must be given to the question of how
capable the liberal ethos is of absorbing such insights and how the insights
might be organically promoted within the liberal construction. A mere
assertion of premodern truth, without any attempt to mediate it in language
that renders it minimally intelligible from a liberal perspective, would be
futile. A way must be found to give the philosophic-Christian tradition a
public voice; otherwise, it will go the way of all traditions compelled to
shrink to a wholly private level.

It is one of the principal contentions of this study that such a means is
available, although not sufficiently recognized, in the traditionalist critique
itself. The very act of critique contains within it the implication of what
is required to remediate the defects. By undertaking the resistance and
diagnosis of what is at fault within the liberal polity, we correlatively evoke a
vision of the alternative that would overcome it. The therapeutic growth of
the soul is the means by which disorder is defeated by order. That process is,
moreover, not one that occurs simply in the critics of liberal thinking but is,
as we have seen, an unfolding that has also emerged from the crisis within
liberal society itself. The analysis of the critics and the self-diagnosis of the
liberal tradition are convergent, even if they are not coincident. They provide
the opportunity for the critics to inject their more profound diagnosis at a
stage within the intraliberal conversation that will enable the dialogue to
move forward toward a horizon beyond the contemporary liberal preserve.
This suggestion is simply another way of stating MacIntyre's account of how
one tradition manages to integrate its rivals "in such a way as both to correct
in each that which . . . by its own standards could be shown to be defective
or unsound and to remove from each, in a way justified by that correction,
that which barred them from reconciliation" (*Three Rival Versions of Moral
Inquiry*, 123).

The difference between my approach and MacIntyre's is that I do not
consider the liberal conviction to be an unalterable fixed quantity. I take
seriously the suggestion that it is a tradition and that, like all traditions, it
rests not on its overt formulations but on the underlying resonances that give
its principles life. Thus, the possibility remains of expanding the admittedly
limited existential base that now underpins liberal order. By building on the
fragments that still constitute a liberal tradition, it is possible to discover
the firm reality on which to build a greater development. Anything else, as
Oakeshott has reminded us, will be utterly ineffectual. It would comprise
only the erection of a superstructure on a foundation of air, unconnected

with the real living world of human beings today. The principal object of this study is to show how such a meditative expansion within liberal politics can take place. Beginning with a reflection on the state of crisis within liberal theory and practice, we move through a consideration of the nature and source of the crisis to a realization of the direction that must be pursued in its resolution. It is crucial that we at no point depart from the liberal self-understanding. The outcome is then one that, even if it is several stages removed from the contemporary liberal conception, is intimately connected to it as its own meditative unfolding. It cannot be disavowed by the liberal mind, and it provides a trajectory of the way by which the liberal tradition itself might be transformed.

The first stage has consisted of the self-recognition of the crisis and the outline of the parameters in which the liberal order is both an enduring source of moral authority and incapable of acknowledging the depth of conviction from which it springs. The next stage is to delve more deeply into the liberal tradition to discover what resources might be available to renew it from within. This will begin naturally with a reflection on the source of the liberal contradiction between its convictions and their acknowledgment, which seems to be the core of the instability of the whole construction. Why is it that liberal conviction is so constitutionally incapable of mounting a coherent defense of the principles that it so manifestly holds? With that deeper understanding of its nature in mind, it will then be possible in the third stage of the meditation to take account of the limitations and strengths that conjoin to form the liberal tradition. In that way we will have a means of exploring the extent to which the limits can be expanded and the strengths exploited to constitute a more substantively moral politics. The conversion that MacIntyre and others look to must, like all true conversions, occur within the soul of the penitent.

Part II

Historical Sources and Resources

4

Liberal Achievement of Order from Disorder

The most notable aspect of the liberal tradition has been a preoccupation with the problem of its own coherence.[1] When we return to the formative liberal exponents, to gain a deeper insight into the origins of the crisis that pervades the liberal present, we find that they too were steeped in the awareness of a crisis of order. There is no point of Edenic tranquillity before the chaos and clamor of disputes about order get under way. The consensus is already under pressure when we encounter the first recognizably liberal approaches to the problem of its consolidation. All subsequent periods may appear relatively more coherent only in light of the greater divisiveness of a later phase, not in relation to the looming disintegration each seeks to resist in its own time.

We may indeed define liberal politics as the effort to salvage order within a social context where the underlying cultural consensus has fractured. That means that it seeks to build on the residue of the moral consensus unaffected by the break, while it works to prevent a deepening of the crisis into its radically overt expression. The twin strategies are intended to be mutually reinforcing. The strengthening and expansion of order in practice does much to halt the slide into greater disorder, as the residual virtues are increased through their actualization in concrete individual and social life. At the same time, the refusal to entertain the ultimate implications of the collapse of order saps the disintegrating impulse long enough to allow the emergence of practical virtue to renew its strength. The result is the creation of an order of modest virtue and stability able to withstand the worst possibilities present within its surrounding environment.

But at no point is the liberal tradition in a position to give an account of its own foundations. It is based on the deliberate strategy of avoiding the question of foundations in order to concentrate on the evocation of an order from the residual consensus that remains. There is neither the capacity nor the inclination to confront ultimate questions of justification that, from a liberal

105

point of view, must always appear dangerous and irrelevant. It is far better to expend our efforts on building up the order that is practically possible, rather than inviting an even more radical confrontation with questions that we will not be able to resolve and that, even if resolved, would contribute not a whit to the formation of virtue. Liberal priority is placed on the evocation of whatever order is currently viable.

Liberal order does, of course, depend on a foundation, but not one that can be explicitly elaborated—nor does it need to be. What underpins the formidable liberal effort of reformation is the faith in an order that is strong enough not to require an explication. Behind the successive liberal movements of renewal, one senses the presence of an intuition of order that endures with an impressive unshakability. It is what makes possible the endless creativity and adaptability of liberal forms, stretching from their beginnings in the sixteenth century to the present. It is a faith that no matter how traumatic the crisis of the day happens to be, no matter how unprecedented the split it introduces into human society, there is nevertheless an order that binds human beings together. There is an order between us, and its presence becomes all the more significant in just those times when its articulation is itself a source of greater conflict.

Silence about the foundations does not, however, wholly remove them as questions. Over time the vulnerability of the liberal order unable to coherently invoke its own deepest convictions becomes more apparent. The uncertainty surrounding its justification becomes increasingly an uncertainty of its justification. Fearful of the evaporation of the faith that has hitherto sustained the liberal tradition, liberal thinkers turn more consciously to the problem of deepening its inspiration. No longer content with the surface allusion to contract and self-interest, increasing prominence is given to the articulation of its real foundation in the liberal democratic virtues. Liberal order is perceived as a problem of virtue precisely because of its customary silence on its sources. The quest for the liberal "habits of the heart" is thus one that extends almost from the beginning up to our own day.[2] It too is part of an abiding liberal pattern of uncertainty about its own resources with the correlative effort to recover and renew the sense of order in danger of being lost within it.

Key to the success of this enterprise is the capacity of the liberal symbolism not only to evoke a stabilizing consensus but also to develop the advances and refinements it has managed to introduce along the way. Liberal principles represent more than the residue of classical and Christian traditions that have survived into the modern world. They also constitute a unique refinement and deepening articulation of the older traditions. By being compelled to narrow the presuppositions of order to its essentials, the liberal persuasion has correspondingly illuminated central elements of the philosophic-Christian tradition with renewed emphasis. The focus on the inviolable dignity of the free, self-determining individual is recognizably from the classical-Christian orbit, as it is compatible with the other world religions as well, but liberal for-mulations give it a prominence and a sacredness that are also recognizable as an advance from the earlier traditions. Philosophy and especially Christianity recognize their own truth in the liberal reverence for the person. That is the source of the liberal appeal.

The dimensions of the liberal tradition are, in other words, complex. Unraveling them requires making careful distinctions if we are not to engage in blanket condemnations and equally fruitless commendations. Part II of this study is devoted to a nuanced examination of the historical tradition as it is available through the reflections of some of the leading liberal theorists. There is no assumption that the philosophical articulation of liberal order is mirrored in actual political practice. The two are clearly separate but related. Theoretical reflections, if they are serious, arise out of the problems introduced by the practice; they reflect the presuppositions that also inform the practice, even if they are capable of diverging from the practice; and they are intended to enlarge the conception of order that also underpins the concrete political world. Taken with suitable cautions about their detachment from practice, the reflections of theorists provide a uniquely profound insight into the self-understanding that constitutes a historical order. Conversely, the historical developments also illuminate the world of theory that derives its point of reference from actual events. Theory and practice are mutually illu-minating, neither taking place in a self-contained realm apart from the other.[3]

With this orienting insight in mind, we will examine the principal dimen-sions of the liberal tradition as they have just been sketched. The present chapter will examine the evocation of order from disorder, which has been the liberal genius from the start. We will sample the successive phases of disintegration in which the liberal tradition has succeeded in assembling an order capable of commanding the allegiance of societies split by profoundly divergent viewpoints. In the next chapter we will trace the parallel line of increasing liberal concern about its own foundations and the correspond-ing series of attempts to expand the moral sources of its order. These attempts have generally taken the form of enlarging and departing from the philosophic-Christian tradition that has formed the background of the liberal construction. Finally, in Chapter 6 we will attempt to identify the core of the liberal appeal, in its secularization of the Christian understanding of the person, which has been the key to its evocative success as a public symbolism. The irony of the traditional truth of the liberal emancipation from traditions will hardly need to be underlined.

An Embracing Order of Law

The splintering of Christianity following the Reformation was probably the greatest shock that the modern political order has had to absorb. It intro-duced, within and between societies, deep divisions that seemed impossible to avoid and about which a compromise seemed impossible to reach. If men disagreed about the most important matter, the manner in which they should serve God, how could they trust one another in anything else? We are perhaps inclined to give too much emphasis to the crisis of pluralism that afflicts our own society and not enough weight to the gulf opened up by the religious conflicts of the early modern era. After all, they did not have the example of several centuries of the liberal solution of tolerance to demonstrate how a public order can be maintained in the absence of agreement on fundamental questions. It seemed unthinkable that people who disagreed so radically could trust one another in anything. The whole basis on which a res publica, or common order, was based seemed to have been shattered.

The depth of the crisis was, moreover, likely to be driven home with some frequency as a result of the numerous individuals and groups who were prepared to invest their energy and blood in the cause of spiritual uniformity. The wars of religion of the sixteenth and seventeenth centuries may in hindsight appear fruitless and nugatory, but religious and political exigencies of the day rendered them virtually unavoidable. Very few shared the flexibility of the *politique* mysticism of Jean Bodin and others who were capable of discerning the one divine truth embodied in varying degrees within all the world religions. His wonderful colloquium *The Heptaplomeres,* in which seven representatives of all the religions of the world (including one who represented none) enter into a sympathetic and dispassionate conversation, was not even published until the nineteenth century.[4] Much more typical was the kind of strident Puritanism confronted by Richard Hooker as he sought to deal with the reality of a significant minority bent on imposing their viewpoint on the whole community.

The portrait of the vociferous dissenters Hooker faced is surely as impressive as any of the ideological protagonists of our day. He recognized that the demand to make Scripture the rule of life, and overrule civil law, would mean not the rule of God but the rule of the private opinions of his interpreters. The consequences were exemplified in the Puritan demand for Presbyterian Church governance and the assertion of the superiority of the community presbyters over all other authorities temporal and spiritual. What astonished Hooker was the passion with which the scheme was promoted, a zeal that demonstrated a will to impose the scheme even though it meant the overturning of the whole public order of the common law and monarchical governance of England. Since they believed it was "the absolute commandment of almighty God, it must be received although the world by receiving it should be clean turned upside down; herein lieth the greatest danger of all" (40).[5]

Hooker understood the danger when men abrogated to themselves the authority to interpret the will of God for the community. "For my purpose herein is to show that when the minds of men are once erroneously persuaded that it is the will of God to have those things done which they fancy, their opinions are as thorns in their sides never suffering them to take rest till they have brought their speculations into practice" (47). Eventually, they would come to feel free to disregard all laws, convinced that their divine valorization permitted all things to them. The crucial step in this process of self-exaltation was in the supersession of the judgment of the community with their own opinion. Hooker pinpointed the fatal turn as the assertion of their conception of ecclesiastical governance " 'whether her Majesty and our state will or no' " (48). He recalls them to their inescapably human status and perspective in words that echo down the history of liberal philosophy: "Think ye are men, deem it not impossible for you to err" (49).

In a situation where men are capable of error, their opinions have no more than the force of probability and their disagreements will likely be endless. For the sake of peace, Hooker insists, it is essential that humans be governed by a public law. "So that of peace and quietness there is not any way possible, unless the probable voice of every entire society or body politic overrule all private of like nature in the same body" (32). He is willing to concede that the Puritan dissenters are among the best men but insists that does not always mean they are the best within society. What makes "their disposition so unframeable unto societies wherein they live is, for that they discern not aright what place and force these several kinds of laws ought to have in all their actions" (125). They commit the cardinal error of confounding the different kinds of law and refusing to recognize that they must all be ordered by the public authority of the community.

Hooker goes on to illustrate what he means by the example of food. We might think that what and how much we are to eat is a matter entirely for our own discretion, and that we are guided in this only by the law of reason that counsels moderation. But Jews and Christians are also bound by certain specific regulations concerning what and when and how food may be eaten. Sometimes food takes on a religious significance, as in the paschal celebration and the Eucharist. The commonwealth too may from time to time issue certain injunctions, which we are required to obey, on the manner of utilizing food. In these as with the instructions of the Church on fasting "unless we will be authors of confusion in the Church, our private discretion, which otherwise might guide us a contrary way, must here submit itself to be that way guided, which the public judgment of the Church had thought better" (126–27). Becoming a member of a society means that we accept the public order of law where otherwise our private judgment might have substituted. We do not insist on our own abstract assessment of things but recognize that the "one and the self-same thing is under divers considerations conveyed through many laws, and that to measure by any one kind of law all the actions of men were to confound the admirable order, wherein God hath disposed all laws, each as in nature, so in degree distinct from other" (127).

The difficulty, as Hooker well knew, was in getting such passionate men to recognize that the complex hierarchy of law ought to control the ardor of their convictions. A first step was to elicit the acknowledgment that their conception of ecclesiastical governance was, at best, only probable and could not be conclusively established from Scriptures. Even the Scriptures did not stand alone because they relied on the presence of other principles that confirmed that they are the revelation of God. Hooker recognized that this could not come from the Scriptures themselves. That must come from the testimony of our own nature that recognizes in Scripture the voice of God. Scripture in turn then lends its authority to the law of nature discovered by our reason, which, by itself, is often dark and difficult to fully discern. It is a complex reciprocal foundation "that nature and scripture do serve in full sort, that they both jointly and not severally either of them be so complete, that unto everlasting felicity we need not the knowledge of anything more than these two" (116). Only the Catholic emphasis on tradition is omitted as inessential.[6]

Instead, Hooker locates the seat of authority in the interpretation of law in the sovereign. He rejects both the Calvinist and the Romanist assertion of the primacy of the spiritual authorities, whether derived from Scripture or tradition, as against the independence of each body politic. It is not so much that the king ought to be the final arbiter in all disputes but that each multitude is responsible for governing itself, which necessitates a submission to the head through whom the community acts. To Hooker "it seemeth almost out of doubt and controversy that every independent multitude before any certain form of regiment established hath under *God's* supreme authority full dominion over itself, even as a man not tied with the bond of subjection as yet unto any other hath over himself the like power" (141). An allocation of reserved authority to the clergy would be tantamount to giving part of the community authority over the whole. The king's authority is derived from his position as representative of the whole.

The necessity for such an ordered whole, a body politic, is obvious to Hooker because of the realization that "strife and troubles would be endless, except they gave their common consent all to be ordered by some whom they should agree upon; without which consent, there were no reason, that one man should take upon him to be Lord or Judge over another." He proceeds to emphasize the extent to which the formation of a political community with its organization of authority must be grounded in acknowledgment of its very necessity by those who are to compose it. Contrary to "the opinion of some very great and judicious men [that there is] a kind of natural right in the noble, wise, and virtuous, to govern them which are of servile disposition; nevertheless for manifestation of this their right, and men's more peaceable contentment on both sides, the assent of them who are to be governed, seemeth necessary" (90). Like Hobbes and Locke later, Hooker considers it possible for men to live without government but concludes that they are not likely to survive or thrive under such a condition. Government emerges, therefore, as a virtual necessity apprehended by reason and entered through the free consent of all who are to compose civil society.

Within this political order the most significant development is the emergence of the rule of law as the principal form of its governance. In a passage underlined and quoted twice by Locke in the *Second Treatise* (pars. 94, 111), Hooker details the growing dissatisfaction with the rule of one man, regarded as a remedy that was increasingly worse than the disease. Rather than chafing under the arbitrary dictates of a single individual, men came to prefer the rule of law in which a constant and reliable order would be applied to all. "They saw that to live by one man's will, became the cause of all men's misery. This constrained them to come unto laws, wherein all men might see their duties beforehand, and know the penalties of transgressing them" (91). Locke exploits this passage as an argument for placing legislative authority in a collective assembly, but in its context it does not require to be extended so far. It is a simple insistence on the rule of law from the perspective of the need for regularity experienced by those under the law. Hooker does not share Locke's contention that the sovereign must be subject to the same laws no more than he shares Locke's enthusiasm for revolution. But Hooker does expound the basic liberal prescription of the rule of law as fundamental to the creation of an order among individuals who "brook it worst that men should tell them of their duties, [but] when they are told the same by a law, think very well and reasonably of it" (92).

Yet he does maintain the principle of self-government that could later be extended by Locke into the requirement of a legislative assembly. "For in a collective body that hath not derived as yet the principality of power into some one or few the whole of necessity must be *Head* over each part. Otherwise it could not possibly have power to make any one certain person *Head* inasmuch as the very power of making an *Head* belongeth unto *Headship*" (170). It is civil society that by nature has the power to make laws, the consent of the people having devolved that authority on the king as its effective instrument. Hooker quotes the medieval canonist principle, "What touches all ought to be approved by all" (185), to indicate the depth of the recognition that men cannot be bound without their consent. Whether elected or not, the crucial thing is that the legislative enactments of the king must be understood as the actions of all, of the whole society that acts through him. Conversely, the actions of a part of the society cannot be considered as binding on the whole until they have been authorized by its head.

Hooker is steadfast in maintaining this principle. "A law be it civil or Ecclesiastical is as a public obligation wherein seeing that the whole standeth charged, no reason it should pass without his privity and will whom principally the whole doth depend upon" (186). It is for this reason that he utterly rejects the notion that "the clergy might give laws unto all the rest." He acknowledges that the monarch cannot displace the sacramental role of the clergy and is peculiarly unsuited to impose any requirements that touch upon the inner spiritual life of his subjects. Monarchs are equally ill equipped to render competent judgment on theological and juridical disputes within the Church. But they alone are in a position to authorize the results of ecclesiastical deliberations within all these areas. Without that public valorization, decisions of the clergy remain the actions of a part or of private individuals. Only the sovereign can render them binding on the whole.

Hooker supports his position with a wide-ranging array of historical references to the actions of sovereigns in attaching public authority to the actions of the Church. Whatever we may think of the historical validity of all his allusions, there can be little doubt that he has established a core principle of order that applies to any political community. The pivotal difference between the situation of Hooker's day and our own is that we no longer conceive of the problem as that of ordering a Christian community. For us the political umbrella for the religiously divergent tendencies has, even as it was becoming untenable in Hooker's day, completely disappeared. Yet the principle remains that the only way of ordering the external obligations of a society is through the authorization of that part that is charged with the function of its direction. If the Church is to remain a concrete visible community, then it must of necessity be ordered by the political authority within which it resides. This is the case under the later separationist approach as it was under Hooker's integrationist model. At the very least, the state is the authority that determines where the line of separation is to be drawn, what is and is not to be permitted, and must of necessity acknowledge the validity of the purpose that is served by the maintenance of the line of separation.[7]

Hooker's is a deep and nuanced conception of law as the embracing public order that makes possible the freedom of individuals within it. No man is compelled to do anything against his will. "Against all equity it were that a man should suffer detriment at the hands of men for not observing that which he never did either by himself or by others mediately or immediately agree unto" (183). He is subject to no laws to which he has not consented. This is the basic understanding of freedom elaborated by successive generations of liberal thinkers. It means that the law is the embracing order within which the individual is free to govern himself, because the law is itself an expression of the self-governing freedom of the individual. While Hooker may have too hastily glossed over some of the distinctions in consent that we would be inclined to make, such as between original and participatory consent, there can be no doubt that he has clarified the basic liberal conception of law. "A law is the deed of the whole body politic, whereof if ye judge yourselves to be any part, then is the law even your deed also" (26).

Hooker's philosophy is recognizable as the source of Michael Oakeshott's conception of law as a noninstrumental order that makes possible the pursuit of diverse individual purposes. As such, it is a complex hierarchy of order that for its preservation depends on the willingness not to subject its components to any abstract tests of fitness. They may not measure up to such an absolute criterion, although they play an indispensable role in the maintenance of the complex order of the whole. The result of railing against the established order is not the substitution of a better order in its place, but the disintegration of the only order, albeit imperfect, that is available. Hooker was undoubtedly the first to identify the modern proclivity to hold reality up to such absolute judgments. "He that goeth about to persuade a multitude, that they are not so well governed as they ought to be, shall never want attentive and favorable hearers; because they know the manifold defects whereunto every kind of regiment is subject, but the secret lets and difficulties, which in public proceedings are innumerable and inevitable, they have not ordinarily the judgment to consider" (52).

We recognize our own professional instigators of unrest, the news media and social revolutionaries whose very livelihood depends on maintaining an audience ever attentive to criticism of the public order, in such remarks. But what makes Hooker in many ways the founder of a liberal order is that he also homes in on the crucial defense that liberals have also struggled to articulate over the centuries. That is, an order of law that makes freedom possible may indeed be a compromise of a great many contingent factors, but it is the only real order that exists until it is in turn molded into something better. Hooker provides a wonderfully evocative metaphor that, like so much of his language, resonates down the centuries. He explains,

> The stateliness of houses, the goodliness of trees, when we behold them delighteth the eye; but that foundation which beareth up the one, that root which ministereth unto the other nourishment and life, is in the bosom of the earth concealed: and if there be at any time occasion to search into it, such labor is then more necessary than pleasant both to them which undertake it, and for the lookers on. In like manner the use and benefit of good laws, all that live under them may enjoy with delight and comfort, albeit the grounds, and first original causes from whence they have sprung be unknown, as to the greatest part of men they are. (53)

States, like trees, can be thoughtlessly cut down, but they grow only with difficulty and over time.[8]

Contemplating the Abyss

The main outline of a theory of law originating in the free consent of all and regulating only the outer conduct of the citizens had been the achievement of Hooker. He thought thereby to have dampened the appetite of his countrymen for religious extremism. The main argument he had going for him was the conception of the Church as a concrete historical community indistinguishable from the political community and therefore just as much in need of government: "Visible government is a thing necessary for the Church" (168). That means acknowledgment of the only concrete government that is available, the monarch of the realm of England. So long as membership in the Church and in the state were coterminous, then they constituted the same concrete community that, under different aspects, could resolve itself for action only through the one visible head. Otherwise, the Church would be incapable of governing itself; it would be without a head.

But what would happen when the process of polarization had gone so far that membership in the Church no longer overlapped with citizenship? Thomas Hobbes witnessed that deepest rupture in the English civil war when a preponderant part of the state no longer saw enough interest in maintaining it. They had become so taken with their vision of the alternative that they were willing, contrary to Hooker's counsel, to sacrifice the real order in which they lived to its precarious ideal attainment. It struck Hobbes, too, as a kind of madness in which the imaginations of men become fired with an enthusiasm that eclipses all rational deliberation of the costs and likelihood of their realization. Hobbes was the first modern thinker to grapple with the full manifestation of revolutionary intoxication, that peculiarly modern disease that blinds men to the real consequences of their actions as they struggle to bring about an impossibly utopian future. How is this possible? How does it take hold of a whole society? And what are the steps that can be taken to staunch the madness and restore some modicum of sanity?

These were the questions that Hobbes confronted. By facing them unflinchingly and following out the depth of their consequences, his work has acquired a timeless importance as a meditation on the worst possibilities within the modern world. Hobbes contemplated the abyss of pluralism. He saw it not simply as the endless frictions and disagreements of our politics but as the cataclysm that overwhelms the political when it is invaded by men who would prefer to live without any order rather than compromise on the order of their visions. Beyond disagreement, this impulse strikes at the very possibility of agreement. The permanent validity of Hobbes's work is that he has elaborated, in contemplation of the extremity of political disintegration, the exigencies for the restoration of order in civil society.[9] The danger of civil war is thankfully not an ordinary proximity of political life, but the structure of the essentials of order evoked by its prospect are of almost universal applicability under more comfortable political conditions. Liberal order that presupposes a more reliable consensus than was available to Hobbes is nevertheless articulated in the shadow of his meditations of its own nightmare possibility.

Hobbes is the one who looks most acutely at the core liberal problem, noting (in words echoed by Alasdair MacIntyre) that "when every man follows his own opinion, it is necessary that the controversies which arise among them, will become innumerable and indeterminable" (*Man and Citizen*, 364). He understood as few thinkers before or since that the diversity of opinions among human beings and the impossibility of appealing to a means of resolution universally compelling define the parameters of political order. Conflicting estimations of the good are not new to politics or to political theory. Plato was fundamentally concerned about them in his debates with politicians and Sophists. His solution, as it is outlined in the *Republic* (581a-82a), a dialogue devoted to the problem of different interpretations of justice, is to propose that only those who have experience of the full range of the human good are in a position to judge. When Socrates finally confronts the question of which is the best way of life—that of pleasure, of power, or of virtue—he replies that it is only one who has experience of all three, the philosopher, who can determine between them. The difficulty is that the representatives of the other ways of life are not well placed or even inclined to acknowledge the superior vantage point of the philosopher. Everything depends on the spiritual authority being surrounded by a tradition of respect that restrains the less experienced from pressing their ignorance too far. But what happens when traditional reverence breaks down and the suspicion erupts that it was only a cloak for the self-aggrandizing power of the wise? That is the situation to which Hobbes responds.

That is also why there are no philosophers in the classical sense in his or liberal political theory. Philosophic wisdom can no longer exercise its own direct authority. The only authority that can win recognition in the public square is what can be rendered plausible to the ordinary citizen. The virtue and wisdom of the philosopher must disappear behind the veil of interests whose conflict defines the public arena. Hobbes was compelled to face the great problem of order, largely avoided in classical and medieval philosophy, because the line of division in his time was no longer between lower and higher conceptions of the good. The split was, rather, around rival interpretations of the highest good that, precisely because they involved the highest things, did not augur well for resolution or compromise between them. From the division of opinion Hobbes understood "there will breed among men, who by their own natural inclinations do account all dissension an affront, first hatred, then brawls and wars; and thus all manner of peace and society would vanish" (365). How then can order be created between men who cannot agree on the most fundamental things?[10]

It is not, as is commonly asserted, that Hobbes had a "pessimistic" view of human nature. Equally anachronistic is the attempt to assimilate him to the later Nietzschean nihilism of the final collapse of philosophic Christianity. Hobbes had to deal with passionate and disordered individuals, but they were not without relationship to a spiritual order beyond themselves. He explicitly rejects the assessment that "men are wicked by nature, which cannot be granted without impiety" (100). The root difficulty is that without any means of reconciling their differences, they cannot trust one another and so must act as if they assume that all men are in fact, if not by nature, wicked. "For though the wicked were fewer than the righteous, yet because we cannot distinguish them, there is a necessity of suspecting, heeding, anticipating, subjugating, self-defending, ever incident to the most honest and fairest conditioned." It is not that men are unfit for society or are not by nature inclined to live in a polity, but that their best inclinations must be constantly checked by distrust and dread of one another.

The picture Hobbes draws of humanity is still recognizably within the philosophic-Christian orbit, even though it is tilted toward the recognition of the darkest potentialities of our nature.[11] The presence of an Augustinian component in Hobbes's anthropology has long been remarked, but this has often not been accorded its full positive significance. It means not only that he was able to analyze the ulterior motives behind even the most exalted human actions, his celebrated diagnoses of vanity and pride as the mainsprings of our endeavors, but also that such self-seeking was not permitted to define all that there is to human beings. Besides the passionate striving for satisfactions, there is the recognition of the limitation of such an unending pursuit of fulfillment. It is a great error to read Hobbes as acceding to or even as presupposing the acquiescence of most men in this circle of futility. He is careful to characterize it as a process confined to this life.

Thus, Hobbes defines felicity as "a continual progress of the desire, from one object to another, the attaining of the former, being still but the way to the later." The insecurity of human life compels us to seek not only our present satisfactions but the means of obtaining future satisfactions as well. It is not that we cannot be contented with less but that we never know whether we will have enough to ensure our future requirements. As a consequence, Hobbes identifies as "a general inclination of all mankind, a perpetual and restless desire of power after power, that ceaseth only in death" (*Leviathan,* 160, 161). But he is careful to frame this entire discussion of the "manners" of human nature with the stipulation that it applies only to this life. It is only when we consider "the felicity of this life" (160) that we are compelled to admit that there is no summum bonum. Life is motion, and its happiness "consisteth not in the repose of a mind satisfied" (160).

In this sense, Hobbes remains explicitly within the general Christian anthropology that recognizes that the greatest good is not attainable in this life. Indeed, it is the sharpness of his awareness of the imperfection of all finite goods that enables him to characterize human life as a quest for that which can never be attained. This is the basis for his understanding of the essence of life as motion.

> The greatest good, or as it is called, felicity and the final end, cannot be attained in the present life. For if the end be final, there would be nothing to long for, nothing to desire; whence it follows not only that nothing itself be a good from that time on, but also that man would not even feel. For all sense is conjoined with some appetite or aversion; and not to feel is not to live. (*Man and Citizen*, 53–54)

The restlessness that characterizes this life is defined by the contrast with "the kind of felicity God hath ordained to them that devoutly honour him, [which] a man shall no sooner know than enjoy" (*Leviathan*, 130). In this life that eternal joy is "incomprehensible," but its prospect points up the incompleteness of everything here.[12] Such remarks might be dismissed as rhetorical covering for Hobbes's darker assessments, but that hardly seems tenable in the context of his thought as a whole. Not only is there the extensive elaboration of a Christian commonwealth, including the impressive demonstration of the consistency of his ideas with revelation, but the human nature with which he deals is constituted by its awareness of a law of nature given by God as well. Hobbes is emphatic that all men by nature can know God. Some may be misled by their own superstitious errors and the manipulations of their priests into identifying the divinity with the forces of nature. Others may be so "imprudent" as to be atheists, like the fool who said in his heart that there is no God. Their error is not injustice, which always consists in breaking an agreement, but in not recognizing the authority to whom we should submit (*Man and Citizen*, 284–85). As such, atheists are enemies of God and subject to his law involuntarily and may be treated as enemies by all who are part of God's kingdom, including the civil magistrates who represent that kingdom on earth.

Knowledge of God by nature is attainable, according to Hobbes, when we follow out the cause of all things without consideration for our own fate or fortune. We allow the meditation to unfold rationally and dispassionately until it reaches its culmination in the uncaused cause whom we call the incomprehensible God (*Leviathan*, 170–71). Hobbes admits that it was "almost impossible for men, without the special assistance of God, to avoid both rocks of *atheism* and *superstition*. For this proceeds from fear without right reason; that, from an opinion of right reason without fear" (*Man and Citizen*, 310). The impression that Hobbes himself inclined toward atheism is perhaps gained from one or two remarks about revelation that are frequently quoted out of context. In his discussion of how we come to believe in a revelation of God that we have not ourselves received, he points out that we have no alternative but to accept it from those who claim they have. Hobbes seems to suggest that this is an utterly unsupported basis because he concludes the chapter with the observation that "whatever we believe, upon no other reason, than what is drawn from authority of men only, and their writings; whether they be sent from God or not, is faith in men only"

(*Leviathan,* 134). This needs to be balanced against the more frequently enunciated principle that men of judgment "in supernatural things require signs supernatural" (180) and in the past have received them in the form of miracles, prophecies, and "extraordinary felicity" (180). Most important, it must be read in the light of Hobbes's overall program to establish the conviction that our only indubitable guide to revelation is what is declared so by the state (*Man and Citizen,* 72). The conclusion to which he is drawing us is "that in all things not contrary to the moral law, (that is to say, to the law of nature,) all subjects are bound to obey that for divine law, which is declared to be so, by the laws of the commonwealth" (*Leviathan,* 333).

Hobbes, too, does not escape the circularity of reason and revelation that was acknowledged by Hooker. Reason leads man to the recognition of the sovereign as the authenticator of revelation, and revelation confirms the law of reason that establishes the authority of the sovereign. Hobbes repeatedly affirms his intention of demonstrating that the law of God in nature and revelation are continuous with the civil law.[13] The circularity did not strike him as problematic because the law of God was of only the most general kind; it became concrete through its specification by the legislative authority of the state. Divine law provided the moral imperative for the content of the civil law. "Theft, murder, adultery, and all injuries, are forbid by the laws of nature; but what is to be called *theft,* what *murder,* what *adultery,* what *injury* in a citizen, this is not to be determined by the natural, but by the civil law" (*Man and Citizen,* 185). The circularity was therefore only apparent because it is ultimately the recognition of a divinely willed natural law that is the source of the obligation that receives virtually all of its specification within the state.

Hobbes recognizes, however, that even that divine obligation is not ultimate, and in this sense he is the originator of the modern liberal perspective that derives all from the consent of the self. He insists that the obligation, even to God, must be based on consent. Those who have not confessed their dependence on God and acknowledged his authority are not his subjects. They are not obliged by his law as free subjects. Instead, they are subject to the law in the coercive sense. As enemies of God they may be treated in the same way as all enemies are treated in the state of nature when there is no common order between us—that is, with regard only to what is necessary for us and without consideration for any rights of theirs. Atheists are punished by God or by kings constituted by God "not as a subject is punished by a king, because he would not keep the laws, but as one enemy by another, because he would not accept of the laws" (*Man and Citizen,* 285). This is simply an application of the principle that it is of the essence of free human beings that they can be bound only by their own consent. Hobbes is very clear that the conqueror has no rights as such over the conquered. "It is not the victory that giveth the right of dominion over the vanquished, but his own covenant" (*Leviathan*, 256). Human society is not the natural organization of the hive; it is artificial in the sense of being constituted by the agreement of those involved (225–26).

The question on which all his reflections concentrate is how to make that agreement in such a way that it will be stable. This is the transition from the state of nature to civil society. The state of nature merely describes human life without government and is, as such, an estimation of the resources available for the formation of the state and of the process by which they converge toward its construction. We have already noted the awareness of a law of nature already present in that state, although it is surrounded by the uncertainty concerning its performance by others. The major element enunciated by Hobbes is that we are obliged not to do anything contrary to our self-preservation. We have both a right and an obligation to use all means we judge necessary to preserve ourselves (*Leviathan*, chap. 14). But that still does not give us license in regard to others. Despite this latitude it is possible to break the law of nature in the state of nature, as in, for instance, injuring others when it is not necessary to our own preservation (*Man and Citizen*, 116). The state of nature is, as Hobbes constantly reminds us, a state without a common superior and therefore one where human beings who may be peaceably disposed to one another must nevertheless act on the assumption that they are enemies.

Under such conditions individuals must take steps so "that if there needs must be war, it may not yet be against all men, nor without some help" (*Man and Citizen*, 118). This consideration prompts the quest for "fellows" who may be obtained by constraint but are more reliably secured by consent. Indeed, it is only consent that binds them together by a moral obligation and removes the state of war. Given the approximate equality of injury that human beings can inflict on one another, we could never rely on our ability to continuously compel the obedience of others. Only a bond that has been internalized gives any hope of security because it is only then that the presumption of enmity has been lowered and we have some reasonable prospect of the continuation of peace in the absence of its enforcement. That is still not sufficient, because we know "how little men are kept to their duties through conscience of their promises" (*Man and Citizen*, 176), but it is a necessary starting point. The weight of obligation can be placed on men in no other way than by their own consent.

What prepares the way for the acceptance of this obligation is the realization of the intolerable condition of the state of nature. It is not enough to present the more attractive prospect of "commodious living" that might be obtained in the state of civil society. Hobbes realizes that the passions of men must be cooled in some way and especially the key one of pride, the desire for preeminence or "glory." What can be done to break the arrogance of men who "scarce esteem anything good, which hath not somewhat of eminence in the enjoyment, more than that which others do possess" (*Man and Citizen*, 168)? It is one of the most profound insights of Hobbes's work that he recognizes the depth of this problem. To make men rational it is necessary to break the hold of this irrational impulse to establish their superiority at all costs. The experience that makes them sober is the fear of violent death. This is the key realization that the whole elaborate description of the unending war of the state of nature is designed to evoke. Hobbes summons all his literary genius to construct the overwhelming impact of his meditation, which reaches its apex in that matchless cumulation of epithets describing life in the state of nature. It visualizes the elimination of all that constitutes civilization, a state in which industry, culture, navigation, building, and instruments have all disappeared. There is "no knowledge of the face of the earth; no account of time; no arts; no letters; no society; and which is worst of all, continual fear, and danger of violent death, and the life of man, solitary, poor, nasty, brutish, and short" (*Leviathan*, 186).

It is this realization that induces the rationality that conforms us to the laws of nature. The first of these is the obligation "to seek peace, and follow it," although never at the cost of abandoning the right to defend ourselves. The second law of nature specifies the means by which a relationship of peace is established. "That a man be willing, when others are so too, as far-forth, as for peace, and defence of himself he shall think it necessary, to lay down this right to all things; and be contented with so much liberty against other men, as he would allow other men against himself" (*Leviathan*, 190). Hobbes distinguishes between a contract, where a reciprocal transfer of rights actually takes place, and a covenant, where only one side actually delivers and the other promises to deliver. Covenants in this sense are the more normal form of an ongoing relationship, and then the crucial question becomes their reliability. Words alone are not sufficient to guarantee fidelity, "for nothing is more easily broken than a man's word" (192). Only the fear of the consequences of infidelity, derived from an oath that calls on divine punishment or from the physical power available for enforcement, can promise stability.

The covenant does not, however, rest on the sheer coercive power because, as Hobbes recognizes, all conjunction of power is itself dependent on voluntary support. That is why the third law of nature is "that men perform their covenants made" (201). This principle is the source of justice and is derived from the rule of reason that forbids us to do what is destructive of our life. Hobbes often sounds as if he is saying that it is the power of coercion that sustains contracts, as in his remark that "the validity of covenants begins not but with the constitution of a civil power, sufficient to compel men to keep them" (201). But then what sustains that civil power? His point is the more subtle one that the presence of an enforcing power frees us from the suspicion of noncompliance that would incline us too to suspend the fulfillment of our commitments. He is emphatic that we have an obligation to abide by our covenants and that it is irrefragable, not only where there is a power to enforce it but also whenever the other has already performed his end of the agreement (204). Then there is no possibility of our being abused and no excuse for not fulfilling our obligations. A person who would take such advantage of others undermines the whole trust on which society is based and "can in reason expect no other means of safety than what he had from his own single power" (205). Obligation is the irreducible foundation of a commonwealth.

This insight is also what sheds light on Hobbes's understanding of what holds civil society together. Given his assessment of the self-serving proclivities of human nature and of the necessity for the public authority to draw its strength from the members, we might expect the arrangement to be somewhat unstable. Is it not likely that there would be wholesale attempts to cheat whenever individuals felt they could get away with it? Is this not indeed even more likely in an agreement that men have entered to preserve and benefit only themselves? What is it that prevents the complete disintegration of the political order based on such a covenant? This is the notorious weakness of all social-contract explanations of the grounds of obligation, recognized at least as far back as Plato.[14] Hobbes, too, is patently aware of the insupportability of an egoistic agreement. Even self-serving agreements presuppose a background of virtue, at least that of fidelity to agreements, if they are to be more than strict exchanges.

His solution was to emphasize the obligation we have to abide by our covenants, only removing the inhibiting barrier of suspicion of nonperformance by others—the sole legitimate ground for our own reneging on promises. The whole elaborate account of the genesis of civil society in conformity with reason and revelation is to convince his readers of the legitimacy of the state and of their inescapable obligations to support it. This is why the law of nature dispensed by God is so important to Hobbes. It is not simply that men enter into society out of an interest in preserving their lives, but that they are under a natural and divine obligation to do all that they can to preserve themselves. That includes supporting the whole process by which human life is preserved. Hobbes's discussion seems to turn on the recognition that deception can gain only a limited good but that its effect is to undermine the whole possibility of agreement with the deceiver in the future. The criminal attacks the foundation of political order and separates himself from the community (205–7).[15]

What makes it work is that the numbers of those who dissent from the common order will, on Hobbes's estimation, always be small. This is the point of his insistence that "the number of them who conspire in a mutual assistance be so great, that the accession of some few to the enemy's party may not prove to them a matter of moment sufficient to assure the victory"

(*Man and Citizen,* 167). That is decisive for the majority who have kept themselves in readiness to fulfill their obligations according to the law of nature, because they can count on the public authority being sufficient to restrain or punish the breakers of their trust. In this sense, the public power of compulsion, while it is not the source of law, is its indispensable condition. It is what enables the law-abiding citizens to remain such and relieves the necessity of every man having to shift for himself. Before the emergence of a city there is "nothing else but some mutual contracts, which oblige not any man (and therefore are no laws) before that a supreme power being constituted, which can compel, have sufficient remedy against the rest, who otherwise are not likely to keep them" (*Man and Citizen,* 273).

Once there is an authority to enforce the laws of nature on the recalcitrant, the laws lose their conditional character for us, binding only so long as a man does not "make himself a prey to others" (*Leviathan,* 215), and become obligatory.[16] As Hobbes unfolds them, the laws of nature are elaborations of the virtues required of those who enter into the society intended to provide mutual assistance. Thus, the fourth law of nature that prohibits ingratitude is directed to the temptation to avoid fulfilling one's obligations of the covenant, thereby causing those whose contributions have already provided benefits to repent of their gifts. The result would be the collapse of trust and mutual assistance and reversion to the state of war (209). The other laws are of a like character, specifying the qualities needed to sustain the reciprocal cooperation, such as: each should "strive to accommodate himself to the rest"; readiness to pardon offenses, to moderate the demand for revenge, and to avoid all indication of contempt for others; the acknowledgment of every other as one's equal, relinquishing all claim to special privileges for oneself; and so on. We recognize these qualities as the virtues of the liberal state, in which primacy is given to those elements that render citizens agreeable to one another above all others, rather than the ethic of the saint or the hero.

What convinced Hobbes that the breach of these laws could be reliably prevented is the element in which he differs from the succeeding liberal tradition, but in which he is probably more consistent than any of his subsequent liberal critics. This is the absolute authority he assigns to the sovereign. The extreme experience of the English civil war had convinced him that the security of the state is dependent on the recognition that there are no constitutional limits to its power. Later liberal tradition has tended to focus precisely on the issue of constitutional restraint on authority, but that should not conceal the reality that they have also tacitly or obliquely acknowledged the cogency of Hobbes's principle. No state can predict in advance the limits of authority it will require; extreme necessity may compel even liberal democracies to adopt extraconstitutional measures in their self-defense. "This same may be confirmed by experience, in all the cities which are or ever have been. For though it be sometimes in doubt what man or council hath the chief command, yet there is such a command and always exercised, except in time of sedition and civil war" (*Man and Citizen*, 182).

The fatal defect in establishing a government is the failure to see that its power must be absolute in order to ensure that it will have a sufficiency of power to overwhelm the dangers that threaten it. Thus, it is "that a man to obtain a kingdom, is sometimes content with less power, than to the peace, and defence of the commonwealth is necessarily required" (*Leviathan*, 364). If the government's power is limited or it can be called to account by some other institution, then it is the latter that is supreme and the government is not truly sovereign. Hobbes rejected the notion that sovereignty could be limited. He recognized that the supreme authority in the state was morally bound by the laws of nature and of God and avowed the wish that they confine themselves within such limits. But he could discover no way to institutionalize this except that "they who do set the limits must needs have some part of the power, whereby they must be enabled to do it, [in which case] the government is properly divided, not moderated" (*Man and Citizen*, 195).

The great task on which Hobbes had set himself was to convince his countrymen that they could join in a commonwealth in no other way than by the acceptance of the unchallenged authority of the sovereign. We have seen how he demonstrates that the readiness to obey the natural law, to observe justice, can only become effective if there is an authority to define the law and ensure that lawbreakers are brought to account. Now we must examine the argument he makes that the authority of the law enforcer must be absolute and that the subject can have no legitimate grounds for complaint or resistance. The covenant through which the sovereign is created from the pledging of all the strength of individuals cannot be compromised by reservations or restrictions. It is a pledge that once given cannot be revoked no matter how burdensome the impositions of the sovereign may become.

The core of the argument by which Hobbes sought to convince self-willed human beings to accept the public authority as the final arbiter of all disputes is based on his concept of representation. There can be no basis for complaint against the sovereign because by virtue of the covenant the subjects have authorized all his actions as their own. The identifying mark of a city as opposed to a multitude is that the multiplicity of individual wills has been reduced to one. Hobbes defines the commonwealth as "One person, of whose acts a great multitude, by mutual covenants one with another, have made themselves every one the author, to the end he may use the strength and means of them all, as he shall think expedient, for their peace and common defence" (*Leviathan*, 228). He emphasizes the extent to which the covenant is more than consent or concord in the pursuit of the common good, such as occurs in ants or bees that all subordinate their individual needs to the common purpose (*Man and Citizen*, 168). Civil society is a conjunction of the plurality of human wills that nevertheless remain diverse. They retain their individual differences and have not been submerged in the common project. Rather, their divergences have been contained in the only way that they can without their elimination, through their acceptance of one will as the authority that settles their disputes. "This is more than consent, or concord; it is a real unity of them all, in one and the same person, made by covenant of every man with every man" (*Leviathan*, 227). By this means, "the great Leviathan" or "mortal god" is created that forms an order out of that which is otherwise without order.

Since there is no other order apart from that instituted by the sovereign authority of the commonwealth there can be no grounds on which the latter can be rendered illegitimate. That is why for Hobbes the covenant is irrevocable. There is no time, except when the commonwealth has collapsed, that the subjects are released from or can suspend their obligation to support it. The sovereign cannot be accused of breach of covenant because there is no covenant before the existence of the sovereign. He does not hold his authority conditionally but is the unconditional condition for all agreements. Nor can he be accused of injustice toward the subjects because before him there is no justice or injustice. He is the one who determines what is just because apart from him it is simply the state of war in which individuals compete with one another for survival. What is to be considered just or unjust is therefore relative to the order of a commonwealth that is sufficient to enforce the determination, and the city is not tied to its own laws since they are the city's own creation and it is free to change them as it wills. The sovereign or supreme authority "contains the wills of all particular citizens. Therefore neither is he bound to the civil laws, for this is to be bound to himself; nor to any of his citizens" (*Man and Citizen*, 183–84).

Hobbes is willing to push this line of reasoning pretty far, although he does so without asserting that the sovereign is free of all law in his decisions. He is still subject to the law of God, although there is no human means of calling him to account before it. Subjects never surrender their right to defend themselves or those for whom they are responsible when they are about to be injured by the sovereign or anyone else. Hobbes's reasoning is that they retain this right for the simple reason that they cannot surrender what they cannot separate from themselves. But the subject has no legitimate grounds for grievance against the sovereign if deprived of his goods or even his life. An action such as that of David in causing the death of Uriah may be contrary to the law of nature, but not to the subject or against the law of the state. "Not to Uriah," Hobbes explains, "because the right to do what he pleased, was given him by Uriah himself: And yet to God, because David was God's subject; and prohibited all iniquity by the law of nature" (*Leviathan*, 263).

The only crack in the legitimacy of the public order, in which Hobbes acknowledges not just the inevitability of a self-preservative resistance but the validity of resistance, is where it touches one's eternal salvation. This had, of course, been the area of most heated controversy, and Hobbes's inability to completely foreclose the possibility of conflict is testament to the difficulty of establishing an order beyond grievance. He begins by narrowing the area of conflict in two ways. First, Hobbes insists, like Hooker, that by the law of nature and revelation the king or sovereign is the only one authorized by God to interpret his word. As the one who speaks for the community, the sovereign is the only one who can make decisions on its behalf; any others who try would be merely asserting their private viewpoint. Second, Hobbes insists that what is necessary for salvation consists in the most elemental faith in Christ and obedience to the laws. The possibility that the sovereign might obstruct this most basic of commitments is bound to be relatively slight, and anything else he may command is not of such importance that it can affect our eternal salvation. "But if the command be such, as cannot be obeyed, without being damned to eternal death, then it were madness to obey it, and the counsel of our Savior takes place (Mt 10:28) 'Fear not those that kill the body, but cannot kill the soul' " (*Leviathan*, 610). In the extreme instance it is clear the command of God is still to be preferred even to that of the mortal god (*Man and Citizen*, chap. 18).

What is prohibited by divine law cannot be permitted by the civil and what is commanded by the former cannot be prohibited by the latter. But what may be done by divine law can be forbidden by the civil, and then it becomes a part of divine law. Hobbes emphasizes the continuity of the two. The laws to which Christ commands our obedience are no other than the laws to which all men are subject, and each must take their content from the city in which they dwell (*Man and Citizen*, 341–43). There is no separate spiritual authority of the Church because the Church is the mystical body whose head is Christ. The concrete community of Christians is identical with the concrete community of the state, and its head can only be the individual or body that is authorized to act on its behalf. The Church is, on Hobbes's often forced reading of Scripture, an invisible community that will be realized in heaven.[17] The community of Christians is that which is concretely governed by the political sovereign. From him they receive the interpretation of God's law, for only he can authorize it as publicly binding on all members of the community (*Leviathan*, chap. 42).

Hobbes admits the inconveniences of ceding so much authority to the sovereign who must rule unchecked by any other human restraints. But he always comes back to the insistence that the resulting hardship, compared to "the greatest, that in any form of government can possibly happen to the people in general, is scarce sensible, in respect of the miseries, and horrible calamities, that accompany a civil war" (*Leviathan*, 238). Besides, he rejects the notion, which goes back to Aristotle, that the fundamental difference between regimes is between those that are governed in the interest of the ruler or in the interest of the citizens. For Hobbes this is a nonessential distinction, connoting only the mildness or severity of rule, not a fundamental difference of regimes. His reasoning is that "all the profits and disprofits arising from government are the same, and common both to the *ruler* and the *subject*" (*Man and Citizen*, 222). If a state is well governed, then it redounds to the ruler as well as the subject, but if it is misgoverned then the ruler too will suffer from the deterioration of the commonwealth. The relationship is clearest in the case of monarchy, and that is the basis for Hobbes's preference for this form, because the monarch must necessarily view the state as his own and care for it as people do their patrimony. But he is willing to accept other forms and endorses a type of democracy in which the people are content with selecting the magistrates but do not interfere with their administrative function (*Man and Citizen*, 233).

At bottom, forms of government are all the same for the fundamental difference remains that between a people and a multitude. "The *people*," Hobbes emphasizes, "rules in all governments. For even in *monarchies* the *people* commands; for the *people* wills by the will of *one man;* but the multitude are citizens, that is to say, subjects" (250). It is because in a monarchy "the king is the *people*" that he can do them no injury. All is ultimately referred back to the concept of representation in which a people or a state is constituted. Having made the sovereign their representative, the multitude have authorized all his actions as their own and therefore cannot legitimately refuse to acknowledge them. The only alternative, on Hobbes's conception, is to withdraw their authorization, in which case, the sovereign is no longer or never was their representative. The abiding difficulty for Hobbes is that he can conceive of no way of limiting the authority of the sovereign that would not be equivalent to the removal of his authority to resolve their disputes.

Such a step would be disastrous in a social setting where nothing is simply and absolutely good, "nor any common rule of good and evil" between men (*Leviathan*, 120). Each defines *good* as whatever is an object of his appetite or desire and defines *evil* as what is regarded with distaste or aversion. Even when we talk of an object that is commonly good to all men, such as health, Hobbes explains, "this way of speaking is relative; therefore one cannot speak of something as being *simply good;* since whatsoever is good, is good for someone or other" (*Man and Citizen*, 47). This is not to assert the absence of a moral or natural law, but the improbability of coincidence on it given the diversity of human perspectives. Hobbes takes seriously the irreducible plurality of human nature and in responding to its challenge is one of the founders of the liberal approach. Ultimately, what is good, he goes on to suggest, must be referred to God for whom all that he "created was good"

(47). That is the point of Hobbes's demonstration to wayward human beings that the only order that can contain them derives its obligatory force from the divinely willed order of nature.

The difficulty is that the diversity of loves and hates creates enough uncertainty about their common sense of a divinely willed order and of the reliability of their conformity to it that we are inevitably compelled to act as if there is no such common rule between us—that is, until there is an authority to define it. It is only when there is a sovereign, Hobbes repeats, that we can talk of acting justly or unjustly. "Where there is no common power, there is no law: where no law, no injustice" (*Leviathan,* 188). Then we have a definition and a surety of the performance of others that renders our own conformity obligatory. But in the state of war everyone must decide for himself what is appropriate to his self-preservation, and no one can challenge his assessment because there is no common measure. In that sense, there is no standard prior to the existence of the sovereign by which the justice of his actions can be judged. Such is the logic of the starting point of the radical plurality of human perspectives. Thus, there is no way of calling the power that relieves the anarchic chaos to account for its own abuses.

Evocation of Liberal Consensus

Hobbes was willing to accept the consequence of sovereign unaccountability, but most of his successors have not. Most prominent among those who sought a different line was the man who, more than anyone else, formed the idea of liberal democracy, John Locke. His central idea was that the sovereign is a part of the political compact, not simply its indispensable condition. As such, the sovereign is received on the basis of the trust that is shared by all the partners to the contract. There is still the assurance of compelling recalcitrant members who are tempted to renege on their commitments. But, most important of all for Locke, there must be a means of calling the most powerful partner, the government, to account for its breaches of the public trust. That entails an appeal to standards of justice prior to the creation of government and a definition of the common good prior to the formation of the political order. Elaboration of that prevailing moral consensus evokes the sustaining continuity of liberal democratic order up to the present. Where Hobbes has confronted the limiting case of mutual distrust, Locke has articulated the normally reliable common sense that avoids the necessity of giving priority to the extremes of division. In that way Locke has exercised the greater influence in liberal circles, although the shadow of Hobbes has always been in the background.

Hobbes is certainly more profound than Locke in the analysis of problems to their roots and in the correlative development of fundamental modes of response. But Hobbes's reflections reveal their true significance only when we have reached the limiting situation. In the normal course of events, division and distrust between human beings does not extend so far. Locke becomes the more attractive (if less rigorous) guide, precisely because his ambiguous analyses reflect the unclarity of the situation in which we find ourselves. We do not exactly know what the limits of our agreement are, but we do know that we operate from a bedrock of consensus concerning what is good and what is bad. Nor is it generally necessary for us to test the limits of our divergences in order to know that a substantial convergence exists between us. Thus, it is a great mistake to read Locke as a guide to the liberal institutional structure. He is first and foremost an exponent of the spirit that animates the various institutional forms that are considered liberal. Locke's account of the institutional relationships is incomplete and notoriously replete with inconsistencies, but as an evocation of the animating consensus of liberal democracy it has scarcely been surpassed.

The confidence he has in the existence of a common sense of order permits him to focus attention on the secondary consideration of making its political expression responsible. Unlike Hobbes, whose first and only concern is to ensure that there will be a political order, Locke is free to explore the means by which the political articulation reflects the impulse to self-government in practice. It is not enough to claim that all the citizens have authorized the actions of the sovereign as their own; there must be a means by which the consent they have given can be given concrete expression in the continuous unfolding of government. Not content with mere political life, Locke is intent on the pursuit of the good political life. That is, he sets out to discover the means by which the political order can more fully realize the freedom of its members. In order to accomplish this, he is even willing to risk its destruction through revolution.

What gave Locke the kind of security that permitted him to countenance and engage in revolutionary activities was the overwhelming sense of the ease of restoration of order given the preexisting community between human beings. Contrary to the caricature of Locke that still prevails of an individualist, possessive or otherwise, it ought to be emphasized that Locke is preeminently a theorist of community. Political order is not crucial because he is confident in the prepolitical order that already joins us together. Before there is any civil law, each of us is governed by the law of nature "by which law common to them all, he and all the rest of mankind are one community" (*Second Treatise,* par. 128). The state of nature is in this sense already an ordered community and, "were it not for the corruption, and viciousness of degenerate men, there would be no need of any other; no necessity that men should separate from this great and natural community, and by positive agreements combine into smaller and divided associations" (par. 128). The sense of a common law of nature makes possible the formation of agreements and cooperation in the state of nature. This may be a state without government, but it is not a state without order.

Locke, too, understands that agreements and contracts are not self-sustaining. They depend on a prior readiness to acknowledge them as binding that renders them obligatory whether they continue to be advantageous or not. Contracts for "truck" and other services are equally binding on men who have freely made them whether they are on a desert island or in a civilized political state: "For truth and keeping of faith belongs to men as men, and not as members of society" (*Second Treatise,* par. 14). Curiously, it is Locke's insistence on the viability of such a state of nature as a real possibility that creates the impression that he considers political society an option that depends on individual choice. It is optional only because, for Locke, human beings are already within an ordered relationship to one another. Political society is an extension and specification of the order that governs the state of nature and establishes it as already a state of community.

The state of nature, while it is a state of perfect liberty and equality between human beings, is "not a state of licence." It is governed by a law of nature that reason teaches to all mankind. The source of that law, Locke emphasizes, is the one omnipotent creator of us all who has not given any one of us a position of superiority or advantage over any others. "For men being all the workmanship of one omnipotent, and infinitely wise maker; all the servants of one sovereign master, sent into the world by his order and about his business, they are his property, whose workmanship they are, made to last during his, not one another's pleasure." From this condition of equality in relation to one another and responsibility for our actions toward the God who created all of us, Locke deduces the two fundamental principles that define the law of nature. "Every one as he is *bound to preserve himself,* and not to quit his station wilfully; so by the like reason when his own preservation comes not in competition, ought he, as much as he can, *to preserve the rest of mankind"* (*Second Treatise,* par. 6). Locke also quotes Hooker's further interpretation of the law of nature as requiring the Christian injunction that we be prepared to love others as we would wish to be loved by them (par. 5).

From the law of nature the rights that human beings possess are derived, rights that are antecedent to and foundational to the political order. Locke specifies many of these natural rights, beginning with the right to property as the enjoyment of the fruits of our own labor. The right to property is established from the principle that "every man has a *property* in his own *person"* (par. 27). No one has a right to the work of our hands but ourselves and, by extension, that which has become ours through the operation of labor. "Whatsoever then he removes out of the state that nature hath provided, and left it in, he hath mixed his *labour* with, and joined to it something that is his own, and thereby makes it his *property"* (par. 27). Not only is the right to property thus established as part of the divinely ordained order of nature, but its enjoyment is also contained by law. Contrary to the picture of Locke as a protocapitalist, it is quite clear that he limits acquisition to the natural limits of that which "any one can make use of to any advantage of life before it spoils" (par. 31). These limits established by God and reason are breached only through the convention, also established before the advent of civil society, of money as a means of storing wealth without perishing. It is evident that Locke acknowledges, without approving, a situation that has made possible a "disproportionate and unequal possession of the earth," because he emphasizes that this consequence of money could be altered once we enter society. "For in governments the laws regulate the right of property, and the possession of land is determined by positive constitutions" (par. 50). That is, the government might again tilt the ownership of property toward those with the most natural title to it, "the industrious and rational" (par. 34).[18]

In the same way, nature already structures the obligations human beings have toward one another before there is a civil society. The society of the family is natural, and the obligations of parents to care for their children and of children to honor their parents (as well as the obligation of spouses to remain faithful to one another) are prior to any regulations that may be placed on them. None of these relationships amounts to an unconditional grant of authority. Locke argued strenuously against the patriarchal absolutism of Robert Filmer. But Locke was also careful to insist that the duties of parents and children toward one another cannot be suspended by any later legal accretions. Neither parents nor children can be discharged from the natural obligations they owe one another (pars. 56, 63, 69). Even the contract between husband and wife has a natural status that is prior to the authority of the magistrate, who "doth not abridge" the rights of either side "but only decides any controversy that may arise between man and wife about them" (par. 365).

Where Hobbes emphasizes that the political order is the source of all specificity of rights, Locke maintains the priority of the order of rights in nature before the advent of the means of their adjudication. Political authority is limited by the order of rights that men hold in nature from their creator. Foremost among these are the rights and obligations to preserve their lives, liberties, and property, both for themselves and for those for whom they are responsible, as well as that of all others whose rights do not endanger their own. The determination of the boundaries of these rights is not usually open to disagreement. While Locke does acknowledge the "inconveniences" of men being judges in their own cases, he does not consider that this will imperil their sense of justice overall. Perhaps the best illustration of this is his reflection on the situation where we are robbed of our property by a thief. Like Hobbes, Locke views this as a state of war between two human beings, where, even though no force has been used, "I have no reason to suppose, that he, who would *take away my liberty,* would not when he had me in his power, take away everything else" (par. 17). We have no choice but to treat him with the utmost suspicion and are therefore justified in killing a thief who has, as yet, made no attempt on our lives. But, Locke insists, that is the limit of the injury we can do him. We cannot then deprive him of his goods, beyond the recovery of our own, for the right to receive the thief's goods "belong to the children to keep them from perishing" (par. 182). He acknowledges that this may be a "strange doctrine" (par. 180), that we may deprive a man's life but not his goods, but insists that it arises from the rights of the innocent that are not in any way compromised by the breakdown of comity in the particular instance.

Locke does not draw the Hobbesian conclusion that because the reciprocal recognition of rights has failed in one case then the entire order of rights has been rendered unreliable. Until there is a manifest threat, we can operate on the assumption that we share a common sense of reason with others and that this consensus is sufficient for the emergence of an authoritative order between us. The emphasis is placed, rather, on the elaboration of a political structure that reflects and preserves the order of nature. Where Hobbes focuses almost exclusively on the conditions that can secure the public authority from disintegration, Locke is largely unconcerned with this problem in his mature writings, preferring to attend to the conditions that make the political power responsible. The animating center of his construction is his opposition to all forms of absolute political power. His preoccupation is not how to create the power of law but how to render the power itself law-abiding.

The historical background described so extensively in Richard Ashcraft's study is not strictly necessary to pick up this dimension of Locke's thought. It is certainly useful to know that the *Two Treatises of Government* were written as "exclusionary tracts" around the crisis of 1681, in which Parliament sought a means of excluding the Catholic James II from the inheritance of the throne from his brother, Charles II. Just as useful is the effort to trace the points at which the rhetoric of the text was later enhanced to direct it more effectively toward James after he had succeeded to his brother.[19] But any careful reader can discern the animus that flames up in the author when the possibility of absolute rule is broached. Locke's fervent opposition to everything that tolerates the arbitrary rule of a single will is what makes him the leading figure in the liberal impulse that defines itself by its opposition to political absolutism.

Clearly, the inconveniences of the state of nature are slight compared to the horror of an absolute prince. Locke often has difficulty in finding language strong enough to express his condemnation. In an interpolation probably added in 1689 he declaims that such an individual may be destroyed by anyone "for the same reason, that he may kill a *wolf* or a *lion;* because such men are not under the ties of the common law of reason, have no other rule, but that of force and violence, and so may be treated as beasts of prey, those dangerous and noxious creatures, that will be sure to destroy him, whenever he falls into their power" (par. 16). The reference is clear because Locke proceeds to talk about all who try to get us into their "absolute power" as deserving of such treatment according to the state of war (par. 17). The motto Locke attached to the title page of *Two Treatises of Government*, with its incendiary quotation from Livy against those who "will not be placated unless we yield to them our blood to drink and our entrails to tear out," was not chosen for its decorative effect.

For Locke, the great evil is the arbitrary power of absolute government that, if it were accepted by men, "were to put themselves into a worse condition than the state of nature, wherein they had a liberty to defend their right against the injuries of others" (par. 137). Accordingly, the crucial aspect of the compact that draws men out of the state of nature is the character of the authority it establishes. The whole point of the decision to quit the state of nature, which is still governed by the law of nature, is to obtain a means of resolving the controversies that arise but do not permit men to be judges in their own cases. We must create a common authority to whom all can appeal as the embodiment of the law. Such a purpose is inconsistent with the admission of an absolute monarch who, by definition, remains outside of the means of settling disputes. As with all "who have not such an authority to appeal to, for the decision of any difference between them, there those persons are still *in the state of nature*. And so is every *absolute prince* in respect of those who are under his *dominion*" (par. 90).

The remedy is to make the monarch as well as every other member of the community subject to the rule of law. Then it is not the rule of the will of one man or one group that is supreme, but the law that all have made through the consent they have given. An articulation of the consent is, for Hobbes as well as for Locke, the sole foundation for legitimate government and the only thing that distinguishes it from slavery. Locke defines political society as "where every one of the members hath quitted this natural power [of judging and enforcing the law of nature], resigned it up into the hands of the community in all cases that exclude him not from appealing for protection to the law established by it" (par. 87). In place of private judgment the community acts as "umpire, by settled standing rules, indifferent, and the same to all parties." The mark of those who are in civil society is that they "have a common established law and judicature to appeal to." To be within civil society, and not in the state of nature wherein all disputes are likely to end in a state of war (par. 21), the monarch must become subject to the rule of law along with everyone else.

This is done by placing the sovereignty in the community itself. Locke, as we have noted, twice quotes and underlines a passage from Hooker in which the rule of law is asserted as infinitely preferable to the rule of a prince, for

" '*to live by one man's will, became the cause of all men's misery*' " (par. 94). Princes, too, must be subject to the rule of law, and its source must be located, therefore, in the consent of the whole community as the lawmaking authority. For this reason men have concluded, Locke observes, that they "could never be safe nor at rest, *nor think themselves in civil society*, till the legislature was placed in collective bodies of men, call them senate, parliament, or what you please." There is a common rule to which all can appeal only when "every single person became subject, equally with other the meanest men, to those laws, which he himself, as part of the legislative had established." None, Locke emphasizes, are outside of the law if they are within civil society.

The question of what ensures that the law itself will be responsible does not seem to trouble Locke excessively.[20] He is aware of the problem because he insists that the legislative authority does not thereby acquire arbitrary power over the lives and fortunes of the people. Since it is simply the aggregate of the powers that each of them had in the state of nature, the power of the legislature is bound by the same natural limits as each was obliged to observe in that condition. "For no body can transfer to another more power than he has in himself; and no body has an absolute arbitrary power over himself, or over any other, to destroy his own life, or take away the life or property of another" (par. 135). Locke is emphatic that the legislative authority extends only to the promotion of the public good, understood as the preservation of the lives, liberty, and property of the subjects. The obligations of natural law rest with even greater gravity on us in the state of civil society because of their greater specificity and reliability. The rules and actions of legislators must "be conformable to the law of nature, i.e. to the will of God, of which that is a declaration, and the *fundamental law of nature* being *the preservation of mankind*, no humane sanction can be good, or valid against it."

The reason for expecting that a body of legislators will be more faithful to observance of the laws is that the legislators also remain individuals subject to the laws they have made. That is the meaning of the rule of law that Locke goes on to elaborate. It excludes rule by extemporary decrees, requiring instead rule by "promulgated standing laws, and known authorized judges" (par. 136). In particular this requires that property, the nucleus of the order of rights that radiate from the property each has in his own person, never be taken from the subjects without their consent. That is, the deprivation of property always requires scrupulous adherence to the process by which men are governed only by laws made through their own participation (par. 138). Locke offers a striking illustration of the seriousness of the principle of consent by reflecting on the situation of the authority of the general over the soldier. This is a microcosm of the absolute authority that the state, even a limited constitutional one, must from time to time exercise over its members. The authority of the state to enforce the law within its prescribed jurisdiction must be absolute, but, Locke argues, it is not thereby rendered unlimited. Thus, the general can order the soldier to expose himself to the risk of imminent death and execute him for disobedience to the charge, yet he cannot "with all his absolute power of life and death, dispose of one farthing of that soldier's estate, or seize one jot of his goods." The absolute authority of the general is limited strictly to the military purpose for which it was instituted (par. 139). In the same way all who are part of the government must exercise their authority in such a way that they do not betray the trust placed in them. Thus, Locke places as the last of the conditions on the legislature the prohibition against transferring lawmaking power to anyone else (par. 141), because that would be to break the bond of consent on which the entire construction has been erected.

Everything returns to the principle of consent as the only legitimate foundation for the exercise of public authority. Hobbes recognizes it as the only legitimate starting point, but Locke extends it as a requirement for the operation of government itself. Where Hobbes is concerned only with securing the existence of the sovereign, Locke accepts the sovereign's existence as unproblematic and concentrates on the process by which power can be guided by the restraints of the law of nature. His solution is to allow the formative influence of the law of nature as it exists within each of us to continue to determine the direction of public policy through the requirement of continuous consent of the governed. The crucial assumption is that the law of nature continues to exist within the diversity of individuals or at least in a sufficiently consensual form in their aggregate. He does not face the extreme pluralism contemplated by Hobbes, only the more ordinary circumstance of considerable uncontroversial agreement with differences at the margins.

Locke, as we have seen, recognizes the need for circumspection even in admitting a popularly representative legislature. The legislators still need to be reminded that they are the means to the self-government of society, not its paternal tutors. Locke is even willing to build certain institutional checks, what James Madison later referred to as "auxiliary safeguards," into the system. Most prominent is his suggestion that the legislative and executive authorities ought to be separated. It is, he considers,

> too great a temptation to humane frailty apt to grasp at power, for the same persons who have the power of making laws, to have also in their hands the power to execute them, whereby they may exempt themselves from obedience to the laws they make, and suit the law, both in its making and execution, to their own private advantage, and thereby come to have a distinct interest from the rest of the community, contrary to the end of society and government. (par. 143)

The bedrock of Locke's faith in the virtue of popular government is that the rulers are also the subjects and will not impose policies that would injure the common good that is their own. The representatives cannot separate themselves from the consequences of policies whose full weight must be borne when they return to the private state. Deprivation of property without consent "is not much to be feared in governments where the *legislative* consists, wholly or in part, in assemblies which are variable, whose members upon the dissolution of the assembly, are subjects under the common laws of the country, equally with the rest" (par. 138).

That still does not eliminate the concern that a majority of the subjects through their representatives might seek to oppress a more or less stable minority. Locke's failure to consider this problem can be explained in part by the circumstances, in which the usurpation of power by the monarch was by far the greatest danger. But the absence of this consideration remains one of the notorious weak points of his theory. The best that can be said in his defense is that Locke was writing to evoke the moral consensus that was already present in the surrounding society and has been successfully re-evoked in the succeeding liberal societies. Such a forceful articulation of the law of nature would make its blatant disregard well-nigh impossible. In many ways the *Two Treatises of Government* are something of an education of the people, after the model of treatises that educate the prince. One can assume that the strictures he applies to absolute rulers would equally apply when the popular representatives have made themselves absolute. If the ruler does not abide by the law, then all contracts between men are rendered unreliable, "there needs nothing to dissolve them but power enough" (par. 194). Even if the rulers claim to be free from the laws of the state, "they owe subjections to the laws of God and nature" (par. 195). No one is or can be exempted from the eternal law. "These are so great, and so strong, in the case of *promises,* that Omnipotency it self can be tyed by them. *Grants, promises* and *oaths* are bonds that *hold the Almighty:* Whatever some flatterers say to princes of the world who all together, with all their people joined to them, are in comparison of the great God, but as a drop of the bucket, or a dust on the balance, inconsiderable nothing!" (par. 195).

The term that recurs over and over again, especially in the *Second Treatise,* is *trust.*[21] Government is a fiduciary responsibility that is broken when it exceeds the bounds of its authority and no longer acts for the common good. Tyranny occurs whenever power is exercised without the authority of law. " 'Tis a mistake to think this fault is proper only to monarchies; other forms of government are liable to it, as well as that" (par. 201). It matters not, Locke observes, "whether those that use it are one or many" if the power is used to deprive people of their properties. There is little in the *Second Treatise* by way of constitutional safeguards to guard against the emergence of tyranny, but it is a powerful evocation of the opposition to all forms of the tyrannical exercise of power. The capacity to convey the sense of the overwhelming weight of trust, of faithfulness to law, and of the acceptance of limits on power as the abiding realities has been the secret of the *Second Treatise*'s influence over the centuries. Locke communicates a powerful sense of the majesty of the law that binds even the almighty, compared to which the lawbreakers are the mere dust of history.

That forceful evocation of a community between human beings explains Locke's relative unconcern for ensuring that there will be a community and a state. It also accounts for the other notorious weakness that has attracted criticism over the centuries, the relatively open-ended endorsement of a right to revolution. Even Locke betrays an undercurrent of uneasiness in his chapter on the "dissolution of government," almost as if his own assertion of the right of revolution frightened him. He is careful to explain that such revolutions against tyranny "happen not upon every little mismanagement in publick affairs" (par. 225). But after all the qualifications and explanations, the striking aspect of Locke's discussion of revolution is that he leaves open the question of who is to form the revolutionary force. Unlike the earlier tradition that always emphasized that revolution is not an action for private individuals to initiate, Locke seems to place no such requirements for garnering community authorization.[22] As Ashcraft has pointed out, Locke really does intend "the people," an undifferentiated mass, as the carrier of revolutionary resistance.[23] This may be one of the weaknesses of his theory, but it is consistent with the indeterminacy in which he is content to leave the problems of order. If he has succeeded in his intention of communicating the liberal spirit of restraint and respect for law, then there will be less to fear from the self-assertiveness of the people.

This also explains Locke's nonchalance about the great danger of locating such power in the people, that it will prove impossible to hold the civil society together. He has been frequently criticized for underestimating the difficulty and increasing the danger of disintegration by placing such emphasis on the social contract. What is to prevent its collapse when the suspicion of mistrust undermines its foundation? Locke is careful to reinforce the contract by insisting that it is no ordinary temporary agreement of mutual advantage between men. At the end of the last chapter on revolution he concludes that "the *power that every individual gave the society*, when he entered into it, can never revert to the individuals again, as long as the society lasts, but will always remain in the community" (243). This is a position he had iterated a number of times previously in the text, that anyone who gives express consent to a commonwealth is "perpetually" and "unalterably" bound to it (121). Unlike all other contracts, the agreement that founds civil society is an expression of the law of nature. It is a promise that cannot be removed.

Minimum Consensus of Liberal Politics

For Locke, the foundation of the social contract was not a problem because it was identical with the moral law. The breach of one was tantamount to the breach of the other, neither more nor less. All that the language of contract or compact did was make the situation explicit. Revolution was thus not an act that dissolved the government; rather, it was a response to the situation in which the government had already dissolved itself by breaking the bond of trust on which it had been based. The breach is not simply of a contract or agreement but of the moral law on which all agreements are premised. Hence it is that Locke anathematizes the betrayal of this trust of mutual respect for rights as the most serious offense possible. It is immaterial who does it for, "whoever, either ruler or subject, by force goes about to invade the rights of either prince or people, and lays the foundation for *overturning* the constitution and frame of *any just government,* is guilty of the greatest crime, I think, a man is capable of, being to answer for all those mischiefs of blood, rapine, and desolation, which the breaking to pieces of governments bring on a country" (*Second Treatise,* 230). The "compact" is merely shorthand for the maintenance of the moral commitments on which community is based.

But how much consensus is needed? Can order be maintained with much less consensus than Locke presupposed? Evidently, the answer is yes, because order has been maintained even though we have expanded the toleration of diversity beyond the limits suggested by Locke. He had, for example, excluded atheists, Catholics, the intolerant, and advocates of civil disorder (*A Letter Concerning Toleration,* 50–52). We are daily confronted with new demands to expand the boundaries of the permissible and the protected, however unpopular or unsavory the activities of some of the claimants may be to majoritarian sensibilities. We are pressed more urgently with the question of the limits, if any, to the consensus needed to hold the public order together. Locke identified the presence of a consensus that made a liberal political order possible. The form assumed by contemporary liberal politics is defined by the question not of the existence of a consensus but of its limits. What is essential to the consensus of a liberal democracy?

The man who confronted this question and whose response has shaped the self-understanding of the liberal constitution up to the present is John Stuart Mill. It is no accident that Mill is the last great liberal thinker because we continue to live in the context formed by his thought. The debates in which we are engaged are framed in Millian terms; he is the starting point for the disputes and the remedies with which we continue to grapple. Not only is he the point at which the liberal tradition acquires the self-consciousness of a name, but he is also the one who gives it a definitive formulation that has been only revised, not overturned, in the succeeding century.[24] Mill's "principle of liberty" continues to be the touchstone of truth in liberal debates, a principle of such self-evidence that it can stand as the measure by which all other proposals are to be judged. For all of the objections leveled against it, Mill's principle still stands as one of the few points of public agreement in a contentious world. That is why Mill may be regarded as the father of contemporary liberal politics.

The context Mill confronted is essentially the same as our own. In contrast to the earlier generations of liberal thinkers, the locus of problems has shifted from the struggle to secure popular self-government from reluctant monarchs to the difficulties and dangers generated by mass democratic politics itself. The risks to liberty, Mill announces in the opening of *On Liberty,* come not from the tyranny of political rulers but from "a social tyranny more formidable than many kinds of political oppression" (7). There is little danger of government abusing the rights of the majority because under a republican system the means are readily available of conveying popular displeasure and, if need be, throwing the culpable out of office at the next periodic election. But the safeguard of popular control contributes little to the security of minorities and individuals. If they are the target of political oppression, then it will, more likely than not, be with the approval of popular opinion whose instrument is the political power. What then is there to restrain the abuse of popular power?

That is the question Mill came to focus on with increasing sharpness over the course of his writings, which reach a culmination with *On Liberty* (although it is a mistake to isolate that text from the long series of preparatory reflections and his other writings). He saw that with the decline in independence of the political class, an aristocracy, and with the disappearance of all the qualifications and barriers that had restricted the access of ordinary individuals to political power the task of the day had become the formation of the now all-powerful force of public opinion. An enthusiastic supporter of the expansion of the franchise and an advocate of its universal extension to include women, Mill was nevertheless deeply concerned that the experiment in popular government turn out right. His reading of Tocqueville and others had sharpened his own awareness of the dangers of the democratic process.[25] Like Hobbes and Locke before him, he set to work to accommodate "the struggle between liberty and authority" in a way that would be evocative of a publicly authoritative order in this new context.

The measure of his success is that Mill's formulation still holds the field as the criterion of order that contains the ring of truth. His principle of liberty, "that the sole end for which mankind are warranted, individually or collectively, in interfering with the liberty of action of any of their number is self-protection," defines the line that characterizes the consensus underpinning liberal democracy up to the present. The intuitive rightness of his distinction is reflected in the unquestioned acceptance as a general approach to the resolution of social and political conflicts. We acknowledge as proper the idea that "the only purpose for which power can be rightfully exercised over any member of a civilized community, against his will, is to prevent harm to others. His own good, either physical or moral, is not sufficient warrant" (*On Liberty,* 14). The presumption is that human beings must be allowed to lead their own lives and be free to make their own mistakes, so long as no direct harm results to others. It is a principle well established in liberal history and in its philosophic and Christian predecessors, but Mill formulates it with a sharpness that has come to define the contemporary era.[26]

Mill's philosophy makes clear the way in which people of widely different opinions and viewpoints might live together without sliding into an attitude of mutual suspicion and mistrust. Where differences have been accepted as legitimate, the pressure to enforce conformity has been eliminated and with it the tendency to interpret all actions and expressions as stratagems in a campaign of compulsion. Mill's principle avoids the suspicion of ulterior motives behind the intentions of others by affirming the public consensus concerning the limits of compulsion. In this way an atmosphere of trust is created that goes a good distance toward lowering the antagonistic tensions between people who disagree and making possible the conditions for cooperation on projects of mutual necessity and benefit. The key to the stability of the consensus is the recognition of the appropriateness of the criterion for the exercise of authority the maxim defines.

For Mill the principle of liberty is essential to his project of staking out an area of freedom for the particular minority that plays the critical role in the progress of society. He recognized the stultifying effect of the pressures for social conformity as the great danger in an era where mass tastes and opinions dominate. Social pressure could be more tyrannical because it was more universal than any older forms of oppression, leaving "fewer means of escape, penetrating much more deeply into the details of life, and enslaving the soul itself" (9). The effect could be deadly, Mill foresaw, for everything unconventional and original, including all of the new ideas that could eventually advance the wisdom of the human race. The principle of liberty would preserve a realm of independence into which official interference could not penetrate, even though it would be impossible to insulate individuals from the more pervasive effects of opinion. Yet, the principle would have the effect of promoting the recognition of the value of independence itself.

In a more positive sense, the principle of liberty is the means by which the number of such independent, self-responsible individuals can be enlarged. Mill, like Tocqueville, understood the importance of the formation of character within the democratic era and devoted a considerable part of his reflections to the task. His *System of Logic* included the chapter "Of Ethology, or the Science of the Formation of Character," confronting one of the most crucial intellectual questions of his day. Not surprisingly, Mill never felt bound to follow his own suggestions of environmental determinism for such a science but continued to reflect more concretely on the process by which moral maturity is produced. In economics he advocated cooperative associations of workers, not primarily for their economic benefits but because they were the indispensable means by which the workers acquired the virtues of democratic self-government (*Principles of Political Economy,* chap. 7). In politics Mill favored local initiatives and private responsibility, because, even if the task was more efficiently performed by government, "the business of life is a large part of the practical education of a people" (312). In ethics only the "person whose desires and impulses are his own—are the expression of his own nature, as it has been developed and modified by his own culture—is said to have character" (*The Logic of the Moral Sciences*, 73). Liberty is essential to the development of our human capacity for self-government.

The misconception is often picked up from a casual reading of *On Liberty* that Mill was primarily concerned with defining an area of untrammeled personal freedom, much in the manner of our own superficial enthusiasts for private rights. One of the long-standing criticisms of the essay is that its notion of liberty is compatible with a despotic regime, that it neither requires nor promotes a consideration of our obligations toward the common good.[27] But that is to overlook the viewpoint from which the whole book is written. Mill alludes to the viewpoint in the final chapter, insisting that "the absorption of all the principal ability of the country into the governing body is fatal, sooner or later, to the mental activity and progressiveness of the body itself" (125). The well-being of the state depends not on maintaining a population of contented consumers of private liberty but on promoting a vigorous spirit of independence that is to be attained only by allowing men to take charge of their own affairs.

The worst form of government is that in which there is a democratic constitution without the practice of democratic institutions pervading it. Then, Mill warns, the rhetoric of self-government will be quickly overtaken by the impulse to secure the means of domination, as everyone realizes that it is only access to political power that can secure them against the domination of others and ensure the realization of their interests. In a passage that sounds eerily similar to a description of our own politics of interest-group competition for influence, he explains how

> in proportion as all real initiative and direction resides in the government, and individuals habitually feel and act as under its perpetual tutelage, popular institutions develop in them not the desire of freedom, but an unmeasured appetite for place and power: diverting the intelligence and activity of the country from its principal business, to a wretched competition for the selfish prides and petty vanities of office. (*Principles of Political Economy*, 314)

This situation can be avoided only by extending the reality of self-government to encourage all levels of society "to manage as many as possible of their joint concerns by voluntary co-operation" (313).

Some of Mill's most evocative writing on this theme comes in his essay "The Subjection of Women," which brought many of his ideas to passionate clarity. The justification for extending the franchise to women and amending the property and divorce laws to secure their independence ultimately turns on the realization that this is the indispensable way to human happiness. Mill asks us to consider that "the ennobling influence of free government—the nerve and spring which it gives to all the faculties, the larger and higher objects which it presents to the intellect and feeling, the more unselfish public spirit, and calmer and broader view of duty, that it engenders, and the generally loftier platform on which it elevates the individual as a moral, spiritual, and social being—is every particle as true of women as of men" (*On Liberty and Other Essays*, 577). The alternative, he reminds us, to the self-esteem and satisfaction of determining our own lives is the perverse compulsion to seek a substitute for our own lack of independence in attempting to control others. Love of liberty and love of power are the opposing poles of the political spectrum.

That is the substance of Mill's argument in the essay "The Subjection of Women." The unjustified authority that men exercised over women, especially in marriage, was detrimental to the men as much as to the women. While Mill was undoubtedly guilty of rhetorical excess in the weight of significance, for good and for evil, that he placed on the relationship between the sexes, there can be no doubt that he understood it as a microcosm of the basic political choice of direction within liberal democracy. We cannot expect the equality that men encounter in public society or the virtues of mutual respect to take much hold on them if in returning to their domestic settings they are free to behave as absolute tyrants toward their wives and children. Nor can we expect that women will develop the qualities of forthrightness and responsibility if they are alternately pampered or brutalized as the private possessions of their husbands. Like society as a whole the family too must be defined by the conditions of justice and equality that make it the most effective school for the virtues of freedom (*On Liberty and Other Essays*, 518). "The desire of power over others can only cease to be a depraving agency among mankind, when each of them individually is able to do without it; which can only be where respect for liberty in the personal concerns of each is an established principle" (578).

The principle of liberty is thus proposed not as a means to establishing a zone of indifference around largely self-absorbed human beings. Rather, it is envisaged by Mill as a means toward the emergence of genuine community because it is based on the mutual recognition of one another as persons—that is, as beings whose humanity can only be fostered by being freely chosen. Through the practice of such mutual respect the virtues that sustain it would themselves be imprinted. By exploring the modes of voluntary cooperation between individuals who are free not to cooperate, the spirit of community takes hold more deeply in them than any external exercise of power could make possible. They become individuals more worthy of respect because the exercise of their liberty has made more evident the value of its recognition, and each in turn becomes more capable of acknowledging the same qualities and virtues in others. A mutually reinforcing circle of freedom is the vision of order that Mill puts before us.

The nobility of Mill's vision is the source of its long historical influence. He is clearly within the line of thinkers, going back to Hobbes and Locke, whose successful construction of the liberal tradition arises from their capacity to evoke exactly that sense of the indubitable rightness of their order. Mill, like many of the great nineteenth-century liberals, tapped into that rich vein.[28] It is evident in his assertion that human happiness consists in the liberty to exercise our faculties to the fullest, that there is nothing more oppressive than the feeling of having wasted one's life because of the inability to make use of the energies and gifts we possess. In a passage that seems to come from the heart, at the conclusion of his reflections on the position of women, Mill makes a passionate plea to men not to add to the evils that by nature occur to human beings. The core of his resonance with the liberal democratic spirit is captured in his assertion that "every restraint on the freedom of conduct of any of their human fellow creatures (otherwise than by making them responsible for any evil actually caused by it), dries up *pro tanto* the principal fountain of human happiness, and leaves the species less rich, to an inappreciable degree, in all that makes life valuable to the individual human being" (581–82).

Yet, despite Mill's estimable ability to evoke the vision of liberty that underpins the liberal consensus, he is also the point at which the disintegration of the consensus also becomes visible. More than Locke, Mill has been accused of incoherence, of indeterminacy, and of sheer eclecticism, and there is more than a grain of validity to the complaints. His reflections cover an impressive range of subjects, from economics to logical method to moral and political theory, and exemplify a variety of approaches from utilitarianism to Aristotelianism to positivism, which make it difficult to reconcile their diversity into anything resembling philosophical coherence. Indeed, Mill is the last great liberal thinker largely because he is the last to attempt to hold all of these areas of reality together within an overall approach. His inability to formulate their underlying coherence accounts in good measure for the paucity of subsequent attempts to render their unity transparent. After Mill liberal philosophy assumes the shape we have already observed, which, with the possible exception of Rawls, is content to work away on the articulation of portions of the whole that can no longer be comprehensively formulated.

At the same time, we should not exaggerate the incoherence of Mill or of the subsequent tradition. Mill's philosophy does have the coherence of a single inspirational center, as indicated by the preeminence of his principle of liberty. The centrality of this emphasis casts a light over the different areas and problems to which he turns and gives a very strong sense of the constancy of approach in all his philosophy. The problem, therefore, is not of a lack of unity but that its unity cannot be articulated by Mill. He is the first of that characteristic pattern of contemporary liberal thinkers that are distinguished by their inability to satisfactorily account for the source of their convictions. Mill exemplifies what Charles Taylor has identified as the strange contradiction in which such thinkers "are constitutionally incapable of coming clean about the deeper sources of their own thinking." They are motivated by the strongest moral ideals of freedom, virtue, and altruism, but their very ideals seem to drive them to deny the ideals' existence (*Sources of the Self*, 88). With Mill we see this problem in its earliest manifestation, as he is not so much silent about his sources as unable to reconcile them and unavoidably communicates the impression that none of them really function as such a source.

Mill's *Autobiography* recounts in touching detail his youthful quest for the authenticating source of his moral impulse. Having grown up with his father's agnosticism he could not be said to have rejected Christianity, for he had never embraced it. The absence of a religious background explains much of the enthusiasm of Mill in his early years. When he first read Jeremy Bentham's work, it had the impact of a religious conversion on him. "I now had opinions; a creed, a doctrine, a philosophy; in one among the best senses of the word, a religion; the inculcation and diffusion of which could be made the principal outward purpose of my life" (68). Mill eagerly embraced the calling of social reformer and unstintingly expended his energies on a variety of causes intended to promote the happiness of the greatest number. He had unbounded confidence in the power of utilitarian philosophy and in its political expression through the institutions of representative government and the complete liberty of thought and discussion.

But the poverty of utilitarianism was brought strikingly home to him in the course of his autobiography. After devoting years to the cause Mill one day permitted himself to ask the fatal question: "Suppose that all your objects in life were realized; that all the changes in institutions and opinions which you are looking forward to, could be completely effected at this very instant: would this be a great joy and happiness to you?" The answer that unavoidably welled up within him was a stark "No!" after which, Mill recounts, "the whole foundation on which my life was constructed fell down. . . . I seemed to have nothing left to live for" (112). He had discovered what Hobbes had understood as the defining characteristic of life, that it is essentially a movement whose fulfillment cannot be attained. Hobbes was able to frame his insight with the recognition of eternal felicity as life's final goal, but for Mill there was only the prospect of immanent satisfactions within this world. Once the highest goal had been attained, life would cease to possess any meaning. There would literally be nothing for which to live.

Happiness, he came to realize, cannot be the object of our actions in life. Mill did not have the clarity that the language of a transcendent end provided to Hobbes and Locke, but he did grope toward its secular equivalent. He could not get away from the acknowledgment that somehow happiness, our own and others', was the goal, but he no longer felt it was to be attained by directly aiming for it. "The enjoyments of life (such was now my theory) are sufficient to make it a pleasant thing, when they are taken *en passant,* without being made a principal object. Once make them so, and they are immediately felt to be insufficient" (117–18). With that admission, of course, went any sense that happiness is the goal. Happiness continues to be the general goal, but it is itself defined in terms of other things, which demonstrate that mere subjective satisfaction is not the ultimate. What is important is the right kind of happiness. "I fully admit that this is true: that the cultivation of an ideal nobleness of will and conduct should be to individual human beings an end, to which the specific pursuit either of their own happiness or of that of others (except so far as included in that idea) should, in any case of conflict, give way" (*The Logic of the Moral Sciences,* 143).

Mill's own account of utilitarianism spells its death knell. It founders on the rock on which all such attempts, as far back as Plato's *Gorgias,* to define the good in terms of pleasure have shattered. That is, it recognizes the impossibility of denying the difference between good and bad pleasures. "It is quite compatible with the principle of utility to recognize the fact that some *kinds* of pleasure are more desirable and more valuable than others" (*On Liberty and Other Essays,* 138). Mill goes on to recommend that we take into account the "quality" as well as the "quantity" of pleasure and, in proposing that we pursue the former over the latter, subverts the notion that pleasure itself is the goal. It is not, as Socrates had compelled his interlocutors to concede, pleasure as such that is the goal but only that which is good (*Gorgias* 497). Yet Mill is not prepared to acknowledge the logic of his own recognition and continues to assert that the greatest pleasure or happiness of the greatest number must remain the axiological justification for all our actions. It is a curiously revealing piece of writing in which a thinker's own performance directly refutes his conclusions.

Mill's essay "Utilitarianism" is among the most illuminating examples of the liberal tension we have earlier remarked upon that is characterized by an utter inability to acknowledge the profound moral sources of the convictions publicly espoused. He insists that even though virtue and heroic self-sacrifice may be the highest ideals, their value is measured by their contribution to the happiness of the greatest number. The utilitarian is not opposed to the sacrifice of individual happiness for the good of others but insists only that the sacrifice is not in itself good and is of no value if it is wasted (148). The telos must remain that of service toward the common good, not the empty pride of becoming virtuous. It is the reality of virtue that counts, not its trappings. But at this point the principle of utility ceases to play any regulative role in the determination of action, for it has become indistinguishable from the realization of justice as the highest form of utility. Instead of utility being the measure of justice the traditional measure has been restored, so that justice becomes the criterion of what constitutes social utility.

Mill concludes his reflections in this way by warning against the short-circuiting of justice on the way to maximizing collective utility. There is no higher utility, he argues, than fidelity to the indefeasible demands of justice. Even when extreme circumstances compel us to deflect justice's requirements (as in stealing food to save a life), we do not justify our actions on the ground of expediency but maintain that the situation was not one in which the requirements of justice applied. "By this useful accommodation of language, the character of indefeasibility attributed to justice is kept up, and we are saved from the necessity of maintaining that there can be laudable injustice." Mill still proceeds to maintain that justice is "simply the natural feeling of resentment, moralized by being made co-extensive with the demands of the social good" (201), but it is all too evident that expediency is no longer its measure. It is rather that justice is the measure of expediency, for Mill is unwilling to countenance even the implication that there could be such a thing as "laudable injustice."

The value of Mill as a thinker is that he brings the inner tensions of the liberal tradition to the light of self-consciousness. His account of justice as being concerned with "certain social utilities which are vastly more important, and therefore more absolute and imperative, than any others are as a class" does not sit well with his recognition that it is "guarded by a sentiment not only different in degree, but also in kind . . . from the milder feeling which attaches to the mere idea of promoting human pleasure or convenience" (201). The difference we are tempted to suggest is that justice will not bend to the expedient, even of the most remote and general kind. Mill himself illustrates this in his refusal to embrace the positivist utilitarianism of August Comte, which he recognized as "the completest system of spiritual and temporal despotism which ever yet emanated from a human brain" (*Autobiography*, 163). We are back at the fundamental principle from which his thought springs, that "there is a circle around every individual human being, which no government, be it that of one, of a few, or of the many, ought to be permitted to overstep" (*Principles of Political Economy*, 30). The idea of the "sacred" liberty of human beings may be justified by utilitarian argument, but it does not depend on it.

The weakness of the utilitarian arguments in *On Liberty* are well known. Mill himself even seems to acknowledge them when he concedes that liberty of discussion will lead to a situation in which the "narrowing of the bounds of diversity of opinion" will remove one of the utilitarian justifications for permitting disagreement to flourish (*On Liberty*, 50). If disagreement is no longer needed for allowing the truth of competing ideas to be tested in the competition and to be apprehended more accurately through the contest, then there will be less of a necessity for requiring untrammeled liberty of debate. The paper covering of the utilitarian justification falls away, and we recognize what its substantive inspiration had been all along, that "it is the privilege and proper condition of a human being, arrived at the maturity of his faculties, to use and interpret experience in his own way" (64). The idea of self-realization is essential to the "distinctive endowment of a human being" (65). We realize that even the utilitarian perspective is one that has been heightened and enlarged by Mill.

Bentham's famous phrase, "everybody to count for one, nobody for more than one," was originally intended to refer to the equality of each individual's pleasures within the utilitarian calculus. But Mill, whether deliberately or inadvertently, gives it the much nobler interpretation of "the equal claim of everybody to happiness in the estimation of the moralist and legislator" (*On Liberty and Other Essays*, 199).[29] The explanation of the shift is unimportant because it appropriately captures the transformation of utilitarianism effected by Mill. He may continue to subscribe to the Benthamite account of the source of utility in the collective impulse of self-interest, but Mill had gone far beyond Bentham in his understanding of the real foundation on which individuals could be counted upon to subordinate their individual welfare to that of all. Service toward others arises from the convergence of influences that "tend to increase in each individual a feeling of unity with all the rest; which feeling, if perfect, would make him never think of, or desire any beneficial condition for himself, in the benefits of which they are not included" (166). It is this mystical unity with all humanity—parallel, he acknowledges, to the religion of humanity of Comte whose politics he abhorred—that constitutes "the ultimate sanction of the greatest happiness morality" (167).

The difficulty is that universal altruism has no place within the secular order constructed by Mill. He may indeed be correct that the readiness to respect and preserve the dignity of all human beings can ultimately be sustained only through a kenotic outpouring of self toward all. But there is no readily apparent connection between this selfless humanitarianism and the assertion of the liberty of self-determination that is the centerpiece of his philosophy. They may indeed converge for a few exceptional individuals, such as Mill himself, for whom self-realization is defined in terms of service to humanity. But there is no necessary connection, and for the vast majority the promise of moral progress may simply never materialize. Most people may be content to settle down with their personal freedom and devote themselves to the narcissistic gratifications of a consumer society. Even for the idealists the problem is that Mill cannot explain the relationship between self-actualization and universal love. It stands as a bare postulate.

The virtue of Mill is that he at least brings the problem into focus, although he is unable to go very far toward resolving it. He makes us aware that the liberal order of mutual respect, which he understands as moving toward the inclusion of economic as well as political independence, requires an existential order that is not simply a given within the ordinary range of human experience. Yet he has no means of accounting for its formation except to acknowledge that it would play the same role that religion had in an earlier era and to recognize that it is the inspirational impulse enkindled within himself by contact with the reforming fervor of his father, Bentham, Harriet Taylor, and other kindred spirits. Because the tension is so close to the surface, Mill provides perhaps the clearest illustration of the incompatibility between the nobility of convictions and the paucity of their sources. He exemplifies the liberal inability to articulate its own depths. What makes him a major figure is that he still retained a profound awareness of the tension that in the legion of epigones is still present but below the range of their conscious reflection.

The incommensurability between principles and experience becomes transparent in the Millian resort to progress as the covering that will eventually close the gap. Even in his day it was a covering that was becoming threadbare, as Nietzsche's diagnosis was quick to expose. There are enough passages in Mill's work where the romantic rejection of progress, at least as it is characterized by its principal engines of economic and industrial growth, is sounded with profound weariness. Mill longed for solitude, a world with fewer people who could concentrate on their own inner development in communion with nature, and proclaimed all the virtues of a stationary economic state. He saw only too clearly the hollowness of the pursuit of unlimited material growth and recognized the abyss of dehumanization brought about by advancing mechanical progress. Mill was a zealot for population control throughout his career from beginning to end. For all the talk of progress in his writings he does not come across as a believer in its inexorably beneficial effects.[30] He is, rather, a believer in a very specific kind of moral progress, which he experienced in his own life, the ultimate source of which remained something of a mystery in his writings and reflections.

The casual reader might well conclude that Nietzsche was correct and that the liberal philosophy presented by Mill was an elaborate house of cards. Without any substantial structure or foundation it was doomed to fall before the first crisis could shake it. This, as we have seen, was not the case, for liberal persuasion has weathered the storms that were expected to overwhelm it. Nor would it be fair to take Mill's inarticulateness as an indication of a lack of depth behind his convictions. Both Mill and the liberal tradition, for all their faults, embody a spiritual openness whose roots go deeper than their own explanations would incline one to suspect. Perhaps the most convincing indication of the inner vitality of that tradition stretching from Locke to Mill and beyond has been the continuing concern with its own inner resources. Ever fearful that its own rhetoric of individual liberty may be all there is to it, the liberal tradition has been preoccupied with the spiritual foundations of its convictions. Mill, for all his confidence bordering on priggishness, exemplifies this liberal uncertainty. A valid way of reading his work is to see it as one long quest for contact with the inspirational realities that he knew an earlier age had found in religion. The best evidence for their presence within Mill and the liberal tradition is to be found in the enduring knowledge of what is absent or only incompletely present within it. To that self-reflection we now turn.

5

Struggle as Source of Liberal Richness

The awareness of living within a consensual order whose roots have not and, perhaps, cannot be fully articulated has been the source of the notorious liberal uncertainty of its foundations. This uncertainty has drawn upon the liberal political tradition the undeserved ignominy of the contrast with the spiritually and philosophically more coherent traditions, and it has impressed liberal self-understanding with an unnecessary sense of its own inferiority in the intellectual world. None of these consequences are in themselves detrimental, a modest sense of one's own limitations is generally a good starting point, but they do lead to an undervaluation of the richness of the liberal tradition. We still have difficulty appreciating the extent to which the liberal tradition is *the* dominant tradition in modern political thought. With a few notable exceptions, the divergences between modern political thinkers have been differences within a largely liberal horizon, which has proved to be an arch of amazing amplitude and variety.

What has sustained this great creative impulse is the awareness of a spiritual depth that has not been adequately captured within the liberal articulations. There has always been a rhetorical gap between the liberal surface, with its discussion of rights and protections, and the passionate sense of moral rightness with which it is asserted. The tradition has been characterized by the awareness of this lack of existential depth and the correlative sense of what is needed to fill the void. Liberalism has been like a quest that cannot be defined as an utter loss. It is an absence of that which is present in a certain way, however inchoate, because it already knows that of which it is in search. The continuing vitality of liberal order derives in considerable measure from this tension of the search for its own spiritual foundations. For this reason a large aspect of the tradition may be viewed as the attempt to explicate the spiritual underpinnings that are needed to sustain its convictions.

The criticism of the lack of substantive justifications is not, in other words, the prerogative of only the critics of liberal politics. It is central to liberal self-awareness itself, as demonstrated by the successive attempts to expand the liberal foundations. Far from the impoverished exterior that is often mistaken for the essence of the liberal endeavor, its most fundamental level is to be identified with such vigorous self-rejuvenating efforts. It is a process that goes all the way back to the tradition's beginnings and must be examined if we are to get a measure of the existential strength that has sustained the liberal construction for centuries. The struggle to articulate the moral formation of character, which it recognizes as its own indispensable presupposition, brings us close to the heart of the liberal impulse.

It goes without saying that the effort is not always successful. Indeed, the continuing series of attempts would hardly be needed if any one of the foundational meditations had proved definitive. It is the instability of the liberal project that gives rise to the unending search for the stabilizing foundations, and it is the inadequacy of each of the proposed alternatives that moves the search for more appropriate evocations. We are today further than ever from a stable or satisfactory formulation. But that should not be permitted to overshadow the formidable seriousness of the search itself. The fact that liberal self-articulations have not reached a stable account does not mean that the attempt itself is invalid or that it is a hopelessly incoherent symbolism. It means rather that liberal order is sustained by a real, demonstrable spiritual attunement whose effects are clearly visible but whose nature cannot be brought into harmony with the minimal public consensus. The exploration of the fertile instability at the heart of the liberal tradition is the subject of the present chapter.

Locke's Reinforcement of Reason and Revelation

The note of uncertainty is sounded in the impetus that set Locke to work on *An Essay Concerning Human Understanding.* "The Epistle to the Reader" that prefaces the study depicts its beginning at a dinner conversation among friends who, "meeting at my chamber and discoursing on a subject very remote from this, found themselves quickly at a stand, by the difficulties that arose on every side." We learn from one of the friends, James Tyrrell, that they were discussing "the principles of morality and revealed religion."[1] Locke concluded from the experience of their perplexity that they had set about the discussion incorrectly, "and that before we set ourselves about inquiries of that nature, it was necessary to examine our own abilities, and see what objects our understandings were, or were not, fitted to deal with." Locke's major philosophical work therefore was intended to provide a more secure elaboration of morality and religion, and it must be read with that intention in mind. The *Essay* ranges widely over the subject of human knowledge, but it always returns to the acknowledgment of the spiritual as "that sort of knowledge which is most suited to our natural capacities, and carries in it our greatest interest, i.e. the condition of our eternal estate. Hence I think I may conclude that *morality* is *the proper science and business of mankind in general* (who are both concerned and fitted to search out their *summum bonum*") (bk. 4, chap. 12, par. 11).

Some sense of Locke's intentions can be gleaned from the "Essays on the Law of Nature," which he wrote almost thirty years before the publication of *An Essay Concerning Human Understanding*. These early writings provide a remarkable insight into the origins of the conviction (to which he returns in all his later writings) that there is an indubitable moral order, "for the nature of good and evil is certain, and their value cannot be determined either by the public ordinances of men or by any private opinion" (*Essays on the Law of Nature*, 121). The source of morality is the law of nature, and Locke's concern is to explain how knowledge of it can be certain yet admit the evident variability we witness among human beings. He suggests that the source of our knowledge lies in conscience and is "innate" (117), but then he backs away from this to the position he elaborated in his later writings. Locke rejects the notion that knowledge of the natural law can be innate because of the extent of disagreement, but he is careful to iterate that it is nevertheless available to all men and therefore binding on all. Its source is neither innate nor traditional (125–26), but from our reflection on sense experience. Specifically, our knowledge of natural law arises from our reasoning from the existence of things to their maker.

It is in these early writings, and not in the *Essay*, that he uses the term *tabula rasa* to describe the mind at birth. The rejection of innate knowledge that follows from this conception of the mind has often been taken as a more radical rupture with the classical and medieval tradition than Locke implied. Not only does he quote Aristotle and Saint Thomas on nature and law, but he also develops a position that is not all that significantly different from theirs. The notion of innate ideas that he rejects is something of a straw man since no one ever defended it in that form, as explicitly formulated knowledge. Locke's purpose was to avoid making the moral law vulnerable to the charge that it was subjective because its knowledge was not universally consistent. His position is actually closer to the natural-law tradition that insists that knowledge of it is available to all but is variable depending on the degree of openness to its ordering influence.[2]

The central pivot of Locke's conception of the law of nature is the idea of a lawmaker. Reason leads us to the affirmation of God as the source of all, and from that acknowledgment we derive all our sense of obligation. In order to be bound by a law, we must first, Locke insists, "know beforehand that there is a lawmaker" and then that "there is some will on the part of that superior power with respect to the things to be done by us" (151). He unfolds his meditation from the observation that we do not owe our existence to ourselves and that everything around us points to a source beyond itself. By thus following out the direction indicated by sense experience and reason, we arrive at the realization of a creator of infinite wisdom, power, and goodness. Having arrived at the realization of a creator, God, to whom we owe everything, we have also arrived at the superior to whom we owe perfect obedience: "For who will deny that the clay is subject to the potter's will, and that a piece of pottery can be shattered by the same hand by which it has been formed?" (157).

There is a striking constancy to this theme in the *Essay* and the *Two Treatises,* where we are called "God's property," and there can be little doubt that we are here at one of the illuminative centers of Locke's thought. This explains the casualness and unconcern about demonstration. He insists that all of this is demonstrable, but Locke can hardly imagine that anyone would be so obtuse as to demand that something so overwhelmingly self-evident would need to be deduced. Law cannot be derived from the general consent of men because, as the "unhappy lesson" of the Civil War has taught, there is scarcely "anything so abominable . . . which the general consent, or rather the conspiracy, of a senseless crowd would not at some time advocate" (161). Nor can law be based on the necessity of self-preservation because then "virtue would seem to be not so much man's duty as his convenience" (181). We are obliged, Locke insists, only to someone who has "right and power over us" and, in this sense, "ultimately all obligation leads us back to God" (183). It is not, of course, simply because we are in God's power and therefore liable to punishment that is the source, but that we recognize that God's authority over us is determinative and just. It is "not fear of punishment, but a rational apprehension of what is right, [that] puts us under an obligation, and conscience passes judgement on morals, and, if we are guilty of a crime, declares that we deserve punishment" (185).

In *An Essay Concerning Human Understanding,* Locke refines this conception without fundamentally altering it. Morality is defined as a mixed mode—that is, a combination of simple ideas always attached to a substance (as in the notions of obligation, justice, right, and so on) that must be attached to specific individuals to become concrete (bk. 3, chap. 5). The process of assembling the ideas is the work of our minds, but that does not mean that they are the reflection of arbitrary or subjective juxtapositions. On the contrary, Locke argues, we can be more certain that they are true than we can be of the existence of substances, precisely because our moral concepts are entirely the fruit of reflection. Our knowledge of substances may or may not accurately reflect the combination of qualities in the real world, but we can be sure of the nature of our moral principles from their internal implications. This is why Locke is so insistent that moral truth cannot be measured by the practice of any particular individuals or society. Simply because no one lives up to the prescriptions advanced by Cicero for the virtuous man does not make them any less valid an account (bk. 4, chap. 4, par. 8).

Locke anticipates the objection that such a conception invites everyone to construct their own definitions of good and evil. No, he responds, or at least no more than in mathematics where men are not free to change the definitions of figures although no one will stop them if they do.

> Just the same is it in moral knowledge: let a man have the idea of taking from others, without their consent, what their honest industry has possessed them of, and call this *justice* if he please. . . . But yet for all this, the miscalling of any of these ideas, contrary to the usual signification of the words of that language, hinders not but that we may have certain and demonstrative knowledge of their several agreements and disagreements, if we will carefully, as in mathematics, keep to the same precise ideas, and trace them in their several relations one to another, without being led away by their names. (bk. 4, chap. 4, par. 9)

Locke was no stranger to moral conflicts—the example of taking property without consent is at the heart of the controversies of his whole life—but neither was he inclined to surrender the contest in hopeless resignation. Moral truth exists in imperious indifference to the predilections of human beings. The source of this confidence was Locke's conviction that the order was ultimately sustained by a divine lawgiver.

Locke's empiricist psychology did lead him to conclude that "good and evil . . . are nothing but pleasure and pain" (bk. 2, chap. 28, par. 5), that they are "the hinges of passion" moving us to action in each instance. But he did not mean that good and evil were relative to the pleasure and pain of each individual, because he bemoaned the tendency human beings have to pursue immediate pleasure without thought for the greater one they may thereby miss. The problem is always to raise men up from being satisfied with "nasty penury" to the larger contemplation of their final good. Were the will to fully contemplate it, Locke remarks, "I do not see how it could ever get loose from the infinite eternal joys of heaven, once proposed and considered as possible" (bk. 2, chap. 21, par. 38). Now the correlation between our actions and the pleasures and pains they bring upon us, in the form of rewards and punishment, is the rule of the lawmaker, God.

There is an important distinction between good and evil in general and moral good and evil. *"Moral good and evil,* then, is only the conformity or disagreement of our voluntary actions to some law, whereby good or evil is drawn on us, from the will and power of the law-maker" (bk. 2, chap. 28, par. 5). Without an authority to enforce the rule, we cannot speak of action as moral, for then it would merely be a matter of following one's own convenience. Only if an action is done in recognition of a rule is it to be properly considered moral, or performed out of recognition for the rule. There are three such rule-making authorities—society, the state, and God—

employing the enforcement power of reputation, the civil law, and the divine law. The first two determine rules that are relative to a particular community and are content with the appearance of virtue. Only divine law is directed toward the reality of virtue apart from its particular appearance. That is why for Locke the divine source of law is so decisive. "That God has given a rule whereby men should govern themselves, I think there is nobody so brutish as to deny. He has a right to do it; we are his creatures; he has goodness and wisdom to direct our actions to that which is best, and he has power to enforce it by rewards and punishments of infinite weight and duration in another life; for nobody can take us out of his hands. This is the only true touchstone of moral rectitude" (par. 8).[3]

The theocentric nature of Locke's vision necessitates a heavy emphasis on the accessibility of the divine will through reason, "the candle of God" within us, while at the same time giving full recognition to the role that revelation plays in strengthening the natural light of reason. The intricate nature of this relationship accounts for the ambivalence with which it is often discussed by Locke, and for the frequency with which it is misunderstood. His reputation as a crypto-deist and fellow traveler of Enlightenment rationalism seems hardly justified in the context of his broad though unfeignedly sincere Christian piety.[4] Locke's position is carefully balanced between a defense of reason against the irrationalism of private revelation and an acknowledgment of the insufficiency of reason without the aid of the revelatory tradition. Nowhere is the delicacy of his judgment more in evidence than in the *Essay*, which is the source most often quoted as Locke's profession of the superiority of reason.

When we read the relevant chapters more carefully, we realize that he nowhere asserts the absolute authority of reason. He deliberately recognizes that revelation may establish its primacy even in opposition to reason, and the confidence he places in reason as the judge of when revelation has occurred is itself rooted in a faith in the God whose workmanship we are. Locke is clearly concerned with the problem of the private authority of religious enthusiasts and takes aim at "this crying up of faith in opposition to reason, [to which] we may, I think, in good measure ascribe those absurdities that fill almost all the religions which possess and divide mankind" (bk. 4, chap. 18, par. 11). He is disturbed by the "absurdities" of religions that draw men away from their real obligations toward God and one another. His critical treatment of religion in this context should be read not simply as a plea for reason but as a defense of religion against its perversion. Locke believes strongly that reason and revelation are continuous, "reason is natural revelation . . . revelation is natural reason enlarged" (bk. 4, chap. 19, par. 4), and he cannot accept that God would allow them to be confused and opposed.

In sorting out their relationship, Locke begins with the recognition that the authority of revelation can be no higher than the certainty we have that it is a revelation. That is bound to be less than the certainty we have of propositions known through reason or our sense experiences. Revelation cannot contradict reason or intuition because that would be to accept that God would undermine his own workmanship. Locke recognizes that revelation deals with what is beyond reason and explicitly declares that reason must then yield to what it cannot fully understand. Locke underlines the possibility that *"revelation,* where God has been pleased to give it, *must carry it against the probable conjectures of reason."* The role of reason is confined "to judge of the truth of its being a revelation, and of the signification of the words wherein it is delivered" (bk. 4, chap. 18, par. 8). Locke's conception is that "an evident revelation ought to determine our assent, even against probability," and he is principally concerned to establish the role of reason (itself authenticated by the Creator) in delimiting the probability of the existence of revelation.

It is advice that is well taken because, as in the example adduced by Locke of Saint Paul persecuting the Christians, even good men are liable to fall into error. We must still consult the light of reason. "God when he makes the prophet does not unmake the man" (bk. 4, chap. 19, par. 14). It is ultimately this faith in the order of God's creation that frees Locke to declare so boldly his faith in reason. *"Reason must be our last judge and guide in everything."* When we keep this faith in mind, the contrast between the *Essay* and his work on *The Reasonableness of Christianity,* which appeared a few years later in 1695, will not be so great. The latter provides an important amplification of the subordinate dimension of the earlier discussion, the necessity under which reason stands for revelation. This should be obvious when we consider that reliance on reason is ultimately vouchsafed by the faith in the Creator, but here Locke goes considerably beyond it to establish the insufficiency of reason left strictly alone within its own province.

Contrary to the interpretation placed on *The Reasonableness* as a reduction of Christianity to a rational moral core, it is intended to establish the reliance of reason on revelation as its own preservation and fulfillment. The rationalist misreading took hold, even in Locke's day, because of his latitudinarian presentation of Christianity that is indifferent to the distinctions between conformist and dissenter (*Reasonableness of Christianity,* par. 252). He is concerned to provide "the simplicity of the gospel" more in line with God's intention that it be for all, not simply the learned and disputatious. To this end he tries to pick his way between the two extremes of those who insist that all were condemned in Adam's Fall and those who insist that none were, between the idea of Christ as the sole restorer of our nature and the assertion of the sufficiency of our own efforts, between Calvinism and deism. Now while there is a distinctly rationalist tone to some of Locke's speculations on what divine justice should require, and even a tendency to flatten the impenetrable mystery limiting our full comprehension, there can be little doubt that Locke tries to preserve a middle ground that is not far from orthodoxy. Unwilling to admit Adam as the scapegoat for the moral derelictions of the human race, he nevertheless preserves the notion of the Fall as a loss for all mankind. It is the loss of immortality, which was never ours by right only by gift, rather than the state of grace or perfection, and "therefore," he concludes, "though all die in Adam, yet none are truly punished, but for their own deeds" (par. 6).[5]

It is not possible to analyze the complexity of Locke's relationship to Christianity here. It is surely enough to emphasize the seriousness of it, as evidenced most sincerely by his lifelong struggle to arrive at a satisfactory personal understanding of the Christian faith. The latitudinarian and even novel character of some of his interpretations of traditional Christian doctrines are best understood within the context of a sincere search for the truth that he shared with many of his contemporaries. Disgusted by the futile and destructive nature of dogmatic disputes, Locke and many others sought to recover a direct, simple Christianity that would rest on the plain meaning of Scripture. It is this intention that explains the extensive attention that Locke devoted to the interpretation of Scripture, especially in his last major project, *A Paraphrase and Notes on the Epistles of St. Paul*. But the faith that a concentrated reading of Scripture would yield a clear meaning, which none but the most perverse could reject, is already present in his 1689 *A Letter Concerning Toleration*. The postscript is an intriguing reflection on the problem of heresy and schism, which Locke characterized as "an ill-grounded separation in ecclesiastical communion made about things not necessary" (61). He cannot understand why heretics and schismatics would insist on propositions that are not in Scripture as being necessary or fundamental and remarks on the arrogance of men who place their own interpretations above the authority of Scripture. "I cannot but wonder at the extravagant arrogance of those men who think that they themselves can explain things necessary to salvation more clearly than the Holy Ghost, the eternal and infinite wisdom of God" (61). Locke is utterly secure in the conviction that the "express words of Scripture" will disclose their meaning to all who read them without preconceptions.[6]

The result of this restriction to the plain meaning of the words of Scripture, the evocation of a nondogmatic scriptural Christianity, is a certain flattening of some of its mystery along the lines associated with deism. After all, the great Trinitarian and Christian dogmas and many others dealing with Christ's salvific action do not lie on the surface of Scripture. But it is a great mistake to identify Locke's project with deistic rationalism.[7] It is more properly an effort to preserve the main outlines of the Christian faith on an uncontrovertible reading of Scripture, thereby deepening the very sources of conviction by which Christianity is sustained. Locke is more inclined to oversimplify some of the setting in order to maintain the integrity of its central convictions. To this end he is prepared to list the essentials of the Christian faith as the acknowledgment of Jesus as the Messiah, the Son of God (*Reasonableness,* pars. 27, 30, 39, 56), and the recognition of the need for restoration by which "the law of faith is allowed to supply the defect of full obedience; and so believers are admitted to life and immortality, as if they were righteous" (par. 22). To this he adds that the acknowledgment must be more than a verbal admission of faith; it must entail a genuine effort of repentance, including a request for forgiveness and the resolve to lead a better life (pars. 167, 181). That experience is the center of Locke's Christianity. To the extent that he flattens out some of the mystery, it can be attributed not so much to a rational reductionism as to an overriding concern to heighten the meaning of the moral order at its core.[8]

It is in relation to the moral law that Locke indeed heightens the significance of Christianity. In answer to the question "What need do we have of a Savior?" he explains that although reason could arrive at the idea of one God and of his law for man, it would never be delivered to us as clearly or as completely as Christ has done. The passions of men and the intellectual limitations of many, combined with the deceptive machinations of the priests of various religions, all conspire to prevent the human race as a whole from making much progress in the understanding of the moral law. "It should seem," Locke concludes, "by the little that has hitherto been done in it, that 'tis too hard a task for unassisted reason, to establish morality, in all its parts, upon its true foundations, with a clear and convincing light" (par. 241). Even in the case of the best thinkers, the philosophers, their achievement consisted in making out only a part, never the whole, of the moral law with all its majesty in the order emanating from its divine source. "And he that shall collect all the moral rules of the philosophers, and compare them with those contained in the new testament, will find them to come short of the morality delivered by Our Savior, and taught by his apostles; a college made up, for the most part, of ignorant, but inspired fishermen" (par. 241).

What was missing from the "scattered sayings" of the wise men was an apprehension of the rule of morality as law, carrying the full force of obligation because it derives from the divine lawmaker. Their prescriptions were viewed as necessary "bonds of society" or as "laudable practices," but never as a law of irrefragable authority over us (par. 243). Only if we understand morality in this sense as law do we see it clearly as an authoritative order, independent of our estimations of it because it derives from a source absolutely capable of imposing rewards and punishments on us. Then it rises to the level of becoming what Locke termed a "demonstrable" order, as indifferently objective as mathematics. For most men it is only the hearing of a law authoritatively declared, "the hearing plain commands, is the sure and only course to bring them to obedience and practice" (par. 243).

But even for the minority with the ability and the leisure to pursue the demonstration of its truth through reason, the moral law of Christ and the apostles cannot but impress them with its perfection. It is such that "as it suits the lowest capacities of reasonable creatures, so it reaches and satisfies, nay, enlightens the highest" (par. 243). The purity and completeness of the law of Christ is, for Locke, the most compelling evidence of its divine origin and authority. Impressed by the witness of Christ and the apostles, men have not been tempted

> to mix (as we find in that of all the sects of philosophers, and other religions) any conceits, any wrong rules, any thing tending to their own by-interest, or that of a party in their morality: no tang of prepossession or fancy; no footsteps of pride or vanity, no touch of ostentation or ambition appears to have a hand in it. It is all pure, all sincere; nothing too much, nothing wanting; but such a complete rule of life, as the wisest men must acknowledge, tends entirely to the good of mankind, and that all would be happy, if all would practice it. (par. 243)

Besides this confirmation and illumination that revelation casts on the moral law, there are also the truths beyond reason that cannot be known in any other way. Among these Locke includes the apprehension that Jesus died for sinners, to restore the expectation of eternal life for the faithful, the certainty of the rewards and punishment of the next life, and the promise of the assistance of his Spirit in our moral struggles "though we perceive or comprehend not the ways of his operation" (par. 246). He does not consider it beneficial to elaborate the theological mysteries any further, because his concern is to demonstrate the way in which Christianity broadens and deepens fidelity to the moral law. Revelation, for Locke, is "natural reason enlarged," and this eminently practical purpose must be kept in mind in assessing his reluctance to expand on the theological mysteries. It is enough to articulate the essential outline as it effects our fulfillment of the moral law (par. 252).

By thus simplifying the meaning of revelation he sought to bring reason into line with it. This may be taken as the deepest level of Locke's reflection. He wished to make revelation appear more reasonable, not so as to eliminate or reduce it to reason, but so that reason might more effectively operate as a guide to action by its openness to a truth that is continuous with it but unreachable by reason alone. In that sense, the reason to which he refers so frequently in his writings is not a wholly neutral, scientific instrument; it is reason formed by the faith in the goodness of the order of God's creation and revelation.[9] This is demonstrated in a passage from his journals, just after a reflection on "the crying up of faith in opposition to reason" (which found its way into the *Essay* [bk. 4, chap. 18, par. 11]), in which he emphasizes the necessity for a humble faith if we are to reason rightly. Those that are ready to modestly perform their duties toward God and their fellow men will discover all that is required for them to know. Locke continues:

> The same cannot be said of those who begin at the other end, who, giving way to their own desires, making themselves their own god and their own

end, will not hearken to any of the truths of natural or revealed religion, till they can have all objections answered, all scruples removed, and will, if there remains but a little doubt in the whole system, reject the whole, because some one part has some difficulty. It is not, I say, likely that these men should find truth, because both they seek it unreasonably, i.e. otherwise than rational men and they themselves too do in other cases, and also they seek it not for that end for which God designed it, which is not as an improvement of our parts and speculations, but of our love of Him and charity to our neighbor, and that increase of our knowledge should make our lives better. ("Faith and Reason," in *Essays on the Law of Nature*, 281 and also 277)[10]

It is a remarkable expression of the unfeigned spiritual humility (why dissimulate in a private journal?) that Locke considered essential to making men reasonable. Its social presence through Christianity is the bedrock on which his liberal consensus ultimately rests.[11]

Rousseau as Theorist of Crisis

The evocation of latitudinarian Christian piety by Locke was evidently not capable of stemming the tide of skepticism and rationalism that was already beginning to sweep across Europe in his own day. His attempts at a moderate reformulation of Christianity were maligned as deist, and his empiricist account of knowledge was put to very different uses than any he intended. The reductionist and materialist psychologies of the Enlightenment, with their implications of a determinist analysis of human nature and their narrowing of divinity to the point of irrelevance indistinguishable from atheism, were all consequences that the radical French *philosophes* could attribute to the influence of their great English mentor.[12] The story was of course different outside of France. In America, Locke was read in a thoroughly orthodox manner as is evident in the deepening application of his thought through the theological reflections of Jonathan Edwards and others in the movement of religious revival known as the Great Awakening.[13] Similarly, the revolutionary and founding generation in America scarcely recognized the radicalized extension of Lockean ideas that had taken over the leading wing of the French Enlightenment.

Whatever may be said for the more traditional elaborations of the liberal impulse, it was certainly the more radicalized formulations that tested its inner convictions and eventually defined the problem confronted by all strands of liberal reflection. The impending crisis is already becoming visible as the background that provoked the great institutional reflection on order in Montesquieu's 1748 *L'esprit des lois* (The spirit of the laws). While his study is concerned with identifying the proper institutional balance of power that will enable an order of liberty to be sustained, the focus has shifted to the crucial underlying level of the spirit that defines the whole character of the political order. Montesquieu remarks that he has "written this work to prove it: the spirit of moderation should be that of the legislator; the political good, like the moral good, is always found between two limits" (*The Spirit of the Laws,* bk. 29, chap. 1). He calls his readers back to the "natural empire" of reason (bk. 28, chap. 38) from the excesses of the passion to dominate as if we were ourselves the whole and not simply a part. Like Locke, he emphasizes the importance of Christianity as a warrant of the integrity of morality and "the only bridle that can hold those who fear no human laws" (bk. 24, chap. 2). Montesquieu thus brings us to the brink of the abyss that opens up when faith is lost and there are no means of restraining the wild surging of passion other than the brittle barrier of the law itself. He asks what will happen when the citizens have lost the mores that underpin the law: "Punishments will cast out of society a citizen who, having lost his mores, violates the laws, but if everyone loses his mores, will punishments reestablish them?" (bk. 19, chap. 17). Montesquieu contemplates the problem of a moral crisis that cannot be surmounted by ejecting everyone from the society, but it was the next great French political thinker, Jean-Jacques Rousseau, who confronted it in all its depth.

Rousseau is the first theorist of crisis in the liberal tradition.[14] The writing that brought him to public attention, the prize-winning discourse on the arts and sciences, forcefully proclaims the state of crisis in which the much vaunted progress of humanity has left us. Contrary to the enlightened self-understanding of the current age as the apogee of human history, Rousseau declaimed the "depravity of soul" that had been the cumulative effect of all the progress achieved by the arts and sciences. He went on to show that vanity, dissolution, and luxury were not only the actual but also the inevitable outcome of this progress, which was driven largely by the urge to gratify and serve such impulses. Even the growth in knowledge could not stand on its own merits when it is so easily debased by "those vain and futile declaimers [who] go off in all directions, armed with their deadly paradoxes, undermining the foundations of faith and annihilating virtue" (*First Discourse,* par. 40). Rousseau's essay, a veritable broadside against the very idea of the Enlightenment, unequivocally established the distance between the corrupting refinement of the trappings of morality and the true inner reality that can have its existence only within the human heart.[15] That contrast is what launches him on the quest for virtue, which is the central axis of his lifework. "O virtue! Sublime science of simple souls," he concludes, "are so many efforts and so much equipment really required to know you? Are not your principles engraved in all hearts, and is it not enough, in order to learn your Laws, to return into oneself and, in the silence of the passions, to listen to the voice of one's conscience? That is true Philosophy, let us know how to rest content with it . . ." (par. 61).[16]

That withdrawal into himself in order to listen to the voice of conscience within and from there to reconstruct the public order of virtue was the task on which Rousseau expended his energies. In undertaking this task he often appears to suggest that the inner impulses of the heart are the pure fount of virtue and that all that is evil and dark comes from the accretions of society upon us. He asserts "as an incontestable maxim that the first movements of nature are always right. There is no original perversity in the human heart. There is not a single vice to be found in it of which it cannot be said how and whence it entered" (*Emile*, 92). He goes on in the same passage to explain that the fundamental impulse of the *amour de soi* or *"amour-propre"* is in itself neutral.[17] Everything depends on the relations or object to which it is directed. "Therefore, up to the time when the guide of *amour-propre*, which is reason, can be born, it is important for a child to do nothing because he is seen or heard—nothing, in a word, in relation to others; he must respond only to what nature asks of him, and then he will do nothing but good." So long as action is undertaken under the guiding impulse of nature and never out of the manipulative falsity of appearance, we can rely on the innocent and abiding goodness of nature to preserve it without any taint of calculation, deception, or guile. But really such action would be neither good nor bad; it would, like the amour propre that moves it, simply be neutral. This is confirmed by Rousseau's depiction of savage man as not being evil "precisely because they do not know what it is to be good" (*Second Discourse*, 27).

Goodness and evil are moral categories that presuppose a level of reflection and an element of choice that merely following our natural impulses precludes. What, then, does Rousseau mean when he insists that our natural inclinations, the "heart," are the infallible guides to goodness in human life? It would appear to mean the natural impulses as they are disclosed to someone who is capable of reflecting on them and who may even have to return to them from a certain detachment bred of socialization. Contrary to the popular conception of Rousseau as favoring a return to the state of nature or the condition of the noble savage, it seems that he wants merely to make use of such a meditative exercise as a way of removing the corruptions of civilized man. The purpose is not to return to the primitive state but to bring its rejuvenating and purifying force into the present. This is the same with the entire romantic inspiration that flows out of Rousseau, virtually none of which really calls for an abandonment of the achievements and advances of civilization.

It would be more correct to say that Rousseau does not abandon the distinctions of traditional morality, although he no longer makes use of them in the same way. For example, despite his insistence on the goodness of unfeigned nature he still recognizes evil too as a reality within the human heart. Otherwise he would have had great difficulty in explaining the genesis of evil in society. He could not have attributed all of it to the corrupting influences of social institutions. Where did the scheme for institutions that allow the possibility of manipulative behavior come from, or what accounts for the ready reception their deceptions receive within the human heart? We see Rousseau struggling with this problem in his *Second Discourse: On the Origin and Basis of Inequality among Men,* where he must explain the transition from the moral independence of the state of nature to the corrupting subservience of property and civilization. He presents it as a series of accidents, of unforseen discoveries in agriculture and metallurgy that encouraged the formation of the idea of property, and finally of a grotesque subterfuge by which the poor and weak were deceived into committing their strength to the preservation of the very inequality that so harshly held them in subordination. An accumulation of explanations does not quite add up to plausibility in depth, and we sense Rousseau's unease with the account as an "unfortunate accident" (179). How did the great property owners become so evil and the propertyless so craven, living, as they did, in the state of robust truthfulness of nature? The genesis of evil remains a mystery.

All that matters, however, is that Rousseau recognizes its existence. His purpose can be defined more accurately as a listening to the good or true heart of man, not simply a naive submission to whatever impulses emerge from within. Despite the rhetoric of sentiment he so frequently employs, Rousseau recognizes the capacity for wickedness as well as goodness. What is important is listening to the voice of conscience, which is the voice of God, the voice of our true selves. This analysis of good and bad selves, which is in line with the tradition from Aristotle and Saint Augustine, comes out most completely in the "Confession of the Savoyard Vicar." The evil he witnesses on the earth leads him into a meditation on its source within the soul of man. He is drawn to a Pauline analysis of the nature of man as defined by a struggle between "two distinct principles: one of which raised him to the study of eternal truths, to the love of justice and moral beauty . . . while the other took him basely into himself, subjected him to the empire of the senses and to the passions which are their ministers." Then in a passage that virtually quotes the Pauline conflict within the soul (Rom. 7:13–25), he describes the turmoil of the heart. "I want and do not want; I sense myself enslaved and free at the same time. I sense the good, I love it, and I do the bad. I am active when I listen to reason, passive when my passions carry me away; and my worst torment, when I succumb, is to sense that I could have resisted" (*Emile,* 278–79).

It is not that we are the source of goodness and that it is the world that is bad or makes us bad. This is an impression that many readers have taken from Rousseau, but his real position seems to be that God has created the world good and willed it to be good. In confronting the existence of evil, Rousseau counsels man to "seek the author of evil no longer. It is yourself. No evil exists other than that which you do or suffer, and both come to you from yourself" (282). His whole point is that we must learn to follow the principles "written by nature with ineffaceable characters in the depth of my heart. I have only to consult myself about what I want to do. Everything I sense to be good is good; everything I sense to be bad is bad." It is the inner voice that unfailingly informs us we are doing wrong when we seek to advance ourselves at the expense of another. "We believe we are following the impulse of nature, but we are resisting it. In listening to what it says to our senses, we despise what it says to our hearts" (286).

Rousseau's whole enterprise is directed toward the recovery of the moral sources of the self, to use Taylor's phrase, as the foundation to the public order. He recognized that the rationalism and superficiality of French society had undermined the traditional moral and religious sources that Locke could still count on in his time. The fashionable ridicule of religion and the exposure of hypocritical virtue had done their work in subverting faith in the reality of order. Without that indispensable bedrock of confidence in the validity of moral convictions, of the certainty of honor and virtue as the only enduring realities that make human life worthwhile, there was left only the hollowness and cynicism that has been an intermittent feature of the moral landscape ever since. It was because Rousseau had such a deeper understanding of the connection between order and virtue that he could foresee, during the age of absolutism, that Europe was "approaching a state of crisis and the age of revolutions" (194).[18] Within that impending upheaval all that was superficial would fall apart, only what was from nature would survive.

That is why the education of Emile and of society would have to follow the simple maxim of eschewing appeals to what is from morality. They must learn to do everything out of conviction, inner feeling, never from a desire to please or to conform with social expectations. Rousseau's educational approach is to bring his pupil carefully through the developmental stages of the moral life, so that the virtues imprinted are genuinely the boy's own and he is never propelled prematurely forward to a stage where he would be inclined to feign what he does not really experience as his own conviction. Much of the tutor's effort is directed toward limiting the pupil's desires to what is within reach of his own capacities to attain. It is very important, Rousseau emphasizes, to remove the incentive to pursue what is beyond his own strength by manipulating the cooperation of others. The all-important sentiment of acceptance of his own lot and limitations is dependent on preserving the sense of the inflexibility of the boundaries of his satisfactions. They are impervious to his complaints and his machinations. In this way he will eventually bring his desires and his powers into harmony and become, on Rousseau's definition, the free, happy man. "The truly free man wants only what he can do and does what he pleases. That is my fundamental maxim" (84).

All that he does flows from the inner promptings of his own soul. It has the solidity and durability of conviction that can stand against the shifting winds of social fashions and the false desires of the senses. Reason could never bring about the inner growth of the soul that is necessary to sustain the pain of self-denial that the path of virtue may require. Left to itself, reason would be inclined to raise the Nietzschean question of: "where is the precise reason for me, being myself, to act as if I were another, especially when I am morally certain of never finding myself in the same situation? And who will guarantee me that in very faithfully following this maxim I will get others to follow it similarly with me?" (235). Something more is required in order to move us, especially when it involves substantial cost to ourselves. Reason is too thin a motive where self-interest is absent. What is required Rousseau identifies as a growth of the soul. "[W]hen the strength of an expansive soul makes me identify myself with my fellow, and I feel that I am, so to speak, in him, it is in order not to suffer that I do not want him to suffer" (235). It is this openness of compassion that Rousseau characterizes as the essence of justice and of the Gospel. It may be stretching the gospel formulation to assimilate love of the neighbor to self-love, but it is surely not far from the gospel sense of loving others *as* ourselves.

The more we yield to the deepest impulses of our nature the more we are united with all others. In being most ourselves we are most intimately members of the human community. This is the political direction in which Rousseau's principle of listening to the voice of nature within is leading. It is a dimension of his larger recognition that "the less of myself I put in the judgments I make, the more sure I am of approaching the truth. Thus my rule of yielding to sentiment more than to reason is confirmed by reason itself" (272). In the quest for true virtue that is the fulfillment of the self and of the whole, the great difficulty is in recognizing it. The battle is "between my natural sentiments, which spoke for the common interest, and my reason, which related everything to me" (291). The conflict would have alternated without resolution, the Savoyard priest explains, if he had not seen clearly the difference of direction that separates the impulses of vice and virtue. "The difference is that the good man orders himself in relation to the whole, and the wicked one orders the whole in relation to himself. The latter makes himself the center of all things, the former measures his radius and keeps to the circumference. Then he is ordered in relation to the common center, which is God, and in relation to all the concentric circles, which are the creatures" (292).

Ultimately, therefore, faith in the order of nature is faith in the God who guarantees that it is a whole in which we live. "If the divinity does not exist, it is only the wicked man who reasons, and the good man is nothing but a fool" (292). This is why religion plays so prominent a role in *Emile* and in the *Social Contract*. Not only does the presence of God ensure that we live in an order of justice in which the good will ultimately be rewarded and the evil punished, but it is also the relationship with him that brings about the inner order of acceptance of the human condition and conformity with the divine will. The meditations of the priest are like the singing of "the divine Orpheus" bringing about the true inner worship that is the fount of virtue. He explains to his young listener,

> Not to be contented with my condition is to want no longer to be a man, it is to want something other than what is, it is to want disorder and evil. Source of justice and truth, God, clement and good, in my confidence in You, the supreme wish of my heart is that Your will be done! In joining my will to Yours, I do what You do; I acquiesce in Your goodness; I believe that I share beforehand in the supreme felicity which is its reward. (294)

Rousseau's emphasis on religion parts company significantly from his Enlightenment contemporaries, many of whom were content with a skeptical tolerationist approach or a rational deism that was indistinguishable from indifference. Nor can his approach be counted as mere pious rhetoric because of the indispensable role that religion plays for him in underpinning the moral order. All of this becomes clear in the section of *Emile* where he attacks the "philosophist party" for the assertion of their own superiority to the "fanaticism" of Christianity. Rousseau presents an extensive defense of religion that, even if fanatical, represents a "grand and strong passion which elevates the heart of man," in contrast to the abjectness of irreligion that cannot avoid contracting all our interests to the boundaries of the self within this life. Atheism, for all its tolerance, "thus quietly saps the true foundation of every society. For what private interests have in common is so slight that it will never outweigh what sets them in opposition." Even skeptical philosophy's claim to provide the conditions for toleration and peace does not compensate for what has been lost. "His principles do not cause men to be killed, but they prevent them from being born by destroying the morals which cause them to multiply, by detaching them from their species, by reducing all their affections to a secret egoism as deadly to population as to virtue. Philosophic indifference resembles the tranquility of the state under despotism. It is the tranquility of death. It is more destructive than war itself." But worst of all, philosophy will hardly be able to maintain its own virtues in the absence of a religious sanction. "It still remains to be known whether philosophy, if it were at its ease and on the throne, would have a good command over vainglory, interest, ambition, and the petty passions of man. . . . Philosopher, your moral laws are very fine, but I beg you to show me their sanction" (312–14 n).

It is not simply that religion operates through the threat of punishment or the promise of rewards in the afterlife, but that it fully internalizes the order within which we live. The sanction consists in living in the divine presence, whose loving illumination draws us forward and makes us dread the loss of our deepest hold on being. This is the "new interest" that religion gives

Emile and all others in remaining faithful to the moral order even when there is no one to see and it costs us much to do it. Rousseau explains:

> He does this not only for love of order, to which each of us always prefers love of self, but for the love of the Author of his being—a love which is confounded with that same love of self—and, finally, for the enjoyment of that durable happiness which the repose of a good conscience and the contemplation of this Supreme Being promise him in the other life after he has spent this one well. Abandon this, and I no longer see anything but injustice, hypocrisy, and lying among men. Private interest, which in the case of conflict necessarily prevails over everything, teaches everyone to adorn vice with the mask of virtue. (314–15)

It is because Rousseau was so preoccupied with the formation of virtue that he devoted such prominence to the spiritual substance informing it. He was not the first theorist to explore the requirements of a civil theology—we have already seen Hobbes's discussion of the subject—but Rousseau was clearly the first to propose a civil religion that would subsume the role of Christianity as well. Where Hobbes had been concerned to define the relationship of the sovereign to the dogmas of Christianity, Rousseau proposes a naturalized form of Christianity that will supersede the denominational presentations. The whole point of the conversation of the Savoyard vicar is to show how the inner worship of God in the heart, which is the source of virtue, is the true natural religion of man. It is because this religious impulse is so important that Rousseau separates it from the revelations that constitute particular religions and that are, as a consequence, an obstacle to the universal acknowledgment of their inner truth. Far from disparaging natural religion as Christians do, Rousseau insists, we must recognize that it is the source of the sense of God that is less powerfully conveyed through the particular revelations: "The greatest ideas of the divinity come to us from reason alone. View the spectacle of nature; hear the inner voice. Has God not told everything to our eyes, to our conscience, to our judgment?" (295).[19]

Revelation is less secure because in the different religions God speaks in the different human voices of those peoples and times. Nor does it coincide with Rousseau's sense of divine justice, that God would require all men to know him through a particular revelation that can be accessible only to a limited portion of the human beings within history. And then there are the problems of establishing the authenticity of the ministers of revelation. The very fact that there are disputes renders the whole process implausible: "Is it reasonable, is it just to demand that all of mankind obey the voice of this minister without making him known to it as such?" (298). Even the claim that miracles are sufficient to establish divine authorization does not answer the difficulty, because "after the doctrine has been proved by the miracle, the miracle has to be proved by the doctrine, for fear of taking the Demon's work for God's work" (299).

It is in this way that Rousseau readmits revelation after going through all the difficulties concerning its authenticity and transmission. He declares that he has closed all the books to open the one in which God speaks clearest, the book of nature. But then he goes on to admit that "the majesty of the Scriptures amazes me, and that the holiness of the Gospel speaks to my heart" (307). He is impressed by the moral purity of the Gospels and by the figure of Jesus whose divinity is established by his life and death. That is the greatest proof of the text's authenticity, for "the Gospel has characteristics of truth that are so great, so striking, so perfectly inimitable that its contriver would be more amazing than its hero" (308). Yet for all that, the Savoyard priest finds many "unbelievable things" in the Gospel and before such contradictions can maintain only a respectful silence. He regards all the particular religions as all true in their different forms of public worship, because the outer is merely a reflection of the essential worship of the heart. This is what enables the priest to carry on within the rites of his own church, practicing them now with even greater reverence, while abhorring their erection into dogmatic absolutes of intolerance.[20]

When viewed in this context, what Rousseau has to say of Christianity in the *Social Contract* appears less puzzling. There he harshly rebukes Christianity, and even Christ, for destroying the unity of the state and causing "the internal divisions that have never ceased to agitate Christian peoples" (*Social Contract,* bk. 4, chap. 8). At the same time, he identifies the "religion of man," the true inner worship of the heart, with "the pure and simple religion of the Gospel" (bk. 4, chap. 8). The apparent contradiction is dissolved in light of the fuller account in *Emile* in which Rousseau demonstrates how the inner natural religion may be held together with the particular expressions of Christianity, especially to the extent that the former is the means of recognizing the divinity present in the latter. But to that assimilation of the two, Rousseau adds an additional element in the *Social Contract* that is in response to a profound limitation of even this purified natural Christianity—the element of social cohesiveness or particularity.

The problem with Christianity, which might well be generalized to all transcendent religions, is that it detaches men too much from earthly things. A society of true Christians, Rousseau explains, "would be so perfect that it would lack cohesion." Christians would be dutiful, but, without much regard for the success or failure of their efforts, their meekness and resignation would make them a prey to any emerging tyrants in their midst. They are too removed from this world to be much use within it. In other words, "they know how to die, but not how to conquer." The solution, Rousseau proposes, is "a purely civil creed whose tenets the sovereign is entitled to determine, not precisely as dogmas of religion, but as sentiments of sociability, without which it is impossible to be a good citizen or a loyal subject" (bk. 4, chap. 8).

He frames the discussion of the civil religion with this remark that the sovereign is not entitled to determine the dogmas, because that would be to get involved with purely religious questions that concern not this world. They lie beyond the boundary of "public utility," which is the limit of the sovereign's authority. Equally, the sovereign cannot compel anyone to believe, but he may banish him, although "not for impiety, but for being anti-social." He may even put to death one who, once having publicly subscribed to the tenets of the civil creed, later "behaves as if he did not believe them." Such a person, Rousseau remarks, has committed the "greatest crime," which is not impiety, but that "he has lied before the law" (bk. 4, chap. 8). The severity of such punishments may initially strike us as shocking, but they become more plausible in the context of Rousseau's goal of establishing a civil religion. That entails a force of social cohesiveness that would fill the gap opened up by the Christian detachment from this world. The seriousness of the punishments for lying before the law or for being antisocial is surely designed to inculcate a sense of the solemn majesty of the political order.

That interpretation is confirmed by the tenets of the creed that Rousseau lists as a belief in a benevolent, providential God, the rewards and punishments of the afterlife, and "the sanctity of the social contract and the law." Negatively, there is only one injunction, that "there shall be no intolerance," which Rousseau extends to include theological as well as civil intolerance. The two are inseparable because it would be impossible to live in peace with those whom we regard as God's enemies, but the most decisive consequence is that once again the social unity would be broken. Once theological intolerance or exclusivity is admitted, "the sovereign is no longer sovereign, even in the temporal realm. From then on, priests are the real masters, and kings are only their agents" (bk. 4, chap. 8). The means by which Rousseau sought to build and maintain social unity was through the loyalty to the political order represented by the sovereign.

Now it is questionable whether his prescription of a civil creed actually accomplishes that goal. It might well have been necessary for him to go considerably beyond the unification effected by the sovereign and the law in order to do this. It is equally questionable that such social solidity can ever be achieved within a context formed by the differentiated perspective of Christianity. Rousseau has been much criticized for his characterization of Christianity as disruptive of social unity, but he points toward a genuine tension that has always existed between Christianity and the political order. Many Christians would, after all, agree with him that a "Christian republic" is a contradiction in terms. "Those two words exclude one another" (bk. 4, chap. 8). At best, "Christian" and "republic" have lived in uneasy relationship in actual states, and social cohesion has often been bought at the price of Christian universalism. Rousseau's solution no more than acknowledges this inner tension and reflects the uneasy accommodation that has in fact operated within liberal states—that is, to exclude the sovereign from engaging in the interpretation of dogmas while, at the same time, measuring the political impact of religion in terms of public utility.

His genius was to have seen more clearly than his predecessors the impossibility of separating religion and politics. The moral and political order cannot subsist without the underpinning of spiritual substance. What Rousseau fails to emphasize is the degree to which the transcendent order also functions as a check on the political. He is in a sense so concerned with the formation of virtue that he pays relatively little attention to the restraint of vice. This is what accounts for the romantic naïveté that permeates his writing, conveying the strong impression that if only the intimations of his heart could be communicated to all men a perfect political harmony would ensue. For Rousseau it is not that there is no evil in human nature, only that the voice of conscience is a reliable guide to goodness and can be trusted to function without prejudice or suspicion. The most glaring illustration of this overemphasis on the goodness of conscience is found in the *Social Contract,* which has often drawn on itself the charge of being proto-totalitarian in its disregard for individual protections against the misuse of power. It does not seem that Rousseau abandons the liberal emphasis on individual freedom— indeed, in a sense he is led in this direction by a more single-minded emphasis on freedom—but that he feels no need to institute a check on a political order that so perfectly reflects the intuitions of the heart.[21]

He is captive to the preoccupation with the inner virtue of liberty from which his reflections begin. The *Social Contract* is a liberal utopia, Rousseau's translation of the virtuous freedom of nature into a political order. It is his solution to the problem of combining the free self-expression of the state of nature with the advances and benefits of civil society. It is "the republic [in which] all of the advantages of the natural state would be united with those of the civil state, and freedom which keeps man exempt from vices would be joined to morality which raises him to virtue" (*Emile,* 85). The challenge was how to construct a political and social order in which the incentives to dissimulation and manipulation would be entirely absent and each individual would be compelled to follow the free virtuous promptings of his own nature. It is in this sense that each would be, in the most infamous phrase of Rousseau's entire oeuvre, "forced to be free." Despite the ominous overtones that this, in its own context, innocent remark has for us, his intention was emphatically to promote the untrammeled exercise of freedom that would alone ensure the emergence of civic virtue. By bracketing for the moment the later historical baggage that attaches to it, we can begin to read the *Social Contract* as one of the great evocations of the virtue that sustains a liberal democratic order.

Its centerpiece is Rousseau's conception of the "general will" by which civil society governs itself.[22] This is his solution to the problem of how the individual can be subject to law yet free at the same time, the reconciliation of the conflict of freedom and authority with which the book begins. It answers the central liberal conundrum: " 'To devise a form of association which will defend and protect the person and possessions of each associate with all the collective strength, and in which each is united with all, yet obeys only himself and remains as free as before.' " It combines the freedom of nature in which each follows the immediate impulses of his own heart with the tangible security of a legal political order. The danger of some individuals dominating others, as occurs in present political society, is avoided by removing any opportunity for the separation of some one or few from the social whole. In that way, "in giving himself to all, each man gives himself to no one, and since he acquires the same right over all the other associates as they acquire over him, he gains the equivalent of everything he loses, plus greater power to preserve what he has" (*Social Contract*, bk. 1, chap. 6).

Much of the treatise is spent detailing the manner in which the general will is to be constructed so as to prevent it from becoming the instrument of any particular interests and thereby subverting its character as general. Thus, Rousseau insists that the sovereignty of the general will cannot be alienated, divided, or delegated, all of which would introduce an interest separate from the whole. The actions of the general will have the general interest for their object and as such are general laws for the whole community. The general will cannot be corrupted in the sense of intending other than the common good, but it can be misled if the people no longer act as a people. Only if it is without factions or differences can the general will always follow the natural impulse toward the common good. Once that condition is observed, Rousseau insists, there is no danger for the individual.

The social contract requires only that individuals give up what is necessary for the good of the community, but the community is the judge of what is required. Once all decide together and all are equally affected by the outcome, there is no likelihood that some would be exploited or dominated by the rest. The power of the sovereign and the nature of the general will do not extend beyond the making of laws directed toward the whole community. What they determine will in its nature be identical with the common interest so that, he concludes, "individuals do not really give up anything when they enter into the social contract" (bk. 2, chap. 4) and bind themselves under the same conditions and have the same rights. Just as the sovereign cannot impose a law on itself that it cannot remove, so it cannot have an interest contrary to that of the individuals who compose it. There is no need to interpose safeguards between the individual and the sovereign because they are one and the same. Thus, Rousseau readily accepts that "the social pact gives the body politic absolute power over its members," while he acknowledges that the individual can be required to submit only "that part of his power, possession and freedom which it is important for the community to control" (bk. 2, chap. 4). The danger of abuse is eliminated by the identity of interest within the general will. "Each of us puts his person and all his power in common under the supreme control of the general will, and, as a body, we receive each member as an indivisible part of the whole" (bk. 1, chap. 6).

Everything turns on the maintenance of a truly general will, so that the aggregation of the particular wills sums all the minor differences between them into an accurate reflection of their common good. The virtue of the community is preserved through its preservation free of all taint of faction (bk. 2, chap. 3). Politics is then not so much a matter of counting votes as it is of determining what the general or common good is. "When, therefore," Rousseau observes, "the opinion contrary to mine prevails, it proves only that I was mistaken, that what I thought was the general will was not" (bk. 4, chap. 2). In the most crucial instance where an individual has a private will different from the general, and even contemplates the advancement of his particular interest at the expense of the common interest, the social contract "tacitly includes one stipulation without which all the others would be ineffectual: that anyone who refuses to obey the general will shall be compelled to do so by the whole body." Rousseau goes on to remark that this "means nothing else than that he shall be forced to be free," which he explains "is the condition which gives each citizen to his country and thus secures him against all personal dependence" (bk. 1, chap. 7). Under any other alternative the individual would be subject to a particular will, the will of another, and would therefore not be free. Only in this way is he subject to the will of no one because he is subject to the will of all, which is as nearly identical with his own will as is practically possible. To the extent that he is as similarly situated as all others in the general will, the common good is coincident with his particular good.[23]

It may be, of course, that he has a different perspective or different inclinations from the majority, even though their circumstances are similar, but Rousseau did not choose to dwell on that possibility. For this reason he has earned the unbroken enmity of all those who insist on the incommensurable heterogeneity of human beings. He has even been dismissed as illiberal because of his unconcern about the preservation of an area of inviolable individual liberty, which even a person's own good does not authorize invading. It is hard to deny the validity of such objections. Once the determination of the exercise of my freedom is no longer mine, but is surrendered to the collective wisdom of the community, it is difficult to maintain that it is fully respectful of human freedom whose essence is to be freely and intelligently self-determined. Even Rousseau's defense that it is to avoid the even greater coercion contained in the alternative of subjection to the particular will of another cannot quite remove the stigma. It is no longer the exercise of *human* freedom, a self-exercise. The fact that the compulsion may be exercised for the sake of human freedom cannot erase its nature as compulsion. All of that is before we even consider the likelihood of abuse under the more ordinary circumstances of politics, where factions and interests cannot be eliminated and are likely to see their effectiveness magnified under the free-flowing politics envisaged by Rousseau.[24]

The best that can be said is that Rousseau provides the most profound illustration of the extent to which the liberal tradition can be drawn in its quest for the inner order of its regime. Rousseau recognized the nature of the problem, requiring something like a suprahuman "legislator" who would be capable of "changing human nature, so to speak," in making social beings out of the individuals provided by nature. It could not be accomplished by reason since men lack the rationality required before they enter into the social unity, nor by force since any compulsion would undermine the very humanity the social contract seeks to promote. The only possibility is the lawgiver's own quasi-divine "greatness of soul" that, in Rousseau's inimitable phrase, must "lead without compelling and persuade without convincing" (*Social Contract*, bk. 2, chap. 7) as the viable means of inculcating the virtues of the general will. The prospects are, even on Rousseau's own admission, dependent on a miracle for their realization. The *Social Contract* and *Emile* might be read as his own attempt at actualization. But even then they can hardly escape the charge of irrationally dangerous one-sidedness.

Other than in the uniquely homogenous and small-scale circumstances envisaged by his social contract, the arrangement by which individuals surrender all to a whole that they hope will not be dominated by interests hostile to their welfare invites the worst form of tyrannical abuse. The totalitarian reverberations of Rousseau's rhetoric cannot be wholly exonerated by its substance.[25] Even the defense that it is primarily concerned with the evocation of virtue does not, and perhaps least of all, mitigate its one-sidedness. The central defect of Rousseau's philosophy is not that he rejects the possibility of evil in human nature, but that it is systematically eclipsed by his overriding focus on the liberation of the impulse of virtue. Not only does the possibility of wickedness not enter into his political theory, but it also is never seriously confronted as a perennial temptation of the human heart itself.[26] He has little of the Augustinian or Dostoyevskian insight into the great attractiveness of evil. It is an abyss that invites us to plunge headlong out of the sheer exhilaration of tasting what is forbidden.

All of that seems to escape Rousseau at a certain level. Moral ambivalence is a phase to be overcome, rather than a permanent feature of the human condition. In that sense, his great evocation of the natural impulse to virtue, while it carries great edificatory impact, is a testament to the dangers of focusing exclusively on the problem of virtue itself. Rousseau undoubtedly makes clear the correlation between individual interest and the common good, between the spontaneous exercise of individual freedom and the formation of an ordered community of the whole. He impresses on generations of readers the utter lack of any incompatibility in principle between the welfare of the individual and of the public whole. At root the individual's fulfillment is bound up in service to the community. Many of Dostoyevsky's characters express the same illuminative insight that paradise is already within our grasp if only we open ourselves to realize it. Marx, too, read Rousseau in this light, as his vision of the communist transformation of human nature makes plain. What is absent from all of them is a reflection on the dark propensities that remain in human nature, even among the converted, and that necessitate an ordered structure of liberty to sustain a concrete polity. That is the task, in deliberate continuity with Rousseau, undertaken by Hegel.

Hegel's Completion of Virtue with Concrete Order

Rousseau had heralded the great crisis of virtue that would sweep over liberal democracy, but his focus on its refraction through the individual was as much contributory as remedial. By becoming absorbed in the spontaneous impulses of the heart he had run the risk of overlooking the calculating tendencies that could never be entirely eradicated. Rousseau's pure individual is possible only under the rare circumstances enjoyed by the young pupil, Emile, and even then is suspiciously incomplete. The improbability of the realization of the social contract is brought home in the multiple layers of difficulty that Rousseau himself acknowledges must be overcome. Most fundamental, the virtue that is to be created by the institutions would have to preexist before them, and "before the laws exist, men would have to be what they are to become by means of those same laws" (*Social Contract*, bk. 2, chap. 7). Neither the divinely authorized lawgiver nor the tenets of the civil religion were sufficient to answer the problem of the prior formation of the individual.

As a consequence, Rousseau was vulnerable to the charge of abstraction hurled by many critics but none with more forcefulness than Hegel. He understood that "the beautiful soul" of the wholly natural individual was a pure abstraction that invited nothing so much as the free play of caprice, an irresponsibility that exposed the lack of seriousness at its core. Hegel struggled from his youth against the derailment of the bright vision of liberty that had occurred in the French Revolution and whose intellectual culpability he had placed squarely at the feet of Rousseau. The latter had, in Hegel's view, properly discerned the foundation of the state, for "by adducing the will as the principle of the state, he is adducing a principle which has thought both for its form and its content" (*Philosophy of Right*, par. 258). The difficulty was that he, like Fichte and others, still conceived the individual in solely individual terms and the state as an accidental conjunction of individuals' wills in the social contract. When it came to the overthrow of an actual state, the revolutionaries were convinced that they could reconstruct an order out of such purified individuals. "The will of its re-founders was to give it what they alleged was a purely rational basis, but it was only abstractions that were being used; the [concrete] Idea was lacking; and the experiment ended in the maximum of frightfulness and terror." Abstract reasoning, by enthroning the individual will as absolute, "destroy[ed] the absolutely divine principle of the state, together with its majesty and absolute authority."[27]

Despite the formidable evocation of virtue in Rousseau's natural individual, Hegel had hit on the weak point of its reliance on a wholly individual affirmation of truth. Absent was any sense of the "divine principle of the state" apart from the ancillary of the civil religion, which merely confirmed what the individual had already endorsed in the social contract. The real issue was how such individuals were to be formed and, in the absence of the social and political institutions of liberty, to acquire the virtues that would be necessary to sustain the order of which they partook. Rousseau himself had been aware of the difficulties, but he had never made them thematic in the way Hegel sought to confront them. By doing so Hegel added a decisive layer to the collaborative liberal cake by dramatizing what had been known but never before highlighted in the tradition—that is, the radical insufficiency of the individual as the exclusive foundation of order. He represents the end of the language of the social contract that had, as we have seen, never been taken literally but had always been invoked to suggest the primacy of individual consent. Hegel, along with Burke, Bentham, and many others around the beginning of the nineteenth century, forcefully declaimed the arbitrariness with which the contract theorists had infected the public order. While not wishing to abandon the liberal emphasis on consent, they no longer wished to see it reduced to the hazards of individual willfulness.[28]

Hegel's work in particular constitutes a massive effort of reorientation within the liberal tradition, in an attempt to evoke the integral unity between the individual and the concrete historical order in which he lives. Hegel's goal was to demonstrate that, while the public whole is derived ultimately from the free participation of the individuals who compose it, it is not simply a product of the fortuitous conjunction of their individual impulses for cooperation. The political order is not merely a convenient afterthought to their drive toward individual self-fulfillment. It is of the essence of who they are as individuals. Without the social and political order that forms them, they would hardly even be the individuals they presently are. All that they are has come to them through the historical transmission of the community, most of all their enjoyment of individual liberty, which is made possible through the tradition of political order that sustains it.

For Hegel the reconciliation between the public and the private is part of the larger historical sublation of the tensions that have defined human existence. It is a process that reaches its culmination in the dialectical *Aufhebung* (transcending) of the opposition between man and God. Many commentators have made the mistake of not recalling this philosophical background as the setting for Hegel's *Philosophy of Right,* a mistake made all the more egregious by Hegel's own repeated reminders that the state is "objective Spirit," or the form of rationality in external political institutions, as opposed to the transparent rationality of "absolute Spirit" in religion, art, and philosophy.[29] It is for this reason that individual states are ultimately the instruments of the absolute, out of whose finite dialectic arises the universal Spirit of the world *(Philosophy of Right,* par. 340, and the conclusion to *Encyclopedia of Philosophical Sciences).* For even though tainted with contingency, passion, and particularity, the state moves toward the same self-affirmation in the recognition of itself as "objective Spirit," or as Hegel so shockingly phrases it, as "the march of God in the world" (*Philosophy of Right,* addition to par. 258).

Without hastily assuming we can determine Hegel's meaning exactly in this language, it is safe to assume that it is part of his intention to impress on liberal individuals the substantive nature of the state. *Philosophy of Right* is itself the dialectical meditation by which the political reconciliation is effected. By reading it, the contemporary liberal individual is shown the way from the contradictions inherent in his own position to their resolution in the transparent unity of the state. The traditional liberal conflict between rights and duties, the particular and the universal, are transcended. "In the state, as something ethical, as the interpenetration of the substantive and the particular, my obligation to what is substantive is at the same time the embodiment of my particular freedom. This means that in the state duty and right are united in one and the same relation" (par. 261). The modern state is in this sense "the actuality of concrete freedom" and derives its "prodigious strength" from its ability to interrelate the individual and the political. It is not only that the individuals see their interest protected by the state but also that they recognize their individual interest in service to the state. "The result is that the universal does not prevail or achieve completion except along with particular interests and through the cooperation of particular knowing and willing; and individuals likewise do not live as private persons for their own ends alone, but in the very act of willing these they will the universal in the light of the universal, and their activity is consciously aimed at none but the universal end" (par. 260).

The movement toward this final integration begins from the traditional liberal starting point of the individual, which, specifically, is the "formal right" of the individual to exercise the freedom of his personality. The freedom of the human will, the capacity to determine ourselves toward any particular goal yet to remain capable of detaching ourselves from all determinations, the pure self-identity of the "I am I," is the basis for the assertion of the formal right to freedom. It is embodied in the social recognition of its existence in the ownership of property, the exchange of contracts, and the acknowledgment of wrong. Subjective freedom becomes objective through the common recognition of its right. In each of the three instances selected by Hegel, the acknowledgment of right is merely contingent, depending on the fortuitous convergence of individual wills without any more reliable source of legitimation. Even the recognition of wrongdoing is only an immediate assertion of injustice, appearing in the form of the call for revenge to recompense an injury. It points toward a more stable expression of the universal order shared by human beings, which is so recognized precisely because it is the order that arises from their own free subjectivity. That is the transition to the second "moment" of morality.

It is an order that is recognized as binding precisely because it is the universal law created by their own subjective willing. This structure comes to light in the elaboration of the self-consciousness of the wrongdoer or criminal whose punishment is not only "implicitly just" but also explicitly just "in his objectively embodied will" or action. "The reason for this," Hegel explains in a line that can be traced all the way back to Plato, "is that his action is the action of a rational being and this implies that it is something universal and that by doing it the criminal has laid down a law which he has explicitly recognized in his action and under which in consequence he should be brought as under his right" (par. 100). That is the emergence of a common standard by which disagreements and wrongdoing might be judged. It is the establishment of a common order, no longer dependent on particular wills as in the formal right of property and contract, but now explicitly recognized as their own universal necessity. The proximate source of this in Hegel is, of course, Kant's categorical imperative, and as with that concept the central difficulty becomes the relationship between the universal moral law and the particular subjective wills.

In general, the relationship is characterized by the aspiration "ought-to-be" or the demand that the subjective will conform itself to the objective law that is its own universal. Conversely, the individual will can insist that it ought not to be subject to any law other than that which it itself has made through the universalization of its will. This recognition that the duty that binds us must be derived from ourselves, Hegel acknowledges, is the great merit of Kantian and modern philosophy (par. 133). But it is also the source of untold mischief in the invitation it contains to promote subjective preferences to the status of a universal law. At best, the Kantian call of "duty for duty's sake" is no more than an empty formalism, the demand that we remain consistent with the choices we have made. There is no way of deciding what is or is not a duty or of deciding between them, because on the Kantian basis "no immanent doctrine of duties is possible" (par. 135). At its worst, the demand for consistency suggests that the content of action is irrelevant, that all that counts is the formalism of its assertion as universal, which thinly disguises the reality of the elevation of subjective caprice and impulse above every other consideration.

Hegel had understood all too clearly the temptation contained in the assertion of sincerity as the sole criterion of goodness. He knew that it was potentially a mask for every manner of evil that could now step forward under the guise of its good intentions. In a blistering paragraph he excoriates the hypocrisy of "a stage at which subjectivity claims to be absolute," which he sees as a twisting of the profound philosophy of the modern era, "just as it has arrogated to evil the name of good." He meticulously details the stages of hypocrisy beginning with the agent's awareness of the conflict between the universal to which he should conform and the particular end he proposes for himself. It initially takes the form of "naive hypocrisy" in which the individual seeks to deceive others of his good intentions, advances through "probabilism" (which justifies his action through the discovery of some reason that supports it), and proceeds to the assertion that the mere willing of the good is sufficient irrespective of the consequences of the action, finally conceding his real subjectivism in the acknowledgment of his subjective opinion as the real criterion of good and bad action. The defense of consistency cannot sustain itself because its content is given by subjective caprice, impulse, or whim and reveals that it is therefore not to be taken seriously. Morality appears to fall apart in the subjectivism and irony of the beautiful soul (par. 140).

The situation is remarkably similar to that depicted by Richard Rorty's account of the contingency or subjectivity of all moral absolutes and the necessity of acknowledging the irony of liberal reason that must act as if its convictions were ultimate while knowing they are merely predilections. But Hegel cannot rest satisfied with this evocative aspiration, because he knows that it will shortly unravel into the labyrinth of self-serving egoism that is a permanent temptation of human beings. The intentions of the beautifully souled individuals had, after all, not been enough to prevent the Reign of Terror. More positively, he knew that what sustained his conviction of a moral order was not simply the awareness of its subjective origin. He knew, as Rorty and our contemporaries do not, that along with the subjective component, moral conviction is in its essence the profound sense of participation in an order of reality independent of our wills. The dialectical cast of Hegel's mind enabled him to comprehend objectivity and universality as the other truth of the subjectively affirmed moral law. In light of the incompleteness of each of them in isolation from the other, we begin to recognize them as moments in the new whole of what Hegel calls *ethical life (Sittlichkeit)*. "The identity of the good with the subjective will, an identity which therefore is concrete and the truth of them both, is Ethical Life" (par. 141).

Hegel goes on to define ethical life as "a subjective disposition, but one imbued with what is inherently right" (par. 140). It is the concrete order of a society in which the content of an individual's duties is known through law and custom, but, unlike traditional society where such institutions are merely present as powers external to the individual, in the final form of ethical life the individual understands and wills their existence. The whole public order is rational through and through. It is a harmony of the individual and the universal in which both sides have acknowledged their incompleteness without the other. The public institutional recognizes the individual as its own foundation and has the welfare of the individual as its aim; the individual recognizes his subjective indeterminacy without the order of duties derived from his station in the social and political whole. It is the perfect coalescence of rights and duties in which the moral "ought" has been removed because the individual's rights have been recognized as coincident with his duties. Transparence has been achieved in the recognition that we cannot have one without the other, for "an immanent and logical 'doctrine of duties' can be nothing except the serial exposition of the relationships which are necessitated by the Idea of freedom and are therefore actual in their entirety, to wit in the state" (par. 148).

The first moment of ethical life is the immediate substantiality of this unity in the family. It is immediate because it is simply present as a lived or felt unity, not mediated through differentiation and reintegration. But all the elements that can later be differentiated are present, and the family clearly provides Hegel with a model of the unity eventually obtained in the state. Most important, it is a unity in which the individual in giving himself to others does not thereby lose himself but gains his substantive identity and fulfillment in the process. Hegel remarks that the union of man and woman in marriage is initially a self-restriction, "but in fact it is their liberation, because in it they attain their substantive self-consciousness" (par. 162). Through marriage, the care of their common property, and the birth and education of children, each member subordinates him- or herself to the whole but thereby receives all the care that the whole can give. "Hence in a family, one's frame of mind is to have self-consciousness of one's individuality within this unity as the absolute essence of oneself, with the result that one is in it not as an independent person but as a member" (par. 158).

The multiplicity and insufficiency of families means, of course, that they do not exist on their own, but must find their livelihood in the larger social order. That next phase of ethical life Hegel terms *civil society*, which he understands as the common order in which human beings compete and cooperate in the task of gaining a livelihood. It is not simply the economy, because an economy functions only within a political order that orders its sustaining conditions. But civil society is the public arena in which individuals appear to be engaged in the promotion of their self-interest, although its truth is that they are also engaged in the maintenance of a common order that makes their individual pursuits possible. Initially, that construction of a public whole is indirect through the increasing interdependence of workers in a complex division of labor by which a "system of needs" is built up. "When men are thus dependent on one another and reciprocally related to one another in their work and the satisfaction of their needs, subjective self-seeking turns into a contribution to the satisfaction of the needs of everyone else" (par. 199).

Even in that form, however, the individual does not step forward in his purely private or particular character. He participates in the order of civil society as a member of a definite class—the agricultural, the business, or the universal public-servant classes. The classes are formed around the awareness of their common interests in defending their rights, the most fundamental being the administration of justice. The principle of right becomes valid and binding only when it has been made determinate in a system of positive law, which in turn can be applied to particular cases only through the judgment of courts of justice. "The principle of rightness passes over in civil society into law. My individual right, whose embodiment has hitherto been immediate and abstract, now similarly becomes embodied in the existent will and knowledge of everyone, in the sense that it becomes recognized" (par. 217).

Continuous with this recognition of the rights of individuals is the demand that the welfare and livelihood of each be equally protected. The security of all is taken care of through a police force, but that still leaves the great problem that civil society may not adequately serve the material needs of all. There is no guarantee that individuals will be successful in the struggle to pursue their welfare in the reciprocal arrangements of civil society. Hegel quite clearly perceived the pressures that were building within the capitalist economies in which the concentration of wealth and the division of labor resulted in the creation of a large dependent class of workers unable to guarantee their own well-being. He saw the impending crisis when "the standard of living of a large mass of people falls below a certain subsistence level" to create "a rabble of paupers" (par. 244). At the same time civil society lacked the resources to deal with the crisis, the steps it was likely to take would only aggravate "the evil which consists precisely in an excess of production and in the lack of a proportionate number of consumers who are themselves also producers" (par. 245). Civil society is pushed to search for a solution by moving beyond its own limits in search of new markets for its excess goods and new colonies for its excess population. But it also must unfold an ethical response in which the substantial unity of the individual with the universal is acknowledged. This, Hegel maintains, occurs in the emergence of "corporations," which function as a "second family" for their members by promoting their interests, compelling their cooperation, protecting them against poverty, and providing for their education (par. 251). Like the family, the corporation organized along vocational lines is the means in civil society by which the "particular welfare is present as a right and is actualized" (par. 255).

Yet the corporation is still restricted because the end that defines it is not present as the transparent identity of the rulers and the ruled. For this reason, Hegel explains, "the sphere of civil society passes over into the state . . . which then reveals itself as the true ground of these [earlier] phases" (par. 256). The state is explicitly the unity that is only implicit in the family and civil society. "The state is absolutely rational inasmuch as it is the actuality of the substantial will which it possesses in the particular self-consciousness once that consciousness has been raised to consciousness of its universality" (par. 258). It must not be confused with civil society, a mistake Hegel identifies with the traditional liberal ascription of the protection of the liberty and property of its members as the end of the state. That is to make the state subordinate to the individual interests and membership in it as something optional. The state is rather the self-realization of the individual, not a means toward it. "Since the state is mind objectified, it is only as one of its members that the individual himself has objectivity, genuine individuality, and an ethical life." It is because the state is the culminating expression of freedom that it is "an absolute end in itself" and "has supreme right against the individual, whose supreme duty is to be a member of the state" (par. 257).

The Rousseauesque idea of the individual whose freedom is realized through the general will is here elevated to a new level in which the individual grasps his freedom as the universal. Not only do the particular needs "gain explicit recognition for their rights," but "they also pass over of their own accord into the interest of the universal," which they recognize "as their own substantive mind" (par. 260). It is no longer a question of straining to bring the individual interest into conformity with the common interest; persuasion and compulsion are no longer necessary in the ethical unity of the state where "my obligation to what is substantive is at the same time the embodiment of my particular freedom" (par. 261). Externally, this unity is the organic differentiation and integration of the components of the state; internally, it is the political sentiment or patriotism that binds the individuals to the whole. Hegel recounts the relationship as one in which the opposition between the individual and the state has been entirely overcome in the recognition that the interest of the individual is entirely bound up and identical with the interest of the state. "In this way, this very other [the state] is immediately not an other in my eyes, and in being conscious of this fact, I am free" (par. 268).

He acknowledges that it is appropriate to explore the relationship between the state and religion in this context, since religion is often attributed with the capacity to effect the inner integration of the citizens. Hegel acknowledges that religion is indeed the "groundwork" of the ethical and political realm, but it is no more than a starting point. Religion is not yet the actuality of order. "The state," in contrast, "is the divine will, in the sense that it is mind present on earth, unfolding itself to be the actual shape and organization of a world" (par. 270). If religion insists on regarding the state as inessential or merely external, then it relegates its laws to the realm of prejudice and caprice, and they no longer have the authority of universal reason. This is the inevitable consequence of a religion that is something immediate or given, a feeling of oneness with the absolute, which does not yet comprehend the way in which all other dimensions of existence, including the political, are related to the divine source. The state, on the other hand, is mediated through the awareness of the necessary interrelationship of its component parts, and most fundamentally by the reciprocally acknowledged necessity of the particular and the universal interests. Thus, while Hegel admits the importance of the role of religion, and even accepts the possibility that the state may require membership in a particular religion, he insists that religion must not overshadow the divinity of the state itself. To do so would be to consign the political realm to the contingency of passion and conflict or to force the religious injunction for purity of heart on the political realm, because religion is incapable of rendering the determinations of law with the same transparency as the state. Where religion can only intimate the absolute that it feels in its heart, "the state *knows* its aims, apprehends and gives practical proof of them with a clear-cut consciousness and in accordance with principles."

Hegel's position is summarized in one of the lecture additions to this paragraph where he reflects that if we want men "to respect the state, this whole whose limbs they are, then of course the best means of effecting this is to give them philosophical insight into the essence of the state, though, in default of that, a religious frame of mind may lead to the same result." His own project is such an effort, a translation of the divinely willed order of the state into an apprehension of its rational necessity. It is more than a conventionally liberal argument to induce wayward individuals to see that their individual interest is best guaranteed if all support the common interest. Even more than Rousseau's attempt to situate the individuals in such a way that their individual interests will converge on the common interest, Hegel is evoking the transcendent unity of human beings as the inner reality of the state. In the state they pursue not only their individual interests but, more important, their universal interests as well. It is a secularization of the religious impulse. The question is, is it tenable?

There can be no doubt that Hegel had a very profound sense of the role of civil religion, the extent to which every viable state manages to embody a dimension of ultimate reality for its citizens. It is never merely a moral relationship, and certainly not a matter of convenience. The state must be experienced by its citizens as essential to who they are, never as an option. We see Hegel working with such conceptions as a "national religion" (*Volksreligion*) in his earliest writings.[30] What he could not find was a way of rendering the plausibility of such civic religion. It was necessary to find a way of entering into the religious experience that would make its logic transparent within the context of modern human experience as a whole.

Hegel should be read as one of the great thinkers of spiritual renewal. He sought to make contact with the divine source of order. The breakthrough in that odyssey is his understanding of *Geist*, the continuity of divine and human spirit, especially as it is recounted in *The Phenomenology of Spirit*. Without going into the complex debates concerning this divine-human encounter, it is important for us to assess the degree to which their reconciliation could be carried into the political in *Philosophy of Right*.[31]

The most striking aspect of the discussion of the state in the last part of the book is the separation between the inspirational proclamation of perfect unity, which we have summarized, and the examination of the various institutional layers that compose it. It remains an open question whether the various elements of the state share the same inspirational vision that Hegel articulates. We are told that they represent specific components of it, but do they themselves contain the whole spirit? Or is the spirit something else that exists independently of them? Perhaps it is the limit or best understanding they might struggle to attain? If so, then what is to guarantee that they will continue to play their appropriate role in the political order in the absence of a full understanding and conviction? Are we back at the old liberal problem of persuading the citizens to be virtuous? Or does Hegel rely on the evolutionary stage of world spirit, whose instruments the political actors are, to ensure the stability of the whole?

There are more questions than answers, and it is best to confine ourselves to what can readily be determined with confidence. The most obvious is that Hegel has not identified or effected the perfection of the liberal state. It still remains the unstable consensus whose final outcome hangs in the balance between the centrifugal private interests and the public good. Moreover, this becomes evident in Hegel's own description of the state whose institutional components play their role in the whole without necessarily comprehending it. At the end of his account of the state we are left with the suspicion that it is only the author of *Philosophy of Right* who fully appreciates their integral unity, despite all the warnings about philosophy never prescribing what reality ought to be. While the branches of government are not self-subsistent entities, for "each of these powers is in itself the totality of the constitution" (par. 272), it is not clear that this is fully apprehended from their side as well.

In the first "moment," the crown, all that seems to be necessary is that the monarch represent the element of subjective assent that is the foundation of the whole. It is through the concrete personality of the monarch that the subjective "I will" is recorded; the specific monarch "often has no more to do than sign his name" (addition to par. 279). Even the executive class, composed of the police force and judges—the universal class of civil servants who forgo their private interests in order "to find their satisfaction in, but only in, the dutiful discharge of their public functions" (par. 294)—is not so invincibly tied to the public good. Hegel mentions the safeguards against the abuse of their office through their election by corporations and their oversight by the monarch (par. 297). The third moment, the legislature of the Estates, is defined as "the subjective moment in universal freedom . . . integrally related to the state" (par. 301). They are likely to know their own interests, but they are unlikely to know what is rational, since that "is the fruit of profound apprehension and insight, precisely the things which are *not* popular." Hegel is deeply suspicious of public opinion (pars. 317–20) and suggests various precautions, including bicameralism, as a means of checking its rashness. It is clear how each moment plays its part in the order of the whole, but how and whether they have internalized that order remains to be seen.

We are left with the suspicion that it is only Hegel and those who have gone through "the philosophic justification of the state" that have fully acknowledged its nature. Despite the abiding refrain of turning the "in-itself" substantial unity of the state into the "for-itself" transparence of the mutual necessity of its reciprocal parts, it is not clear how that self-conscious reconciliation occurs in the individual members of the whole. The unity remains "for-us," the readers, never the "in-and-for-itself" unity of the members of the political community. Most especially absent is any sense of how the citizens make the transition from the self-interested perspective of civil society to the self-sacrificing service of the substantive order of the state. All of that is eloquently asserted by Hegel in paragraphs 257–71, but other than a few hints in relation to the class of civil servants or the sacrifices required by times of war, we do not get a very precise sense of the way in which that spirit transforms the citizens.

The reason is not hard to find. It is that the philosophical meditation that enables us "to recognize reason as the rose in the cross of the present" (preface) is only available to those who can go through it. Not many citizens will be up to the course on the philosophy of right. Hegel's difficulty is that he has eliminated most other avenues by which men might obtain a sense of their participation in the reality of the absolute. Religion was grudgingly admitted but is, in his estimation, as likely to discredit the state as merely accidental to the substantive reality of the relationship to the eternal God. Hegel is in the paradoxical position of having affirmed more deeply even than Rousseau the bond between the individual and the state, yet to have thinned the threads by which they are connected to the point of invisibility for most ordinary human beings. This accounts for the striking inconsequentiality of Hegel's political theory, which has had little effect on liberal politics or thought, no matter how often it is touted as a misunderstood model. It is a paradoxical result that can be explained only by his absorption with the primary problem of clarifying the relationship between the individual and the absolute, human and divine reality.

Hegel was obsessed with the problem of the "unhappy consciousness," the gulf of separation between man and God. He had an intense longing for unity with God, to the point that the traditional religious forms of unification through prayer were no longer sufficient.[32] From a religious point of view, it might be described as a thirst for reassurance of God's love, a burning desire to know and feel the continuity between the divine and human natures. It was not enough to be reassured that they were or would be reconciled at some future time. Hegel had to see their integration here and now. The only way available was through the narrowing of the relationship between man and God to the inner dialectic of their concepts. Any of the traditional forms of unification through prayer, sacraments, and inwardness all preserve too much of a penumbra of mystery surrounding them. They provide no more than intimations of divinity. Hegel sought the more substantive comprehension of the way in which the human nature is integrated with the divine. The price he paid was a contraction of the relationship to its conceptual dimensions, eschewing all of the traditional religious symbolizations. Only in this way could "the unity of the divine nature and the human" (par. 358) be more than a promise and "the state as the image and actuality of reason" (par. 360) more than an aspiration. Their dialectical realization would already have occurred.

Criticisms of the adequacy of Hegel's conceptual reconciliation can be made but are in this context beside the point. What is most evident is that his principal effort to evoke a publicly effective spiritual order was undermined by the very concentration on conceptual rigor intended to make it more compelling. The rationality of the divine-human integration that was the means of dissolving all possibility of doubt, rendering it the indisputably authoritative order, had the opposite effect of sealing the relationship from all but the most devoted philosophical readers. What began as an effort in public transparence ended in the arcana of dialectical speculation. Hegel's brilliant failure explains why he has on the one hand so profoundly impressed those who read him with understanding, such as the generation of Feuerbach and Marx, and why he has had no such prodigious influence in the stream of liberal political thought for which he wrote.[33] He represents the limit in the struggle to evoke a definitive spiritual order from within the liberal impulse. The next generation would turn again to the more traditional resources of religion itself.

Indispensability of Religion

The turn toward religion characterizes even the most unreligious of the nineteenth-century liberals, John Stuart Mill. Even he turns toward religion or its equivalent, quite unlike Hegel's notion that philosophy might become the means of transcending it. There is even a certain poignancy to the hunger of the agnostic Mill for something to replace the Christianity he had not so much shaken off as simply never known in childhood. His career might be understood as a succession of experiments with various alternatives, beginning with the "creed" of utilitarianism, proceeding to the spiritual crisis precipitated by his collapse into depression, selectively embracing something such as the Religion of Humanity of Auguste Comte, and finally reaching some kind of stability in the concrete humanitarian spirituality of Harriet Taylor. At each stage, however, the relationship is recognizably religious in nature.

Mill proclaims the necessity of finding a new spiritual underpinning if the liberal integration of individual freedom and the common good is to become effective. The "social problem" is at root a spiritual one of bringing about a "social transformation" or "change of character" (*Autobiography*, 175–76), if the spirit of selfishness is to be replaced with the spirit of service. He understood his age to be one in which "the philosophic minds of the world can no longer believe its religion" when, in consequence, "a transitional period commences, of weak convictions, paralysed intellects, and growing laxity of principle, which cannot terminate until a renovation has been effected in the basis of their belief, leading to the evolution of some faith, whether religious or merely human, which they can really believe" (180).

Utilitarianism originally struck him as such a creed. Mill's own internalization of utilitarianism was in the form of a transcendent altruism that inclines each man never to want any benefits not shared by others. He recommends Auguste Comte's Religion of Humanity as having "superabundantly shown the possibility of giving to the service of humanity, even without the aid of belief in a Providence, both the psychical power and the social efficacy of a religion" (*On Liberty and Other Essays*, 166). His only objection to Comte's construction was its coercive political application; Mill seemed to have consistently admired its evocation of the mystical unity of humanity. "It is as much a part of our scheme as of M. Comte's, that the direct cultivation of altruism, and the subordination of egoism to it, far beyond the point of absolute moral duty, should be one of the chief aims of education, both individual and collective." Comte was "right in principle" but only went wrong through the "extreme exaggeration in practice" (*Collected Works*, 10:340).

Mill, however, never got beyond such an endorsement of the need for a new religious awakening. He was offended by the elaborately mimetic Catholicism of Comte's symbolization and never seriously attempted to articulate an alternative. The result is that curious disconnection we noted in the previous chapter between the depth of existential inspiration and the superficiality of political formulation in Mill. Nowhere is it expressed more poignantly than in his essay "Theism" in which, after going meticulously through the arguments against belief in God, he concludes with a heartfelt admission of hope as all that remains. "The whole domain of the supernatural is thus removed from the region of belief into that of simple hope, and in that, for anything we can see, it is likely always to remain." He goes on to voice the foreclosure of expectation that is indeed so characteristic of the entire secular ethos that has come to dominate the world. In the absence of expectation, of the inner openness of soul, no genuine revelation can take place. Even if one rises from the dead they will not listen (Luke 16:31), because, as Mill discloses, "we can hardly anticipate either that any positive evidence will be acquired of the direct agency of Divine Benevolence in human destiny, or that any reason will be discovered for considering the realization of human hopes on that subject as beyond the pale of possibility" (*Collected Works*, 10:483).[34]

Yet this germ of secular hope is no mere empty husk. The appreciation of the formative role of supernatural hope in human life may not amount to a religion, but it may, Mill still contends, be "fitted to aid and fortify that real, though purely human, religion which sometimes calls itself the Religion of Humanity and sometimes that of Duty" (488). Mill saw the religious impulse as an invaluable reinforcement of his own highest aspiration, which he recognized as "a religious devotion to the welfare of our fellow creatures as an obligatory limit to every selfish aim, and an end for the direct promotion of which no sacrifice can be too great." He went on to explain that religious faith, even when based on the slender thread of unfounded hope, "superadds the feeling that in making this the rule of our life we may be co-operating with the unseen Being to whom we owe all that is enjoyable in life." In order for this sentiment to be effective, however, it is essential that it be based on faith in a God who is not omnipotent. Only then can we have that deepest feeling, "the feeling of helping God—of requiting the good he has given by a voluntary co-operation which he, not being omnipotent, really needs, and by which a somewhat nearer approach may be made to the fulfillment of his purposes" (488). Mill's spirituality teeters precariously between the most profound humility and the most grandiose hubris. "To do something during life, on even the humblest scale if nothing more is within reach, toward bringing this consummation ever so little nearer is the most animating and invigorating thought which can inspire a human creature; and that it is destined, with or without supernatural sanctions, to be the religion of the future I cannot entertain a doubt" (488–89).

The most obvious hubris is, of course, contained in the suggestion of the greater human self-importance in the coequal role with God in the work of redemption and transformation. By contrast, this human self-assertion is well restrained in the Pauline desire to make up what is lacking in the suffering of Christ. But the core of Mill's self-aggrandizement is perhaps to be found in his utter refusal to accept as God an omnipotent creator who is, as he insisted, responsible for the evil as well as the good in existence. The distance between Mill and traditional religious forms, especially Christianity, is most evident in this position.[35] How he can contemplate the possibility of a God who is not omnipotent is a measure of the disconnection from the orthodox religious imagination. We recall the adamantly agnostic character of Mill's upbringing and the extent to which his experience of Christianity or any other religion was very much later and derivative in his life. Perhaps the closest he comes to genuinely religious sentiments is in the intimate relationships of his life, preeminently with Harriet Taylor, whose memory he concedes became for him "a religion" (*Autobiography*, 183). What is lacking is the acceptance of that transcendent mystery that is in all differentiated religious forms the core orientation.

It is not, of course, completely lacking, and this is what renders his religious rejection of religion so poignant.[36] Mill refuses a faith that he sees as a reduction of life to self-interest because he is moved by the higher impulse of self-sacrifice. He fails to recognize that he has already reached the "Kingdom of God" or is not far from it in the transcendent purity of his own intentions. Perhaps nowhere is the conflict more palpable than in the conclusion of his essay "The Utility of Religion," when he contemplates the possibility of a life of heroic service of the greater good without the possibility of supernatural rewards or consolations. Admiring the Buddhist aspiration for the annihilation of self, he observes the similarity with his own intimations.

> It is impossible to mistake in this religion the work of legislators and moralists endeavoring to supply supernatural motives for the conduct which they are anxious to encourage; and they could find nothing more transcendent to hold out as the capital prize to be won by the mightiest efforts of labor and self-denial than what we are so often told is the terrible idea of annihilation. Surely this is a proof that the idea is not really or naturally terrible; that not philosophers only but the common order of mankind can easily reconcile themselves to it and even consider it as a good; and that it is no unnatural part of the idea of a happy life that life itself be laid down, after the best that it can give has been fully enjoyed through a long lapse of time, when all its pleasures, even those of benevolence, are familiar and nothing untasted and unknown is left to stimulate curiosity and keep up the desire of prolonged existence. It seems to be not only possible but probable that in a higher and, above all, a happier condition of human life, not annihilation but immortality may be the burdensome idea; and that human nature, though pleased with the present and by no means impatient to quit it, would find comfort and not sadness in the thought that it is not chained through eternity to a conscious existence which it cannot be assured that it will always wish to preserve. (*Collected Works*, 10:427–28)

The most affecting aspect of this entire passage, for which it was necessary to quote it entirely, is the complete unconsciousness of Mill himself of what it contains. He does not need to contemplate an immortality of endless days because he has already glimpsed the reality of immortality. It is the real experience of participating in that which is more serious and enduring than all the finite satisfactions of existence. This is the contact with the most real reality there is, whose mere touch is sufficient to dissolve all the doubts and objections we can propose. Instead, Mill turns away from the great mystery of participation that reveals itself within him, without realizing the depth of reality before him.[37]

Perhaps the reason is to be found in his readiness to call God to account. It is not for him the humble admission of the mystery of the mixture of good and evil in experience. If infinite goodness is good, then it cannot be responsible for all that is evil in the world; thus, it is not infinite. If infinite goodness is responsible for all the undeserved suffering and wickedness we witness in life, then it cannot be good. Like Ivan Karamazov, Mill cannot await a reconciliation. He will have an answer now or refuse to submit to this God. "Whatever power such a being may have over me," he declaims, "there is one thing which he shall not do: he shall not compel me to worship him. I will call no being good who is not what I mean when I apply that epithet to my fellow creatures; and if such a being can sentence me to hell for not so calling him, to hell I will go" (*Theism*, 93). The sense of reassuring contact with the redemptive divine presence, the mystery of the divine suffering of evil that renders the human suffering of evil bearable, without in any way dissolving its impenetrability, is not vouchsafed to Mill. Instead, there is a haughty self-reserve that refuses to bow down before a God whose worship he held "to be profoundly immoral—that it is our duty to bow down in worship before a Being whose moral attributes are affirmed to be unknowable by us, and to be perhaps extremely different from those which, when we are speaking of our fellow-creatures, we call by the same names" (*Autobiography*, 204).[38]

Mill's estrangement from God is only the most extreme of those who recognized the indispensability of a religious background for liberal order but who yet regarded traditional forms of Christianity as opaque. Not all of them were in open revolt against Christianity, regarding God with the jaundiced superiority of an almost gnostic abhorrence. For many it was simply the dogmatic rigidity that had rendered Christianity impervious to the inner resonance so necessary to the life of the spirit and, by consequence, to the leavening moral influence in political life. A classic example of this call for a vitally interior Christianity as the means of political renovation is to be found already in the work of Benjamin Constant. He had devoted his major uncompleted work, *De la religion*, to the evocation of the inner religious impulse, which he insisted was the indispensable foundation to the moral and political order. "Religion is the common center in which all ideas of justice, love, liberty, pity, which in our ephemeral world form the dignity of the human species, unite themselves above the action of time and the reach of vice" (*Political Writings*, 279). Constant was convinced that the neglect and devaluation of religion by educated opinion was entirely the result of mistaking the dogmatic exterior for the interior reality. All that was needed was to open their ideas to the religious depth at the heart of all things. "All that is beautiful, all that is intimate, all that is noble, partakes of the nature of religion."[39]

It is a strongly romantic conception that was part of the larger romantic rediscovery of religion in the early decades of the nineteenth century. Echoes are to be found everywhere, especially among the romantic political thinkers such as Coleridge who transmitted such ideas to Mill.[40] It is from this background that the most orthodox of the political endorsements of religion undoubtedly emerged in the great arch of liberal theoretical reflection coming from Alexis de Tocqueville. The French aristocrat epitomizes the liberal quest for its own foundations, the very ambivalence about itself that has characterized the liberal democratic impulse. Tocqueville embodied and revealed the inner depth of the liberal inspiration. He was a firm believer in the liberal enlargement of the self-responsibility of individuals, yet he saw clearly the dangers endemic to a mass egalitarian social condition, and he sought within liberal philosophy itself the means of overcoming its most desultory and destructive effects. He is the one who articulates most clearly the necessity for a growth of the liberal soul.

The radical extremism into which the French Revolution had debouched had sharpened Tocqueville's sense of the dangers incident to the liberal revolutionary movement. It gave him heightened sensitivity to the contextual dimensions that make a liberal political order possible. Problems that were vaguely acknowledged in the more sedate political traditions of England and America were thrust into the foreground in the reflections of Continental friendly critics of liberal politics. Foremost among these was: Who was to form the characters of the citizens if the citizens were to form the government? How was it possible to ensure that the new emphasis on individual liberty would lead to responsible liberty? Or was it inevitable that in the new egalitarian social setting, public opinion would be the product of the passions of the mob and that the leadership of responsible individuals would no longer prove possible? What would replace the stability and nobility of the aristocracy now that they were no longer the fulcrum of the social and political balance?

The shifting of the burden of government to each individual presupposed that each had to become capable of the kind of responsibility that could support it. All of Tocqueville's writings are directed toward this goal of forming the free, responsible individual within the liberal political order. Without the traditional hierarchical order of society, a greater weight was placed on the structure of order that remained. Foremost among such structures was religion, for without such a spiritual point of reference, individual liberty was likely to dissolve into the abyss of nihilism. Tocqueville had already noted the course of that phenomenon in the French Revolution. He understood that the enlargement of the political into a religious revolution, the movement of de-Christianization, had robbed the political world of the only means of retrieving order from the chaos.[41]

It is because he focused on the spiritual dimension of the upheaval that Tocqueville achieved a depth of insight into the Revolution that has not been superseded. He identified the antireligious spirit of the Revolution as its most shocking aspect, because it is what made possible the eruption of militant idealism on the political scene. It was not that men suddenly became debased and wicked, for they displayed qualities of courage and self-sacrifice that were far beyond any that had been elicited by the ancien régime, but that their virtues were mixed with a ruthlessness and violence that was utterly incongruous. Never before had "so many men displayed a patriotism so intense, such unselfishness, such real greatness of mind." The revolutionaries were a new breed of men "who carried audacity to the point of sheer insanity" and "who acted with an unprecedented ruthlessness" (*The Old Regime and the French Revolution*, 156, 157). It was the combination of idealism and cruelty that was the most puzzling aspect of the convulsion, and Tocqueville was among the first to diagnose its source in the spiritual disorder of their souls.

"The anti-religious spirit of the age had very various consequences, but it seems to me that what led the French to commit such singular excesses was not so much that it made them callous or debased their moral standards as that it tended to upset their mental equilibrium." The evacuation of religion from the hearts and minds of the citizens did not result in the creation of a secular society. A nonreligious society, Tocqueville understood, was not one from which all religion was absent but only one from which the traditional forms had been expelled. The vacuum was not permitted to remain long, for it was promptly filled with a whole new set of secular ideals that "fired the popular imagination." They developed an intense conviction of their own unbounded virtue and of their unlimited capacities for perfecting the order of society. This fanatical faith in the transformation of human nature through their efforts "was in fact a new religion, giving rise to some of those vast changes in human conduct that religion has produced in other ages. It weaned them away from self-regarding emotions, stimulated them to heroic deeds and altruistic sacrifices, and often made them indifferent to all those petty amenities of life which mean so much to us today" (156).[42]

One wonders if Mill had read such passages in Tocqueville or, if he did, whether he recognized his own progressivist religiosity in its lines. Tocqueville's analysis is a brilliant dissection of the disorder of militant humanitarianism, of secular religion. As the product of man's own fitful enthusiasm for perfection, it illustrates the disorder that results when connection with the divine is severed. The way is opened up for man himself to become God, and there is no means of resisting the madness of the schemes of revolutionary activism that ensues. Tocqueville put his finger on the core of the problem in recognizing the most damaging consequence of irreligiousness as the loss of "mental equilibrium." Man no longer knows who he is in the order of things when he no longer knows God; there is no point of reference from which he can orient himself in constructing the order of his life. Everything was possible and nothing was possible. It was a brilliant insight into the lesson that would be the major advance of collective learning through the deepening political convulsions that swept over the modern world in the succeeding century.

Contrary to the Enlightenment understanding of religion as in tension with reason, Tocqueville concluded that religion was at bottom what made men rational. Christianity functioned as the overarching order that made possible the construction of a rational political order. It did not have to inject itself into politics to do this; indeed, he was convinced that Christianity performed its political function best when it was kept separate from the strains and tensions of political life. Free from partisan entanglements, it was less likely to be attacked as the ally of one or other of the political forces, as it had inevitably been attacked as one of the pillars of the ancien régime. In that condition of serene independence above the fray, religion best preserved the transcendent authority that was its most important contribution to preserving the concrete order of personal and political life. Tocqueville was surely among the first to fully appreciate the genius of the American separation of church and state in all its mutually beneficial consequences.

He recounts how, like many visitors to the United States, "the religious aspect of the country was the first thing that struck my attention" (*Democracy in America*, 1:319). On inquiring into the reason for the surprising vitality of religion in an age when it was declining elsewhere, he was informed that it was the separation of church and state that had made it possible. Tocqueville then goes on to speculate that religion is a natural phenomenon in human life whose finitude is bound to frustrate most of the aspirations of the human heart. It arises, "from a human point of view" (321), from the desire for immortality that alone can assuage the infinite longings of our nature that can never rest content with "the imperfect joys of this world." So long as religion rests on this response of the human heart, untainted by any association with the passing realities of political power, it is assured of a continuing vibrancy. "The church cannot share the temporal power of the state without being the object of a portion of that animosity which the latter excites" (321–22).

It is because the influence of religion is thus indirect that it is so powerful in American democracy. The detachment from official entanglements leaves it free to pursue its spiritual mission and liberates its profound natural appeal. The consequences redound to the political realm in the indirect influence that religion exercises in grounding the whole order of liberty. It is because Americans recognize this indispensable role that religion "must be regarded as the first of their political institutions" (316). They understand that "despotism can govern without faith, but liberty cannot." They recognize, Tocqueville explains, that religion is more necessary in democratic forms of government than any other precisely because there is less in the way of political restraints on the people. What, he asks, "can be done with a people who are their own masters if they are not submissive to the Deity?" (318).

The great service of religion in this world, Tocqueville explains in the second volume, is that it provides "clear, precise, intelligible, and lasting" answers to the fundamental questions that frame human existence (2:22). There is scarcely any aspect of our lives that is not ultimately affected by our understanding of God and human nature; the inability to reach any settled conviction on these matters will have a pervasive disorienting effect on all other issues in which we are involved. He talks about the necessary authority religion thus exercises as "a salutary restraint on the intellect," and allows that "if it does not save men in another world, it is at very least conducive to their happiness and their greatness in this" (22). Such remarks, along with a host of others on the political utility of religion, come dangerously close to conveying the impression that Tocqueville is himself indifferent to religion's spiritual value. But that would be a great mistake. It was as evident to him as it is to us that religion can have no political value if it does not step forward in the name of the spiritual truth of the human condition.[43]

A religion that is proposed or promoted as a means of attaining satisfaction in this life will soon find its hollowness exposed. Indeed, it will have no political utility if it does not first have a spiritual utility. The suggestion that Tocqueville was cleverly weaving together a restraining symbolic web calculated to fool the masses but transparent to the cognoscenti is too pseudosophisticated. It flies in the face of his whole understanding of the modern democratic situation in which there is no longer a curtain that shields the machinations of leaders from followers. In modern politics he knew, as we are daily reminded, that there is nothing hidden that is not eventually revealed. Most important, however, is that the authoritative order of religion would work its restraining and moderating effect on the leaders too. It is a prescription for all of human life, public and private, the indispensable means of maintaining our "equilibrium."

More problematic is the notion Tocqueville held of religion as winning uncontested assent. He was surely aware of the divisions and controversies introduced by religious differences, which had been the original impetus behind the separation from politics he valued so highly. His response seems to have been to accept a wide amplitude of variations within a broadly Christian continuum and to expect that the denominations in a democratic age would move closer together in eliminating the inessentials to focus on the central message of faith. The differences would no longer prove significant, especially from a political viewpoint. Once religion was free to work its profound spiritual appeal, it would find a ready response in the human heart and eventually establish itself as the indispensable authoritative foundation of order. Tocqueville emphasizes the extent to which the appeal of religion is precisely its authoritative force. It was this dimension that led him to speculate, somewhat naively, that America and democracies would inevitably gravitate to the most authoritative of denominations, Roman Catholicism (*Democracy in America*, 2:6). Of course, more than a few writers have inclined toward the same conclusion of the expanding appeal of Catholicism precisely because it seemed to most securely retain the transcendent authority of religion.[44]

Such optimistic asides did not, however, distract Tocqueville from the fundamental problem of the decline of religion itself. Even while he is cheering the natural vitality of religion in a secular political order, he warns ominously that "as public opinion grows to be more and more the first and most irresistible of existing powers, the religious principle has no external support strong enough to enable it long to resist its attacks" (2:28). There is a limit to what religion can expect by way of public influence, and his advice is to husband that influence through deference to the majority in all but what is not contrary to faith. Most disturbing of all is the tendency, which Tocqueville honestly confronts, of the declining appeal of religion. He knew, especially in Europe, that believers were "at war with their age" (1:325). Under the pressure some had already fallen away from Christianity, others caught in paroxysms of skepticism no longer knew what to believe, and many "are afraid to avow that Christian faith which they still cherish in secret" (325).

Tocqueville's response to this situation is most revealing, both of his approach and of the inner reserves of the liberal tradition that are called forth by this sense of crisis. He looks to the actual practice of self-responsibility, of defending one's rights and the system that preserves them, as the indirect means of resuscitating the virtues on which such practice in turn depends.

> Do you not see that religious belief is shaken and the divine notion of right is declining, that morality is debased and the notion of moral right is therefore fading away? Argument is substituted for faith, and calculation for the impulses of sentiment. If in the midst of this general disruption, you do not succeed in connecting the notion of right with that of private interest, which is the only immutable point in the human heart, what means will you have of governing the world except by fear? (1:255)

It is noteworthy that he does not consider interest alone, any more than fear, sufficient to create an order. It must eventually return to the connection with right, and ultimately with the idea of "divine right."

This is a strategy repeatedly recommended by Tocqueville throughout the two volumes on democracy and invariably when his meditations have reached their gloomiest. As he sees that we live in an age when "the light of faith grows dim," he contemplates the abyss of mediocrity in which men cease to struggle for anything great or lasting and "give way to their daily casual desires" (2:159). If faith is no longer there to lift them up beyond the narrow perspectives of their egos, then some other means of spiritual enlargement must be found. They must be brought to think of their responsibility for something larger than their immediate selves. "Governments must apply themselves to restore to men that love of the future with which religion and the state of society no longer inspire them." They must teach them, "without saying so," that all that is of value in life comes only through long and arduous labor. When they have thus become accustomed to look toward their goals in the remote future, they will hardly be able to confine their meditations only to this world. They will be drawn naturally into the contemplation of their ultimate fulfillment beyond this life. "Thus the means that allow men, up to a certain point, to go without religion are perhaps, after all, the only means we still possess for bringing mankind back, by a long and roundabout path, to a state of faith" (2:160).

What is decisive is that Tocqueville considers it necessary to follow that "roundabout path" to its theological conclusion. He never suggests that concern for the future alone might be sufficient as a substitute for the religious impulse. He knew that in human affairs as in history there is no resting place without movement. If the direction is not inexorably upward toward the eternal perspective, it will as surely follow the downward pressure toward the dissolution of all order. This is the background behind his repeated expressions of concern for the inner dynamic of the limited virtues of materialism that serve not so much to "corrupt, but enervate, the soul and noiselessly unbend its springs of action" (2:141). It is a serious misreading of Tocqueville to conclude that he believed a "virtuous materialism" might be sufficient to preserve a liberal democratic order. There was always a need for something more and, while even the narrow virtues of self-interest might be enough to get the process going, they would have to lead to something much deeper if the direction was to be sustained.

It is in this sense that we must take his exhortations to democratic man to raise his sights higher, even to vices that are more expansive than the indulgence of his own "vulgar pleasures." Tocqueville returns repeatedly to this call for an enlarged self-understanding that would set them on the course toward true virtue. "Humility is unwholesome to them; what they most want is, in my opinion, pride. I would willingly exchange several of our small virtues for this one vice" (2:262). Pride is, of course, the aristocratic virtue, and it would not be too much of a strain to read Tocqueville's program as the injection of an aristocratic component into the democratic ethos. Unlike the aristocrat who had a circle of compatriots to sustain his freedom from the common viewpoint of the people, nurturing his independence of mind, democratic man is isolated before the overwhelming pressure of public opinion that "drives them to despair" (275). Tocqueville paints so touching a portrait of the individual's predicament because he has himself sensed its oppressive weight. "I dread, and I confess it, lest they should at last so entirely give way to a cowardly love of present enjoyment as to lose sight of the interests of their future selves and those of their descendants and prefer to glide along the easy current of life rather than to make, when it is necessary, a strong and sudden effort to a higher purpose" (277).[45]

The means that he recommends to oppose this contraction to immediate self-interest, which is the inevitable consequence of increasing equality of condition in society, is immersion in the vigorous exercise of freedom. This is the genius Tocqueville discerns in American institutions, that liberty is employed to counteract the ill effects of equality. By leaving men free to govern themselves, to take charge of their own affairs, they are quickly brought to the realization that they must depend on the voluntary cooperation of others, and not for the immediate task but over the long run. They become engaged in the task of cooperatively pursuing their common interest (2:109). There are a multitude of opportunities, from the self-government of townships to the composition of juries, that all conspire to promote that sense of manly confidence in assuming responsibility for the public good. "By obliging men to turn their attention to other affairs than their own, it rubs off that private selfishness which is the rust of society" (1:295). Freedom is the indispensable means of overcoming the deleterious effects of equality (2:113). Reflecting on the difficulty of rousing a democratic people to engage in warfare before the danger is actually on their doorstep, Tocqueville reiterates the need to infuse some of the aristocratic love of liberty, or at least their loathing of being conquered, into them. They must never forget "that nothing but the love and the habit of freedom can maintain an advantageous contest with the love and the habit of physical well-being. I can conceive nothing better prepared for subjection, in case of defeat, than a democratic people without free institutions" (2:301).

But once they have begun to take a stand on the value of what transcends their own private lives, then they have taken the first step on the path that leads to the full recognition of the transcendent constitution of order. It is a dynamic in which human beings are inextricably involved because of the infinite thrust of their aspirations and the all too finite nature of their existence. Tocqueville well understood the spiritual restlessness that, especially in the American, poured itself out in a "bootless chase of that complete felicity which forever escapes him" (2:145). It was a cloud of sadness that tainted even their pleasures and was the source of the outbursts of fanatical religiosity he witnessed on the western frontiers. The soul of man has "the taste for what is infinite and the love of what is immortal. . . . He may cross and distort them; destroy them he cannot" (142). The choice is either between following out the spiritual intimations of transcendence or oscillating wildly between self-absorbed materialism and eruptions of "religious insanity."

In a democratic age the most natural tendency will be toward an all-dissolving materialism, so that the maintenance of an equilibrium will be dependent on the presence of a countervailing spiritual direction. The outbursts of religious enthusiasm are more a symptom of the suppression of the spiritual impulse, rather than a valid manifestation of it. Tocqueville's emphasis is to articulate the order as a whole in which we recognize the overarching principle with which his study of democracy begins, "that liberty cannot be established without morality, nor morality without faith" (1:12). For this reason he counsels that when religion has "struck its roots deep into a democracy that you do not disturb it; but rather watch it carefully, as the most precious bequest of aristocratic ages" (2:154–55). But what of the more common situation when faith is not so unshakable? What can political authority do to sustain that on which its own authority rests? His answer is that it is "not easy to say" what government can do to promote religion; at any rate it cannot do very much without endangering the impulse they wish to see flourish. Indirectly, however, governments can be of decisive influence by communicating the seriousness of their own convictions. "I believe," Tocqueville concludes, "that the sole effectual means which governments can employ in order to have the doctrine of the immortality of the soul respected is to act as if they believed in it themselves; and I think it is only by scrupulous conformity to religious morality in great affairs that they can hope to teach the community at large to know, to love, and to observe it in the lesser concerns of life" (156).

The advice is no doubt sensible, but is it sufficient? There is something quaint about the recommendation that government set a good moral and religious example, especially in a democracy. For if the government is a reflection of the people, how can we be sure that it will be in any way spiritually better then they are? Tocqueville's advice begs the question: What can we do to make sure the government believes its religious morality? He was no doubt aware of the difficulty in the hesitant way he framed the discussion, observing that religion is a precious bequest from aristocratic ages. The implication is that it can only be preserved, not rediscovered, in a democratic age that balks at the notion of spiritual authority and truth. Tocqueville was enough of a child of his time to know the modern predicament. Neither his prescription of a reaffirmation of the spiritual foundation of virtue, nor Hegel's evocation of the spiritual reconciliation of the divine and human natures, nor Rousseau's call for a civil religion of inner virtue, nor Locke's concern for a reformulation of the truth of Christian reason, could realize any of these aspirations. Yet they are not for that reason brilliant failures that accomplish nothing.

That is the great error of so many contemporary writers, themselves generally liberals of various stripes, who proffer an easy dismissal of the liberal philosophical tradition, without reflecting that this is the central tradition of the modern world. There is no other. That reason alone should give pause to the dismissal and prompt a reexamination of what for almost five centuries it has been trying to do. In the preceding chapter we examined the unfolding of the liberal evocation of the minimal public consensus of order that can be realized in a period of philosophical and religious divergence. The present chapter has followed the correlative process to the construction of the liberal consensus, that of the increasing concern about the sufficiency of the inner spiritual resources to sustain that order. The instability of the order, riven with tensions and conflicts, and the inconclusiveness of the search for the foundations of virtue, never more self-conscious than today, have often been taken as indicative of the hollowness of the entire liberal enterprise. The considerable effort of renovation we have here chronicled should have been enough to expose the superficiality of that complaint.

Simply because the search for the foundations of liberal order have not yielded definitive results is not in itself proof that there are none. Indeed, such a formidable effort drawing on the greatest political philosophers over the centuries is a powerful indication of the substance of the liberal convictions. Without the presence of powerful inner convictions whose truth was to be articulated, what would have sustained the momentum of the effort? It is integral to all meditative reflections that there can be no search unless we are already in possession of some knowledge of that which we want to find. Throughout the quest we have followed it was evident that the inquiry was sustained by the immovable conviction of the rightness of the liberal political order. All that was in doubt was the means of articulating its truth, of finding the formulation that would evoke the necessary sustaining virtues. It is true that the history of liberal political thought has largely been the history of the crisis of liberal politics, but it has been the depth of conviction of the rightness of the liberal approach that has sustained the vigor of the critical self-examination required. There are probably few criticisms of liberal aspirations that have not been made by liberals themselves. That robustness of liberal discussion is the most powerful testament to the inner strength of the tradition itself.

The preceding two chapters have, in other words, taken the measure of the liberal tradition, but we have not yet identified the nature of the inner resonances that sustain it. We have seen the character of the consensus it has formed and plumbed the depth of the concern that has animated the repeated efforts to infuse its virtues, but we have not highlighted the precise nature of the inspiration itself. We have noted its effects, and we have followed the course of its self-examination and self-rejuvenation; now we must attempt to identify the character of the impulse itself. There is no doubt both in the history of the liberal tradition, and in the contemporary manifestations examined in Part I, that there are powerful resonating forces behind it. The liberal idea of limiting political authority correlative to the expansion of individual responsibility exercises an almost irresistible appeal on our imaginations. Typically, that appeal is attributed to the "something" universal in human nature. Such responses only beg the question of why the appeal exercises so strong a force at some times and places and not others. Can we identify with any more precision the sources of its attraction and why it has so powerful a hold over us? If we can do that to some extent then we will be that much closer to an articulation of the heart of the liberal tradition. It will be the *animus animi* of the liberal soul.

6

Source of Liberal Appeal
Secular Christianity

The genius of the liberal construction has been its capacity to authoritatively evoke order while remaining silent about its sources. It has simultaneously refined the requirements of order and enlarged the range of its appeal within a historical context of profound philosophical controversy. The movements are correlative since it is precisely its capacity to separate from unnecessary conflicts that has enabled it to win so wide a consensus of support. But like all philosophical compromises it is unstable, and its preservation depends on deflecting the pressure to fully confront the source of its instability. The result has been the rich profusion of liberal philosophical attempts to reach an uncontested account of its own foundations. Mill and Tocqueville represent the end of that process, in the sense of a patent admission that liberal convictions cannot survive unaided but must be sustained by a larger spiritual impulse. Hegel is in many respects the culmination of the effort to articulate a self-transparent evocation of the liberal polity. The succession of contemporary evocations are, with the exception of Rawls's neo-Kantianism, self-consciously fragmentary contributions that presuppose a whole that can no longer be coherently articulated.

Yet the theoretical disarray, we have emphasized, has not automatically been reflected in an existential dislocation. Liberal politics and liberal philosophy have proved their durability and, although always in danger, seem to have postponed their demise with impressive regularity. The thesis of this study is that liberal resilience is to be attributed to the presence of a profound spiritual impulse that has remained, despite the disturbances, as the still point of the turning external world. One senses its presence in the complacency with which theoretical inconsistencies and inconclusiveness are accepted by liberal writers and leaders. It is not so crucial that all of the loose ends have not been tied up, because there is a deeper certainty of the rightness of the whole

199

approach. It is often a matter of indifference that the liberal construction has not been given a comprehensive definition, when it is the medium through which what is most important about human beings is being expressed and realized.[1] All that matters is fidelity to the transcendent inspiration that is its source.

So far we have seen the effects of that powerful impulse, both in the consensus it has maintained and in the succession of attempts at rejuvenation. Now we must focus on the nature of that impulse itself in an attempt to articulate what liberals themselves are content to leave inarticulate. It is the nature of that which is most deeply held, that of which we are convinced without question, that it does not need to be explained or defended. It is that in terms of which everything else is measured but does not itself stand in need of justification. The search for foundations is always necessarily incomplete, for it comes to rest at that which we do not perceive as needing foundational support. In that sense, all foundations adduced are inevitably only intermediate. For liberals it is that ungrounded ground that provides the powerful inner life of their convictions. Like Winston Churchill, they are capable of making enormous efforts in its defense without ever having to explain why it is worth defending.

The task of making the implicit explicit involves going beyond the contours of the liberal vocabulary to the engendering symbols and experiences behind them. We must follow the trail of intimations within the conceptual writings to their vital animating center. Unfamiliar as such an approach may be, it is not in any way esoteric or speculative, for the illuminative inspiration is not concealed but lies ready to hand within the writings and actions themselves for those who are careful to discern it. After all, it is precisely the resonance with this impulse that is the carrying power of the whole liberal enterprise. What is needed is a heightened sensitivity to those texts and passages that convey its burning intensity, that signal the dimensions of sacredness and awe before a reality regarded as the ultimate horizon of our existence. Once alerted to their presence, we discover that the sedate liberal elaborations are sustained by a spiritual inspiration of impressive power and depth.

The only adequate way of describing it is in the language of religion. It may seem a stretch to characterize the appeal of the liberal tradition as that of secular Christianity, including the integration with Greek philosophy, but it reflects the theoretical necessity of using the appropriate vocabulary. Something is missed if we flatten out the resonances to a purely secular construction. There is a palpable aura of the sacred surrounding certain liberal expressions of the transcendent dignity of the person that call for the characterization as religious or quasi-religious. To adumbrate them in any other terms is to lessen the resonances they undoubtedly have and to miss the horizon-constitutive role they play within the liberal experience. It expresses the notion of something at once awe-inspiring and imperious, surpassing a purely human calculus of estimation. We recognize its imperative because it is the mystery before which we too bow low. It is the horizon of our lives too.

Not that there is anything surprising about such a realization once we reflect on it. Despite the liberal secular language emphasizing its separation and independence from religion, it is only natural that evidences of the Christianity it has left behind should have found their way into it. One might even say that liberal order is the trace of Christianity in a world from which it has withdrawn. For even after a spiritual symbolism has lost much of its transparence and no longer functions with uncontested authority, one can expect that many of the expectations it has generated will continue to exist. Even when Christianity no longer shows clearly the way to their fulfillment, the aspirations it has stirred up in the course of its history are not so easily dissipated. They continue a subterranean existence, their origin no longer apparent to so many of those who share them. And then there is the continuity of philosophy and Christianity as living traditions that continue to wield considerable appeal within the enclaves of modern societies where they flourish privately. The legions of Christians, churched and unchurched, should not be underestimated in any assessment of the inner resources of liberal order. Both the residual and the ongoing presence of Christianity exert a powerful pull within the liberal soul.

It is an influence that deserves to be taken seriously on its own terms rather than dismissed as a temporary rhetorical cover for a different underlying reality. So long as the liberal convictions have not become a substitute for the Christian faith, so long as they do not function as a substitute religion, then there is nothing derivative about their status as a secular reflection of Christianity. It is only when the line between the two is blurred and politics masquerades as religion that an artificial hybrid results. Then the effect is patently contrived and is held together only by the resort to subterfuge and force. Yet the experience of such quasi-religious movements, in the great revolutionary ideologies, should not cloud our sensitivity to the subtler manifestations of the religious spirit in the more moderate development of liberal order. Given the historic presence of Christianity it would even be surprising if there were not some traces in the political framework, which remain perfectly legitimate so long as an awareness of the difference between the two spheres is retained.[2]

The interrelationship can be seen as mutually illuminating. Just as Christianity is in some fundamental sense the truth of the liberal conception, so liberal order can be considered the political truth of Christianity. Something like this reciprocal illumination has been occurring in the best understanding of the two. Just as the liberal tradition can be understood most profoundly as the political reflection of Christianity, so the political implications of Christianity are most deeply reflected in the liberal construction of order.

They are two sides of the coin of the self-consciously moral advance embodied in the emergence of liberal democracy. This is what has given liberal philosophy its moral self-confidence, even superiority, in its sense of having superseded previous spiritual and political forms. It is the core of the rivalry that occasionally erupts with Christianity. But the mistake of emphasizing their opposition is readily recognized in the extent to which the advance is an advance within the parameters of the Christian framework. In that sense, liberal principles represent a deepening of the manifestation of Christianity, and Christianity is the truth of what is being realized within it.

The objection most likely to be made to this suggestion is that their continuity can be understood as easily in relation to the underlying dynamic of human nature or the human condition. The centrality of freedom can hardly be claimed as the exclusive prerogative of one particular tradition. The idea that there is a neutral essence of humanity that can serve as the touchstone has long been a part of the liberal framework, but it has effectively been undermined by a succession of critiques ending in deconstructionism. The problem with an appeal to human nature has always been that we never find any raw depiction of it that does not already have the skin of interpretation covering it. The deconstructionists are right that any account of human nature is historically contextualized, but they are wrong in concluding that they are all relative. The historic accounts themselves assert their status as true and require a sifting of their claims in order for us to assert the reality of our own human natures. That means that we must make the historical investigation of discovering the most adequate account and take up our own responsibilities within its framework. The historicity of truth means that we take seriously the differentiation of truth in history. Just as there is no access to reality except through the language forms that structure our experience, so there is no serious language engagement without relating to the reality from which it arises.[3]

There is no detached perspective from which we can weigh the truth claims of the various historical traditions. We must make our judgments from within the process and cannot avoid the decision. That means we must sift what has historically become available to us for the account that most resonates with our own experience, knowing all the time that our judgment must be open to questions and critiques posed from other traditions or from outside of them. The only confidence we can have in our judgments arises from this readiness to confront objections to them. But we cannot avoid taking a stand within the framework of one or other of the available traditions, if only provisionally. The responsibility is ours to ensure that we have sought out the deepest and most illuminating framework within which to conduct the inquiry. In relation to liberal politics, Christianity is that most embracing and most profound horizon, the one that illuminates most powerfully the impulse that moves it at its best.

The sense of rightness we find expressed within liberal self-reflection is best explained within the spiritual horizon of transcendence. Without that perspective, the liberal assessment of the finiteness of all political achievements and the infinite dynamic of the human person make no sense. They really are absurd residues of a vanished world that we are at a loss to know how to deal with. We are disturbed by the prospect of their disappearance because we know that the liberal order we favor cannot hold together without them. But we no longer know how to render them intelligible. Without an acknowledgment of man's participation in a movement toward transcendent reality, a movement common to all the world religions, then we are stuck with the puzzling aftereffects of a world inherently short of our expectations and a valuation of human beings out of all proportion to their social roles and contributions. Everything in the world can be defined in quantitative terms; only if there is a dimension transcending all limits is there the kind of ultimacy to human beings that liberal democracy has aspired to preserve.[4]

The crisis of liberal politics from which the study began can now be more exactly formulated as a crisis of the spirituality that underpins it. Rather than the intellectual problem so much debated in contemporary philosophy, where the search for an uncontestable account of its foundations is the holy grail tirelessly pursued, the real difficulty lies at the existential level of the spiritual convictions that have historically been reflected in the liberal construction. The problem is not even in the nature of the questions themselves, for even if we abandon the search for foundations as futile there will still be the need to recover the existential impulse that sustains order when it is no longer convenient or attractive. The need is neither to make liberal convictions intellectually coherent or to become comfortable with their incoherence. It is to render the liberal order spiritually transparent. We must find the means of rejuvenating the deeper resonances of the spirit, still fitfully present, whose affirmation of the indefeasible rightness of liberal order makes all the fragmentary incoherence insignificant.

The reason I am relatively sanguine about the prospects of such renovation is that the resonances are not wholly absent in the contemporary world, and they have been brilliantly captured within the richness of the liberal historical tradition. Because they have been successfully communicated before in the modern world, we have both the model and the encouragement that they can be spread forth again. While it is not likely that a religious revival or consensus will emerge to dominate the public square, there is no reason why the sub rosa form it assumed within the liberal symbolization could not continue to evoke a spiritual response. Having found a way of embodying the transcendent finality of human existence, the liberal tradition still possesses the resources that can stir the embers of conviction to flame again. What is needed is an identification of the inspirational outbursts from which that movement of enlargement of the liberal soul can begin again. It is no accident that so many successful political campaigns have been built on the appeal to "traditional values," for there is still a readiness in liberal societies to follow the call of what is deepest within them. Argument and policy have never carried the day; they have always been the means of articulating what was sensed to be right before the articulation got under way. To the capacity of the liberal tradition to tap those wellsprings of spiritual resonance we now turn.

The Dignity of Rational Creatures

The success of Locke in evoking a liberal democratic order may be attributed in large part to his ability to communicate the invincible force of his convictions. For all the incompleteness and incoherence of his thought there is a central passion that unifies it all. That is the transcendent value of freedom. The indispensability of liberty is the core of his thought and of the political form in which it is expressed. Locke is not the first to make liberty a theme, but he is surely preeminent in the centrality he gives it within the political order. It becomes for him the transcendent human good, the sine qua non of all other goods, that without which no other goods can be attained or if attained are not worth having. We recognize in Locke the authoritative invocation of liberty as the defining characteristic of humanity that has become the defining differentiation of the modern self-understanding. It is because we share the conviction that its authoritative rightness strikes us too.

Not only does the emphasis on freedom function as a transcendent principle, but it is also a distinct refinement of the Christian understanding of man. The discovery of the infinite worth of each individual is made within the Christian experience of the love of God infinitely poured out for each one in the sacrifice of Christ. That realization is unfolded in the radical equality of all human beings, individual infinities whose value cannot be weighed against one another or the whole but acknowledged only in their transcendent destiny. Within that relationship with God, now made transparent in the revelation of Christ, the condition that makes it possible from the human side is freedom. The capacity for movement toward fulfillment with the transcendent God is contained in the infinite freedom of human nature. Only a being that was God-like in his independence could enter into relationship with God. Freedom is at the heart of the love of God for man and the answering love of man for God.

Locke makes clear this connection of freedom and the religious understanding in the *First Treatise* where he argues against the idea that some men have been given by God dominion over others. They are all, he insists, made in "the image of God" (par. 30), and each exercises the dominion over himself that God has granted to him. That freedom is indispensable to the full exercise of his humanity and in particular in the unfolding of his central responsibility toward the God who created him. In *A Letter Concerning*

Toleration Locke places the case for liberty squarely on its indispensability to man's relationship to God. Just as we cannot love by force so we cannot be saved by coercion; the relationship is neither true nor of value if it is not constituted by the free assent of our will. That is why, Locke affirms, "the principal consideration and which absolutely determines this controversy is this: Although the magistrate's opinion in religion be sound, and the way that he appoints be truly evangelical, yet, if I be not thoroughly persuaded thereof in my own mind, there will be no safety for me in following it. . . . Faith only and inward sincerity are the things that procure acceptance with God" (34). Faith is necessarily a matter of freely emergent conviction, "men cannot be forced to be saved whether they will or no" (35).[5]

In faith, as in everything else in life, it is the freely donated assent that constitutes the value and attraction of what is done. That irresistible appeal of liberty is central to Locke's *Some Thoughts Concerning Education,* where liberty is identified as the "true relish" that unlocks the heart of the child to the formative influence of education. "We naturally, as I said, even from our cradles, love liberty, and have therefore an aversion to many things for no other reason but because they are enjoined to us" (par. 148). It is by taking advantage of this natural love of what is gained freely that the child can be brought through the rigors of learning and led to the maturity of the virtues. Locke's whole educational philosophy may be summarized as the exploitation of the appeal of everything that is discovered through the free exercise of our faculties. As far as possible, learning is to become play. But Locke was not an educational utopian and understood the evil proclivities of human nature as well; man is not all the pure desire for knowledge and virtue. "I told you before that children love liberty; and therefore they should be brought to do the things are fit for them, without feeling any restraint laid upon them. I now tell you they love something more, and that is dominion: And this is the first original of most vicious habits that are ordinary and natural" (par. 103). The love of power and dominion "shows itself very early" and must be combated by the teacher or parent who will demonstrate very firmly that nothing will be gained by such a course, whereas the virtues of civility and kindness will obtain all the rewards and approval. Thus, Locke recognized the essential supportive role of habit, "working more constantly and with greater facility than reason" (par. 110), but he did not confuse it with the free inner assent to what is good for its own sake, the heart of the life of virtue. He wished to see the young charge progress from the incentives of praise and blame to the rank of "a gentleman, whose business is to seek the true measures of right and wrong" (pars. 187, 200).[6]

If they are to attain their proper maturity, men cannot be permanently under the jurisdiction of others, because that would be to deprive them of the freedom whose exercise is central to their humanity. It is in this sense that men are equal. They are not equal, Locke admits, in age, virtue, qualities, or advantages, but they are "in respect of jurisdiction or dominion one over another, which was the equality I there spoke of, as proper to the business in hand, being that equal right that every man hath, to his natural freedom, without being subjected to the will or authority of any other man" (*Second Treatise,* par. 54). Children, because they do not yet have the full use of reason, are naturally under the tutelage of their parents, but that dominion ceases once they reach the age of their majority and are capable of taking care of themselves. To treat them otherwise would be to deny their rational natures and to treat them as less than their parents. The assignation of permanent jurisdiction to some men over other men is tantamount to a rejection of their rational natures that can function only in freedom.[7]

Such an overriding emphasis on consent is often contrasted with the classical insistence on the principle of authority, and the complex relationship requires some clarification. On the one hand the Greeks are the ones who discover *nous* or reason as the constitutive center of the person. It is the free activity of reason pursuing its own ends for its own sake that constitutes for Aristotle the essence of a liberal way of life. Liberal is contrasted with a material and utilitarian exercise of humanity. But the Greeks conceived this truly liberal life as possible only for the elite who possessed the requisite leisure and capacity to pursue it. All others could participate in it only through obedience to the philosophic order that emanated from leaders or laws that possessed the reality. Christianity in particular breaks this hierarchical mold and pushes the Greek discovery of the free inner self in a more universal direction. It does this by emphasizing the fallibility of all human beings, their equidistance from divine perfection, and the necessity of receiving the redemptive gift of Christ as the means of overcoming their fallen condition. That definitively tilts the discovery of the inner life of the soul toward the modern conception of the equal right of each to govern himself irrespective of the probability of failure. Anything less would constitute a rejection of the revelation of the transcendent depth of divine Love within each of us. Of course, the political necessity of invoking some approximate hierarchy of wisdom is not in any way lessened. The story of liberal political societies becomes largely one of balancing the transcendent principles at their core with the pragmatic necessity of ensuring rule by the optimally virtuous and intelligent. God's infinite love may not respect differences of persons, but our political survival is crucially dependent on a system of selection. This is the whole point of elections that in principle can be contested by all but cannot in fact be won by all.

Similarly, for Locke consent is always tied to an authoritative moral order. The state of nature, he emphasizes, is not a state of license or one without direction. It is a state of lawfulness, governed by the law of nature, but it is a rational order in which we participate through the free exercise of our reason. It is a state of law constituted by the self-governing reason, not a law that we are compelled to follow whether we will or not. In that sense, the state of natural freedom is not a state without law, but one in which man follows the law through the rational apprehension of its moral authority over him. The political freedom men enjoy or ought to enjoy is derived from the rational freedom they possess as the condition of fulfilling their moral obligations. It is for this reason, Locke emphasizes repeatedly, that they can be bound by no other obligations except those to which they have freely consented. Just as God invites men to freely participate in the order of his governance, so all human relationships must be based on the acknowledgment of the free participation of their members as the condition of their worth. If the commitment is coerced or commanded, then it is to that extent less adequately human.

Law is properly, then, not a restraint on freedom but its fulfillment. "For law, in its true notion, is not so much the limitation as the direction of a free and intelligent agent to his proper interest, and prescribes no farther than is for the general good of those under the law" (par. 57). It is the intelligent self-direction of those under it and is justified in reference to their common good. If they were capable of attaining their ends without it, then "the law as a useless thing would of it self vanish." There is no conflict between law and liberty in this sense, for "the end of law is not to abolish or restrain, but to preserve and enlarge freedom." Locke knew, of course, that law will not always be experienced so benignly or positively. There will be an element of coercion and restraint, but its justification must be that it is at root what makes freedom possible. Safe from the arbitrary domination of others, each is free to live rationally in accordance with the moral law of nature. The civil law is both an expression of his freedom and the means of its expanding realization.

It is this centrality of freedom that makes its suppression so intolerable for Locke. We are clearly at the heart of his experience in those passages where he is dealing with the threat represented by an absolute prince. Locke reserves his most emotive language, none surpassed by the bloodcurdling quotation from Livy affixed as the motto to the *Two Treatises,* for the moments when he confronts the prospect of the betrayal of the trust of civil society in the hands of a tyrant. The vehemence of his response to Filmer's *Patriarcha* is explained by the same passion, for he saw the patriarchal argument as a cover that was increasingly being used to legitimize absolute rule. Nothing stirs Locke and, not coincidentally, the liberal tradition so much as the appearance of tyranny. All his political involvements, which exposed him to considerable personal risk and hardship, were directed against what he saw as an unmistakable pattern of deprivation of liberties that would end only in the complete subordination of the nation.

Absolute power was the perversion of the idea of civil society. For Locke it represented nothing less than an assault on his very humanity. Not only does it deprive us of the means of defending ourselves against injury, but each is also "as if he were degraded from the common state of rational creatures, is denied a liberty to judge of, or to defend his right, and so is exposed to all the misery and inconveniences that a man can fear from one, who being in the unrestrained state of nature, is yet corrupted with flattery, and armed with power" (par. 91). It is to reduce men to the status of animals, who may indeed be taken care of by their master, but not out of any love he bears them but from the "love of himself and the profit they bring" (par. 93). Locke returns to this analogy several times throughout the *Second Treatise* to underline the connection between self-government and the free exercise of rationality that defines being human. To argue for the unlimited power or authority of the prince is to assert that "the people under his government are not a society of rational creatures entered into a community for their mutual good . . . but are to be looked on as a herd of inferior creatures, under the dominion of a master, who keeps them, and works them for his own pleasure or profit" (par. 163).

Locke recurs to the depiction of subhuman beastliness as the only adequate identification of the tyrant who has broken the sacred bond of trust on which civil society is based. They may be hunted down like a wolf or a lion, "because such men are not under the ties of the common law of reason, have no other rule, but that of force and violence, and so may be treated as beasts of prey, those dangerous and noxious creatures, that will be sure to destroy him, whenever he falls into their power" (par. 16). The danger contained in any unlawful encroachment on the liberty of the citizens is not defined by the specific injury of the case, but by the metaphysical chasm it opens up whereby he who would take away one's freedom "must necessarily be supposed to have a design to take away everything else, that freedom being the foundation of all the rest" (par. 17). The threat against freedom must be seen as an assault on the core of our humanity. It breaks the bond of mutual trust and respect that ties us together and undermines the whole possibility of civil society.

Locke invests this social agreement or compact with all the aura of the sacred he can summon. It is in the nature of human beings to be rational self-governing beings, no one of whom has a right to exercise power over another except through the latter's consent. Any attempt to encroach on that self-governing prerogative would constitute a breach of the only legitimate basis on which society can be established. This is why the location of the legislative power is "sacred and unalterable in the hands where the community have once placed it," for without this authority "the law could not have that, which is absolutely necessary to its being a law, the consent of the society, over whom no body can have a power to make laws, but by their own consent" (par. 134). The depth of the passion that inspired Locke and liberal revolutionaries in general is palpable in the utterly impervious character of this requirement.

It was the moment at which their essence as human beings was at stake. The choke point Locke knew would be the regulation of property because it is through the freedom to dispose of our property, founded in the property each possesses in his own person, that we are capable of exercising freedom. If princes or rulers can by their own wills dissolve the contracts made by men, then there is no property and no freedom. The consequence is that "all the grants and promises of men in power, are but mockery and collusion" (par. 194). Neither property nor agreements are any longer possible once their breach has been perpetrated by those in authority. Locke's response is to measure such an outrage in the transcendent perspective of God. "I will not dispute whether princes are exempt from the laws of their country; but this I am sure, they owe subjection to the laws of God and nature." No one, he goes on to say, can exempt them from the imperious obligations of the eternal law. "They are so great in the case of *Promises,* that Omnipotency it self can be tied by them. *Grants, Promises,* and *Oaths* are Bonds that *hold the Almighty.*" In that transcendent perspective we see all things rightly. Locke reveals that the source of his conviction is that preeminent divine reality of right, in comparison with which all human subterfuge falls away as dross: "Whatever some Flatterers say to Princes of the world who all together, with all their People joined to them, are in comparison of the great God, but as a Drop of the Bucket, or a Dust on the Balance, inconsiderable nothing!" (par. 195). One word of truth outweighs the whole world.

Divine Stature of Man

The necessary dependence of a liberal order on religion is a recurrent refrain, as we saw in the last chapter, that arises from the inherent incompleteness of the liberal symbolism. The evocative consensual nature of its construction, leaning heavily on a level of citizen virtue it cannot directly sustain, leads to repeated invocations of the larger spiritual underpinning implied. Individual freedom is acknowledged as the indispensable condition for the emergence of true virtue, the capacity to choose what is good for its own sake, while virtue is correlatively the requirement for the proper exercise of freedom. There is enough uncertainty about the convergence of the two that reflection is naturally directed toward the spiritual sources for the growth of the soul, which are principally available through religion. It is for this reason that so many of the great liberal theorists have emphasized in one way or another the formative role of religion. In the present chapter we turn to another dimension of the liberal enterprise in examining the extent to which it has managed to absorb the religious impulse within itself.

Locke reveals the continuity between Christianity and liberal freedom, but it was Rousseau and Kant who did most to turn the liberal impulse into a secular Christianity. That does not necessarily imply a rejection of traditional

Christianity, although the danger is clearly present and becomes manifest in the militantly secular liberalism of the later centuries. Neither Rousseau nor Kant are anti-Christian, but they project an exaltation of the human that contains the seeds of the absolute human independence from which the later revolt could spring. With them it is still very much a refinement of the Christian transcendent dignity, and no overt or implied rivalry seems to be intended. We see that the appeal of the later self-assertion of human dignity is a Christian one and that they are not necessarily in conflict with Christianity itself. Indeed, we will see in the last section of the present chapter that a valid reading of Christianity would recognize the liberal democratic form as its own highest political expression.

That line of development begins its meandering path in Rousseau's single-minded recovery of the interiority of virtue. His castigation of all moralizing as the death of education and insistence that only what comes from the heart can be counted as true virtue (*Emile*, 390) is the first step. It set him on the search for a form of life that would be purified of the inclination to manipulate others in order to have our way. The secret was, initially without the knowledge of Emile, to convince him that nothing could be gained by such machinations and that reality was impervious to his demands and complaints. Confronted with an impermeable world he would learn to confine his desires within the limits of his powers, and thereby he would be perfectly one with his own impulses. Later, after meeting Sophie, Emile has to take a conscious role in his own formation and, by agreeing to an enforced separation between them, develop the requisite detachment from even his own most deeply felt desires that would enable him to be free. The result would be a man utterly without subterfuge because he is without the need for subterfuge, a man at home with himself and his world because he has no needs beyond what is within the powers of his attainment. All that he does flows freely from the goodness of his heart because no shadow of calculation intervenes between what he desires and what he can attain.

The point is not simply to listen to his heart because, as Rousseau acknowledged, one's heart was sometimes in conflict with itself or hankered after what was not possible. It was to listen to one's heart of hearts, the true self, which was only possible if one had gained the peace of inner detachment: "The fear of losing everything will prevent you from possessing anything. As a result of having wanted to follow only your own passions, you will never be able to satisfy them. . . . How will you know how to sacrifice inclination to duty and to hold out against your heart in order to listen to your reason?" (444). Tell me, he asks the young man in love, "at what crime a man stops when he has only the wishes of his heart for laws and knows how to resist nothing that he desires?" He must now learn to free himself even from the very best inclinations of his heart, his love for Sophie, and accept her loss and the finitude of their love, if he is to return with a love purged of all falsity and illusion. "Be a man. Restrain your heart within the limits of your condition. Study and know these limits. However narrow they may be, a man is not unhappy as long as he closes himself up within them" (445).

Emile is counseled to leave Sophie in order to learn the detachment from perishable things that can free his soul to attach itself only to what is imperishable. It is not a stoic resignation, a grim determination, that forms the core of this experience. Rousseau is quite clear that it is the filling of the soul with transcendent virtue that is the purpose of the kenotic surrender of all that is most dear. If he had remained as he was with her, then inevitably they would have sought the imperishable and the perfect in a relationship that could never be more than transient and imperfect. Illusion and deceit would have entered their world. Rousseau advises him to accept what he has already received as the best that can be attained and not to look for the "more than" that is bound to fall short. "Except for the single Being existing by itself, there is nothing beautiful except that which is not" (447). He had earlier alluded to the idea that "a truly happy being is a solitary being. God alone enjoys an absolute happiness," but had gone on to admit that "I do not conceive how someone who needs nothing . . . who loves nothing can be happy" (221). Now he seems to say that he does understand how detachment can lead to happiness, to the deepest happiness. It is perhaps not too far-fetched to suggest that the soul of Emile has grown in the course of the book to the point where he can perceive the greater reality of that independent Being. He now has a sense of the fullness of divine reality that can be open to all because it transcends all. Toward the close of the book, Emile acknowledges that his master has "made me free in teaching me to yield to necessity," and he resolves to persevere on this course. "If I were without passions," he recognizes, "I would, in my condition as a man, be independent like God himself" (472).

It was not, of course, that Rousseau ever achieved that state of divine autarky, but that it functioned as the inspirational telos of his thought. Rousseau's prescription for the attainment of virtue was not only to follow the spontaneous promptings of our heart but also to listen to the heart that had been shaped by the contemplation of all things sub specie aeternitatis. The culminating inspiration of his moral pedagogy was the Christian longing to see all things in God. When viewed in that perspective, we see all things rightly and are not confused in the measure we apply to them. Behind it is the incredibly powerful sense that it is only transcendent reality that is real and that all other realities of our experience are to that extent less real. The soul that is once touched by this realization must hunger for ascent toward what is lasting and true and the profound realization of the limitation of all the satisfactions available to us within this world. Behind all of Rousseau's variable impressive efforts to evoke the pure inner virtue that he recognized would be needed to sustain a self-governing order, there is the pull of the same Christian experience of the union with perfect transcendent reality as the source of its appeal.[8] Despite its dissolving tendencies, Rousseau's moral theory manages to retain a distinctly Christian character. This becomes clearest in the hands of the man who gave it formal philosophical shape.

Immanuel Kant is the one who gave philosophical precision to Rousseau's emphasis on the self-governing individual. Kant's analysis of the self-determining nature of reason represented a milestone in the unfolding of the liberal self-understanding. His achievement was to have made the necessity of self-determination unmistakably clear. Freedom of thought, the foundation of all other freedoms, is not simply a desirable option within a developed social condition, but "signifies the subjection of reason to no laws other than those *which it imposes on itself*" (*Political Writings,* 247). It is a necessity anchored in the nature of reason itself. Without free self-determination it is impossible to characterize an activity as rational, merely as the causal effect of certain forces on a human being. Embedded within our whole notion of moral action, that it springs from a good will that chooses its course for the sake of the goodness it wills, is that "the principle of action is free from all influence by contingent grounds" (*Groundwork of the Metaphysics of Morals,* 88). This is, of course, the famous categorical imperative, the absolute requirement of acting morally under all circumstances irrespective of what we derive from it.

Autonomy, the sense in which the will is free because it determines the laws it will follow, is the centerpiece of Kant's moral philosophy: "What else then can freedom of will be but autonomy—that is, the property which will has of being a law to itself?" (*Groundwork,* 107). The negative concept of freedom is that the will is independent of all alien causes, but positively it is what it is because it follows its own law of being free. "Thus a free will and a will under moral laws are one and the same" (108). The will is not causally determined as are all things in the sensible world because it determines itself to action on the basis of its willing of itself as a universal law. The categorical imperative that defines the rational will is that it follows the principle: "Act only on that maxim through which you can at the same time will that it should become a universal law" (84). In this way the action is willed for its own sake, its universal character free from all the contingencies of interest and circumstances. It is that action done out of pure duty, irrespective of inclinations or effects, that can alone "be an object of reverence and therewith a command" (66).

What is most intriguing is the point at which Kant wonders what it is that can move the will that has thereby established itself in its imperious independence. "But on this basis," he observes, "we can as yet have no insight into the principle that we ought to detach ourselves from such interest—that is, that we ought to regard ourselves as free in our actions and yet to hold ourselves bound by certain laws in order to find solely in our own person a worth which can compensate us for the loss of everything that makes our state valuable. We do not see how this is possible nor consequently *how the moral law can be binding*" (110). Kant admits that this is a "kind of circle" from which he does not see any means of escape. It is part of the larger antinomy between freedom and necessity that arises from our participation in the world of reason, things in themselves and, the world of sense, things as they appear. The one is governed by the free exercise of reason, the other by the pull of interest. We do not understand the relationship between them. "Hence for us men it is wholly impossible to explain how and why the *universality of a maxim as a law*—and therefore morality—should interest us" (120).

All that we can know, Kant maintains in one of those statements of heroic rationality, is that "the law is not valid for us *because it interests us*" (120). It is indeed the very sparseness of incorruptible duty that is the source of the moral appeal. There is a purity, a transcendence, in this stance that has no attraction beyond itself and is best reflected in the epithet of "dignity" that Kant assigns to it. "It is precisely in this," he observes, "that the worth of character begins to show—a moral worth and beyond all comparison the highest—namely, that he does good, not from inclination, but from duty" (64). Utterly bereft of all resources of support and encouragement that could move him toward the good, Kant's rational individual fulfills his duty solely from a sense of duty, because it is the universal law that he recognizes within his reason. He is a self-governing hero alone in the universe. In that sense, he deserves to be treated as an end in himself, the self-justifying condition of all other goods, that alone which is good in itself and therefore ought never be treated as a means. "Reason thus related every maxim of the will, considered as making universal law, to every other will and also to every action towards oneself: it does so, not because of any further motive or future advantage, but from the Idea of the *dignity* of a rational being who obeys no law other than that which he at the same time enacts himself" (96).

It is this splendid independence, the knowledge of one's fidelity to what is true no matter the cost, that can "compensate us for the loss of everything that makes our state valuable." In one respect it seems to lead toward that characteristic modern hubris in which human autonomy has grown to such proportions that it can stand independent of the whole world and even God himself. Kant would not, for example, have us act from the motive of gaining our eternal happiness or even out of service of God. That would be to seek our own interest and the essence of good action is that it is defined as good, as that which can be universally willed, irrespective of our own preferences and benefits. Indeed, he often seems to suggest that the goodness is problematic when the action coincides with our own interests, and that it is only action that is contrary to our interests that we can be sure conforms to the purity of goodness. That would seem to set Kant down the road of defiant independence even from God.

But it can also be read as the culmination of the Christian inspiration. Behind the demand for fidelity to duty for duty's sake is the Christian longing for purity and perfection that will not be satisfied even by the consolations of the spiritual life itself. The drive toward transcendence will not fall short of its goal. It will not be satisfied with the feeling of divinity, but only with the attainment of the reality. There is much of the language of Christian perfection in Kant, and it is more than a rhetorical penumbra to the rational analysis. While the rigors of the categorical imperative do not depend on the pull of Christian meaning, and its demands are self-justifying, the Christian tonality does provide an important insight into the attraction of the imperative itself. It is for this reason that the designation as secular Christianity, pronounced by Nietzsche and many others, is not far off the mark. Kant himself seems to acknowledge this in the deliberate invocation of the theological context as the necessary completion of the moral analysis.

Reason can be secure against error only if it confines itself within the parameters of its spatiotemporal experience. It has no access to what lies outside those limits, but it cannot avoid adumbrating the realities that lie beyond them. This is in the nature of "a felt need of reason" (*Political Writings*, 243) that directs us toward realities beyond reason but that are nevertheless necessary for the functioning of reason, especially practical reason. Kant particularly included as such "postulates of reason" the idea of God and the immortality of the soul. Thus reason cannot establish the existence of God who lies beyond the sensory world of our experience, but it must postulate his reality as the indispensable foundation of its own moral order.

> It does so not in order to derive from it the binding authority of the moral laws or the motive for observing them (for they would have no moral value if the motive for obeying them were derived from anything other than the law alone, which is apodictically certain of itself), but only in order to give objective reality to the concept of the highest good—i.e. to prevent the latter, along with morality *[Sittlichkeit]* as a whole, from being regarded merely as an ideal, as would be the case if that [being] whose idea is an inseparable accompaniment to morality *[Moralität]* did not itself exist. (243)

This is not an easy passage to interpret. Why, we might ask, is it necessary to be assured of the reality of the highest good if it is not to play any essential role in the formation of the good will?

The answer is that Kant is already convinced in his own rational will that morality is not simply an "ideal," a pure "ought" that may or may not be realized. He knows it already as a reality in the self-governing rationality of his will. It is the most real reality there is, what calls him to fidelity as the ultimate meaning of his existence compared to which the loss of everything else in life pales into insignificance. His participation in the transcendent order is not a mere postulate, but the most convincing reality of his existence. God is, in this sense, not the ground or motive for his good conduct, but the culmination of it in transcendent Being itself. The postulation of God and the immortality of the soul is the affirmation of the transcendent finality of the person who transcends the finitude of all interest and inclination. As such they are not postulates, but extrapolations from the experience itself.[9]

Kant presents us with a purified Christianity, purged even of the attraction of transcendence, in its utterly selfless elimination of all motives but the love of what is right. Even if religion is no longer the motive, the process can be described only in religious terms. Kant talks about the difficulty of explaining this appeal of that which is beyond all appeal. It contradicts our ordinary experience "that no idea can so greatly elevate the human mind and inspire it with such enthusiasm as that of a pure moral conviction, respecting duty above all else, struggling with countless evils of existence and even with their most seductive temptations, and yet overcoming them—for we may rightly assume that man can do so." Then he goes on to draw the conclusion that it reveals the spark of divine being that ultimately draws man from the very depths of his soul. "The fact that man is aware that he can do this just because he ought to discloses within him an ample store of divine capabilities and inspires him, so to speak, with a holy awe at the greatness and sublimity of his true vocation" (71).

The clearest indication of the transcendent impact of the good will is to be found in Kant's faith in its transfigurative power in the conflict with evil. Although Kant tossed off the infamous remark that "the problem of setting up a state can be solved even by a nation of devils (so long as they possess understanding)" (112), it does not seem to have reflected his deepest perspective on the problem. He recognized the possibility of "radical evil" within man and was dismissive of the romantic notion that goodness could result from the natural processes themselves (197). Nor, despite his subscription to the outlook of the Enlightenment did he believe that "the basic moral capacity of mankind will increase in the slightest, for this would require a kind of new creation or supernatural influence" (188). But when he contemplated the imperious exigencies of the good will he recognized its transcendent power that is capable of transforming evil into good. This was the source of his melioristic historical vision.

Man, he recognized, cannot escape the concept of right. Its dreadful presence will impose itself upon him and prevent him from being openly opportunistic. The inexorable march of right will assert itself within the human heart and society, persisting in its disturbing effect until it is accorded due recognition of its preeminence. "We may therefore," Kant observes, "offer the following advice: 'Seek ye first the kingdom of pure practical reason and its *righteousness* and your object (the blessing of perpetual peace) will be added unto you' " (*Political Writings*, 123). No goal, not even the loftiest social good, must be allowed to stand in its way. Let justice reign, even though the whole world perish, may "sound somewhat inflated, but it is nevertheless true." Its truth is contained in the conviction that right is a superior reality to evil and that, in the conflict between them, right is bound to prevail so long as its full transcendent stature is allowed to emerge. The "courage of virtue . . . does not so much consist, in the present case, in resolutely standing up to the evils and sacrifices which must be encountered, as in facing the evil principle within ourselves and overcoming its wiles" (124).

The transcendent power of right within his own soul had convinced Kant that the same process would sooner or later spread to the social scale. If we assume "that the pure principles of right have an objective reality," then they must inexorably expand to the point that they crowd out the unreality of historical political practice. "For all politics must bend the knee before right, although politics may hope in return to arrive, however slowly, at a stage of lasting brilliance" (125). The "sacred" character of rights will govern the political reality more and more as the progress of reason and guilt at its violation draw in an ever larger circle of human beings. The expectation of moral progress in some general sense is an inseparable idea from Christianity, and Kant, while acknowledging that its structure is "beyond our understanding," insists that it also cannot be dismissed from our historical situation. "If we suppose that mankind never can and will be in a better condition, it seems impossible to justify by any kind of theodicy the mere fact that such a race of corrupt beings could have been created on earth at all" (124–25).

No doubt there is a kind of brittleness to Kant's secularized Christianity. To the extent that it has become more secular it has to that degree lost touch with the full amplitude of Christianity itself. This is most apparent in the naïveté of the treatment of evil that seems never to confront the deepest suspicions that it might infect even our most exalted convictions of right and consequently that caution, self-examination, and humility must remain our watchwords. It is equally in evidence in the gullibility of the Enlightenment view of historical progress that, from the hindsight of our own moral catastrophes, appears terminally obtuse. Whatever the providential order of history we must now confess, with a good deal more humility, that God's ways are indeed inscrutable to us. But having noted all those qualifications, it must also be admitted that Kant conjoined a powerful evocation of transcendence with the liberal aspiration of self-government. He showed that the liberal reason, the source of the call for self-government, is at its best a fidelity to the imperious exigencies of morality that has hitherto received its fullest expression within the Christian ideal. As a consequence, the prodigious influence he has exercised, extending up to the liberal idealism of Rawls and our contemporaries, arises from the resonance that his philosophy evokes within a Christianly formed civilization.

What Kant did not do was to connect his philosophy with Christianity, to make clear the extent to which it depended on the Christian inspiration and correlatively exemplified the philosophic refraction of that inspiration. That was the task of Kant's successors, but especially Hegel.[10] We have already seen Hegel's elaboration of the constitutive spiritual order of the liberal state, and there is no need to add anything further to that account. What this chapter is concerned with is the inner appeal of the liberal order, and it will suffice to focus on Hegel's clarification of that nexus. His contribution is to have highlighted what Kant overlooked, the recognition of the liberal order as the culmination of Christianity. The appeal of self-determination is the transcending of all motivations of interest and inclination, a rational appeal, but it is a real transcendence into the mode of divine spirit intimated by Christianity.

Hegel recognized that Kant had clarified the movement toward self-transcendence but had not identified the nature or significance of his discovery. He had not understood it as the secular form of Christianity or the Christian form of the secular. Kant had not recognized the Christian character of his philosophy. He had articulated the human capacity to transcend all the limitations of interest and inclination, in willing the universal, but had not adverted to its identity with the religious overcoming of self in union with the transcendent divinity. God and the immortality of the soul do not have to be introduced apologetically as "postulates," for they denote the reality of the self-transcending movement of the soul. They are realized in the experience itself. Hegel is the one who reminds the Kantian good will that its own very selflessness, transcending even its desire for God, is the reality of transcendent being made actual. It is the mode of our participation in the lasting of divine Being.[11]

The power of Hegel's construction is that he shows that the divine is not merely an aspiration or a postulate, but is to be found at the outer limits of our experience. Kant had shown what those limits are, but Hegel demonstrated that knowing the limits is already a knowledge of what is beyond them. We do not have to look for the divine in that beyond that is defined as precisely that which cannot be attained, but have merely to open to the recognition of its presence as constitutive of the structure of our experience. The liberal state, as the most faithful embodiment of the human capacity for transcendent self-determination, is the participation in the spirit of divine Being. It is "the march of God in the world," although it is not God. Hegel had identified the secret of the appeal of Kant's categorical imperative as the appeal of that which lies beyond all appeal. It is the participation in transcendent reality itself that constitutes the movement beyond all considerations of motive or return. The categorical imperative is not a means to this participation; it is it, and there is nothing further behind it.

In that sense, Hegel adds nothing to Kant's analysis. He merely expands its meaning and in that lie all the consequences. The effect is to liberate the spiritual power of morality so that it no longer appears as a precarious individual effort, but as the formidable movement toward more eminent reality with a force of its own. It is revealed, as it had covertly exerted its irrefragable pull within the earlier analysis, as the irresistible presence of transcendent being. The separation of religion and morality, which had seemed so prominent within the modern liberal disposition, was exposed in its untenability. Kant had strained it to the point of breaking, and Hegel gave the final impetus that dissolved it entirely. Not only did the liberal order not separate from religion, but it could be properly understood only as an unfolding of the Christian movement toward self-transcendence. Just as self-government is rooted in the human necessity of self-determination, the latter is rooted in the capacity for self-transcendence revealed in the Christian participation in the utter transcendence of God. Liberal order is the deepest political expression of Christianity.

Ironically, Hegel is also the point at which the liberal exaltation of self-determining transcendence comes closest to eclipsing Christianity. The danger of absorbing the divine substance into the human is well illustrated in the messianic self-aggrandizements that occur after Hegel. His own construction teeters on the brink with its enormously skillful interconnection of the liberal and the Christian drives toward participation in transcendent reality. The result can be so successful that it constitutes a world sufficient unto itself, suggesting that there is no participation in Being except through the inner elaboration of rational liberal self-determination. All the threads are interwoven so successfully that there seems to be nothing left over. There is no need for any other transcendence once its necessity has been exhausted within the liberal interrelationships. It was an impressive intellectual achievement, but, more significant, it had a powerful spiritual impact. All that was missing was the rest of reality outside of the self-conscious relationship. There is the reality in depth of God and man, the world and society, which cannot simply be absorbed into the internal dynamics of the relationship of self-transcendence nor be rendered wholly transparent to our understanding. All that we have is a perspective on reality through our participation; we cannot comprehend it. The effort to expand our vision beyond that vantage point can only result in the tragic distortion of the reality in which we live.[12]

The result was that the Hegelian synthesis fell apart, and its good and bad parts went their separate ways. The evil consequences in the megalomaniacal schemes for revolutionary transformation of reality—as they were unfolded in Marxism, anarchism, fascism, and nationalism—have overshadowed the positive components of Hegel's deep understanding. No one has taken up his theme of the Christian realization of the liberal impulse with comparable depth and range. It has been left to float as one of the disconnected suggestions within our fragmentary intellectual and political landscape. Many have suspected that there is such a connection but, without the necessary philosophical means, have been unable to establish the relationship so firmly enunciated by Hegel. Missing has been his sensitivity to the inner dimensions of the experience of self-determining transcendence that would make it possible to recognize its equivalence to the Christian movement of pure abnegation of self that draws the soul toward God.[13] The best that can be said of Hegel's immediate liberal successors is that they had an intimation of the connection, but lacked the philosophical resources to articulate it. The rectification of that defect is the principal purpose of the present work.

Transcendent Source of Liberty

Even though the Christian constitution of liberal order has not subsequently been articulated with the philosophic depth of a Kant or a Hegel, it is not surprising to discover powerful intimations of the relationship as it confronts the crises of the next two centuries. They are centuries of a more self-consciously liberal direction precisely because, as we saw in the last chapter, of the challenges that faced it. The crises that periodically seem to sweep over the liberal tradition in the period up to the present derive in part from those challenges, but also from the uncertainty of the liberal tradition bereft of profound philosophical foundations. We have seen the results in the profusion of attempts at finding such a foundation, but there is also the less noticeable deepening of the convictions themselves. Even in the absence of a coherent unfolding, the confrontation with the destructive abyss before it has always caused a deepening of the liberal resolve and a return to the spiritual traditions that have historically underpinned it. When liberal convictions are pinned to the wall, Nietzsche observed, they will reveal their true foundation as Christianity.

Despite the claims of the revolutions through which he lived, Tocqueville declared, "I do not clearly perceive that they are liberal" (*Democracy in America*, 2:333). The nineteenth century, for all its liberal reputation, was really the age in which liberal thought began to comprehend the gathering storm that would politically overwhelm it in the twentieth century. Few identified the structure of that impending catastrophe with more acuity than Tocqueville. He understood it as a perversion of the very principles of liberal freedom itself in its contest with the correlative impulse toward equality. His writings call us again and again to the distinction between these intermingled but rival principles. The liberal revolution, which had begun with the demand for freedom, was in danger of selling its birthright for a mess of equality purchased at the cost of that same freedom. "They had sought to be free in order to make themselves equal; but in proportion as equality was more established by the aid of freedom, freedom itself was thereby rendered more difficult of attainment" (333). No one evokes the specter of this new, more dreadful (because more pervasive) despotism than Tocqueville in his reflections on the tyranny of universal equality.[14]

Nothing was more desultory to his mind than the prospect of the egalitarian society, because "when men are all alike they are all weak, and the supreme power of the state is naturally much stronger among democratic nations than elsewhere" (299). Equality was only possible through that shrinking of men to the status of interchangeable atoms, no one exercising any more power, influence, or prestige than any other. But that also meant that they were equally poor in the resources for taking care of themselves. They might be equally powerful, but they were also equally powerless. Unable therefore to find the means of satisfying their needs in themselves or in others, they were left with no other protection than that provided by the state. The latter loomed larger in the lives of individuals who conversely had less independence over against it. It was "a new species of oppression" that menaced democratic nations, for which the old words *tyranny* and *despotism* were no longer appropriate because "it would be more extensive and more mild; it would degrade men without tormenting them" (335).

That was the core of the problem foreseen by the most prescient of the nineteenth-century thinkers and acknowledged as the commonplace reality of our own century. At stake was the very humanity of these men who, in their egalitarian powerlessness, were ready to turn over the care of their lives to an all-powerful guardian. The portrait he paints is arrestingly close to the comprehensive security apparatus of our own welfare state. Its force of penetration makes it worth quoting in full.

> Above this race of men stands an immense and tutelary power, which takes upon itself alone to secure their gratifications and to watch over their fate. That power is absolute, minute, regular, provident, and mild. It would be like the authority of a parent if, like that authority, its object was to prepare men for manhood; but it seeks, on the contrary, to keep them in perpetual childhood: it is well content that the people should rejoice, provided they think of nothing but rejoicing. For their happiness such a government willingly labors, but it chooses to be the sole agent and the only arbiter of that happiness; it provides for their security, foresees and supplies their necessities, facilitates their pleasures, manages their principal concerns, directs their industry, regulates the descent of property, and subdivides their inheritances: what remains, but to spare them all the care of thinking and all the trouble of living? (336)

Tocqueville well understood the insidious dimension of equality that has "predisposed men to endure [these things] and often to look on them as benefits" (337).

They deceive themselves with the illusion that they are still governing themselves, merely because they have preserved the "outward forms of freedom." Their divergent passions are that "they want to be led, and that they wish to remain free." Instead of confronting the impossibility of their aspirations and learning to overcome them, they give way to the conceit that they are not being controlled because they have elected their controllers. Tocqueville recognized the cruel reality of this illusion because it robbed them of their most precious possession, not simply their freedom, but the growth of their humanity that only the exercise of free self-responsibility makes possible. Like the aristocrats of French society under the ancien régime, democratic man had become victim to the comforting illusion that it was possible to maintain all of the privileges of their station without shouldering any of the obligations. "Every man allows himself to be put in leading-strings, because he sees that it is not a person or a class of persons, but the people at large who hold the end of his chain" (337).

The answer, however, is not to be found in turning away from equality by attempting a restoration of some form of aristocratic privilege. Tocqueville, despite his sympathy and deep appreciation of the role of an aristocracy as a bulwark against despotism, was "persuaded that all who attempt in the ages upon which we are entering, to base freedom upon aristocratic privilege will fail" (340). His own stature as a thinker is demonstrated in this steadfast refusal to take the easy way out by indulging in respectable, but ineffectual, evocations of a vanished past. Only those who have weathered the storm can claim the victory over it. Rather than turn his back in condemnation of the spirit of the age, Tocqueville endured it, contemplated its depth, and found his way through to a transformation that pointed beyond it. He is one of the great heros of the liberal canon because he suffered through its crisis to a reconciliation of its most radical disjunction between liberty and equality.

Tocqueville's most profound insight was that liberty and equality could not be separated. At root they came from the same source, the equal right that each human being possesses to decide how they are going to live subject to no other restraints than the law that applies to all. Once the logic of this understanding of a common human nature—highlighted by the teaching of Jesus Christ "that all members of the human race are by nature equal and alike" (17)—has taken hold, it is not plausible to expect that it will be reversed. A direction has been set that renders a return to the hierarchical order of aristocracy virtually impossible. "Nothing can be imagined more contrary to nature and the secret instincts of the human heart" than this assignation of permanent authority of one group of men over the rest. "Aristocratic institutions cannot exist without laying down the inequality of men as a fundamental principle, legalizing it beforehand and introducing it into the family as well as into society; but these are things so repugnant to natural equity that they can only be extorted from men by force" (438).

There was no alternative but to confront the abyss of egalitarian power-lessness and find within it the forces of resistance capable of surmounting it. The desire for equality must be taught to yield to the desire for liberty. It was the urge to live freely that had driven the movement for the abo-lition of all illegitimate privilege and authority; the same impulse can be the means of resisting the descent to nothingness without liberty. We must not, Tocqueville warns, "confound the principle of equality itself with the revolution which finally establishes that principle in the social condition and the laws of a nation" (*Democracy in America*, 2:332). His whole work might be seen as one long contemplation of the nightmare of egalitarian despotism as a way of resuscitating the contrary force of liberty that is alone capable of opposing it. In that project Tocqueville was moderately successful both as a warning within the liberal tradition and, more important, in pointing toward a therapeutic expansion of the resources of the liberal order itself. He identified the existential depths from which the liberal inspiration springs through an enlargement of the soul beyond the liberal boundaries.

The prospect of imminent self-destruction is what awakens in Tocqueville one of the most powerful evocations of liberty in the modern world. Re-flecting on the drift he witnessed toward socialism, which he traced back to the political economists of the eighteenth century in their preference for governmental solutions, he speculates on what it is that makes men accept so lowly a condition of existence as to live under the tutelage of others. The contrast with those who cannot endure the idea of not being their own masters is striking. They have lost that transcendent spark that moves men to set aside all considerations of practicality and efficiency, even life itself, as secondary compared to the freedom to "speak, live, and breathe freely, owing obedience to no authority save God and the laws of the land" (*The Old Regime and the French Revolution*, 169). It is difficult to pinpoint the exact nature of that impulse, but we can know that it is that condition without which no other benefits are worth having. "It is easy to see," Tocqueville observes about those nations who have chosen a comfortable slavery, "that what is lacking in such nations is a genuine love of freedom, that lofty aspiration which (I confess) defies analysis. For it is something one must *feel* and logic has no part in it. It is a privilege of noble minds which God has fitted to receive it, and it inspires them with a generous fervor. But to meaner souls, untouched by the sacred flame, it may well seem incomprehensible" (169).

The challenge was to fan the "sacred flame" to light in those souls left relatively untouched by it. A means must be discovered of stirring to life what a liberal order depended on but could not directly produce. The key was to be found, Tocqueville was convinced, in the very condition of equality that threatened to overwhelm liberty. In the equality of their social condition modern men and women lacked any ready-made hierarchy of responsibility. Instead of throwing off their problems onto the government or their social superiors, they must be persuaded to undertake the initiatives themselves. Their individual powerlessness must become the occasion for prompting the exercise of liberty in schemes of voluntary cooperation within their local communities. Individually they can do nothing so they are compelled to act together, but the only means of concerting their actions is through the persuasion that draws them into a free convergence of their efforts. It is the very circumstance of their equal isolation and impotence that calls forth the necessity of a free conjunction of wills. This was the genius of the American arrangement, as Tocqueville understood it and made it the centerpiece of his own political theory. The circumstances in which they were placed and the political tradition they brought with them conspired to develop highly the "art of association," of winning the free cooperation of all in accomplishing the public good. "Thus it is by the enjoyment of a dangerous freedom that the Americans learn the art of rendering the dangers of freedom less formidable" (*Democracy in America*, 2:127).

Such voluntary associations are not the most elegant or efficient. They lack the rationality of a centralized administration, but they are a hundred times more powerful and beneficial for a society. Compared to the European experience of oscillating wildly between servitude and license, Tocqueville found in the American polity a stability that was more reliable for all its untidiness. Ultimately, there is no real political power except through the voluntary union of wills; a coercive structure renders only the appearance of power that dissolves once the constraint is relaxed. Even in the case of absolute governments it is always patriotism or religion that is the source of their power, not the apparatus of compulsion (1:97). Democratic regimes, lacking even the elementary means of coercion, are from the start thrown onto the need for such sentiments of cohesion. If they wish to avoid the despotic recourse, then they must turn in some way to the American example of encouraging the elaboration of liberty.

The result, Tocqueville observed, is not only a more reliable means of addressing public problems but also the more invisible, although more crucial, avenue of the inner growth of the citizens in self-responsibility. "Feelings and opinions are recruited, the heart is enlarged, and the human mind is developed only by the reciprocal influence of men upon one another" (2:117). Through exercising the art of association they acquire a taste for cooperation and develop the virtues indispensable to the maintenance of the order in which they live. This explained why in America, composed of such a diversity of human types and backgrounds, with so little of a common world to bind them together, he nevertheless found a level of patriotism and commitment to the common good that was higher than any in Europe. The Americans had hit on the way of linking the individual to the community that had little to do with the satisfaction of interest. Or, rather, by letting the satisfaction of their interests depend on their own efforts, the American scheme encouraged the emergence of those virtues that as the highest expression of freedom direct men beyond the calculation of interest. It exemplified Tocqueville's observation that, in the contemporary democratic setting, "the only means we still possess of interesting men in the welfare of their country is to make them partakers in the government" (1:252).

The self-government of the townships of New England was so natural that it "seems to come directly from the hand of God" (1:62). But everywhere he went in America, Tocqueville was struck by the self-reliant dignity of a people taking care of themselves, spontaneously forming into groups or associations in order to address public problems that elsewhere the government might be expected to resolve. The value of permitting and encouraging people to take the initiative themselves, for all of its untidiness, was incalculable. More than any of the practical benefits that accrued was the growth of the soul that occurred in the discovery of the value of freedom itself. The exercise of that free self-direction itself was recognized as the transcendent end of the whole order, outweighing the value of any of the particular goods obtained through the structure of cooperation. It accords perfectly with Tocqueville's recommendation to not put as much store on doing great things as on making men great, "to set less value on the work and more upon the workman" (2:347).

He was not overly sanguine that this counsel would be followed, for the concluding pages of *Democracy in America* are as heavy with foreboding as anything written in the past two hundred years. But he knew that the movement of liberty was inexorable. The impulse that had devolved into the demand for equality had its roots in the aspiration for liberty. For that reason it could not be reversed without endangering liberty itself. Only the transcendent force of liberty contained an antidote strong enough to counteract the poisonous effects of the resentment behind egalitarianism. By learning through experience to know the pull of the noble cord of freedom, of the gift of self in the service of others, men could discover a force within themselves stronger than envy and self-gratification. They would make the discovery that lies at the core of Tocqueville's worldview, "that nothing but the love and the habit of freedom can maintain an advantageous contest with the love and the habit of physical well-being" (2:301). Just as the movement toward equality seemed irresistible to human modification, so only the transcendent force of freedom within it seemed capable of initiating its transformation.

Tocqueville was deeply impressed with the sense of the providential forces at work within history. Man was not simply at the mercy of his own resources. The contemplation of the vast social and political movement toward equality, the irresistible movement toward universal participation in government, and the democratic revolutions all put him in mind of the inscrutable divine providence that governs the whole process. In his introduction he recounts how the whole book "has been written under the influence of a kind of religious awe" at the prospect of the unfolding movement of history. For centuries it has been moving inexorably in the constant direction of an expansion of the liberty that guarantees equal participation in government. The progressive movement toward ever broader social equality has "the sacred character of a divine decree," and any attempt to check or oppose it would be like trying "to resist the will of God" (1:7). Such remarks should not be dismissed as rhetorical window dressing—his French readers on his own admission were as likely to be atheists—because they represent a spirit of reverence that pervades the work as its defining horizon. They represent the faith on which his conviction of the nobility of liberty rested and the source of his confidence in the vindication of its rightness. Even in the face of the real dangers it invited, Tocqueville had a faith that made it impossible to turn aside from liberty.

A similar sense of the transcendent force of liberty is discernible behind the writings of Tocqueville's greatest nineteenth-century reader, Mill. Often it is buried beneath surface appeals to the utilitarian value of individual inventiveness, but it cannot be completely concealed. Only a transcendent valuation of liberty accounts for the intensity of the convictions expressed. Mill never considers that liberty might be weighed within the utilitarian calculus. Rather, it is what constitutes the measure of utility. This becomes evident in the occasional outbursts where he throws utility overboard and steps forward to declare the indefeasibility of a transcendent order of right. In searching for an explanation of what it is that makes human beings so incapable of settling for anything less than the attainment of their full moral stature, he could find no better name for it than that "sense of dignity . . . which is so essential a part of the happiness of those in whom it is that nothing which conflicts with it could be, otherwise than momentarily, an object of desire to them" (*On Liberty and Other Essays,* 140). The reflections in *The Subjection of Women* provoked a particularly strong affirmation of freedom as "the first and strongest want of human nature" (576). He conceives it as a force with such ennobling power that he regards it as the only effectual means of quelling the contrary impulse of domination in human nature. "The desire of power over others can only cease to be a depraving agency among mankind, when each of them individually is able to do without it; which can only be where respect for liberty in the personal concerns of each is an established principle" (578).

As so often in the history of the liberal tradition, the scale of the threat confronting it galvanized some of the most powerful declarations of the indispensability of freedom that have ever been made. If the nineteenth century was the time when liberal convictions first came under the characteristically modern threat, it was also the time of its most enduring self-affirmations. But it was not within liberal circles that its deepest confirmation was to be found. Tocqueville and, to a lesser extent, Mill had reestablished the transcendent dimension of liberty within a social setting where the liberal impulse was in danger of becoming the victim of its own success. As liberal principles had led to a dramatic expansion of the franchise, the prospect of democratic despotism reared its ugly head. There was no guarantee that the newly enfranchised masses would use their freedom responsibly. They might just as readily turn it over to populist demagogues or pervert it into a means of forcing their prejudices on more-independent-minded minorities. How was it possible to ensure that freedom would not be abused and, if it was not possible to guide it, how could liberty be asserted as the highest value?

These are the questions that disturbed the nineteenth-century liberals and all their successors. Its presence in the background casts a pall over the confident expectations of historical progress, because it suggests that the "experiment" in self-government might ultimately prove stillborn and that men cannot be entrusted with their own liberty. The problem, as they conceived it in large measure, was to develop the institutional structures to absorb the enfranchised masses without jeopardizing the order of the liberal state. Mill's "Considerations on Representative Government" is a classic of this type of reflection on the reforms that might be introduced to preserve a liberal order when it becomes a mass democracy. His proposals were directed at moderating the two principal dangers of the poor quality of elected representatives and their propensity to engage in "class legislation" (chap. 7). The American founders were even more prescient concerning these problems and developed an impressive array of Constitutional devices to moderate the majoritarian tendencies of a popularly elected government. The subsequent experience of liberal democracies has largely been one of muddling through the dangers, pragmatically adjusting reforms in light of trial-and-error experiences to arrive at moderately stable constitutions. But the fundamental question has not been confronted, and that failure contributes more today than ever to the confusion afflicting the liberal tradition. Is liberty worth the risk?

To find an appropriately weighty response, it is necessary to look beyond the usual liberal range to a thinker who is not generally included within it but whose spiritual depth enabled him to reach a level of insight indispensable to, yet not easily accessible from, the liberal perspective. Fyodor Dostoyevsky provided the most profound defense of liberty of the century in large measure because he was not tied to the boundaries of the liberal vocabulary. He was willing to acknowledge that the value of liberty needed to be defended, and not simply treated as the mute premise of all further discussion. In an age when liberty was about to come under attack he recognized that its indispensability would have to be established, however difficult that might prove to be. If that required a meditation on the value of liberty beyond the parameters of an immanentist analysis, then Dostoyevsky was prepared to follow it through. In this way the Russian novelist became the one to articulate the connection with transcendence that was inchoately present but nowhere fully explicated within the liberal tradition itself. Dostoyevsky uncovers the Christian depth of the liberal impulse.

The most celebrated locus for this reflection is of course "The Legend of the Grand Inquisitor." It is the point where Dostoyevsky fully confronts the question of whether the value of human liberty outweighs all the evil and misery that appears to be its unavoidable consequence. In what does its pricelessness consist that it outweighs all of the destructiveness it makes possible? The great merit of Dostoyevsky's analysis is that he poses the question with a depth and intensity that explore its outermost limits. He does not attempt to soften its impact, because he wants to test the case for liberty in juxtaposition with the strongest case that can be made against it. The result, he knew, would be the attainment of a strength of conviction that could withstand the assault of the worst attacks that could be mounted against it. Dostoyevsky, while not generally counted a liberal thinker, has earned his place in the liberal canon because at this one crucial point he contemplated and surmounted the most devastating assault on liberty.

The legend recounts the unannounced return of Christ to earth in sixteenth-century Seville. It is the height of the Spanish Inquisition and against the background of the practice of auto-da-fé, Christ reappears to disturb the peace. The old cardinal, the Grand Inquisitor, has "solved" the problem of order by keeping his charges in a state of unthinking subservience. They have turned over the direction of their lives to him, and he alone carries the burden of the responsibility for decision; relieved of the need to think for themselves they can live out their days in endless carefree contentment. Proud of his achievement in establishing this perfect order, the Inquisitor pronounces their inability to obtain the means of subsistence without his tutelage. "No science will give them bread so long as they remain free. In the end they will lay their freedom at our feet, and say to us, 'Make us your slaves, but feed us'" (*The Brothers Karamazov*, 300).

The greatest challenge to this somnolent utopia is the humble presence of Christ walking among the people. All can sense who he is, the Inquisitor most of all, and he orders his arrest and detention. The greatest part of the story is taken up with the conversation that takes place between them in the darkened dungeon to which the old cardinal has descended for this most intimate of meetings. He knows that Christ is the one before whom he must be judged, for it is only Christ who is the measure of the love that must govern human life. The claim to be acting in the name of humanity, to have placed the service of human beings above all other considerations, must stand in the light of Christ's transcending love. For this reason the Inquisitor is drawn to the interrogation to test the strength of his own resolve. Only if it can stand before the divine gaze can he be assured of its indomitable self-sufficiency, of his own unqualified rightness.

The challenge for Dostoyevsky is to find a plausible means of presenting this transcendent encounter. How is it possible to represent Christ without softening or reducing his awful divine presence? It is a well-known problem of religious art—but especially in an age when the divine no longer elicits the response of awe, and reactions can verge on the blasé. Dostoyevsky solved it in an utterly convincing manner by presenting Christ as the silent interlocutor, yet the most powerful presence in the dialogue. It remains a dialogue, and we obtain a profound sense of the reality of Christ, by virtue of the depth and intensity of responses he evokes in the old cardinal. The conversation never becomes a monologue because the Inquisitor, who has come down to conduct the interrogation, is the one who feels compellingly under interrogation. It is the Inquisitor's response to the divine judgment so implacably, yet unaccusingly, embodied in Christ.

The Inquisitor is, moreover, up to the occasion. It is as if he has been preparing for the contest all his life. He has an answer to the judgment that he has failed humanity by asking men to settle for less than their full human stature. He knows that in convincing them to abandon their freedom he has colluded in their descent into the subhuman. But he is confident that his motives can withstand the examination. His trump card is the condition in which the divine accession to human freedom has left us. The Inquisitor is quite prepared to countenance the immodesty of the assertion that he has "joined the ranks of those *who have corrected Thy work*" (308). They have rendered Christ superfluous and now resent the prospect of his return that can serve only to disturb the work they have undertaken in his name. But it is no longer Christ's work, for that was ineradicably flawed through the affliction of human freedom. The Inquisitor is prepared to defend the superiority of his judgment.

The gift of freedom, he asserts, is only of value to those who are capable of using it wisely. What of the many for whom it is an unutterable burden, who can find no other use for it but to destroy themselves and one another? What is the value of caring for and saving only the elect? Even the elect have begun to raise their banner of freedom against God. "But with us all will be happy and will no more rebel, nor destroy one another as under Thy freedom." Of course the Inquisitor will continue to persuade them that in surrendering their freedom they are exercising and preserving it. "And shall we be right," he asks with unflappable slyness, "or shall we by lying?" It is a performance of matchless subtlety from a man who knows exactly what he is doing and has been completely in charge of every situation in his life.

> They will be convinced that we are right, for they will remember the horrors of slavery and confusion to which Thy freedom brought them. Freedom, free thought and science, will lead them into such straits and will bring them

face to face with such marvels and insoluble mysteries that some of them, the fierce and rebellious, will destroy themselves; others, rebellious but weak, will destroy one another, while the rest, weak and unhappy, will crawl fawning to our feet and whine to us: "Yes, you were right, you alone possess His mystery, and we come back to you, save us from ourselves." (306–7)

There is even a touch of nobility about the role of the Inquisitor and his assistants who have sacrificed their own souls for the sake of the contented millions. "There will be thousands of millions of happy babes, and a hundred thousand sufferers who have taken upon themselves the curse of the knowledge of good and evil" (308). The unthinking masses will live out their subhuman lives, and "beyond the grave they will find nothing but death." Only the suffering elite will face the prospect of judgment, but these nobly guilty few will surely be able to hold their heads up high on that day. They will be able to "stand up and point out to Thee the thousand millions of happy children who have known no sin. And we who have taken their sins upon us for their happiness will stand up before Thee and say: 'Judge us if Thou canst and darest'" (308). The Inquisitor is among those who had been prepared to follow Christ into the desert, "I too prized the freedom with which Thou hast blessed men, and I too was striving to stand among Thy elect." But then he turned away and "would not serve madness." He could not accept that "billions of God's creatures had been created as a mockery" to the freedom they will never be able to use (310). "I left the proud and went back to the humble, for the happiness of the humble" (308).

The sincerity of his intentions is belied only by the disturbing consideration of the alternative to the divine gift of freedom. He is perfectly correct that many, perhaps most, human beings are destined to make a cruel misuse of their freedom. But what is the alternative? Is it the embrace of the beastlike imbecility of the Inquisitor's happy masses? Is there not something even worse about their slobbering dumbness precisely because it has been adopted so self-consciously? They seem to have sunk to a level of degradation that has removed all that makes them human. In their brute ignorance they seem to have lost all that made them worth serving in the first place. Even the Inquisitor can barely conceal the contempt he harbors for the very beings for whom he has sacrificed his soul. Having failed miserably in their efforts to rule themselves they slouch toward the one who can control them, "the beast will crawl to us and lick our feet and spatter them with tears of blood" (306). Is the solution to the self-destructiveness of human freedom the abandonment of their humanity?

There can be no denying the depth of the quandary in which we find ourselves. We cannot reject our freedom without losing our humanity, nor can we avoid the admission of the untold misery it has brought upon us. The flaw of the Inquisitor was his insistence that the tension must be resolved. It is the state of mind that insists that the uncertainties of the human condition be removed, that we shift from the state of struggling fidelity to our deepest intimations to the perfection in which all things have been settled. He represents the type of the dark utopian who is prepared to accept a world less than it might be, if he cannot attain the ideal that cannot be realized. What he cannot tolerate is the ambivalence of the human situation characterized by a freedom that can neither be perfected nor annihilated. It is an ambivalence that pervades the liberal perspective that might be identified as a fidelity to all of its tensional components. The crucial question it provokes is: What can sustain that fidelity in the face of the temptations to abandon it?

The question is posed by the way in which Dostoyevsky unfolds the self-disclosure of the Inquisitor. He articulates with a clarity that remains unsurpassed the concern that had troubled all the great nineteenth-century liberals. If men are to enjoy an ever expanding domain of freedom, how can we be sure they will exercise it responsibly? What is it about human beings that makes them worthy of the risk of the horrible abuse of freedom? The Inquisitor's reflections bring that question to the point of transparence. He shows, but he does not say, that the tensional demands of the human condition can be accepted only if they are underpinned by an acceptance of the mystery of its pulls that are experienced but never fully comprehended. The relationship of its dimensions cannot be definitively penetrated from the human side. The assurance of their order can be provided only by the revelation of the transcendent goodness from which they have been derived. We can sense but we cannot get beyond the good in which we participate. The attempt to escape the condition of the pulls and counterpulls to stand in judgment over it, the impulse to dominate or resolve the whole, can only ruin our attraction toward the good.

What provokes this realization is the silent unaccusing presence of Christ. He says nothing throughout the exchange but we know him through the ever more shrill assertions of the Inquisitor who cannot be at peace so long as the unconditional acceptance of Christ is there before him. The inner contradiction of the Inquisitor's position becomes inescapable. He has rendered men less than human out of love for them but in the process has deprived them of all that makes them lovable. The contempt in which he holds mankind is no longer disguised. Standing over against it is the inexpressible depth of divine love incarnate in Christ. The implication could not be clearer that it is transcendent love that redeems the mystery of the relationship of human freedom and human evil. Only Christ can sustain the tension without straining against it because he alone has plumbed the depths that lie beyond the limits of our experience. His infinitely forgiving presence could not be more perfectly conveyed as the foundation of freedom than in the gaze he turns on the Inquisitor of love too deep for words.

The turning point in the story is the outburst of Alyosha who interrupts Ivan, the rebellious author of the account, with the exclamation, "But . . .

that's absurd! Your poem is in praise of Jesus, not in blame of Him—as you meant it to be" (309). Ivan who had recounted the story with the ostensible purpose of demonstrating the force of the Inquisitor's critique of Christ, cannot follow his character all the way. He is not yet ready to embrace Christ, but he cannot avoid admitting the spiritual truth of his presence. The elaborateness of the Inquisitor's reinterpretation of the three temptations of Christ, as three lost opportunities to bring contentment and peace to an admittedly truncated mankind, serves only to underline the mendacity of his position. Love of human beings, a love that reaches as far as the full acceptance of their freedom, is not possible without Christ. He is the one who has shown the indispensability of the freedom that makes it possible for men to grow toward their full human stature, reaching even into their participation in divine being itself. Christ can sustain the tension between freedom and failure because he has suffered through it to the limit. The acceptance of his passion and death at the hands of men is the love that loves men even in their sin, that triumphs over all the evil they can inflict because it has overcome evil itself. Christ's redemptive sacrifice on Calvary is the affirmation of freedom at its deepest level.[15]

Without God the mystery of the interrelationship of freedom and irresponsibility becomes insupportable. There is no grounding for the transcendent valuation of freedom nor any assurance of the durability of goodness in the conflict with evil. The liberal elevation of the inviolable self-direction of the person is based on a faith in its value and its vindication. It is a faith that can be intuited but not fully validated because it reaches into regions beyond our human ken. The inability of the liberal tradition and, correspondingly, of our contemporary expositors to give an account of their own convictions is derived from this fundamental human limitation. We are participants within reality, not spectators above it. What we know can be gained only from the intimations available to us from within the participatory experience. It entails the meditative unfolding of the intuitions we already possess even before we begin the process of extrapolation toward and beyond the limits of our perspective. At its core the movement is sustained by faith, a sense of the goal that is inchoately present in our inquiry as the assurance of that which is sought. The Inquisitor cannot sustain that opening of the soul in tension toward what is not yet there because, as Alyosha blurts out, "he does not believe in God, that's his secret!" At last, Ivan admits, "you have guessed it" (310). Without the love of God there is no infinite dimension to sustain the love of man. They are just contemptible finite creatures, never more than the sum of their attributes.

The liberal faith is at its root the Christian faith that the value of a human being cannot be quantified, that by any measure that is applied the infinity of the person escapes the posited determinations. Freedom is that dimension of limitless openness integrally connected with what makes it possible for a human being to transcend all finitude. It is what makes possible the movement toward the transcendent and for that reason must be preserved despite the tangible costs that on any finite scale of reckoning tend to outweigh it. That recognition is what has sustained liberal order from its inception. It is the animating conviction that does not need to be fully articulated in order to make possible the unquestioning acceptance of the primacy of human self-direction despite the evident social and political risks. But when such acceptance has become opaque, its necessity no longer self-evident, then the need for explication is thrust upon us. A considerable part of the liberal tradition has historically been occupied with just such an effort of reevocation.

The faith remains Christian, but the Christian sources are no longer dispositive. As a consequence, much of the effort of rearticulation has been directed toward the development of a consensus that implicitly evokes the Christian residue that remains when revelation is no longer publicly authoritative. That vibrant and creative series of reevocations runs, we have seen, a wide gamut of formulations. Some, as in the case of Hegel, strain the limits of orthodoxy; others, as with Tocqueville, are content to stay close to the traditional religious forms. The great merit of Dostoyevsky's analysis is the clear demarcation of the breaking point. The secularization of the Christian faith in the transcendent value of freedom cannot survive the loss of faith in the participation in transcendent reality. By itself the liberal faith in the unconditional worth of the person, the free donation of self in love, cannot be sustained. It depends on the recognition that the person is always something more than we see before us. That which is not present must be allowed to govern that which is. Without a recognition of the human openness to the reality that is beyond all reality, the political expression in the preservation of inalienable rights becomes a hollow shell. It is a quaint historical relic to be swept aside as soon as Inquisitors with the necessary bluff and brusqueness come on the scene.

Dostoyevsky's meditation establishes a limit beyond which the secularization of liberal politics cannot go. It is incompatible with dogmatic atheism. Once faith in transcendent reality is firmly rejected, faith in the transcendence of human nature cannot survive. But beyond that there is a wide amplitude for liberal openness that stops short of pushing presuppositions to the limits. A means must be found of evoking that intermediate consensus on the dignity of the person that is yet surrounded by a penumbra of depths that are acknowledged but nowhere clearly delimited. The meditations we have followed in this chapter, culminating in Dostoyevsky, remind us of the historic and philosophic nature of the liberal construction. It has always been anchored in a transcendent appeal that by its very nature transcends any effort at its immanent determination. The problem of the intangible foundations of liberal principles is not a discovery of contemporary deconstructionists. It is integral to its moral constitution from the start. The secret of the success of the liberal order has always been its capacity to preserve that sense of connection with the depths that lie beyond articulation, by rendering their authority with sufficiently evocative force that the need for further explication was largely moot. Liberal order has always been a consensual symbolism that relied on unspoken recognition of a depth beyond the public definitions. In this chapter we have gained a sense, not only of what those depths are but also of why they are in principle resistant to articulation.

Now we must turn to the contemporary task of reassembling the raft of consensus that floats over an ocean of unknown depth and extent. The only means available to us are the materials that survive in the historical tradition, the elements of the consensus that are still seaworthy. We must attempt to pull them together and if possible fasten whatever other supports come our way if we are to sustain and expand the basis for our order. There is no possibility of fashioning our vessel de novo, for we are already at sea. That means that we must begin the attempt to reformulate liberal political theory by expanding the intuitions that are already present and effective within our politics. Gradually, the meditation can be unfolded toward its limiting point, but there is no necessity to reach it, nor can we make any progress if we begin with the assertion that we have already found it. What our inquiry has yielded so far is a sense of the living vitality that has sustained the profusion of liberal evocations and an insight into the inner spiritual appeal that is at its core. That does not provide us with any detailed model of how to proceed in our own pluralistically fragmented world, but it does provide an important sense of historical context and example so indispensable to knowing who we are. We have seen how liberal political order has been sustained in the face of the difficulties that confronted it; now we must explore the extent to which it can continue to be a living tradition of retrieval and reevocation today. How is it possible to enlarge the liberal soul in the present?

Part III
Outline of a Renovation

7

Incompleteness of Liberal Order

The crisis of liberal meaning adumbrated in the first part of our study is not, we have seen, a peculiarity of the contemporary hermeneutical blind alley. That opacity may exacerbate a situation in which all prospect of philosophical or religious agreement appears to have collapsed, but it does not create the fragmentation of traditions. We might even characterize the contemporary deconstructionist genre of liberal reflection, exemplified by Rorty and acquiesced in by Rawls and so many others, as merely the culmination of a lengthy historical process of disintegration working away at the heart of the liberal impulse. This end result is surely the insight of Nietzsche and Dostoyevsky. Indeed, it is somewhat disingenuous of the deconstructionists to announce their discovery of liberal nihilism as if it were a novelty in the modern world. It is a possibility that has lain at the core of the liberal project from the start. All that is new is the extent to which it has become the dominant self-realization among liberal intellectuals and increasingly within liberal societies.

Fortunately, nihilist liberalism does not have the field to itself. Restorative and resistant forces are also at work in the countermovement of the reconstruction of order from fragmentation. Otherwise, we would be faced with the prospect of a precipitous slide into the nightmare of the Hobbesian state of nature where we are compelled to treat every other human being as our enemy, and the life of man, bereft of all civilizing achievements and influences, cannot be other than "solitary, poore, nasty, brutish and short" (*Leviathan*, 186). The reality is that liberal societies for all their contentiousness have not reached the stage of civil war, carried on by political or other means, and have shown themselves capable of the remarkable efforts of resuscitation that have historically confounded friends and foes alike. Even the liberal intellectuals who tout their own psychic disintegration as our social future are not in their heart of hearts truly nihilist. They are, as I have tried to show, liberals first and nihilists second. Indeed, their embrace of the nihilistic collapse of all foundations can be read as just a more radical and serious effort to ground their liberal convictions on the uncontestable immediacy of practice. When all positions and premises become vulnerable, it is time to retreat to what is beyond formulation in the living reality of life. The depth of conviction with which liberal principles continue to be held belies the confession of their insupportability.

What the deconstructionists fail to recognize is that the liberal tradition is perennially fraught with the insecurity of its justification. Even when the broader religious traditions formed a more substantial background of support for its principles, concern was still voiced about the degree of convergence between them. Had the connection between Christianity and the public order been strengthened or weakened? Was the new prominence accorded individual freedom going to lead toward a heightening of individual responsibility or was it going to unravel into irresistible license? The great liberal theorists, as we have seen, were in the forefront of reflection on these questions and tireless in their search for new evocations of the spiritual core of liberty. The proliferation of attempts to reevoke the underlying consensus of the liberal polity is testament, not to its instability or poverty, but to the rich fund of inspiration on which it continues to draw. It is not so much that liberal order exists without a consensus or underlying agreement; it is that its animating convictions cannot be fully harmonized with the conceptual limitations of its language. The abundance of liberal articulations arises from an enduring vitality of inspiration, but the limitations on its full elaboration have resulted in the instability of its successive evocations. Liberal philosophy cannot be satisfactorily expounded within the immanent framework of liberal formulations. That is the conclusion we reached at the end of the last chapter.

Many commentators, such as MacIntyre, Strauss, Voegelin, Grant, and others, have largely concluded there is nothing more to be said and that liberal democracy is therefore a hopelessly incoherent symbolism. There is no denying the plausibility of this conclusion, especially as we witness the spiraling cacophony of voices in our own public square. But even if it is a case of a fool rushing in where angels fear to tread, I cannot altogether suppress the equally powerful evidence of an order that works despite its manifest and multiple deficiencies. For all its incoherence, liberal democracy continues to function as the overarching framework of our large and complex social existence and, despite everything, is the one authoritative measure of moral truth accepted in the relativized plurality of spiritual traditions. None of this can be counted a negligible achievement, nor is its order merely ephemeral. For better or worse we must live within this tension-ridden order that is the only publicly available definition of our world.

What it requires is that we acknowledge the ambivalence of the liberal complex of symbols that cannot be brought into any definitive formulation. Instead of throwing up our hands at the impossibility and incoherence of the liberal construction, we must recognize the gap between convictions and justifications. It does not mean that the liberal order rests on empty space but that it arises from existential depths that cannot be fully adumbrated. The tension is a source of richness, but it is also a source of danger. A means must be found of acknowledging the gap without tumbling to the conclusion that relativism or nihilism is the liberal truth. This will require a fundamental reorientation both by liberal defenders and by critics who have for so long operated on the basis that the liberal construction is a self-contained symbolism. It implies a sweeping innovation to acknowledge in principle that liberal order is incomplete. It is inherently incapable of standing on its own feet. The perennial accusation of its insubstantiality must be taken seriously as the starting point for reflection on the liberal order.

Once that step has been taken, the way is cleared for a focus on the existential resonances that have all along been the real source of the liberal appeal. We begin to see that the struggle to evoke more adequate formulations has been less a quest for a definitive demonstration than a vehicle by which the inner resonances are heightened and enlarged. The task of consolidating and expanding liberal order is recognized as similar to the struggle to realize any order. It is to be gained only by entering into the struggle. The liberal truth, as with all truth, discloses itself most adequately only to those willing to order their lives in accordance with it. The challenge of liberal order today is less that of finding a noncontestable account of its foundations or premises as it is in living out more fully the intimations that are its deepest inspiration. The tensional structure of liberal politics turns out to be simply a special case of the participatory structure of order in general. Its moral sources reveal themselves more fully only as we participate more fully within them.

The process is two staged, as the division of this final section of the book indicates. The first, covered in the present chapter, involves the acknowledgment of the incompleteness of liberal order, the extent to which it would be incomprehensible without a background of presuppositions that are not themselves established by the liberal framework. Recognition of the transcendent dignity of the person, for instance, cannot be derived from any finite valuation of achievements or contributions.[1] The second component, to be treated in the following chapter, consists of the meditative enlargement of the existential presuppositions that become tangible only as they are lived out more fully. The gap between the logic of liberal principles and the background assumptions is closed when the reality of transcendent valuation impresses itself upon us as the only reality that counts. The growth of the liberal soul consists in the heightening of the inner convictions that have sustained it from the beginning but could never be incorporated into its formulations.

Indispensable to the growth of the liberal soul in enlarging the range and solidity of its convictions is the recognition of its own need for such meditative expansion. Our strategy in the present chapter will be to begin with the most immediate intimations of a transcendent horizon framing the liberal order, then turn to the means available for sustaining the recognition of what is beyond formulation. We will discover, as has been suggested, that the principal means of preserving the transcendent openness of the liberal tradition has been the very dissatisfaction with its own formulation that has made it a tradition in quest of itself. This converges with the broader contemporary odyssey of rediscovering the depth of traditional wisdom, especially philosophy and Christianity, and coalesces with the central realization that order is known and sustained only through participation within it. Finally, we arrive at the recognition that the liberal order is really a special case of the "between character" of all symbolizations of order requiring, even more than most, the realization of its order as the means of discovering its sustaining truth and reality. Liberal order is a special case because it is precisely a heightening of the transcendent dimension of human finality, as that has been disclosed and transmitted within Christianity. We discover that it is not so much the liberal formulations that are incomplete as it is the character of human existence whose transcending of all finite summations renders it so.

Intimations of Transcendence

Once we move away from the conventional picture of liberal rationality and interest, we begin to see it as a very different kind of symbolism. The surface appeal may be to the freedom to pursue individual gratification, apparently at the expense of any devotion to virtue or community, but a deeper examination reveals that a good deal more is involved. It is not the satisfaction of desire that is paramount, for, without freedom, gratification hardly even appears worth having. Beyond any calculation of benefits is the incalculable benefit of self-responsibility. Even when the gift of freedom appears to be an obstacle to the effective fulfillment of desires and a manifest source of human misery, this does not appear to constitute sufficient warrant for abolishing the guarantee of freedom. It is of the essence, if not *the* essence, of what human beings are that they are entitled to govern their own lives. Once they cease to exercise their free self-responsibility, they lose the use of what constitutes their humanity, sinking below the human level to some unactualized form of existence. In abandoning their liberty they lose, as Dostoyevsky's Inquisitor discovered, the activity that makes them worthy of veneration and service. No longer living as ends in themselves they seem fit, even in their own minds, to become only instruments within some larger scheme of things beyond themselves.

Yet it is impossible to avoid the observation of the profligate expenditure of resources implied in the acknowledgment of human freedom. Men seem to profit so little from the privilege they are accorded and seem to wreak so much misery on themselves and others as a consequence. It is true, as the Inquisitor also discovered, that only a small fraction of humanity seems to be capable of living up to the promise of their stature as free, self-responsible beings. Do all of the others, then, live only to provide the chaotic material from which those few admirable free souls might emerge into spiritual brilliance? Surely this seems a cruel and wasteful disposition of beings, who, for all their obtuse dumbness, still carry within them the seed of transparent intelligence. No answer seems to be forthcoming, and the preservation of an order of liberty seems to hinge on our capacity to sustain the tension between freedom and failure without seeking to resolve or dissolve it.

It can be sustained, Dostoyevsky seems to suggest, only on the basis of faith in redemption, the assurance that somehow somewhere all that seems to be lost is restored and gathered up into the transfiguring fulfillment so long as we are willing to receive it. This is the historical meaning of the death and resurrection of Christ. Nothing is changed in the state of our existence within this world; Christ accomplishes no immanent transformation of history. But he is experienced as the turning point of history because it is in him that the mystery of redemption is accomplished. We do not know how or when, but the nature of his victory over evil and death is recognized as final, extending its effects to all men and all ages and requiring no further additions to render it complete. In the mystery of Christ's sacrificial action, the mystery of human freedom and sin is redeemed.[2]

For the moment all that we have is the assurance of redemption, which, of course, is not confined only to Christians but is a dimension of the human condition experienced in varying degrees of compactness in all times and places. We know that we are more than we are at any given time. We recognize that each of us is more even than the sum total of all the states and achievements we go through from birth to death. There is something that escapes all categorization and quantification about a human being. No attempt to sum up what a person is can plumb the limit or value that might be placed on him or her. It is a dimension of radical openness that goes beyond all immanent or finite conditions of existence. The only adequate language to identify the inexpressible depth of mystery that is a human being is the language of transcendence. The liberal language and practice of reverencing the inalienable rights of man is its refraction within a political universe that is no longer explicitly connected with any transcendent order of being.

For that reason the liberal formulations appear puzzling and problematic, as if they are ultimate assertions resting on a vacuum, until we realize that they are the means of evoking the response of transcendent reverence without articulating it. What makes it possible is that the assertion of the transcendent dignity of the person occurs within a historical milieu strongly constituted by the transcendent religions and their influences. Even when

Christianity or Judaism no longer exercise the same authoritative appeal, they continue to shape the way in which we experience the world. Few live in the grim everydayness of the secular world.[3] Our horizons are structured by the transcendent expectations that we are more than we are at any given moment, our lives are more than the sum total of our finite attributes and achievements, and there is more to all of life than the dreary summation of sameness that is the only conclusion from any cold-eyed examination of human history. The finite is surrounded and amplified by a penumbra of mystery; otherwise it would not make sense to disregard the calculable in the name of the incalculable.

It is, of course, the case that what does the calculating cannot be included in the calculations. The operator must be of a different order of reality from the operations; otherwise he would not be able to detach himself sufficiently from them to render a judgment.[4] But what preserves this separation and works to resist the inevitable tendency to absorb the human agent within the ordering of the instruments of production? A formidable force is required to resist the omnivorous pressures of instrumentalizing rationality that seeks to draw all things within its parameters. To the extent that we have not wholly succumbed to this Faustian fatality, credit must be given to the spark of transcendence inchoately preserved within the liberal language of rights. Together with the spiritual traditions that continue into the modern world, the liberal evocation of transcendence has sounded a note of noble impracticality in the face of the relentless efficiency of technique.

The secret of the liberal success, as we have seen, has derived from its correlative movements of submerging its foundations in silence while heightening its spiritual core. The latter is of particular importance because it endows liberal politics with the aura of a spiritual advance that is of enormous significance in rendering it self-sustaining. Moreover, it is a claim not without a certain plausibility. For although the centrality of emphasis on individual freedom and responsibility—the understanding of the person as a self-responsible originator of all values, ends in themselves—is already there within the spiritual traditions, it is given a new prominence as a result of its isolation as a principle within the liberal tradition. The prominence accorded self-responsible liberty suggests that it is a new discovery, but it is not the principle that is new so much as its employment as the driving impulse within the social and political order of existence. Even the Christian centuries, the liberal worldview maintains, did not have the courage or consistency of their valuation of the inviolable freedom of the soul. It was left to the tolerationist liberals to expand the freedom of the Christian into the political realm.

The belated acknowledgment of the Christian inspiration of the liberal order by the churches is perhaps the best evidence of the cogency of the claim. Protestant denominations were first to recognize the practical benefits accruing to them from the liberal guarantee of tolerance. As a consequence, it is difficult to identify the point at which this converges with a theoretical endorsement of the liberal order, but that certainly takes place in the protracted struggles over disestablishment in various countries. The situation is clearest in regard to the Catholic Church, which withheld its unequivocal assent until the Second Vatican Council. There it emphatically sided with the liberal freedom of religion as taking precedence over all authoritarian arrangements and thus sided with the liberal primacy of emphasis on individual self-determination as the sine qua non for the reception of all truth.[5]

The danger is that the unquestioned moral truth of liberal principles will further erode the sense of independence from its own spiritual sources. It is not necessary to recall the militantly secular and anti-Christian brands of liberal politics to become aware of the degree of indifference embodied in the more moderate Anglo-American forms. The separation is such that it is possible at any time for the liberal public order to assert its superiority, if only subtly, to the naively exclusivist professions of the denominations. It is a degree of separation that has enabled later liberal self-understanding to contemplate the rejection of the very spiritual sources that are its own roots. For if faith in the transcendent finality of human life disappears, then it is difficult to sustain faith in the irreducible and irreplaceable depths of the person.[6] If there is no transcendence then there are no rights without equivocation or negotiation. Nothing stands above the marketplace assessment of value.

The liberal assertion of the indispensability of self-determination, while it heightens the moral appeal of its construction, also runs the risk of leaving it exposed without any intelligible means of support. It is a stretching of the tension of freedom that is perpetually in danger of straining to the breaking point. The peculiar brittleness of liberal conviction manifests itself in the twin tendencies toward shrillness and inflexibility. Self-determination and autonomy are professed with such absolutism that, often overlooked, is the equally indispensable value of using freedom well. At the same time, rigidity and disdain are often the responses to the inevitable human failures to measure up to the responsibilities of liberty. Under such pressures it would not be surprising to see the experiment in liberty come apart, especially if its support is confined to the slender thread of the Kantian concentration on the purity of the self-determining will.

Faith in transcendence must be anchored in something more than this rarified achievement, for it must be sustained in the face of the recurrent human failures to sustain the exigencies of liberty. It requires a more substantive understanding of transcendence so that it is not dislodged at the sight of the shocking human capacity for collapse into immanence. Liberty must be sustained, despite the discouraging record of irresponsibility. A faith in its reality and in its eventual actualization is the only means of remaining faithful to its appeal, even when it can hold out only slim hope of securing immanent success. Something like the Christian promise of redemption, the reassuring divine presence that removes all doubts and confirms its mysterious efficacy within history, is a virtual necessity within a continuing liberal order. The attempt to do without such a spiritual context, especially to assert our indifference and superiority to it, can only subvert the faith in liberty itself.[7]

If everything is reduced to the aggregated contingencies of human life, as Rorty has proposed, then it is difficult to sustain the reverence and solidarity that he also recognizes as the source of liberal order. There must be an acknowledgment of depth beyond expression if persons are to be recognized as the unquantifiable and illimitable sources of rights. We can understand the difficulties that Rorty and many contemporaries have with the notion of a human essence. Almost as soon as it is defined, the human being seems to escape the boundaries of any specifications or categorizations.[8] But if all is to be explained in terms of finite historical contingencies, which stretch indefinitely into the past and the future without coalescing into an essence, then it is difficult to sustain any sense of an ultimate value in the expanse of unrelieved finite sameness. At the heart of the liberal order is a lively respect for the mystery of the person, the concrete individual before us, whom we sense is always more than he or she has or will disclose. A person is an epiphany of the infinite within the finite.

That realization cannot, of course, be defined or demonstrated because it is in the nature of that which is transcendent that it escapes all finite formulations. It may be symbolized or pointed to, and this is the mode of communication in all the great spiritual traditions that employ indirection. The deconstructionist liberal reflection of Rorty and the later Rawls, which is representative of the broader self-understanding of liberal society, seems to recognize this, but they lack the theoretical means of acknowledging the force of that which cannot be reduced to language. As a result, they conclude that it must be nonexistent. They rail against a metaphysics of essences because the essences adduced all turn out to be contingent formulations in historical space and time. What they cannot comprehend is how there might yet be a transcendent essence, which cannot be captured within the specificities of historical language, but that is nevertheless the mysterious source of the multiplicity of such putative definitions.[9] Yet their own railing against such contingently formulated essences is motivated by the awareness of the unformulable transcendence that ultimately escapes our language categories. It is a precarious position, as many commentators have noted, not least because of the difficulty of keeping alive that which you deny is a reality.[10]

A breakthrough is required that would enable our contemporary deconstructionist liberals to recognize the depths from which their own convictions arise. Instead of harping on the contingency of all their affirmations of principle, and thereby disposing of all sense of connection with what is enduring and true, they might begin to understand why they are driven to become liberal ironists disposed to cling "unflinchingly" to what they know is shifting. Not only is the position of the liberal ironist difficult, if not impossible, to maintain, it is also unnecessary. The formulations may share the finitude and contingency of everything that exists under the sun, but the movement from which they proliferate has its roots in that which transcends all finitude and contingency. It is this that has compelled them to become ironic liberals even if they can no longer remain simply liberal. It is the reality whence all formulations and convictions spring, although it is its transcendent nature to escape all specifications.[11]

A move away from literalness into something like the analogical imagination is required to deal symbolically with that which cannot be symbolized but is nevertheless the potent source of symbols. Liberal politics is in need of an understanding of Eliot's poetic indication of "the point of intersection of the timeless with time," although it is not merely poetic but the mode of its own deepest reality. We must advert to that which cannot simply be reduced to any set of declarative statements but that forms the contextual awareness surrounding all our exchanges with one another. That is the "something more" that is always there, but never specifiable, in all our conversations. We know that we and the other before us are more than what has been or can presently be stated and even more than we could ever express, an inexhaustible depth whose limits cannot be plumbed by a lifetime of reflection and articulation. It is this awareness that has always been the center of resonance within liberal order. The guarantee of self-directing autonomy is its only adequate expression.

Without adverting to the prearticulate intimations that are its own deepest inspiration, liberal self-analysis will be forever at cross-purposes with its most ardent convictions. The result will be the disorientation and dislocation we witness in our own liberal polities, as they oscillate wildly between moralizing and permissiveness without encountering any coherent principle or measure. This is the forgetfulness of morality as a practice identified so perceptively by Michael Oakeshott, whose converse is the succession of ever more frantic attempts to impose through regulations and abstractions what cannot be located in reference to any concrete common sense. My analysis goes beyond Oakeshott's in emphasizing not only the unformulable concreteness of practice but also the transcendent irreducibility that Oakeshott seems unwilling to single out as its most crucial dimension. Although the game of cricket cannot be reduced to the rules, there is a different mode of irreducibility when we contemplate the "thou" with whom we are in relationship. Then it is the mystery of the transcendent finality of the person that is at stake.[12] The consequence of operating in denial of what is most crucial in human relationships is a fundamental dislocation of all else in our lives.

The need for a measure by which to judge the order of things has never been greater. Only if we have a sense of what is ultimately important can we begin to establish a working sense of the priorities that can ensure the right proportion between the values we must weigh. Without it we confront the contemporary cacophony of rights claims, all of which have some validity but cannot be reconciled together with any modicum of harmony because we no longer understand whence such rights derive or what the order between them ought to be. It is all the more crucial to clarify the sense of the source of rights, not only because their application is a concrete practice, as Oakeshott emphasizes, but even more because their origin lies within the transcendent dimension of human existence. Their source, though powerful and inescapable, is in its very nature beyond all tangible identifications. The apprehension of the right measure is all the more crucial, as the Greeks discovered, when it is to be characterized as the "unseen measure."

Tradition as Quest for Its Source

Liberal order, as we have seen, has not been a bare longing for the transcendent measure that will inform it. The tradition has from the beginning been the tradition of the quest of the source from which it is derived. It has been the uncertainty of its evocation of the transcendent order within the medium of the secular that has given rise to the profusion of attempts to render it transparent. Liberal politics is defined as the translation of the transcendent worldview into the finite public realm, and it is, as a consequence, fraught with the perennial uncertainty of not adequately embodying its inspiration. Since it cannot fully acknowledge the transcendent source of its movement, it is perpetually in danger of suggesting that it is self-contained and without any principle beyond itself. The risk of forgetting its own foundations, especially because they must remain implicit, is one of the structural hazards of the liberal symbolic construct.

The primary means of keeping alive the awareness of its inspiration has been the continuing search for ever more transparent evocations. By engaging in the movement or quest for ever more compelling formulations, the liberal tradition has recurrently preserved the awareness of the measure by which its order is to be judged. The quest for a more trenchant account of what constitutes liberal order is continuously evaluated in light of the larger sense of who we are and of what our mode of being in the world must be. The result of these quests might appear to be a succession of attempts to construct an immanent or secular public order, but, to the extent that they remain faithful to their transcendent inspiration, they sustain the awareness of the silent presupposition by which all that they propose is to be measured.

The difficulty of explicating the transcendent criterion is, moreover, not simply a consequence of the determination to avoid the controversies of religious symbolization. Its essential difficulty arises from the impossibility of rendering the transcendent dimension satisfactorily in any immanent language. The revelatory traditions struggle to overcome this difficulty with some awareness of the analogical character of their language, which insists that God can be represented only so long as we are aware of the degree to which all representations do and do not embody that which is beyond all finite realizations.[13] The difficulty is even greater with the general language of politics where, without the discipline of any well-defined spiritual traditions, the possibilities of distortion are abundant. We have no satisfactory way of explaining why a human being is always more than the sum total of all of the descriptions that can be applied to him or her, no matter how exhaustive. For this reason we have no good way of explaining why men and women are all equal and utterly inviolable sources of rights, deserving of the dignity that goes beyond any and all achievements within this world. The language of transcendence is never the language of anything specific because it aims beyond even the sum of all specifics. It is the language of the "more than" all that can be mentioned.

The inevitable consequence is the tendency to conclude that the language of rights is, as Bentham asserted, "nonsense upon stilts" because its source cannot be adequately specified. How can we even be sure that there is such a depth beyond all expression if it can never be directly and immediately identified? Even the language of a depth prior to and beyond language is notoriously suspect, and the difficulty of dealing with it is the reason why our contemporary skeptics have shied away from all consideration of it. The defender of the notion of transcendence, not as a dogma but as the inexpressible and inexhaustible source of all dogmatic formulations, is in the uncomfortable position of describing something that as soon as it is named ceases to be what it is. Once it is given a distinct identity, it partakes of all the contingency and reducibility of everything else in the historical world. We are inclined to look askance at the notion that we can talk at all about that which cannot really be named. How do we know that the transcendent dimension even exists?

The impossibility of demonstrating it might prove so discouraging that we would be inclined to abandon the attempt were it not for the formidable effect of its influence within the liberal tradition. While none of the formulations succeed in capturing it, there is no denying the depth of inspiration from which they arise. What skeptics and deconstructionists fail to recognize in their assessment of the conditioned contingencies from which every statement of principle arises is the inchoate spiritual vitality from which they emanate. The formulations are a series of attempts to define what is there before the attempt, but they come more fully into consciousness by virtue of the struggle for articulation, without ever fully exhausting the impulse in a comprehensive and definitive formulation. It is not that there is a depth of inspiration that exists prior to the struggle for articulation; rather, the depth becomes more luminous through the attempt to give it expression. There would be no effort at identification if there was not a movement of the soul before the attempt at language mediation.

It is precisely the effort to unfold foundations within the liberal tradition that keeps alive the underlying inspiration most effectively. There is a depth prior to articulation, but the depth lives only through the struggle to articulate it. The awareness of the interplay between linguistic symbols and experiences is what has enabled the tradition of liberal philosophizing to continue and to flourish, serenely accepting the incompleteness and incoherence of the successive formulations proposed. The faith in man's transcendent finality, which is the source of the construction, is also what sustains the repeated nondefinitive attempts at its expression. It matters less that the formulations are imperfect and incomplete than it does that they are guided by the underlying sense of the transcendent trajectory of human existence. It is the spiritual openness of the person that is the source of their rightness, not the cogency of their particular formulations.[14]

The struggle for transparence is of crucial importance because it is through the unfolding articulation that the underlying intimations come to actualization. The formulations are not a matter of indifference simply because they are not absolute. Particular forms become opaque, and it is through the effort to think them through again that the spirit behind them is gathered up and retrieved by being made to live again. That is the point of the survey of the liberal tradition in the second part of this study. It discloses the way in which a tradition lives through the unending quest for the tradition itself. At each stage it is guided by a common inspiration, and the inspiration is itself sustained through the successive efforts at its elaboration, even when the various attempts are only partially or variably successful in unfolding what is within them. We begin to realize that there is no liberal tradition apart from the ongoing struggle by liberal societies and thinkers to render an account of the reasons for who they are. Perhaps this is the deepest layer of the contemporary moment of danger—that so many seem to have become unwilling to continue the quest in light of its inconclusiveness.

Such pessimism seems to arise from a misunderstanding of what a tradition in general is and especially of the transcendentally grounded tradition of liberty. It seems to derive from the misconception that the point of a meditative elaboration of convictions is to arrive at a demonstration that will stand on its own feet. They labor under the impression that a philosophical articulation ought to produce a solution or answer, a knowledge of something quite other than the intimations with which it began. Liberal order, because it is a minimal statement of consensual apprehension of order, has always risked the suggestion that it is capable of standing without presumptions or predispositions and that it constitutes a self-sufficient exposition of the exigencies of social and political order. But that has never been the self-understanding of the liberal tradition at its most vibrant. The great liberal theorists appear to have been much less concerned with the development of a system than with a faithful unfolding of the sense of their intimations of what is right. Incoherences and incompletenesses seem to have troubled them relatively little.

Locke is only the most obvious illustration of this pattern of sublime indifference to the tensions and inconsistencies within his thought. It is unlikely that he or the millions who have subsequently embraced the Lockean form of liberal democracy were oblivious to the intellectual strains of the construction. Much more plausible is the reading that they regarded such concerns as peripheral to the main thrust of elaborating the underlying sense of an order that conforms adequately to the transcendent dignity of human beings. We have seen that it is this measure of what is required for the proper treatment of rational beings that is the crucial issue for Locke in the determination of the form of government. His most vociferous denunciations are reserved for the advocates of absolute rule who insist that men are incapable of guiding their own lives and must submit to the paternal authority of the prince. He is especially provoked by the claims of Filmer and the Anglican clergy that this is a divinely ordained state of things in which the vast majority of human beings are to be kept in a state of perpetual tutelage to a royal few.

What particularly exercised Locke about this suggestion was not the potential for injustice, which he fully recognized, but the denial of the proper human status to beings who are to be kept in a state of perpetual childhood or nonage. Unlike children whose subjection to paternal authority is designed to bring them to the maturity of self-responsibility, the subjects of an absolute prince have no other function than to serve as the playthings of their utterly autonomous ruler. In losing even the potential for self-direction they lose the dignity and the value that separates them from the world of objects or beasts whose only purpose is to serve their master. It is of crucial importance to establish the God-given character of this human capacity for rational self-government, for Locke understood that this was the way to demonstrate its universality as defining the human condition. This is the significance of the *First Treatise*'s rejection of the claim to the divine right of kings. Not only is it unfounded in Scripture and the line of divine authorization is indeterminable, but it perverts the very notion of what a human being ought to be. If they are no longer rational creatures capable of exercising responsibility for their own lives, then they sink to the level of beasts of burden or of prey serving no other function than the satisfaction of their masters.

That realization is what creates the bond of comity between human beings, enabling them to come together in the formation of a community. The absolute prince and the criminal are, to Locke, the ones who have sundered that bond and betrayed the mutual trust that is the only basis on which men can join together in civil society. The rupture is the breach of a sacred trust that, even if it is begun in small and seemingly minor steps, cannot be known to have any limits other than the most extreme tyrannical rapine of the lives and properties of the citizens. Locke reserves his most apocalyptic language to emphasize the almost metaphysical character of the evil introduced by the breaking of the bond of respect for the rights of others. It was his own involvement with the protracted confrontations between Parliament and Charles II that had provoked the awareness of just what is at stake in the encroachments of royal power beyond the law. Nothing less than their status as human beings could ultimately be threatened.

The source of that awareness was articulated only to the extent that Locke considered it necessary in elaborating his resistance to the forces of oppression. This is the point of his speculation on the state of nature and of the condition of freedom under the God-given law of nature in which men originally find themselves. We are "God's property," not anyone else's, and it is incumbent upon us to fulfill the directives placed upon us by our maker— that is, to preserve ourselves for his service and, so far as possible, to secure the same well-being for all others. We must live in conformity with the moral law that is the specification of the law of nature and be prepared to punish breaches of it in others, especially when the deprivation of property or liberty indicates the intention of enslaving a human being. But the punishment of such breaches is as far as we may go. We have no right to deprive criminals of their property, this "strange doctrine" as Locke acknowledged, that we cannot take the property of a thief, because that is the means of sustenance of his dependents. In the same way, the general has the power of life and death over his men but cannot deprive them of a penny of their property. It is not, as Locke is so often misunderstood, that he is obsessed with the preservation of property as an end in itself, but that property is the boundary that guarantees the human status of free men and women.

His account of civil society is not a blueprint for government, but an evocation of what political order should be among people who recognize the inviolability of their members.[15] They recognize the transcendent dignity of human beings that requires them never to invade their liberties except through their consent. The only exception is where an individual has forfeited his liberty through a gratuitous attack on the liberty or person of an other. Locke paints a picture of political society erected on the basis of this common recognition, one whose institutions embody respect for the inviolable self-responsibility of the citizens. Everything from legislation through representative assemblies to the protection of rights, the rule of law, and the right to revolution is designed to realize an order of self-government in which each is subject to the rules that they have themselves authorized.

In answer to the obvious question of what is to prevent the majority from imposing its will unjustly on a minority, Locke can do no more than invoke the imperious order of justice that binds all men irrespective of power. It makes no difference whether the injustice is perpetrated by a prince or a majority; in either case it is a breach of the order of right that binds us together and that none are free to disregard. There can be no doubt regarding the depth of apprehension from which this judgment arises. It was ultimately rooted in the order of divine being compared to which the words of flatterers are no more than an insubstantial drop in the ocean of truth. Such depth of conviction naturally inspires firmness in resisting the forces of corruption, but they contain no guarantee that they will triumph in any of the historical conflicts of will. Locke himself knew what it was like to be a member of the unsuccessful minority, as he found himself on the losing side virtually throughout his life.[16] But his faith in an order of right remained unshaken, sustaining him and the liberal political tradition emanating from him.

Nor did he take the apprehension of the moral order for granted. Locke was concerned at the corrosion of the traditional spiritual world, and he wrote the *Essay Concerning Human Understanding* in large measure, as he explains, to find a way toward a more reliable knowledge of religion and morality. Reason was important in the task of sifting the evidence for conclusions that are founded and rejecting the unfounded. But he concluded that reason alone was not sufficient for the full and universally accessible avenue to the truth about human existence. For that revelation disclosed the most powerful truths, with a depth that the most educated could not deny and the simplest could not fail to apprehend. Reason might provide a valuable service to revelation, especially in detecting the spurious claims to inspiration, but reason itself could be guaranteed only through the assurances provided nowhere as completely as in revelation. It is by no means a final account of the order in which liberal democracy lives, but the Lockean evocation proved a remarkably durable one up to the more searching philosophical crises of our own time.

There were others who saw the crisis coming and who struggled in their own way to respond to it. Rousseau was probably the first to really discern its proportions, and his reflections were intended to reach into the depths from which virtue is formed in the souls of the citizens. We have seen the outline of his effort to elucidate the order that discloses itself to us in the inwardness of our hearts. His strategy of removing the layers of social accretions was designed to lay bare the immediate intimations of right. The construction of the social contract he proposed was designed to remove the obstacles as far as possible, as the tutor had done for Emile, for the spontaneous emergence of the virtuous self-elaboration of the citizens. Despite the distorting neglect of the ever present propensity toward evil and domination within the human heart, Rousseau's reflection is an indispensable heightening of the Lockean presumption of the human capacity for discerning the moral order of the universe.

Kant continues the meditation with more philosophical rigor in his systematic separation of all that arises from self-interest in the definition of the one unqualified good, the good will. It is an evocation of the transcendent dignity of the human openness toward moral right that stands as a beacon of inspiration within the liberal unfolding of order.

Hegel pushes the line of reflection almost to the breaking point in the suggestion that it has arrived at the secularization of Christianity. One does not have to agree with his conclusion to recognize its origination in the sense of the heroic destiny of transcendent openness purged of all particularity. The liberal individual formed by the Rousseauesque-Kantian meditation on fidelity to the intimations of duty does indeed appear as the historical carrier of truth in a world bereft of many other sources of order. We do not, however, have to follow Hegel in insisting that this excludes or surpasses the other historical carrier of transcendence, Jesus Christ.

The brightness of the Hegelian apocalypse began to fade even before it had a chance to glow. It was not long before the element of overreaching together with the divergence of reality from the system dislodged again the coherence of the liberal outlook. The succeeding fragmentation of the liberal worldview continues to define the situation up to our own time. To the extent that "liberalism" functions as an ideology even in the nineteenth century, it is relatively weak and displays none of the omnivorous systematizing ardor so characteristic of its intellectual and political rivals. It is no surprise that it found itself so unprepared in the aggressive ideological confrontations of the twentieth century. Instead it was thrown back on the inner depths of its inspiration and is engaged in an effort of self-retrieval and articulation that we have begun to recognize as its permanent mode of being in the world. It is not that the great nineteenth-century liberals—Mill, Tocqueville, Acton, and the others—were second-rate minds or defective in systematic talent. It is that liberal order cannot be reduced to a system because it reflects the ongoing tensions of the human condition itself.

The best that can be done is to follow out the directions indicated by the tensional pulls, tracing them as far as their sources will permit. Like Locke, many of the nineteenth-century theorists of liberty conclude that it is unnecessary to decide between reason and revelation or to attempt the Hegelian subsumption of one into the other. They are twin sources of order in the concrete historical tradition in which we find ourselves, and it is incumbent upon us to use all the resources available to us in our disintegrated context. One of the striking features of the preceding century, and by continuity our own, has been the rediscovery of religion as an indispensable element in the formation of order. Contrary to the expectation that religion might retreat to the privacy of the denominational enclaves already well defined and accepted, we observe the phenomenon of its reintroduction into the public square at least in some denominationally liberated form. Reason and natural virtue, it is suspected, are unlikely to muster the spiritual strength on their own to withstand the energy of passion and the seductions of self-aggrandizement.

On the other hand, reason has already staked out the autonomous sphere of its own self-determining operations as off-limits to the injection of religious or ecclesiastical authority. Even though such authority may be the most effective means of directing us toward the good, it will profit us little, as Locke pointed out, unless we are personally persuaded and embrace it from the depth of our own conviction. The shift to subjectivity or interiority so characteristic of the modern world finds its central political expression in the liberal insistence on freedom of conscience and the independence of reason as the starting point for all reflection on order. It is not, of course, that the necessity for a personal assent of persuasion or faith is unknown in the premodern traditions, certainly not in the Platonic dialogues or the Gospels, but that it acquires a new prominence and weight in the modern odyssey of the refounding of order. The emphasis on subjective conviction is discovered as the indispensable ingredient in any recovery of truth in existence.

What the more conservative liberal outlook of Tocqueville and Mill indicates is that subjective autonomy is not a sufficient condition for the realization of order. There is no guarantee that individuals will live up to the promise of their self-responsibility. They might just as easily settle for the "nasty penury" abhorred by Locke and visualized so powerfully in the voluntary submission of their freedom to the Grand Inquisitor. The liberation of their autonomous self-direction could prove to be the prison of their souls unless they are drawn beyond the confines of the self by the attraction of that which is worth the sacrifice of their comforts and convenience. In that contest, Tocqueville and Mill suspected, only the pull of transcendent goodness can be counted to outweigh the attractions of all that is finite. Any other finite goal would invite the measuring of its benefits against the measurable returns of the alternatives. Only the immeasurable good can draw us with any surety from dissipation in the measurable.

As a consequence, the recognition emerges that the transcendent openness of the person is not a self-sustaining independent achievement. It is the fruit of the historic revelatory traditions, especially Judaism and Christianity, that have created the language of its self-understanding, and it is not readily sustainable apart from that context. There may be the small minority of cases where the impulse toward transcendent right may be carried forward on the implicit resonances of the spiritual tradition. But that is a precarious connection at best. Even Kant discovered that the aspiration toward a transcendentally good will, for all its logical power, can hardly appear real without the "postulates" of God and the immortality of the soul. Not only is the liberal differentiation of the unconditioned good of the person the secular refraction of Christianity, but it depends on the recognition of that connection if it is to withstand the pressures that deny its very reality and value.

The meditation has come full circle, and we are back at the recognition of the divinely grounded order of Hobbes and Locke. Yet the process of completing a circle is never tantamount to remaining in the same place; there is an unfolding of what was contained in the place from which we began. The crucial aspect is that we have not succeeded in stepping outside the circle or standing above the position from which we have taken our beginning. There is no language of transcendence other than that provided by the spiritual traditions in which it has historically been differentiated. The attempt to sever such notions from that context does not attain an independent vantage point from which to view the process as a whole, but merely results in the disconnection of our concepts from the experiences of reality that are capable of giving them meaning. The attempt to sever Christian ideas from their spiritual setting does not result in their secularization, but only in the evacuation of their substance and the inevitable disorientation when we must nevertheless continue to employ them.

There is no language of transcendence that dispenses with the language of movement toward that which is beyond all finite existence or that accounts for the tension between the different realities in which we find ourselves. The search for such a comprehensive or superior viewpoint is really the attempt to place oneself above the struggle to live toward the enduringly good. It can be none other than an application of the desire to escape the tension of fidelity to the intimations of right. In thus placing oneself above the moral or spiritual struggle one does not thereby attain spiritual perfection, but rather its opposite. One has given up on the aspiration for what is good and thereby lost the only means available to us of finding the moral direction of our lives. The result is a profound spiritual disorientation that may temporarily be masked by the claims of higher idealism but soon degenerates into the unprincipled service of one's own ego gratifications. By giving up on the language of the spiritual struggle we do not attain any higher illumination, but only lose ourselves more profoundly in the outer darkness where there are not even the faint glimmerings of right to guide us.[17]

The only knowledge of order available to us is through our participation within it. The conceit that this imperative can be overstepped and that we can attain a direct and systematic comprehension of all the moral ramifications before us is futile. It is only by undertaking the effort to live more profoundly in accordance with the inchoate sense of order already available to us that we begin to gain a larger understanding of its outlines; they disclose themselves more fully as we participate more faithfully in their ordering directions. There is no privileged or superior vantage point on the order in which we participate. No age and no individuals possess an advantage that would enable them to sidestep the human condition in gaining insight into its order.

Wisdom as the fruit of suffering applies equally to the contemporaries of the Greek tragedy as to ourselves and our liberal confreres.

The difficulty is that the modern quest for foundations, especially for a neutral rational explication, has generated the impression that such a scenic overlook is available above the moral struggle itself. The liberal construction has often been proposed or regarded as just such a universally compelling exposition. The great benefit of our contemporary state of advanced disintegration is that the last props have finally been kicked from under that notion. Even liberals, like Rawls, have accepted that their own construction is falling through space in exactly the same way as all other spiritual symbolisms. There is nothing uniquely objective or rational about its structure. It does not rest on any unassailable first principles. But instead of rejoicing in their liberation from the impossible burden of neutrality, liberal theorists still suffer from the depression of severing their addiction to the bottle of neutrality. They have not yet begun to see its liberating or exhilarating dimensions.

Foremost among these is the realization that, if liberal theory is no longer the unique moral language, it is clearly one of the credible formulations and is free to establish its claims in open competition with its rivals. Not having to defend an impossible claim, it is liberated to articulate the real sources of its appeal. It no longer has to apologize for its historical particularity, to stretch the assertions of its universality, but can accept the historically concrete nature of its development while recognizing that none of its rivals for public authority have escaped the same fate of spatiotemporal origination. Instead of bemoaning the historical contingency of all moral languages, as Rorty does, why not simply accept this as the starting point for their examination? None may be definitive in the sense of guaranteeing their unrevisability, but that does not mean that they cannot be compared and ranked in accordance with the most compelling truth that emerges from their juxtaposition. Only individuals thoroughly imbued with the modern longing for escape from the debate would become downcast at this prospect.

The despondency is moreover unnecessary, for the liberal philosophy itself can find its firmest foundation in the recognition that there is no starting place not itself resting on a prior presupposition. The incompleteness of the liberal construction points to its dependence on certain predispositions in whose absence it is difficult to sustain the commitment to the inviolability of the person. There is nothing burdensome or unsatisfactory about that realization once we recognize that this is the inescapable condition for all human reflection on order. No starting point exists outside of an awareness of order, however inchoate or inarticulate. When we first become conscious of questions of right and wrong, our awareness is already structured by some sense of the differences between them and of the direction in which our obligations lie. There is no pristine Eden of unconstructed first premises, because there is no access to the beginning except by getting outside the human condition. All that we can know must be known from within.[18]

The positive dimension of this realization of the participatory and historical character of our knowledge of order is that we are not utterly at a loss. We may not possess definitive understanding of principles and consequences, but we do possess a sense, albeit unformed, of the direction in which we should go. As we follow it out, we can discern its outlines more clearly; we begin to distinguish between the real and mistaken promptings of our conscience, and we begin to test the rival positions and traditions presented to us in the course of our lives. Our ignorance of right is not total ignorance. No human being, so long as they remain human, ever sinks below that minimum knowledge of moral right that is then capable of indefinite expansion toward the good. Similarly, even the most spiritually profound and insightful never break through to a qualitatively higher viewpoint that lifts them above the battlefield between good and evil in the human heart. We rest always on the moral foundation that is already there when we begin the process of reflection, never escaping above it or descending below it.

What this implies is the inescapable significance of the historically differentiated symbolisms of order. Just as individuals cannot escape the contingency of their moral upbringing, so the human race as a whole can have no moral knowledge but what has emerged within its concrete historical unfolding. There is no perspective from which to judge the strengths and limitations of a particular moral position or tradition, except from within the most moral and most differentiated perspective that has become available to us. This is not to imply that the most advanced in depth and nuance is necessarily the most advanced in every respect. But while all perspectives will have their limitations, the central point is that for the moment they are the only moral language available to us. If we are to comprehend them, then they will probably best be understood from within the perspective of the most developed language. As with languages, there will be things that can be said only within a specific language, but the more developed language will suffer from fewer such exclusions.

Even the inevitable question of how we decide which perspective is the most developed or profound is not as impossible as it is often made to appear. It is only by juxtaposing and testing them against one another, especially in the most crucial test of life itself, that we can sift their achievements and shortcomings. No other measures are available to us than the intimations we already possess, which are in turn formed by our participation in one or more of the same traditions. The process is undeniably untidy and inconclusive, but it is not hopelessly contingent, as the deconstructionists would have us believe. We may not be capable of overcoming all the arbitrary prejudices of our own situation, but that does not mean that we are incapable of advancing beyond any of them. It is enough that truth can be pushed forward a little for us to hold a modest confidence in the process of judgment that we cannot avoid anyway.

The liberal symbolization is only a special case of the general situation of all human articulations of order. None are final or complete; all rest on a preconceptual awareness that stretches back into recesses and depths that can never be fully explicated. We never arrived at an unconditioned statement of the reality in which we participate, because our explications must begin from a participation that is already structured by some elementary knowledge of order. The liberal formulation rests on a more deliberate consensus to preserve the implicitness of the foundations that cannot be articulated within its parameters. Its stability depends on the recognition of this dependence and the willingness to resist the inclination to push conflicts to extremes. Disagreements must be held within a moderate range in order to prevent them from spilling over into an assault on the prearticulate foundations that, by their nature, cannot render an explicated defense of themselves.

This incompleteness by consensus is the additional layer added to the more profound incompleteness of the transcendent source of order, a tenuousness that liberal order shares with the transcendent spiritual symbolisms in general. Not only is there an agreement to remain silent about the ultimate foundations, but their transcendent source renders them incapable of adequate articulation even if it were attempted or desired. The transcendent openness of the person as the ground of inviolable and inalienable rights cannot be established on the basis of any finite affirmations, however comprehensive and evocative. It can only be recounted in negatives, as that which is more than any of the measures we might adduce to limit it, as the depth that is beyond anything that can be plumbed even in self-knowledge or self-expression. What establishes the substance of that orientation lies beyond the boundaries of the expressible. It may be symbolized analogically, although the meaning depends on the preservation of the same tensional awareness of the similarity and dissimilarity between the symbol and the symbolized. It is a reality known through the experience of participating in its pull.

In this recognition the contemporary meditation on liberal order converges with some of the most significant other lines of historical recovery. They have to do with the remarkable rediscovery of the viability of the great spiritual traditions—especially philosophy, Judaism, and Christianity—within the modern world. It is perhaps not surprising that the modern "transvaluation of all values," which relentlessly exposes the suspect contingencies behind all elaborations of order or truth, should also generate a hunger and interest in the more substantive spiritual traditions. We find the extraordinary development of the most serious and profound reexamination of all the great spiritual traditions of the world occurring at precisely the same time as the wasteland of their apparent demolition. They are not, of course, unrelated, and it should not surprise us that the seriousness and depth of interest in traditions should occur at precisely the same time as their apparently final disintegration on a global scale.

From our perspective, what is of interest is the recovery of the spiritual traditions of philosophy and Christianity that form the immediate background to our own liberal order. The movement of rediscovery, both existential and intellectual, is of inestimable significance in demonstrating that we are not confined to the desultory choice between nihilism and liberalism, but that there are more robust traditions of meaning and truth available to those who are willing to open themselves toward them. It was the depth of the spiritual crisis that engulfed modernity in the twentieth century that provoked such a far-reaching reexamination of our world, and it is a process that is still under way without any clearly determined outcome in view. But to find the rediscovery of the very traditions on whose rejection so much of the modern world had been premised, exploding again onto the public scene as credible and superior accounts of the human condition and its order, is a remarkable phenomenon in its own right.[19] The special significance from the perspective of liberal politics is that the traditionalist rediscovery reveals the means of access into the very sources from which the liberal foundations of order have been derived. They solve the problem of the incommunicability of the transcendent ground by exemplifying their participation in it.

Participation as the Opening toward Order

It is in the nature of the recovery of a tradition that it is never the same as its original genesis. There is always the awareness of what one has recovered from, and that inevitably removes some of the naïveté and immediacy from the experience. What is discovered or rediscovered is no longer marked with the magic of youthful impassability; now it is known as that which has as tenuous a hold on existence as everything else in life. What has been lost and recovered can be lost again. Moreover, its recovery is marked by the circumstances into which it is reborn; it is never the same as it was in its first incarnation. Particularly prominent in the contemporary recovery of traditions is the self-consciousness of being a tradition and a peculiarly detailed reflection on the nature and conditions of access into them. This is the unavoidable common thread that persists across the expansion of our horizons into classical political thought, Christian or Jewish spirituality, medieval scholasticism, and the myriad of premodern fields from Egyptology to Sinology. They are acutely conscious of the degree to which an understanding of the premodern traditions of order has required an enlargement and enrichment of their modern worldviews. At the same time, they became intensely aware of the degree to which access into such traditions always entailed submission to their ordering authority. The truth is only disclosed through participation.

A concomitant effect of the dramatic impact of the encounter with the great traditional sources of order is a heightening of the contrast with the modernity that has been left behind. The result is often visible in an emphasis on the discontinuity between the two worldviews. A great gulf separates the ancients and the moderns and even those who, as in the gospel story of Dives and Lazarus, would go from one to the other cannot do so. Spiritual richness and spiritual famine seem to characterize the disparity between them. But this is to give too much weight to the accidents of the experience that in essence have demonstrated that a modern human being can absorb the meaning of Plato or Christ. It is equally to misunderstand the nature of the modern world itself that continues to conceive itself within the terms of the philosophic and revelatory dispensations, perhaps even more emphatically when it defines itself in opposition to them than when it maintains its continuity with the traditions.

Our own reflection on the character of liberal order has brought to light its dependence on spiritual and moral sources that are only adequately unfolded within the premodern traditions of philosophy and Christianity. The difference is that we have reached it by way of a meditation from within the liberal tradition. Efforts to retrieve the premodern traditions themselves are of incomparable significance in making available the depth from which the modern world springs and on which its liberal self-expression still depends. Without such a work of recovery, there would be no chance that the liberal political order could be rendered coherent; it would be condemned to wander forever in the half-light of its intuitive twilight that never dawns into the full luminosity of articulate transparence. Liberal formulations that began in response to the breakdown of the philosophic Christian traditions are, as we have seen, the secular presence of their inspiration within the modern world. It could not survive their complete disappearance from the world, which is why the confrontation with the militant ideological alternatives was so critical for liberal order, and it cannot render itself fully coherent except in relation to those sources. The independent reemergence of philosophy and Christianity, not as dominant public authorities but as credible existential and intellectual forces within the contemporary setting, is of incalculable importance for the liberal tradition.

Most significant is the recovery of the full amplitude of participation in the transcendent order of being at a time when the possibility of knowledge of truth and meaning seems to have perished irrevocably. Both Nietzsche and Dostoyevsky defined the crisis of the age in almost identical terms as the recognition that God is dead and that everything is permitted. None of the later epigonic nihilists have improved much on this formulation. It has merely become commonplace among contemporary intellectuals that all assertions of truth or right are hopelessly mired in contingency and irretrievably afflicted with arbitrariness. Out of this prolonged historicist infinitude there is apparently no escape. We are condemned to be perspectivists. But in the midst of this unrelieved contingency there have emerged a number of voices, still crying in the wilderness but proclaiming a very different message. They speak with the voice of the ancient traditions, but they are not mere refugees from the traditionalist enclaves that survive into the modern world. These are thinkers who are confident that they can speak the truth of the traditions to the modern world because they have understood the traditions as the truth of that world.

The dismissal of philosophy and Christianity by a succession of modern thinkers was unwarranted because philosophy and Christianity are not an assembly of unverifiable dogmas. They are not a conglomeration of dogmas at all. This is the key point in the recovery of Greek philosophy by Eric Voegelin, Hans Gadaamer, and Leo Strauss or in the retrieval of the medieval tradition by Gilson, Maritain, or MacIntyre.[20] Such traditions, they have shown, are not constituted around a set of propositions or first principles, and they do not involve the elaboration of speculative consequences as an end in itself. Philosophy and Christianity are first and foremost ways of life, and they cannot be judged except as it is appropriate to judge a way of life. That is, only those who have lived them or imaginatively reenacted their life-forms and experienced enough of the alternative modes of life are properly in a position to render a decision for or against them.

They cannot be assessed on the basis of their contingent formulations that, like all else in existence, partake of the same contingency and finiteness we witness everywhere. Philosophy and Christianity, like all the great symbolic traditions, can only be understood from within the order they articulate. They cannot be understood in terms of the historical chain of influences that is visible on their surface and that their symbols inevitably reflect. What they are about is not the borrowings and revisions of symbols, ideas, and influences that are the stock-in-trade of the contemporary historical analyst. Their truth, in the sense of their real meaning, is what is intended through the symbols, the reality they make tangible within the limits of the human experience. The symbols do not exhaust the reality from which they arise; rather, they emphatically declare their inadequacy to the depiction of that which is experienced through them. For this reason they are utterly opaque as symbolisms without the entry into the engendering experiences from which they live.

What is remarkable about the contemporary traditionalists, philosophic and Christian, is the extent to which they are capable of putting the modern critics on the defensive—that is, to the extent to which any of the opponents take the time to attend to what is being said, for neglect and silence are still among the most effective means of eliminating threats to one's customary modes of operation. Perhaps it would be more accurate to say that they put the modern attitude on the defensive. The new traditionalists compel the recognition that the modern rejection of philosophy and Christianity suffers from the same arbitrariness with which the traditions had earlier been dismissed. It is always a good strategy to relativize the relativizers, but this involves a more substantive opposition. It insists on the limiting nature of all symbolisms of order and demonstrates the necessity of assessing them from within the dimensions of the human condition that they structure and that none succeed in abolishing or transcending.

The sweeping modern dismissal of all spiritual meaning and truth is exposed as an even more arbitrary assertion because it is derived from the illicit assumption of a privileged perspective on the human condition. No one can know if our knowledge of order is utterly contingent unless they have been able to compare the sum total of all our representations with the definitive reality it intends. Just as they are all tainted by the contingency of the process by which our symbolizations are generated over concrete space and time, so it is equally likely that even the most inadequate formulations cannot fail to capture something of the truth that all have sought. Their validity can be measured only from within the perspective of our participation in existence, which cannot be avoided anyway, and that can be guided only by the intimations of order that are already in place before we even begin to reflect on the questions. Symbolisms of order are what structure our experience of reality. They provide the context in which analysis and critique of specific issues can be carried on, but they are not themselves amenable to the same kind of objective assessment. Only from within the perspective of participating in them and only in relation to the landmarks disclosed within them can they be evaluated.

The authority of a spiritual tradition, as with any symbolism that orders the limits of human experience, rests on its capacity to resonate authoritatively with the intimations of order in our souls. This is an inescapable situation. We cannot avoid the inclinations and pulls that already draw us in particular directions even if we believe, like contemporary deconstructionist liberals, that they are utterly groundless. Rorty and Rawls continue to insist on the superiority of the liberal construction and are deeply convinced of the need to reverence the dignity of persons. Nor is it possible to provide any more conclusive demonstration of the truth of the intimations or the spiritual symbolisms in which they are elaborated than that authoritative resonance. We cannot step outside the perspective of human beings to gain any more objective viewpoint on the whole. We cannot penetrate beyond the mystery of the process within which we find ourselves, nor reach any more definitive account of the inescapable structures of order that compel us.

This becomes remarkably clear in the cathartic rediscovery of order that exemplifies the opening of the soul preparatory to the full recovery of the traditions. Albert Camus and Alexander Solzhenitsyn illustrate this meditative expansion of order from the point of virtual moral zero as they struggled to confront, in different contexts, the abyss of nihilism unleashed by the totalitarian destruction of all values in this century. Some sense of what is involved may be obtained by comparing Camus's "Letters to a German Friend" with the later reflections contained in *The Rebel*. In the "Letters" he acknowledged that he could find nothing with which he could oppose the destructive nihilism of fascism. He recognized that fascism is a permissible expression of the universal relativism that can find no common measure of right and wrong and that, like Rorty when the torturers come, he can only accept this as the truth about man today. The difference is that Camus still feels compelled to register his opposition to the fascist evil, even if he cannot say why. That kernel of resistance is what undergoes a remarkable spiritual strengthening and growth in the intervening years up to *The Rebel*. By that stage, Camus had reached a level of confidence in the superior reality of his intimations of right that he could assert them as the measure by which the evil he witnessed in the totalitarian convulsions could be judged. He proclaimed the presence of a limit, a point beyond which one should not go in the treatment of human beings, and that limit functioned as the boundary reality within which we find ourselves. It had become superior to the falsity of the fascist or communist rationalizations of murder: "Analysis of rebellion leads at least to the suspicion that, contrary to the postulates of contemporary thought, human nature does exist, as the Greeks believed. Why rebel if there is nothing permanent in oneself worth preserving?" (*The Rebel*, 16).[21]

Solzhenitsyn exemplifies the passage from the starting point of the spiritually disorientated inhabitant of the totalitarian regimes. Thrown into the camps toward the end of the war he found himself in a world without any firm moral outlines and discovered the extent of his own moral disassociation. Within that strongly nihilistic environment, with neither rules nor customs to guide him, the direction he discovered would have to come from the force of reality disclosing itself within him. It seemed fully permissible to him in the beginning, he recounts in the *Gulag Archipelago*, to go along with the domination of the weak by the strong. He asks the thieves in the camp to throw out a poor old "last-legger" whom he knew had not the strength to resist in order to obtain a bunk for himself. But he gradually came around to the realization that he had lost more in the exchange than any material comfort he may have gained. There is an inexorable order to human existence and to disregard it is not simply immoral or bad form. It is to lose our grip on the reality that makes us human beings. "And thus it is," he remarks of the experiences in which the moral structure of life becomes existentially clear to him, "that we have to keep getting banged on the flank and snout again and again so as to become in time at least, human beings, yes, human beings."[22]

There are many such remarkable examples in the prison-camp literature of the twentieth century or in the autobiographical recollections of individuals who have confronted the philosophical questions in the most extreme circumstances of life and death.[23] What they demonstrate is that even in a nihilistic age when the language of moral imperatives has lost its efficacy, the structure of a moral reality imposes itself nevertheless. Almost without the availability of linguistic formulations, human beings are compelled to reinvent or rediscover the means of expressing what cannot be avoided. Such efforts of existential catharsis and recovery are of inestimable significance precisely because they occur largely outside of any established tradition of discourse. They point to the prearticulate sources from which the traditions arise, and they speak with an authority that is capable of revivifying the traditions themselves. Indeed, they have a spiritual power that utterly overwhelms the overly precious philosophical reservations posed against all affirmations of moral truth.

A similar force is at work in the rediscovery of the traditions. For it is precisely the depth of the moral disintegration of the contemporary world that has provoked the opening to their rediscovery. The effort of recovery is in this sense not a purely scholarly or antiquarian exercise, although scholarship is definitely involved. Philosophy and Christianity become a means of existential order because they are discovered as a spiritual power of formidable proportions, capable of taking over human lives and transforming our whole sense of what is important in reality. They are capable of exercising that kind of influence because they are more than historically interesting symbolisms, more than a factual residue of a now vanished past; they are the most powerful spiritual movements, as capable of drawing forth heroic responses of self-sacrifice today as at any point in their history. It is this sense of the existential force of their appeal that is the source of the excitement surrounding the reencounter with classical philosophy, Jewish, and Christian testaments in the work of the traditionalist scholars today.

They recognize in Plato's *Republic*, for example, an evocation of order that speaks to the same profound spiritual disorder as characterizes the contemporary world. The partners of the dialogue who meet in the atmosphere of easy informality in the Piraeus are identical with the assembly of dead souls who come together in the myth of Er at the end of the dialogue to choose the form of life they will lead in their next incarnation. In each case there is no reliable principle or model for guidance. Neither custom nor society nor appearance are of much assistance in this most crucial choice of what a human being is to become. Souls thrown back on their own resources discover their lack of a sense of direction to guide them; they recognize how easily they are misled by appearance into making the wrong choices that yield a fate of untold misery. They recognize their need for a helper who might form the formlessness of their souls. "From the Hades of the myth," Voegelin observes, "we are transposed back to the Hades of the Piraeus with its equality of the lonely souls and their freedom without substance. Socrates is the man who can help the others, who will enable them to diagnose the right and wrong paradigms of life, who will build up in them wisdom and, thus, add substance to the Arete of which they have only the freedom" (*Order and History*, 3:58).[24]

It might well be wondered how Socrates is to place the substance of order into souls that are without anchor or direction. How is it possible for him to persuade them of that which they have no knowledge? The answer is that they are not utterly without knowledge; there are no souls without some foothold on the realm of solid truth, and that is enough to provide the link on which a more elaborate connection can be built. This is well demonstrated in the *Gorgias* where Socrates takes on the corrupt politician who is equipped with the Nietzschean defense of the will to power as the inescapable reality behind all moral professions. Eventually Socrates wrings from him the concession that it is irrelevant whether our actions serve the enlargement of ourselves, our pleasure, and our power, but only whether they are fitting, noble, or right. Callicles cannot accept that the coward is as good as the brave man simply because he takes as much or more pleasure at the retreat of the enemy as the other. There is an order of what is "right by nature" that human beings know and cannot avoid recognizing, no matter how much they may seek to avoid acknowledging its consequences.

But that knowledge is not present in some completed form, available for guiding decisions and transmitting instructions as if it were a set of instructions such as Locke's innate ideas. Moral knowledge partakes of what Plato called the In-Between (Metaxy) character of our existence, capable of a wide amplitude of realization from minimal awareness to radiant transparence without ever being definitively actualized or finally eliminated. That is why there is the variability in human beings and in their participation in order. The depth of confusion that is possible is well developed in the portrait of life in a corrupt society painted by Glaucon and Adeimantus (*Republic* bk. 2), as they recount the contradictory pressures and injunctions they receive to pay lip service to the conventions of justice while all the time practicing as much injustice as one can get away with. They recognized the contradictoriness of such aspirations and sensed the depth of viciousness that lay behind them, but they could find no good arguments to marshal against the corrupt suggestions nor, more important, the necessary inner resources to mount their personal resistance to the pressures of involvement. The elaboration of the philosophic discovery of natural right requires more than the invocation of its principles. What the *Republic* reveals is that philosophy in its most adequate implementation consists in the meditative expansion of what the soul knows into the defining sense of reality.

This crucial recognition is key to the multitude of modern objections concerning the contestability of all foundations or principles within the moral world. It shows that the classical thinkers, too, were aware of the dimensions of the problem and that philosophy was in fact their response to it. The argument in the *Republic* seems to have reached a conclusion on several occasions only to be propelled forward again in light of the unsatisfactoriness of the position reached. The most significant occasion is when we seem to have arrived at a definition of justice in the formulation that each part of the soul as well as each part of the state ought to perform the task for which they are best suited by nature (443b-c). But then that definition is revealed as no more than provisional, and we are warned that if we really want to understand what it is that makes this order possible, then we must be prepared for the "longer and more arduous way" (435d) that leads up to the light of the Good. The transcendent apex of Platonic philosophy is, in other words, presented as an afterthought that we encounter only as a result of the proddings of the interlocutors in the dialogue.

It is only for those who are truly desirous of finding the way and are sufficiently prepared for the opening of the soul, which is the only avenue of knowledge of the highest reality. To know what justice is and why it is the measure by which we must be guided, we must be prepared to raise our gaze beyond justice itself to that which makes it good and eventually to arrive at that which is goodness itself and the source of what is good in all things. Why indeed should we be just or right, as Nietzsche and the contemporary world ask? Plato's answer is that it is only because we sense in what is just the pull of that which is utterly good without reservation and qualification, that which is the Good, and in which we come to participate more fully the more we follow out the responsive pull of its attraction. It is the opening toward transcendent being, described in the Parable of the Cave, and realized in the ascent toward the Good that is at the center of the philosophical experience. Beyond that nothing more can be said, nor is anything more in need of saying.

The succinctness of the philosophic account of the Good is, Voegelin observes, the central insight of Platonic ethics. "The transcendence of the Agathon makes immanent propositions concerning its content impossible. The vision of the Agathon does not render a material rule of conduct, but forms the soul through an experience of transcendence" (*Order and History,* 3:112). Obviously, experiences of transcendence are notoriously difficult to communicate, as Plato himself acknowledges in his remarks about "turning the soul around" *(periagoge)* in the *Republic* (518d) and in the *Seventh Letter,* but some such powerful sense of what is "beyond being in dignity and power" (*Republic* 508a) must be presupposed as the impulse that gave rise to the movement of philosophy. Even in Aristotle such experiential depths are still discernible on the analytic surface of his reflections, as when he refers to the good life as "living in accordance with the most divine part of ourselves" and as a process of "immortalizing" (*Ethics* 1177b30). But the difficulty of getting hold of it is evident even among the best interpreters such as MacIntyre, who recognizes Plato's "understanding of the form of justice in the light afforded by the form of the Good" but then complains that "it is not itself and could not be the completion of that enquiry" (*Whose Justice? Which Rationality?* 82).[25]

It may be that the recovery of the traditional sources is not as easy as it sounds, even for those well disposed and capable of the task. The modern prejudices, such as that all can be reduced to the rigors of discursive argumentation, die hard, and we are not always inclined to give full weight to the existential factors that are the palpable source of our own attraction to the traditions themselves. The necessity for participation in the moral and spiritual life of a tradition is acknowledged as a condition for its full appreciation, but the expectation that participation itself will disclose dimensions of reality not captured within the symbolic or conceptual formulations is not fully acknowledged. Thus, while MacIntyre understands that "the reader has to have inculcated into him or herself certain attitudes and dispositions, certain virtues, *before* he or she can know why these are to be accounted virtues" (*Three Rival Versions,* 82), he does not seem to take the full measure of the significance of this existential increase in participation. At any rate, it is evident that it is the appeal of such greater existential truth that is the source of the traditionalist reawakening in MacIntyre and the others and the only possible means of overcoming the nihilistic indifference to all professed articulations of truth. By turning more attention to the experiential component, the traditionalists might begin to build bridges to the unsubmerged outposts of conviction that still remain among the pragmatic deconstructionist liberals as well.

Paradoxical as it may sound, the failure of traditionalist intellectual movements has been in taking account of their own significance for the modern world. Having been on the defensive for so long, they often sound as if their only concern was to preserve their own corner of freedom within that world. Their principle weapon of defense has been the critique of the modernity to which, in one form or another, they have been opposed. What they have failed to recognize is that they are themselves a part of that world and that their own successful recovery of the sources of tradition has significance for the wider civilization. If one or a few individuals have discovered the contemporary relevance of Aristotle or Augustine, then that has representative significance for their contemporaries. Most crucial is that they have discovered the means of recovery, especially the existential enlargement of horizon so necessary to moving from the impoverished modern spirituality to the vastly more profound intuitions available in the great traditions.

A way has been found to the moral sources of order, so much presupposed and so long neglected by the modern liberal constructions. The dependence of liberal order on the transcendent foundation of order does not have to remain a pure dependence, drawing on an earlier tradition without any hope of rearticulating it in the present. Now the possibility of a vital reappropriation of the traditions has been revealed. The interminable and inconclusive debates about the grounds of moral principles have been shown to have an end. It lies in the recognition of the termination of our moral intimations in the transcendent reality that discloses itself more fully to us as we participate more fully in its concrete ordering of our lives. There is no ground that does not itself rest on a ground that is already present when we begin to ask the question of the ultimate source and direction of our existence. All that there is, is the order in which we participate through our articulations and actions, whose transcendent finality discloses itself as the pull that is immanent in the "between" reality of our lives.

Transcendent Completion of Liberal Order

Liberal order is a special case of the in-between character of human existence differentiated by the classic philosophers. It might even be regarded as a heightening of the movement of freedom so indispensable to the unfolding of that intermediate status. The degree to which a human being is incomplete, engaged in a process of actualization of what he or she is but is not yet, never reducible to a pure beginning and never reaching a definitive finality, is the underlying reality so powerfully evoked by the liberal construction. It is this conviction that is given expression in the liberal rejection of all preconceived paradigms of the human good or human nature. If there were a substantive purpose to be attained or an objective to be accomplished, then it would make infinitely more sense to subordinate individuals to a common authority who would more efficiently assemble and direct their resources toward their target. But it is the nature of a being whose nature is not determined and whose end is not pregiven that it must engage in the process of freely pursuing that which is to constitute its order. We are not yet that which we aspire to become, and the freedom of movement toward it is indispensable because we do not yet know what that telos is until we have begun to participate in it. The movement is rational, which means that it must be free.

The recovery of the classical philosophic tradition is of enormous significance in making available an understanding of the self-realizing indeterminacy of human nature that forms the background to such crude liberal formulations as the primacy of right over the good. Such inarticulate gropings to express the essentially in-between character of human existence, whose essence is to engage in the quest for its essence without predetermined impositions, appear particularly unsophisticated by the side of the classic analysis. Contemporary Rawlsian liberals are compelled to defend the indefensible position that their liberal order presupposes no conception of the good and, when this defense is rendered impossible, retreat to the incoherence of admitting the historical arbitrariness of their convictions. What they sorely lack is the flexibility of the classical insight into the in-between character of existence, which can maintain the free indeterminacy of human life without abandoning all notion of the good toward which it is straining. What makes Oakeshott the most sophisticated of contemporary nonfoundationalists is that he has absorbed a good deal of this reappreciation of the classical approach. He knows that the rejection of dogmatic foundations does not necessarily mean the loss of all contextual order.

Liberal political philosophy has long been in need of a coherent means of integrating its emphasis on the inviolability of individual liberty with a recognition of the substantive moral order whose actualization is the justification for the preeminence of liberty in the first place. Can we on the one hand insist that men and women must be free to make up their own minds and follow their own mode of life and on the other that there are certain moral principles by which they must be guided and toward which they might be encouraged and constrained to submit? This is the well-known conflict between liberty and authority that has bedeviled liberal politics in one form or another from its inception. Is there not some root incompatibility between freedom from all pressure and the subtle and not-so-subtle conjunction of pressures in a particular direction? Equally, is there not something profoundly contradictory in the defense of a liberty that is exercised only in the direction of reducing and even destroying the capacity for self-realization itself?

Isaiah Berlin's formulation of the conflict between negative and positive liberty is only one of many alternative presentations of the same issue.[26] The peculiar inconclusiveness of the debate, with Berlin and other liberals, arises from the inescapable limits of the liberal frame of reference. It is a false dilemma that we must choose between negative liberty, which is wholly free of any suggestion of coercion, and positive liberty, which is the only conception that carries some implication of rational or moral order. It is possible for human beings to remain free of determining pressures while accepting that their choices are not wholly without overarching direction or structure. The false dichotomy dissolves when we realize that free self-determination is utterly compatible with a spiritual order that is never stripped of all intimations of direction, but whose moral structure discloses itself to us only as we participate and respond more fully in its ramifications. Freedom and order are perfectly reconciled in an order whose dynamic is the realization of freedom. The understanding of human existence as a drama, rather than as a marketplace, makes possible the recognition of choice as free yet connected with an order that is not yet realized until the action has been completed.

The rediscovery of the narrative structure of human existence has done much to redress the imbalance of the excessive liberal tendency toward abstraction and discreteness in imagining human life. But the new "communitarian" liberals have generally been content to locate the context in the concrete richness of human life and have, as a consequence, not broken through to anything approaching the classical philosophical transparence.[27]

It is not merely that human action is located in the inextricable historical complexity of life that makes it impossible to treat it as a series of discrete self-contained choices, but that human life itself is radically incomplete and incapable of exhausting itself even in the sum total of all the interlocking and interrelated historical reality. It is central to the liberal conviction that each individual transcends the sum total of the whole in which they are a part, and this cannot be established simply on the basis of the horizontal expanse of their relatedness. The incompleteness that defines human life is one that cannot in principle be completed within the finite reach of existence, no matter how extended. It is a radical freedom and incompleteness only because it is a reach toward that which is beyond all limits.

But how can that be established in a way that does not entail the specification of how the freedom is to be employed? Can there be a theological grounding of freedom that does not even define union with God as the telos to be attained? Again, we seem to have encountered a question hoary with the trappings of historical lineage. Suspicion that the full realization of human freedom is incompatible with the acknowledgment of a divine creator might be regarded as one of the central, if not *the* central, self-reflection of the modern world.[28] It is an attitude whose greatest impact has been manifested in the revolutionary ideologies that aspire to re-create human nature; but it has played a role within the liberal tradition itself, as is evident in the suspicion with which Mill regarded the notion of the deity and in the militant antiecclesiastical spirit that dominated the Continental liberal spirit. Even within the more moderate Anglo-American setting exemplified by Rawls, there is a noticeable disinterest in anything remotely resembling a theological frame of reference.[29]

The source of the objection in all cases has been a profound misunderstanding of what the relationship to God means to human freedom. It is assumed that obedience to natural and divine law would necessitate the surrender of some significant degree of the liberty of self-determination, because the acknowledgment of such an authority would specify a substantive portion of what is to be decided in how we are to live our lives. Largely overlooked is the realization that the divine telos provides little or no specific instruction as to what concretely ought to be done in each of the changing situations we encounter. That remains as much a problem for the theist as the atheist. What distinguishes them is the degree of seriousness they bring to the task of discerning what is morally required of them in the problems they confront. No detailed instructions are received from the divine side beyond the affirmation of moral seriousness already intuited in the experience. It is not the content of action that is specified by the divine relationship but the spirit in which all the actions are performed. That pervasive presence is manifested in the sense of transcendent significance attaching to the drama of the struggle between good and evil in the human heart. The specifics of right action are either self-evident obligations or become evident through the concrete fidelity to their realization.[30]

The divine ground of morality is no different from the moral imperatives themselves. They do not provide any detailed instruction on their application but are, in Oakeshott's term, *abbreviations* of a practice that can be learned only by engaging in it. Nor are they directed toward the achievement of any substantive purposes. Like the rules of the game, they educate us on how we should pursue the purposes we select, the constraints and recognitions that must form a part of our activities, and most of all the spirit in which the game must be played. But they do not inform us as to what we are to do or what choices we should make. Purposes are confined to the finite and the immanent, and the most important dimension has nothing to do with what specific achievements or contributions have been made but with what a person has become in the process. Beyond all tangibles and measurables lies the intangible and immeasurable necessity of doing all things rightly. It is that without which no other values are worth possessing.[31]

The transcendent finality of human existence is not one more possibility among the list of options available to us. It is not one of the lifestyles that might be selected and pursued; rather, it is what frames all possible choices and makes them of value. It cannot be treated as one of the choices themselves because that would be to deny its transcending embracing role as that whose presence makes all other choices possible. Once it is included in the list of immanent objectives, it loses its unconditional authority and becomes increasingly opaque as a life-promoting direction. Why, indeed, should one be concerned about fidelity to the moral law or divine commands, especially when they are competing against the more massive social and material gratifications for our attention? The authoritative ground of order must be transcendent. It cannot survive its absorption into the realm of immanent possibilities where it must demonstrate its utility like everything else.

We have seen the way in which liberal principles have functioned as just such an unconditioned order within which immanent ethical choices can be framed. The tendency, as in Rawls and Dworkin, has been irresistible to clothe this liberal transcendence with the same aura of sacredness as has traditionally been reserved for religion. The experiential recovery of the philosophic and revelatory traditions confirms the legitimacy of this tendency. While the liberal invocation of sacredness may strike us as rhetorically hollow, the deeper truth is the logic of experience that is disclosed within it. Order in human existence cannot be evoked without reaching, at least implicitly, toward the transcendent horizon that constitutes it. What is right is a participation in the transcendent reality disclosed within its structure. However it is understood, the experience is unavoidably a heightening or a movement toward what outweighs all the immanent realities of our world.

The crux of the liberal dilemma, as we have seen, has been the inability to assert the reality of its experience. Professions of the sanctity of individual rights have teetered on the slenderest of connections with reality and periodically have collapsed into the abyss of a rhetorical vacuum. The situation has become so desperate today that our contemporary liberal theorists have placed an injunction on the raising of such "metaphysical" questions. Perhaps nothing bears such eloquent witness to the absolute necessity of recognizing the reality of the unconditioned transcendent ground of its order. They recognize that if they are compelled to acknowledge the purely conceptual nature of their transcendent presuppositions that nothing will stand in the way of the wholesale disintegration of their moral order. The depth of conviction with which they struggle against this prospect is the most convincing evidence of their own participation in its transcendent reality and power.

What the experiential recovery of tradition reveals is that the erstwhile transcendence of the liberals is not that far away from the only possible acknowledgment of transcendent reality. The philosophic and revelatory traditions have no other access or basis for their affirmation of transcendent reality than their own sense of participation within it. It is not that men and women of an earlier age had a privileged entrée that has now been foreclosed to us moderns. The only source for their apprehension of divine being and of their expectation of our self-transcending movement toward it was their own experience of participating more faithfully in its order. Perhaps the only difference was that they trusted their experience, whereas we are inclined to suspect it. But surely few can be far away from the kind of tentative reflection on experience in Aristotle's halting conclusion to *Ethics* (1177a10–78a10), where he admits he is not sure whether this life of virtue is divine in comparison to the human or merely the life of the most divine part of ourselves. All that he is sure of is that it is the best and the defining one for a human being and that it engages us in the process of "immortalizing" (*athanatizein*).

The alternative to this expansive opening of the liberal experience in line with its inner directional logic is the contraction toward the nihilistic vacuum it is presently struggling valiantly, if pathetically, to avoid. If they step beyond their own metaphysical prohibition to the admission of ontological vacuity, then it will be difficult to sustain the convictions on which they have relied. It will become increasingly difficult to attend to the tenuous pull of what is transcendent if all of their self-understanding proclaims the nullity of the enterprise. It will be tantamount to stepping beyond the *Tao*, the proclamation of man's liberation from all received moral order and the assertion of his utterly ungrounded liberty, which has been invoked already in the more radical epiphanies of the modern spirit. That logic has now been played out for any who care to witness it in the inhuman degradation and cruelty of the concentration camps. When men are no longer bound by any law they are not free; but controllers and controlled are more miserably dominated than ever by the law of necessity through chance and whim. Man's conquest of nature, including the human nature that draws him into the rationally cooperative project of its realization, turns out to be, as C. S. Lewis so succinctly observed, "the abolition of man."

The law that seemed from one perspective to be man's harness of constraint turns out, when viewed in a different light, to be the guarantee of his liberty. Once everything is permitted then nothing is permitted, because nothing is forbidden. We can no longer distinguish between the beneficial and the harmful, the beautiful and the ugly, the true and the false. All have been reduced to the one indistinguishable maelstrom of process from which nothing distinctively human or significant emerges. The oppressive homogeneity of the empiricist reign of quantity that has formed the nightmare of modern man ever since its figuration in Pascal and Swift has finally crowded out all other reality capable of evoking the distinctions between higher and lower on which our humanity depends. Freedom itself depends on our capacity to take our bearings in relation to certain fixed parameters of order. Once there are no longer any eternal points of reference, we cannot distinguish between activity that is free, because it is consciously chosen for a reason, and what is done autonomically under the impulse of the pulls and pushes of our reflexes. Once there are no longer reasons for what we do or at least the possibility of invoking them, our actions too become indistinguishable from the causal sequence of events in which they are embedded. We are no longer the point of being that can stand apart from the events in confronting them. We sink to the barely conscious submergence in them.

It is in relation to a transcendent order that liberty is intelligible, and it is its capacity for unfolding participation in that reality that underpins the recognition of its value. Human participation in reality is not identical with that of all other things in existence. It is not merely a factual existence. The mode of human participation is conscious and intelligent; it is free. Not only are we part of a larger order of things beyond ourselves, but we consciously and freely choose our participation within it at least to a considerable extent as well. In this sense, it is not a given predetermined mode of participation but a free involvement that participates in the manner of the source of the whole itself. Human freedom is an analog of the divine freedom and is free because it is a mode of participation in the divine being. That is what the Old Testament understanding of man as made in the image of God means. Human freedom is not merely a submission to the rules of order, it is a participation in the rule-making intelligence itself.

The liberal affirmation of self-determination is thus in line with the deepest intuition about the place of man in the order of things. This is the insight of Jacques Maritain who was not the only one to underline the continuity between democracy and Christianity but was certainly among the most forceful exponents of the relationship. He recognized not only the compatibility of the liberal democratic forms with Christianity but also their mutual reinforcement. Just as the liberal elevation of the self-governing individual has become the turning point of the political order, so the Christian affirmation of the transcendent dignity of the human participation in the divine creation of order is its ultimate justification. The transcendent calling of each individual, which is the center of the Christian symbolization, in turn finds its deepest expression in the reverence for the inviolability of individual freedom in the liberal construction. The Judaic and Christian understanding of man finds its most consistent political unfolding in liberal democracy, and the latter regains contact with its deepest inspiration in acknowledging its dependence on the revelatory traditions.

The dignity of the person, Maritain explains, derives from his participation in the transcendent being of God because it is endowed with the being of personality. It exists in the mode of self-subsistence, that which like God contains its existence within itself. That is what the interiority of personality means. We do not simply exist as brute facts but as beings who possess their mode of existence consciously and are capable of expressing and communicating and giving ourselves. Only spiritual beings possess that capacity of free communication of self that is not bound to the contingencies of its existence but is ever able to transcend such limits in the communication of the self that lies beyond or deeper than them. "In short, it must be endowed with a spiritual existence, capable of containing itself thanks to the operations of the intellect and freedom, capable of super-existing by way of knowledge and of love" (*Person and the Common Good*, 40). Maritain quotes Juliet's "Thou art *thyself*, though not a Montague . . . Romeo, doff thy name, and for thy name, which is not part of thee, take all myself," by way of illustrating how the personality transcends all factualities in its possession of itself. "For this reason, the metaphysical tradition of the West defines the person in terms of independence, as a reality which, subsisting spiritually, constitutes a universe unto itself, a relatively independent whole within the great whole of the universe, facing a transcendent whole which is God" (40).

Divine self-subsistent Personality has invited us to participate in the same independent being as itself. We are not subordinate to its ordering rule in the manner of all merely finite creation, but as sons of God in the manner befitting the divine being itself, as freely responsive personalities. Oakeshott acknowledges this uniqueness in recognizing that man's government by the divine law is through the mode of "self-chosen actions, in contrast to a divine Will to which he must submit himself and his conduct . . . or to a divine Purpose to which his conduct willy-nilly contributes" (*On Human Conduct*, 158), but he does not seem to take the measure of what it discloses of the human reality. A similar criticism may be raised against Charles Taylor's celebration of the modern conceptualization of freedom as the guarantee of rights in which the indemnified individual himself exercises the defining role. "To accord you an immunity, formerly given you by natural law, in the form of a natural right is to give you a role in establishing and enforcing this immunity" (*Sources of the Self,* 11). What Taylor also does not quite seem to fully appreciate is that there would be neither the capacity nor the rationale for such an immunity if there was not first the divine gift of self-subsistence as its only possible source.

Oakeshott and Taylor fail to follow through to the underlying meaning of their convictions. Having acknowledged the extent to which freedom is a gift, an open invitation to participate in the self-governing order of divine being, they seem unable to recognize the momentous consequences of this admission—that is, that the participation in intelligent self-determination is at the same time sustained by the divine suffering of the evil consequences of the human failure of self-direction. The divine permission of freedom is simultaneously the divine submission to the possibility of disorder. Man's participation in the self-subsistence of divine being is also the divine participation in the human loss of self-subsistence. The gift of freedom is indistinguishable from the mystery of redemptive divine suffering of freedom. They cannot be separated, and it is this indivisibility that opens the reality in depth of freedom. Oakeshott and Taylor, despite the conscientiousness of their expositions, fail to recognize the dimension of depth from which the evocation of freedom arises. They end up echoing the contemporary "rights talk" because they fail to identify the transcendent adumbration of their convictions. They do not seem to sufficiently recognize the extent to which their own admission of the indefeasibility of rights puts them in touch with the transcendent reality that is their only sustaining source. They do not apprehend the sanctity of freedom as itself a participation in the divine.

The significance of this realization, which even Maritain in his eagerness to emphasize the practical convergence of all forms of liberal politics fails to bring to light, is that the commitment to a liberal order is not only grounded in the participation in transcendent Being but is also sustained by the redemptive outpouring of divine grace. The human failure to live up to the high demands of its nature is an inescapable dimension of the same reality. The gift of self-subsistence that is the dependent independence of the human person cannot be separated from the redemptive presence that sustains it. By granting the freedom of self-direction to human beings, making them participants in the divine mode of being and inviting their responsive opening to its fullness, God also revealed the depth of his merciful forgiveness by which he suffers through the interminable history of human evil and rejection. This is the mystery that is revealed in Christ and which Dostoyevsky most clearly of all the moderns illuminates as the center of order in historical existence.[32]

The tensions endemic to the liberal construction find their resolution only in that movement toward transcendent being that is their inspirational source. Taken as a pure aspiration or longing, the movement would be insupportable in its own terms; it is only because it encounters an answering movement of reconciliation from the divine side that it can be sustained. Without that redemptive restoration the liberal commitment to the inviolability of the person would seem insupportable, even futile, in face of the staggering costs in human unhappiness and criminality. Liberal philosophy is a political symbolism for the everyday reality in which expectations are fulfilled within a fairly narrow range of ponderables; it is notoriously ill at ease in confronting the deeper mysteries of the reality within which it finds itself. But from time to time the necessity of pondering the imponderable is forced upon us. It is at that point that the liberal tradition becomes conscious of itself as a tradition and, as such, as dependent on the larger spiritual traditions from which it has arisen and from which it is inextricably sustained even in the present. The fact that we are contemplating that larger horizon today is testament to the depth of the crisis with which we sense ourselves confronted.

The discovery of the incompleteness of the liberal order and its dependence on the larger spiritual traditions for its self-understanding is only the first stage in framing our response. Beyond the acknowledgment of what is required is an elaboration of the way toward it. We cannot await the civilization-wide revitalization of the premodern traditions or expect that they will soon be restored to their previously authoritative position. Nor can we expect that the liberal public order will undergo a dramatic mutation into an utterly different symbolization of its inner meaning. Both are prospects with high indexes of improbability attached to them, however often the longing for some such outcome might seem to substitute for the reality in the minds of certain contemporary critics. The more likely outcome is that we will continue to muddle through and that whatever change occurs will incrementally manifest itself over the long run.

That implies the necessity of devising strategies that will contain the best promise of cumulatively affecting the flow of a current that none are able to control or reverse. The fluidity of the liberal approach is itself the best ally in this task for, as we have seen, it does not consist of unalterably fixed quantities but exists as an evocative public symbolism that floats above unarticulated depths of spiritual and moral consensus. The possibility exists therefore of enlarging the liberal movement toward a more expansive self-interpretation of its meaning. It can be brought incrementally closer to a recognition of its own fullest aspiration and significance. Rather than a reversion to the tired resuscitation of minimalism, which has been one of the enduring historical patterns, this would begin with the recognition that the decline of order cannot be resolved through the acceptance of ever lower levels of attainment.

At some point the accumulated capital must receive new infusions; it cannot be drawn off indefinitely. That realization is the turning point at which our attention is directed toward the spiritual resources that remain, that can form the basis for a new expansionary movement radiating into the order of our individual and social existence. Instead of a contracting retreat, it would entail a real growth of the liberal soul beyond itself. Is it possible, we now must ask, for liberal society to become better than it thinks it can be?

8

Meditative Expansion of Limits

The purpose of this study has been to affirm that liberal order is capable of undergoing a meditative expansion of its limits, a genuine growth of the soul. Whether liberal society will go through such a spiritual transformation is another issue, because the prior question concerns its possibility. It is enough to direct our attention to that issue, without courting the distraction of futurist speculations. We can predict with certainty that the liberal project will not evolve in such a fashion if it has been demonstrated to be impossible. The concern here is with the more practical task of illuminating the possibility and thereby nudging reality in the particular direction. It is thus a work in the tradition of political philosophy, which is a practical reflection on politics and has this object in view even as it elaborates its speculative comprehension. Paradoxically, it is that practical orientation that opens the deepest contemplation of things.

This is particularly the case with the intermediate symbolism of a liberal public order that evokes without articulating an underlying whole. The most revealing question is not what it is but what it is capable of becoming, for only that perspective reveals what it truly is. The depths of the liberal construction, as we have seen, lie hidden or unspoken, and the pivotal issue concerns the degree to which they can be brought to light and thereby reinvigorate without overstepping the limits of liberal self-understanding. The balance is a delicate one, for the liberal formulations have been developed precisely to preserve silence about their foundations yet they cannot permit a total disconnection to occur. It is a precarious tension that, in the nature of all balances, is preserved only through the continuing struggle against imbalance. The meditative expansion of the limits is a necessary but dangerous exercise within the liberal orbit.

The danger is evident enough in the degree of resistance likely to be provoked by the implications of a study that suggests that the liberal construction presupposes an intimation of the transcendent finality of human life. Only if human beings are always more than the sum of the moments and qualities that constitute them does it make sense to treat them with a dignity and reverence that outweighs all other tangible considerations. The difficulty with this formulation is that it points us in the direction of man's participation in transcendent Being. It presupposes some kind of experience of God as the anchor that explicitly holds it all together, and, after some reflection, it presupposes something like the God who reveals his redemptive presence within history in order to affirm the validity of the transcendent orientation. As Saint Thomas explains, the natural desire to know God by his essence would seem to point toward its frustration without the revelation of the gift of divine life through Christ.[1] The problem is that the liberal framework was developed precisely to avoid such explications, and the discomfort level rises palpably the more overtly they are invoked.

Yet that does not obviate the necessity of straining toward the wider spiritual horizon, because without it the indispensable convictions of a liberal order will begin to atrophy and eventually disappear. Such is the crisis of intelligibility plaguing liberal self-understanding today in which it is becoming all too obvious that liberal convictions do not stand on their own and are no longer clearly related to the historical sources from which they derived. The public manifestation of this intellectual confusion is in the moral disorientation of liberal societies that seem powerless to prevent the progressive descent into incivility and lawlessness. How can it be prevented if there is no longer an animating conviction that there is such a thing as right and that it is our responsibility to uphold it? The paralysis of the central nervous system has left the victim powerless to do anything to defend himself against the myriad small assaults against his flesh, although he remains perfectly conscious of the process for a very long time.

The prospect is not an attractive one, and it is its undeniable imminence that loosens the accustomed rigidities to the point that some new thinking is possible. We are unlikely to encounter the tired liberal platitudes of separation between church and state or the irrefragability of self-determination, simply for voicing the suggestion that society depends on the virtue of its citizens and that something ought to done to encourage men and women to be good. A broad-based realization has already begun to take hold that the most serious social problems are largely impervious to programmatic solutions. They lie at the level of moral ethos, and the implantation of character is not a goal that can be attained through the direct implementation of programs. Virtue is a fragile, although ultimately ineradicable, quantity that cannot be commanded but can be encouraged while all the time remaining outside of the power of leaders to control. What the political order depends on cannot be produced by that order, although it can be facilitated or destroyed by it.

Social discussion that arrives at this realization generally adopts, no matter what the starting point from which it began, a conservative orientation as the most logical implication of its conclusion.[2] The difficulty is that it does not take the full measure of the problem or of the obstacles that stand in the way of any efforts to promote character and virtue. The naïveté of much conservative discussion arises from this inability to recognize the degree of fracture that exists over the question of what constitutes virtue or character. It is precisely because of our inability to reach any agreement on what is good that much of the moral disorientation and disintegration has occurred. Nor has this been a sudden or unexpected turn of events. It has been the logical outcome of a direction of modern liberal self-reflection, through a series of lilliputian steps no one of which could be regarded as definitive, until we arrive at the point where we no longer recognize ourselves or the society in which we live. The history of Supreme Court opinions tracking the social evolution more articulately is a fascinating exhibition of this process at work.[3] In order to address the situation it is necessary to do more than focus on the symptoms; the pathology that has produced them must also be considered for treatment. At that point we begin to move beyond the liberal parameters and consider the liberal construction itself as part of the problem.

This is why it has been necessary in the present study to include the liberal tradition itself within the purview of our examination, if we are to get a handle on the deeper roots of the problems afflicting our world. Such a reflection reveals the intractable character of the moral crisis because it reveals it to be a crisis endemic to the liberal construction. The tools available to us for confronting it are peculiarly limited in that they are largely the instruments made available by the same liberal formulations. We begin to see what Nietzsche foresaw and what MacIntyre has pronounced in our own day: politics in a liberal order without recourse to moral argument must be civil war. It becomes a pure struggle for power because the possibility of rational agreement through appeal to a common sense of right has disappeared. The inevitability of this situation is dictated by the impossibility of articulating the grounds of morality within the liberal construction. We have seen, however, that this is not all that there is to the liberal tradition and that it contains resources not fully counted in the Nietzsche-MacIntyre assessment. That is why I am more sanguine about the possibility of enlarging the liberal ethos, although I make no predictions for the probability of such a development.

The inestimable positive value of the kind of far-reaching examination of liberal order undertaken by Nietzsche or MacIntyre is that it loosens up the limits of the construction. It compels us to look at the source of the problems within the liberal approach and thereby forces us to reconsider alternative ways of going about their resolution. What, for example, can we do about the liberal predetermination to do without any overarching reference to a ground of morality? Given the disastrous consequences of assuming that we can dispense with any ultimate points of reference and the evident impossibility of importing some transcendent order de novo, we are prompted to reconsider the liberal dogmatism on such questions and to approach them with less of a sense of absoluteness. We have arrived at the recognition developed in the preceding chapter of the incompleteness of a liberal order. It disposes us toward a greater modesty or openness in considering the possibility of reliance on sources beyond itself. But it is no more than a preparation. Something more is needed to bring about anything approaching a real change of heart, the conversion that MacIntyre adumbrates but does not contemplate.

To effect such deeper change what is required will have to be of a positive or substantive nature. Beyond the preparatory loosening of the dogmatic boundaries there must be something affirmative that enters in—otherwise we will revert to the petty ideological warfare so much the resort of choice when the liberal fig leaf has disintegrated. There must be a more powerful sense of moral truth that overwhelms the objections of the long-standing skeptical disposition. The preoccupation with the contingency of all formulations of principle, which has compelled liberals to retreat to the admission of the contingency of their convictions, can only be overcome by the inner strengthening of those convictions to the point that the objections are rendered irrelevant. It is not that the intellectual criticisms are no longer acknowledged, a kind of anti-intellectual assertiveness, but that it becomes apparent that they do not touch the deepest level of convictions. The growth of the soul makes the difference between the depth and the surface self-evident, so that, while there are no principles without formulations, we see that there is more to the principles than their contingent formulations.

The "something more" is their derivation from depths that cannot be fully mapped by our analyses. There is no getting back to an a priori beginning that itself has no beginning. Wherever our reflections begin, we are already involved in a conception of the order in which we live. The perspective of participation is ineluctable. What we are engaged in is revealed, therefore, only through the heightening of the mode of our participation in it; by actualizing its order more fully in our lives we obtain a clearer and deeper understanding of what it is and what it entails. We make the reality of order present, or more fully present, through our deeper participation in it. The source of illumination is not the brilliance or transparence of the formulations but the more unmistakable moral reality that has been realized in our lives. It is the authoritative revelation of the intimations of order that we can never completely sever, but that is frequently submerged in the flickering consciousness of everyday existence. Once it emerges with an unmistakable force of reality, its authoritative hold on us cannot be denied.

The capacity for a real growth of the soul, although it is the recurrent fruit of moral struggle and reflection, is the great overlooked factor in all the contemporary debates. The operating assumption is that differences and divergences are irresolvable because they are relatively fixed quantities that can be expected to bounce off one another but not to undergo any significant modification. It is the understandably casual assumption that the future will be very much like the present, that what is irresolvable in one set of premises will remain intractable under all foreseeable conditions. What this orientation leaves out is the recognition that the reality in which we exist discloses itself through our participation in it. It is possible for the unalterability of certain dispositions to take on an altogether different complexion once they are measured against the realization of right that has grown within us. What had previously seemed so oppressive loses all power to intimidate in light of the reality that has taken hold of us. Before, certain aspects of experience had dominated our attention, perhaps the painful exertion required in doing what is right, but now that has been outweighed by the powerful attraction of what is right, the reality that illuminates our way more fully as we give ourselves to it. The obstacles and difficulties pale into insignificance in comparison with the good that is becoming real. In the struggle with evil and darkness, the goodness that draws us can grow to the point that nothing else matters but fidelity to it. The unreality of evil is disclosed in comparison to the more enduring reality of good.

Such a process of growth, it is well known, is at the heart of the moral life, but its character and significance are not very well appreciated. Even those who recognize the role of such experiences of moral enlargement, such as Charles Taylor, do not take account of its capacity to point the way toward the resolution of some of the most bedeviling conflicts of our liberal polity. They do not fully apprehend its significance in drawing us toward a level of moral confidence impervious to the cavils of the deconstructionist termites. It is capable of lifting us to the assurance of what is right irrespective of the consequences or opinions of the rest of the world, because it builds on the kernel of moral conviction that can never be abandoned and never radically transcended.[4] Far from being a flight away from the philosophical conflicts, it is that deeper and broader context in which they can be confronted most adequately. The objections appear for what they are, the specific contingent reservations that rest on their own partial grasp of the larger moral certainties that they presuppose. The critiques themselves are measured in the scale of the larger spiritual intimations that are never definitively formulated but are glimpsed more adequately in the process of the growth of the soul.

This final chapter explores the potential that such experiences contain for a renovation of our jaded liberal contentiousness. It begins with a more extensive consideration of the experience of the growth of the soul, which has been the most crucial and among the most obscure dimensions in the history of philosophical reflection. While all philosophy and spiritual symbolizations have been built on it, the experience itself has only recently begun to be identified with any care. Then we will examine the way in which the conflicts of liberal politics might be approached differently if they are viewed, not as interminable dead ends, but as openings toward the dialectical juxtapositions that invite an inner growth to occur. Finally, we will turn to the implications that this reflection holds for the nature of the liberal construction, a reconsideration that is capable of acknowledging the openness of liberal order toward spiritual sources beyond itself. The way might then be open to reformulate the nature of liberal democracy in a way that recognizes this dependence, while preserving the balance of refusing to allow that recognition to undermine the intermediate character of its symbolism.

Growth of the Soul

The struggle against disorder is always a process that begins in hesitation and uncertainty. This is the point of the sketch of the spiritual and moral disorientation in the first two books of the *Republic,* which details the effects of the social confusion concerning the nature and origin of order. The younger generation, who are its victims, are left with an undeniable sense of revulsion but little in the way of a means of resistance against the corrupting pressures. Yet such uneasy confusion is not total disorientation. There remains the unease itself, which, by careful nurturing, can be fanned to light as the fire that will illumine what is wrong and what should be put in its place. There always exists the possibility of a meditative expansion of the inchoate intimations of resistance, which can be gradually unfolded until they become a reality that is capable of standing over against the corrupt social reality and rejecting it. Moreover, this is no instinctive turning away from a reality sensed as disturbing and threatening, the kind of rejection we witness in a wide variety of fundamentalism, but a rationally luminous articulation of the standard by which the social reality is to be judged and the correlative strengthening of the self to the point of asserting its superior rightness to it. Diagnosis and therapy are inseparable moments in the growth of the soul in opposition to the disorder ranged against it.

This is the process by which philosophy comes into being. It is not an abstract exercise in the development of languages of moral or metaphysical reflection, but a concrete response to a historical situation of corruption and oppression in which a person senses that the reality at stake in the conflict is nothing less than the fate of his soul. We have already referred to the remarkable example in the *Republic* of the transition from the point where the philosopher who is compelled to withdraw into a private existence feels his humanity diminished, to the change effected when, as a result of the meditation on the source of order unfolded within him, he can assert the reality of the "city in speech" as superior to the historical reality, even if it is never in fact realized. Nothing has changed in the concrete circumstances confronted by the philosopher. He is still throwing forth his appeal to a city that not only will not accept it, but is already gathering itself toward the decision to kill him. Yet inwardly everything is different. We understand how it was possible for him to grow to the point that he could assert the reality of his soul against the unreality of the corrupt city and, in that judgment, disregard the murderous judgment of the city against him.

A similar pattern is at work in the other great spiritual symbolizations of history. The Moses who led his people to victorious exodus from the fleshpots of Egypt was not a disconnected figure of the revelation narrative. The assertion of the superiority of Yahweh to the cosmological gods of Egypt was an exodus that occurred first in the soul of Moses before it was unfolded in the actual exodus of the Hebrew tribes. Nor was it an event that occurred without preparation. Although it is not articulated as transparently as the philosophic meditation, we can assume that Moses and the Hebrew tribes that followed him were already prepared through their dissatisfaction with the compactness of the Egyptian order. They must already have been drawn in search of the transcendent divinity that revealed himself to them as the "I Am." Only a man who had already prepared himself to follow the divine command is capable of hearing the voice that commands him. "The command could be rejected," Eric Voegelin observes, "only by a man who could never hear it; the man who can hear cannot reject, because he has ontologically entered the will of God, as the will of God has entered him" (*Order and History*, 1:407).

The greatest exemplar of this growth of the soul to the point of its transcendent formation is Christ. In him is differentiated the culminating insight that the only fully adequate preparation of the human instrument to receive the divine imprint is the instrument that has been provided by God himself and is therefore identical with God. The mystery of the union of divine and human natures in the person of Christ is the definitive revelation of the mystery of the interpenetration of the divine in the human order within history. It is for this reason that the triumph of Christ over sin is recognized, not merely as representative but as effective of the divine victory over the evil and mortality of existence. Participation in the Spirit of Christ, a participation in his redemptive overcoming of all evil, is the fullest expression of the human participation in the transcendent order that eclipses the unreality of disorder and death.[5]

Moral conflicts and limitations are not for that reason insuperable barriers because they are not unalterably fixed quantities. They contain the mysterious capacity for growth in which what had previously appeared impossible takes on a different character and becomes a yoke that is easy and a burden that is light. Objectively nothing has changed; the same requirements and conditions are still in place, but inwardly everything has been transformed by the light of the greater reality revealed to us. Nor is it a radically new reality from what had been known at the beginning of the process, but an enlargement of that which was recognizably present from the beginning and that is apprehended more fully through its meditative expansion. The information available remains the same, but its significance has been changed by reason of the different weight that has been given to it. What had appeared so important is no longer so, what had previously only been of minor significance assumes the central role, as the whole scale of measurement has undergone a modification whose consequences ripple through the whole structure of our thought and way of life. That is the way in which, for individuals and whole civilizations, seismic shifts of spiritual meaning occur. Often the symbols employed betray only the slightest hints of the dramatic events unfolding behind them, yet the results are unmistakably clear in the whole new scale of measurement being applied.

It may not sound like the breakthrough so badly needed to confront the fractured moral and political reality of our contemporary liberal polity, but it is all that we have in the circumstances in which human beings find themselves, and it is sufficient to illumine the path immediately before us. So long as we are prepared to follow out the intimations we already have, struggling as best we can to avoid contriving conclusions that serve our convenience, then the direction will reveal itself. The more faithfully we try to live out the little we do discern clearly, the more the larger structure of morality will become apparent to us. There is no other perspective on the order in which we find ourselves as participants, except through the process of participation itself. At the deepest level there is no moral reality to be apprehended except insofar as it has become actualized through our own concrete realization of it. Anything else is a purely external perspective that is bound to be uncomprehending of a reality whose interior remains hidden to us. The role of exemplars and authoritative symbolisms are of pivotal significance in evoking the initial resonances toward good, but they remain largely opaque until we have begun to respond existentially through our own participation in it.

It is, however, that prospect of moral growth that contains the best promise of penetrating the impenetrable contradictions of our moral universe. In part this has always been the function of moral argument that has sought to move from the level of disputes to evoke the underlying principles and verities that are beyond dispute. What is generally overlooked in such arguments, and the reason for their irresolvability in our own time, is the neglect of the significance of moral conversion in the process. It is not simply a matter of reaching technical inferences from premises, because the deeper disagreements concern the relative weight to be given to the various components that enter into the discussion. Should choice be rated higher than the putative right to life of the fetus? Should the wishes of the terminally ill be accorded a higher priority than the intrinsic sanctity of life? The preference is purely arbitrary or a reflection of self-serving bias so long as it is not made in relation to the ultimate order of existence, taking into account the meaning and direction of human life as a whole. That is, the weighing takes place in relation to the transcendent perspective that exists nowhere except in the reflection and fidelity to its actualization.

By submitting more fully to its ineluctable presence the continuum of our participation in transcendent being is enlarged. The "unseen measure" so beloved of the Greeks becomes more present to us, and from its illumination we begin to see things rightly. We are cured of the disordering blindness of the passions as we see ourselves sub specie aeternitatis. We see that we are not irrevocably confined to the limits of the categories that dominate our public discussion, that debates are not condemned to move in the same interminable circles, but that it is possible to move toward a sense of the really real that places them in a vastly more expansive light. Conversion in this sense is evidently not something that can be commanded, nor is it plausible to expect that it will effect a large-scale social transformation. But if this is the structure of the spiritual reality of our moral life, then it must be recognized as the direction to be pursued, irrespective of the prospects of sweeping political success. We might prefer to be creatures whose moral struggles can be resolved differently, but nothing is to be gained by proceeding as if we can disregard the pivotal role of illuminative experiences of transcendence.

The great benefit of this condition of our spiritual life is that the amplitude of growth that is possible provides the basis for faith in a process whose outcome is not fully known when it is begun. When we engage in the struggle with disorder and disorientation we do not have all the answers, but we do sense the direction to be pursued and know that it will be unfolded more fully as we participate in it. The darkness is not total; it is suffused with the irradiating light of the beginning that expands as we follow its illumination. A trust in the order that will disclose itself enables us to enter on the task of confronting the perplexities of existence. It is not necessary to have all the answers ready-made or complete before our struggle begins; nor is it likely that the incompleteness with which our particular engagement will inevitably terminate will reach any definitive theoretical comprehension. We find ourselves in the midst of a process that it is our task to continue without knowing or controlling the whole. What sustains the mystery of our participation in order is the knowledge already present from the beginning of our participation from the beginning.

The structure is recognizable as the narrative structure of the quest recounted in all world literature. Heroes become heroes primarily through their willingness to undertake and to continue the quest, and are distinguished by their faith in a mysterious unfolding order that sustains them despite the odds ranged against them. Many contemporary writers have drawn attention to the inescapably narrative structure of human life, and it has been a useful counterpoise to the modern inclination to distinguish a series of discrete fragments in existence.[6] Our actions are not self-contained particles randomly colliding against one another. They form part of a larger pattern, and we engage in them in relation to that reflection on the narrative whole that is thereby being created. What has often been overlooked in this contemporary rediscovery of narrative is the degree of faith that is required to sustain it and the capacity for dramatically arresting moments of illumination within it. Even those who are disposed to think holistically are not always prepared for the discovery of the growth of the soul by which human beings are drawn beyond themselves into that higher and better state than they were.

Something of that faith is surely necessary if we are to sustain the struggle against the contraction of our humanity that is so constant a pressure in our technological age. Just as it is futile to think that we can turn our backs on the modern world with its symbolic fragmentation and its technological omnivorence, so is it equally impossible to surrender the struggle that would seal the final loss of our humanity. The contest, which is in common with human beings in every age, requires a continuing engagement that cannot be broken off as a result of discouragement and setbacks. It must be pursued in the face of social and historical forces that seem at times insurmountable and irreversible. But such perseverance cannot arise without its own support; it does not occur in a vacuum. If it is to be sustained, it must be underpinned by a faith in the order of the process in which we participate, confident that its meaning and direction are fully present even when they are impenetrable to us and that fidelity to the call to participate is the way toward their realization.

The role of historic exemplars, including recent ones, should not be underestimated in this struggle. We can draw considerable encouragement, for example, from the degree to which the spirit of truth has already triumphed over the most formidable manifestations of the spirit of domination. The collapse of the vast instrumentalized power structures known as totalitarian states, constructions that appeared invincible in their "hideous strength," is only the most visible manifestation of the exhaustion of the inexorable grasp of the power of modernity.[7] Much more significant is the witness of individuals who in their confrontation with the totalitarian convulsion found within themselves a spiritual reality that eclipsed it. The testaments of those who resisted the holocausts and purges of the totalitarian terror is a daunting revelation of the reality of good that overcomes evil. No one can read their testimonies without coming away with a profound sense of the depths that lie hidden within a human being, spiritual resources of proportions that remained unknown even to those who possessed them until the day when they were called forth by the circumstances in which they found themselves.[8] Their existential witness illuminates more clearly than volumes of speculation the power of truth in the contest with falsehood. In their lives, which are by no means perfect or paradigmatic in every way, we see dramatically exemplified the way in which evil crumbles and hides before the enduring reality of good. They made the existential rediscovery, indispensable for our age, that nothing else matters than fidelity to the pull of right.

Beginning as specimens of ordinary human virtue, the circumstances of utter desolation they faced brought forth a remarkable process of spiritual growth that reveals the unsuspected depths of a human being. They were not heroes when they entered the camps but lost souls in the manner of so many in modern society itself. But the extremity in which they found themselves, the utter loss of all the comforting illusions and distractions that anesthetize us against the final questions of our existence, compelled a confrontation with the durability of the fidelity and goodness that extends beyond life itself. They responded to the pull of the transcendent reality that disclosed itself more fully to them as they had progressively lost all that attaches them to this world. From that small beginning they began to live more fully in accord with the demands of irrefragable rightness and to exemplify that formidable growth of the soul by which ordinary human beings undertake extraordinary actions. Instead of living by the law of self-preservation, the survival of the fittest, they embodied a different code that fully accepted the fate to which they had been called. Victor Frankl depicts it most strikingly in his remark about many of his fellow inmates at Auschwitz. "Suffering had become a task on which we did not want to turn our backs."[9]

This is the amplitude of possibility present in human life, and it is by no means confined to those who have gone through totalitarian imprisonment. Trials and crises await all of us in our personal lives, and no one can escape the inexorable approach of death. When we reflect on what matters within that context the overly sophisticated reservations about the contingency of all our moral inclinations pale into insignificance. What counts is not how well we have been able to defend what we know but how well we have been able to live it. When viewed in this light, the epistemological bad faith, the intellectual scrupulousness from which so much of our contemporary philosophizing suffers, begins to reveal its real purpose of relieving us of the burden of fulfilling our obligations as seriously as we should. In the most important examination of conscience, when the hermeneutics of suspicion is turned on the hermeneutics of suspicion itself, we begin to suspect the motives of such extreme punctiliousness. Before the blinding light of concrete moral goodness they dissolve into the shadows from which they arose. We see them as manifestations of an enduring aspiration within human beings to comprehend the whole in which they are, but now recognize that such comprehension is ultimately denied to creatures who have only the perspective of participants within it. The most crucial thing is to ensure that the aspiration does not become unbalanced and unhinge the more fundamental capacity and responsibility for participation itself. Reflective penetration of the process in which we are cannot become a means of escaping from it.

The unavoidability of the existential setting is the starting point for all serious philosophizing today. Not only is it necessary to continue living while we struggle to dissect its meaning, but the meaning itself is disclosed more fully through living it than can ever be captured within the lifeless traces of conceptualization. The clarion call of Kierkegaard resounds through modern philosophy as the indispensable condition for any credible illumination of the most fundamental questions that still define our existence. It is no accident that the greatest philosophical minds of our era, Nietzsche and Heidegger, have for all their shortcomings taken their bearings in relation to the concrete parameters of life itself. The great recovery of the premodern traditions—through Voegelin, Strauss, MacIntyre, Gilson, and others—has occurred through just such a recovery of the existential underpinnings that illuminate the texts that had previously appeared so opaque. We have begun to realize that we cannot dispense with the truth emergent in what Dostoyevsky called "living life," for it provides the only and deepest access to what can be known by us. There are no shortcuts to the discovery of who we are other than living out the intimations already present in our questions to their fullest.

The difficulty of realizing this insight is well illustrated by those who are most sympathetic to it. We discover elements of resistance to the full unfolding of its implications even by a man like Oakeshott who otherwise presents the case for the indispensability of a living tradition so persuasively. He is unsurpassed in the clarity of his insistence on the concrete character of moral knowledge, the impossibility of directing people toward right action by means of general rules of morality. Good action is not even a substantive goal pursued but the way in which a human being goes about the substantive purposes of life. Morality does not consist of an additional or optional objective that can be added to the range of possibilities to be chosen. It is the inescapable order that must be observed if we want to perform the role of a human being well, just as the rules of a game or a language define what must be observed in performing those activities well. As such, morality is inextricably concrete and cannot be separated from the practice of it that is the only source for its apprehension.

What Oakeshott does not identify, which results in the peculiar ambivalence and inconclusiveness of his response to the collapse of the traditions, is the actualization of the moral sources when the practice is resuscitated. He seems to point ineffectually at the importance of traditions without conveying anything of the vitality to be regained in returning to them. There is a hint of that conservative "terminal wistfulness" for a past that is longed for but that we no longer know how to recover. Oakeshott seems to sell his own proposal short, for what sustains historic movements of recovery and conservation is not merely respect for the value of traditions but the greater sense of life regained and transmitted through them. He overlooks the nature of a practice itself, which partakes of all of the tensions of the drama or performance that are available nowhere else but in the enactment itself.

This is a central concern of philosophers preceding even the classical era, although it certainly becomes thematic in Plato's warnings about not mistaking the symbols of philosophy for the actuality itself (see Plato, *Seventh Letter*). It is a tension that is well known in any activity that exists nowhere but in its performance. As in music, we must recognize the degree to which the reality evaporates except in the performance and, conversely, the degree to which good performance recovers more of the reality than might be suspected before it takes place. That is the magic of great musical or dramatic performances, that they surprise us with the sense of something much greater than the sum of their parts, a contact with the reality that transcends the boundaries of our everyday existence. Something similar may be said of great baseball or football games and of all else that involves the actualization of what is inert and unknown before its dazzling appearance.

Both moral action and the philosophical reflection on it share this character of performative actuality. The result is not only the indication of their fragility and inseparability from the practice of them, but also the indispensable invisible resources that the practice itself calls forth. We have all had the experience of being compelled to do certain things out of a sense of duty and then the surprising discovery that the task disclosed itself as attractive or appealing in ways we had never envisaged. By undertaking the first steps we had initiated a spiritual movement that seemed at some point to draw us onward, so that what had come from our own effort became impossible to separate from the love of the goal gradually manifest before us. In the process of taking up the preliminary indications of what is right, so long as we do not falter or resist the unfolding realization, we are drawn into depths of resolution and illumination that we had never suspected as we entered tentatively on the way. We become better than we thought we were, and we see more clearly than we thought we could.

Oakeshott is, moreover, not alone in omitting or underestimating the inner life of the spirit. Charles Taylor, who otherwise displays as deep an insight into the reality structure of moral experience as any, fails to follow out the implications of his insight when he deals with our contemporary disaggregation of meaning. The first part of his analysis of the *Sources of the Self* lays out the perspective from which he intends to present his masterly survey of the complex stratification of the sources of the modern self-understanding. In this prelude to the study he expounds the pivotal role of "moral intuitions which are uncommonly deep, powerful and universal" (4), in establishing the frameworks within which our evaluation of good and bad is carried on. He argues powerfully for the reality of such luminous intimations, rejecting the suggestion that their rational articulation is "so much froth, nonsense from a bygone age" (5). He takes seriously the notion that they provide the deepest ontological insight into who we are and the order of reality in which we live out our lives. The seriousness is indicated by the claim he makes for his own study as an essay in the retrieval of the repressed moral ontology behind the moral convictions of the modern world.

Much of that world is based on a deeply imbedded moral framework that it is unable or unwilling to articulate openly. Taylor is convinced that the exposition of the deepest spiritual intimations, which are the real source for the various moral positions espoused by modern men and women, is the starting point for any adequate consideration of what it entails. He brilliantly exposes the degree of disconnection that exists between the intensity of the profession of moral principles and the utter vacuity of all references to the real motivating sources behind them. This is the reason for the "gaping hole" in their proposals and positions that invariably "leave us with nothing to say to someone who asks why he should be moral or strive to the 'maturity' of a 'post-conventional' ethic" (87). Taylor's analysis of this foundational failure is in that sense superior to MacIntyre in *After Virtue,* for it is not that modern moralists have no justification for their positions, but that they have been incapable of articulating the substantive moral sources indisputably present within them.

They have failed, in Taylor's view, to take account of their own self-constitution through the visionary aspirations that have formed them. He rejects the understanding of ourselves as "punctual" selves, ready-made and complete, free to choose between the competing moral frameworks available to us. Rather, we are in the process of forming ourselves, and there is no point free of all influence, the self-contained self. We are constituted through the process of self-articulation and find ourselves within a moral and language community before the question of who or what we are arises. In that state of questing, between ignorance and knowledge, we are drawn toward contact with the real and the good as a "sacramental" reality, capable of endowing our lives with a meaning and fullness vastly beyond what we know in our everyday existence. Taylor does not shy away from identifying such experiences with those of being lost in "a rapturous state" (48), in which the whole narrative of our lives assumes coherence and direction. Whatever the language that is used, that of traditional spirituality or his own infelicitous terminology of "hypergood," such experiences are the inescapable formative pillars of our moral universe.

We cannot, he insists, get beyond them to any more fundamental perspective. Such glimpses of the highest good, whether it is God or justice or something else, are reached through a process of moral growth that carries its own conviction of truth with it. We reach them through the supersession of error or the expansion of more limited horizons, and for that reason they seem utterly convincing. But since they constitute the ultimate horizon of our moral universe they cannot be critiqued except by going through them to some deeper articulation of the moral hypergood. "My perspective is defined by the moral intuitions I have, by what I am morally moved by. If I abstract from this, I become incapable of understanding any moral argument at all" (73). All moral articulation is, therefore, an attempt to evoke the moral source of our order, to make contact with it and enter more deeply into its powerful momentum. It is "deeply implausible" to assert that all orders are arbitrary or expressions of "regimes of power," because it is "a form of self-delusion to think that we do not speak from a moral orientation which we take to be right" (99). Taylor takes as his task the exposition of the moral sources of those very modern thinkers who "have made it a point of honor not to admit to any such outlook" (103).

The difficulty is that as he proceeds through the masterful survey of the great philosophical and cultural innovators from the ancient world to the present, it seems almost as if he loses sight of the goal. True, he does unfold the inner dynamics of their moral articulations, but, as with his treatment of Plato, it is difficult not to conclude that something has eluded him. It is almost as if there is a hesitation, a lack of confidence in elaborating the full richness of the experiences behind them. Taylor is reluctant to adumbrate the depths not fully captured in the symbolic and conceptual articulations. He does not look for the growth of the soul toward participation in more eminent reality, which he had identified in his preliminaries, when he comes to the interpretation of specific thinkers. This becomes particularly evident in the conclusion of the book where there is the unresolved tension between Taylor's personal avowal of Christianity and the heavily nontranscendent tenor of contemporary reflections on meaning and order. One wonders why they have not been brought into juxtaposition instead of remaining politely apart.

This problem is of a piece with the more widespread reticence, all the more striking in so searching a study, that holds Taylor back from both more sympathetic and more critical treatments of his subjects. Especially in his analysis of the nineteenth- and twentieth-century avatars of the modern spirit does it become clear that the examination is being made with kid gloves. A misplaced gentleness seems to prevent Taylor from investigating romanticism or realism or deconstructionism to their depths. As a consequence, he fails to expose what his preliminary discussion of profound constitutive experiences had led us to expect. We do not really test the degree of spiritual closure and domination present within the great intellectual rebels of our world, nor plumb the depths of authentic spiritual openness that still remain within them as the secret of their appeal. The tragic character of our world, with its great spiritual aspirations and its heartbreaking failure to live up to them, is missed and with it the possibility of moving beyond the present ambivalence into a deeper realization of order. Taylor seems not to believe in the growth of the soul that he had identified in the first part as the way in which the multiplicity and divergence of moral positions is overcome. There he had rejected the demand for some viewpoint outside the conflicts, insisting that "the most reliable moral view is not one that would be grounded quite outside our intuitions but one that is grounded on our strongest intuitions, where these have successfully met the challenge of proposed transitions away from them" (75).

If we take seriously the assertion that there is no vantage point for critique outside of participation in the moral struggle itself, then we must be prepared to descend deeper into the moral vortex in the hope of ascending with an enlarged perspective capable of resolving the dilemmas before us. The faith to sustain such a struggle implies that there is always the possibility of enlarging the hold that we have on the reality of good at any given stage. Neither we nor our convictions are fixed quantities. They can become surprisingly deeper and fuller and better than they are, rising up to the sense of unshakable transcendent reality at their apex. Taylor's inconclusiveness, in what has clearly been one of the most profound meditations on our contemporary predicament, is that he is unable to unfold the consequences of his own acknowledgment of the failure of the modern inspiration. He holds back on his critique precisely because, it seems, he is unsure that he or the modern figures he admires can undergo the kind of growth of the soul required to move toward substantive goodness. But if there are indeed higher goods animating the modern moral evocations, then there should be confidence in their power to enlarge and deepen their appeal as the means of purifying them of the dross mixed within their schemes of universal progress. It is because the liberal construction is deliberately based on just such an acknowledgment of incompleteness and, by consequence, of the possibilities of expansion and contraction that it points toward such an open recognition of conflicts.[10]

Disagreements are not threatening so long as they are not regarded as ultimate, and that is the implicit consensus that has sustained the liberal arrangement ever since the wars of religion. The increasing intensity and extensiveness of contemporary moral conflicts have struck fear into the hearts of many of our fellow liberals, who have begun to despair of ever finding their way to a resolution and taken to imploring us earnestly from taking them seriously any longer. Such an approach is not only impractical, but disastrous for the possibility of maintaining the liberal order itself. What is required is to take seriously the liberal faith that differences, however irresolvable they may appear, are not fixed but merely the visible manifestations of a common human reality that can be explicated more fully but never exhausted. The convictions that define us at any given time are not immovable, they are the results of a movement of self-articulation whose limits cannot be determined. The possibility remains, therefore, of moving toward a resolution of the often profound conflicts that assail us through the even more challenging but more indispensable process of moral growth itself. Just as we have reached them through a process of maturation, it is also possible that we might move beyond them through such a similarly arduous effort.

Confronting the Conflicts of Liberal Society

The recommendation to confront and grapple with the conflicts that assail liberal society flies in the face of the prevailing liberal practice. That has generally taken the form of avoiding the demand for a resolution by shifting the disagreements from the illumination of the public sphere to the obscurity of untrammeled private choice. This has certainly been the predominant pattern reaching from the tolerationist solution to the wars of religion to the expanding privatization of a wide range of controversies in our own day. The approach has indeed become so pronounced that it is often taken for the essence of the liberal arrangement and proof of the irremediable bankruptcy of a public order that stands for no higher good than an unwillingness to disturb the peace.[11] Our present sense of crisis derives in large measure from the suspicion that we may be on the point of evacuating all conviction of the good or the right from the public realm. Once we have gone "beyond good and evil," we sense, like Stavrogin in *The Possessed,* that we will be "lost."

The present study should, however, give pause to such an easy dismissal. The liberal tradition presupposes and has rested on a much deeper and more substantive spiritual order; its impressive durability cannot be accounted for simply on the basis of an expanding inclination to enlarge the privacy of differences. There are more powerful and more enduring impulses at work, and they remain even in our own constricted circumstances. The viability of a liberal public order depends on their presence and influence. All our efforts must be directed toward building on the residue that remains with a view to the enlargement of the indispensable presuppositions of a liberal politics. The prevalence of controverted moral issues is most commonly viewed as the great obstacle to the recovery of a public consensus, but I would like to suggest that it may also be seen from another perspective as a great opportunity. Profound moral and philosophical differences, while certainly dangerous to public order and tranquillity, have the invaluable merit of compelling a profound reflection on what is at stake in our fractured public square. Nothing guarantees a successful outcome to such a radical dialogue, but we are likely to move toward more fruitful conclusions once we approach it with a spirit of confidence in the unspoken bonds that still link us together. Besides, in our contemporary context we have no other alternative to the prospect of civil war being waged by political means.

When the withdrawal of controversy into the private realm has proceeded as far as it has in our day, to the point where the reality of a realm of public agreement and conviction has been placed in doubt, then we have no choice but to confront the conflicts in all their ramifications. Liberal accommodationism has reached a limit when it begins to undermine the liberal construction itself. It is the gnawing sense of the bankruptcy of the moral core of liberal arrangements, confessed in the theorists' abandonment of the effort of mounting a coherent exposition of its grounds and unmistakably tangible in the mounting moral disorder of our societies, that defines the present sense of crisis. It has become clear that the peeling of the onion cannot continue apace forever. A limit is reached when the onion is no more, and we realize that indeed there was a substantive core to the liberal order, for it has now been lost. Before we reach that final point of the endgame it is still possible to awaken to the realities that are at stake in the process. Not surprisingly, it is the radical nature of the controversies that beset us that furnishes the most powerful impetus for this reawakening to the underlying order seeping through the holes.

The nature of a crisis is that it does concentrate the mind. If we still retain some residue of the spiritual inspiration behind the liberal commitment to the transcendent dignity of the person, then we cannot but respond to the emerging threat that seems to jeopardize it. The response, if we retain any sensitivity to what is at stake, draws forth a deeper realization of the reality that underpins our public order and of the indispensable existential and intellectual presuppositions. Conflict can thus heighten the conviction that had lain dormant so long as it was not called upon to assert itself, and become the occasion for a powerful reevocation of the moral sources from which it draws its formidable spiritual strength. We begin to realize that the everyday practice of "going along and getting along" is only partly descriptive of who we are. There are other strata of our selves, perhaps hitherto unsuspected, that are called forth by the movement of resistance to the dangers looming before us. Nothing, of course, guarantees that such a growth of the soul will occur through the forthright admission of conflicts. All that we can be sure of is that without undertaking the struggle, the prospects for enlarging our liberal horizon are indeed slim.

What stands in the way of an honest acknowledgment of differences, one that is open to the possibility of persuasion and change rather than the peace of cold warfare, is the unarticulated suspicion that there are no common grounds between us. Simply because different rationalities and traditions seem to dominate the debate, we are inclined to conclude that there is no longer a reason or a tradition that is shared. This is the unsettling silent anxiety at the heart of the present crisis. In the face of mounting and ever more radical disagreements we have begun to suspect not only that the center cannot hold but also that it does not, perhaps never did, exist. The self-understanding of the liberal polity becomes that of a precariously minimal agreement resting on a complete vacuity of broader sustaining convictions. Instead of the background of unspoken consensus that can be called upon in periods of strain and uncertainty, the liberal ethos appears as a brittle conjunction of interests that disintegrates at the slightest application of pressure. The greatest casualty of the contemporary culture wars, is not any of the specific controverted issues, but the residue of trust in a sustaining order beyond the bare outlines of the liberal polity.

Yet that reservoir of mutual trust has not entirely disappeared. If it had we would be in an even worse condition than we are, and the process of disintegration would encounter far fewer efforts of resistance and recovery. The reality is that our society has, as liberal societies have for much of this century, been involved in impressive efforts of retrieval and rejuvenation beyond the dismal predictions recurrently made about them. Individually it may not appear so impressive that civil rights have been expanded, albeit without precisely determining the limits, or that the expected decline in religion has more often been confounded by its revival, or that the nightmare of technological control of human biology and psychology has encountered stubborn opposition, but cumulatively such efforts of resistance to the ho-mogenizing and dehumanizing drift have been far from negligible. If they are to be more than rearguard actions of reaction, easily dismissed by the prevailing currents of opinion as fundamentalist, then they must assume a different strategy than one designed not to lose. They must approach the task as one they wish to win. Even if winning is not realistic or, if it is realistic, can never be final, the strategy of confronting the full force of the deformative pressures offers the best chance of intellectual and moral success. The pivotal condition for such an approach is the confidence that there does still exist a common sense of order, however fragmented and submerged it may be, that can form the background from which the conversation can arise and toward which it can ultimately appeal.

The always astonishing discovery is that as we rely on the presence of such a never fully articulated consensus we not only bring more of it to the light of explication but also experience the enlargement and intensification of its reality in our own lives. We begin to gain a different perspective or measure on the problems that had previously assaulted us so absolutely. They no longer appear to define the parameters of our lives together. We recognize that they must be viewed in relation to the more enduring realities behind them. Once the conflicts are thus relieved of some of the burden of finality that so often pervades them, all sides can begin to move with more reasonableness toward the resolution, if there is one, that most faithfully embodies the unfolding of our deepest intuitions. If the issues are always defined in terms of political defeat or victory, then no one can afford to relax their standpoint long enough to consider the right that they know to exist on the other side as well. Some of the hard edge of confrontation begins to dissolve only when we are assured that there is a common reality of right order uniting us, even when it cannot be exhaustively articulated, that it is the animating source of the appeal invoked by the opposing positions. Once the confrontational rigidities have begun to loosen, it is no longer beyond the bounds of possibility that the positions themselves may begin to shift and the previously irreconcilable conflicts give way to some more stable resolutions.

An example of what is meant is the only way of demonstrating the possibility, and what better test case than that most radical liberal fracture of the life issues, especially abortion? The conventional picture is that the opposing positions are poles apart and utterly incapable of resolution and that the issue itself is intractable to the normal political process of compromise. On the face of it this view seems unassailable. Only the extraordinary ambivalence within the broad spectrum of public opinion gives reason to suspect that abortion is not defined by the militants at either end of the controversy. Activists may have the monopoly on its articulation, but the social reality is defined by the irresolution strikingly characteristic of the majority in most liberal democracies. The conflict is, in other words, best understood as a conflict within the hearts and minds of most citizens rather than as a conflict between the exponents of the competing principles. If it is such an internal conflict within us, then the controversy takes on a very different complexion and suggests very different methods of searching for a resolution. The appropriate strategy is not primarily that of attempting to secure a political victory, but of undertaking the kind of meditative elaboration of its dimensions that would lead to a genuinely moral resolution. It is because of the failure to advert to this underlying character of the conflict that political victories, when they are achieved, prove so elusive.[12] The controversy, as with any profound moral disagreement, will not be settled until it is settled rightly.

That means paying careful attention to the moral intimations inchoately present in the positions we adopt, intimations that disturb the smooth surface of arguments so glibly and routinely repeated. Despite all the declamations of the relativist or nihilist social setting in which we work out our contemporary existence, we know that we are not utterly bereft of a sense of moral direction. However ill formed and precarious it may be, there remains an ineradicable germ of the right we ought to follow even in a controversy apparently as wide open as abortion. Contrary to the prevailing impression, we are not simply free to choose sides unimpeded by any considerations other than those we have already chosen to invoke. It is not a pure choice of the side we elect to adopt. We know that this is an issue that defines us even before we have begun to give it our reflection; our task is to find our way through the web of factors that we know already reach into our own lives. We are in search of the unseen measure by which to weigh things rightly and at stake is nothing less than our own souls.

The most general parameter of the controversy is the right, acknowledged in *Roe v. Wade,* and other cases of a right to privacy that must be accorded to human beings in the most intimate decisions of their lives. This especially applies in regard to the bearing and raising of children. We are all appalled at the notion that the state or the community might inject itself into an area of personal prerogative, even if there are many occasions on which men and women seem to act foolishly or inconsiderately in such matters and even when there are often significant adverse social consequences of their actions. A state might often have a strong interest in limiting the number of births in general or in limiting the number of children born to parents unequipped to care for them. Yet any effort beyond moral and material persuasion, such as the erection of legal prohibitions, strikes us as an invasion of personal freedom so profound as to virtually obliterate it.[13] If human beings are to be treated as human, and not as controlled breeding animals, then they must remain free to unite and to bear children through their own deliberation and choice.

Having acknowledged the presumptive right to privacy, to the freedom so essential to the exercise of the human capacity to love and to build a family, it is also evident that this does not provide individuals with a license to do whatever they wish to one another and to their children. The right to privacy may erect a barrier to state intervention in the most intimate relationships and decisions of human life, but it does not erect it so high that it can never legitimately be breached. It is evident that the state must interfere when spouses or children are subjected to abuse. There is even a case for state intervention when there is a flagrant or callous disregard for the welfare of unborn children during pregnancy. The right to privacy does not entitle parents to do whatever they wish to their children either in or post utero. The state has a very specific obligation, not just a general interest in the promotion of human life, but toward the precise individuals affected by the misuse of the prerogative of privacy in such cases.

The pivotal question is whether abortion is one of those cases. If we take the infliction of intrauterine injury as requiring some form of public intervention, then abortion would seem to constitute the most damaging assault on the fetus since it is designed to kill. The suggestion that the fetus does not have a right to life until it has the capacity to have a conscious interest in such a life does not square easily with the notion that it can nevertheless be damaged and deserves protection. Does it then only deserve protection against injury that is not fatal, but not against the termination of life that could remove any victim of the injury? This is surely an odd line of reasoning that would make murder unobjectionable while continuing to punish mugging more seriously. By thus following out the threads we begin to gain a sense of the tangle we have created for ourselves once we begin to disregard the most elementary dimensions of our experience. The horrific logic we have constructed gives pause to the notion that we are free to choose how we are to see the world.

It is not the case that the fetus has no rights simply because at the earliest stages it does not have a conscious interest in such rights. The fetus is unlike a future or potential child that cannot be a subject of rights since it has as yet no concrete existence. We may be said to owe something in general to such future generations, but we do not owe any of them anything specific. A fertilized human ovum, by contrast, is already a concretely existing being, containing all that will make it who it is and a distinctly different individual from the mother. It is a separate life from the mother, a human being whose injury or death can occur without concomitant effect on the mother. In that sense, the fetus is not simply a part of the mother and therefore subordinate to the therapeutic interests of the mother. At the same time the fetus does not have all of the capacities of even elementary personality, not even consciousness up to a certain stage. For that reason we do not feel the same way toward a fetus as we do toward persons we know. Miscarriages are not treated in the same way as infant deaths. Yet there is a continuity, and the effort to break that continuity encounters a sense of resistance that is called forth by all arbitrary dispositions.

An argument might be made on the basis of the immortal soul infused and informing each human life from the moment of conception. That language is no longer readily accepted in our secular universe of discourse, but it is still possible to evoke some of the foundations that render it intelligible. What makes a human being a human being is more than the sum total of the chemical organization of its elemental molecular biology. The ingredients do not constitute the whole. Biology may be destiny, and physics may be fate, but neither can explain the miracle of human life capable of comprehending them and of even transcending their exigencies. Whence arises this concrete whole that is a unique, irreplaceable human being whose trajectory points beyond the whole world? It cannot arise as an afterthought or an epiphenomenon, for it is what makes us human beings and not merely biochemical processes. Since it cannot arise at any later point in our development unless it were already present from the start, we can only conclude that it is there from the moment that the unique identity of each human being is concretely formed.

But it is not necessary to invoke such metaphysical arguments, because they depend on a larger intellectual and spiritual worldview whose elaboration cannot be presupposed in the public square. We must move toward such developed understandings from the immediate intuitions that remain the ineradicable boundaries of even contemporary confused liberal politics. The nub of such intimations is the awareness of continuity between the fetus and the fully developed person. The analogy is not with an acorn, which is clearly not an oak tree, but with the sapling, which clearly is a small oak tree. Both the fetus and the sapling are already in the most important sense what they are to become. All the discussion about the point at which the fetus becomes a person or acquires interests and therefore rights serves only to muddy what is indeed very clear. There is a continuity between the zygote or fetus and the child who is born. No accumulation of distinctions can remove that fundamental fact of continuity and the inescapably arbitrary character of any attempt to disrupt its development. There is no point at which its abortion is anything less than the destruction of a human being. It can hardly be regarded as a defense that it is a very small or very immature human being.

Nowhere is the unease with abortion more palpable than in the absolute refusal to consider the possibility of error. Once the fetus has been pronounced clear of all connection with personhood, whether real or legal, it no longer constitutes any kind of specific barrier to the exercise of private liberty. There may still be what Dworkin calls the "detached" reservations surrounding any deliberate taking of life, but such hesitations are of a generic nature, not tied to the particularity of an individual fetus. They cannot constitute a restraint on the full exercise of discretion unless a woman, through her own religious dispositions, has chosen to give them such a status. The presumptive right to privacy overwhelms all hesitations. But what if the cutoff point is incorrect? What if the emergence of personhood is a more extended, less quantifiable process than we had considered? If the right of privacy is a strongly presumptive right that easily "trumps" the elementary status of the fetus, does it so completely overpower the possibility of inchoate personhood undetectable by contemporary science?[14] Should not the seriousness of the potential right to life claims of the fetus give pause to the unquestioning assertion of the primacy of the mother's right to privacy? Any considered evaluation of the competing rights would have to push the criterion of abortion substantially further back than the viability standard of the present. Even granted that the mother's right to self-determination takes precedence, should there not be a margin of error to ensure that it never entails the taking of innocent human life?

The problem of the criterion or limit is the Achilles' heel of the abortion position, just as the diminished actualization of personhood is the source of weakness on the opposing side. The pivotal issue between them is, of course, whether any consistent cutoff point short of conception can be maintained. While it may indeed be the case that the fetus grows in personal significance as it matures and therefore in the dimensions that evoke a heightening sense of responsibility toward it, the question is whether there is any minimum point below which it ceases to count as a human being at all. The record of judicial and other attempts to find such a minimum point of reference has not been encouraging. Consensus has converged on the point of viability at the end of the second trimester, for the obvious practical advantage that the fetus can survive if born after this time, but even this limit fails to carry the weight of an absolute prohibition on late-term abortions. In the companion case to *Roe v. Wade,* the U.S. Supreme Court conceded that abortion could not be prohibited at any point if the life or health of the mother were at stake, and it went on to define health in the broadest terms to include the emotional well-being of the mother (*Doe v. Bolton,* 1973). There was, in other words, a marked reluctance to countenance any impermeable barrier to the performance of abortion under sufficiently serious circumstances.

The bad faith is evident in the contradiction between the espousal of a demarcation line, selected as viability, and the unwillingness to follow through on it. *Roe v. Wade*'s aftermath exposes the pragmatic character of the viability criterion, that it never constituted a moral criterion and could never withstand the pressure for expansion once a more compelling pragmatic urgency presented itself. Yet the necessity for a fig leaf is inexorable. Otherwise we sense that we are approaching a great divide and that once we have gone completely across we will be left without any limits to restrain what we may want or what we may feel compelled to do. One or two intrepids have already gone across to that other brave new world and admitted forthrightly that the arguments that drew us into an expanding practice of abortion apply equally cogently to infanticide.[15] One or two state courts have taken up the challenge flung down by such advocates to proclaim that the arguments against the personhood of the fetus apply equally to newborns with severe deformities. Their status as persons is rendered highly questionable and therefore their Constitutional protections, especially the right to elementary medical care, have contracted to the point of irrelevance.[16]

If the effort to demarcate the point of transition of the fetus to the rights of personhood had been animated by good faith, then it would be expected that some margin of safety would be included in such a definition. Instead of a persistent upward pressure on the line of permissibility, one would expect to find a contrary inclination to err on the side of life. The balance putatively intended between the mother's freedom and the fetus's life would seem to tilt toward the fetus. After all, if we have not demarcated the point of acquisition of the ingredients of personhood rightly, then we will have killed a person who no longer has any recourse for redress. If the mother's right to freely determine her own life has been significantly abridged, it is a partial invasion of her rights. It does not definitively foreclose the enjoyment of all her rights. Decisions of life and death are different in their obvious finality. Errors cannot be reversed and for this reason require an additional layer of caution, beyond a strict calculation of the sheer balance of competing rights. It is a competition in which one side has absolutely more to lose than the other and is in a considerably less advantageous position to assert its interests in the debate. Given the greater solicitude for disadvantaged plaintiffs in all kinds of other areas, the absence of such sentiments toward the most fragile of all plaintiffs is striking.

Yet even such jurisprudential forgetfulness cannot assuage the unease at a practice that all sides, supporters as well as opponents, find profoundly distasteful. No more eloquent expression of that unease can be found than the book-length reflection lavished upon it recently by Ronald Dworkin. In an admirable, if troubling, effort to put the controversy to rest, he honestly confronts the discomfort aroused by the widespread practice of abortion, although he is committed to the avoidance of any attempt to legally reduce access to the procedure. In struggling to articulate what it is about the availability of abortion that remains unsettling to someone who strongly holds to the mother's right to choose without restriction, he eventually zeros in on what he calls the "intrinsic value" of human life. Dworkin distinguishes this from the instrumental, subjective, and personal value a human life has, all of which presuppose the existence of a person with enough self-awareness to value his or her own life and as a consequence to be valued by others. The intrinsic value of life is broader than that of the specific manifestations of it. It is curious that Dworkin can find no other language to express what he means than language that invokes the religious sense of "sanctity."

He is careful to generalize the context of reference for this religious language, but he still must use it to convey the sense of reverence for the mystery of life whence our own individual existences have been derived. His summary of all of the components of that sense of awe or reverence that persists even within a secular context is worth quoting in full.

> The life of a single human organism commands respect and protection, then, no matter in what form or shape, because of the complex creative investment it represents and because of our wonder at the divine or evolutionary processes that produce new lives from old ones, at the processes of nation and community and language through which a human being will come to absorb and continue hundreds of generations of cultures and forms of life and value, and, finally, when mental life has begun and flourishes, at the process of internal personal creation and judgment by which a person will make and remake himself, a mysterious, inescapable process in which we each participate, and which is therefore the most powerful and inevitable source of empathy and communion we have with every other creature who faces the same frightening challenge. The horror we feel in the willful destruction of a human life reflects our shared inarticulate sense of the intrinsic importance of each of these dimensions of investment. (*Life's Dominion*, 84)

While we might quibble with some of the turns of phrase (the language of "investment" is a particularly flat note), there can be little doubt that this is a remarkably powerful summation of the unease with abortion that would be widely conceded in contemporary society once the klieg lights of rhetoric have been turned down. Dworkin hits one of the most prominent nails on the head when he remarks on the "shame" involved in this deliberate "waste of human life."

The scandal of the abortion holocaust in all of the developed world and outside of it is an affront even to the many who are willing to defend the freedom to practice it. Even its supporters wish that abortion was not, in the vast majority of cases, chosen. In an age of heightened sensitivity to the richness and irreplaceability of the natural world, the profligate disregard for the infinitely greater preciousness of human life cannot but be perceived as deeply disturbing. These are not just contradictions to be pointed out in a debating match. They are the poles of ambivalence pervasively present within the moderately decent majorities. Dworkin is doing no more than giving voice to the profound sadness surrounding all contemporary discussions of the issue. He shows the opening that could lead to a more real consideration of the problem, enabling us to move beyond the rigidities of entrenched confrontation. All that is needed is to follow the logic of the regret expressed in his remarks into the recognition that in some sense the gift of life restrains our freedom.

The most disappointing aspect of Dworkin's exemplary openness is his refusal to give substantive weight to the reservations he acknowledges as governing abortion. In an extraordinarily deft piece of footwork, which forms the central theoretical nexus of the book, he manages to concede all of the intrinsic objections to the disrespect of the value of human life while radically undermining all of the force they might be expected to have in restraining the practice. He elides their impact completely into the character of religious positions that, by definition, cannot have any standing in the realm of public policy. Convictions that are held purely on religious grounds can govern only our private opinions and actions; they can have no dispositive authority in law or politics. Law, of course, does not adjudicate the reasons for positions held, so that the existence of reservations ought to be enough to put a brake on the broad public policy of permitting and promoting abortions. Curiously, Dworkin's own way of expressing the reservations has the effect of almost removing their religious content and recasting the objections in secular, publicly acceptable terms. Thus, the willful character of the result is revealed in the transition he makes from this earlier general account of the intrinsic value of human life to the later specific exclusion of such considerations that he eventually reaches. He begins by outlining the derivation of the idea of the value of life from a general, though not exclusively religious, sense of awe at mystery. Yet when he arrives at the development of its implications, it has become a preeminently religious sense and, therefore, one whose impact can be confined to the private sphere. If there is an intrinsic value to human life from its earliest stages, as Dworkin acknowledges can form the basis for the prohibition of late-term abortions, then that must be allowed to play some, if not a determinative, role from its earliest stages as well. One suspects that the procreative autonomy he wished to reach overrode the reservations he acknowledged along the way.

The basic distinction he promotes between derived and detached criteria, derived from the interests and rights of the fetus or emanating from a detached assessment of the intrinsic value of human life, is a plausible though not ultimately decisive distinction. Individual rights cannot finally be separated from the process of the whole in which we participate. There remains a component of intrinsic value in every assertion of individual rights. What is intriguing about Dworkin's position is that he acknowledges a dimension of mystery and depth as the background from which our consideration of rights arises. But he then too-readily slips into his customary estimation of rights as an assertion of interests, so that only those capable of such self-assertion possess the prerequisite for entry into the liberal game. The reality is that the intrinsic valuation of human life and of human beings provides the indispensable underpinning for what otherwise would be simply a bald assertion of interests and rights claims. Having acknowledged the presence of such a dimension of valuation in depth, reaching into the mysteries whence our own existence arises, it is sad that the pressure to reach a conclusion of untrammeled autonomy prevented Dworkin from following the direction he acknowledges.

His argument is an updated application of the age-old liberal temptation to separate the transcendent impact of its principles from the transcendent valuations that animate them. The success of the enterprise, as we have seen, depends on not pushing the distinction so far that the principles lose their capacity to carry the resonance of reverence from which they are derived. Dworkin's relegation of the intrinsic valuation of life to the private realm runs that risk by suggesting the purely private and therefore unserious character of such estimations. The reality is that the sense of the value of human life cannot be separated from the specific individual lives that are at stake. Abortion does not simply represent a disrespect for human life in general but always takes the form of an assault on a specific individual life. Its character as a general affront is contained in its concretely real destruction. The suggestion that only general conceptions of life or worldviews are at stake does not stretch far enough to conceal the specific termination of life that is entailed. Unlike a disagreement about religious or philosophical beliefs, where each side agrees to tolerate without coercing the other in any way to conform their convictions, abortion is a practical disagreement that commits us to acquiescing or supporting a particular course of action. Those who oppose it are asked to countenance murder, not merely accept broader spiritual differences with others. Quite contrary to Dworkin's easy disposition of it as a merely philosophical dispute, it is a prime example of the impossibility of severing the connection between philosophy and practice. It is not merely about rival or divergent worldviews but about how we are going to treat one another.

Toleration could be adopted as a resolution of confessional disputes in the early modern period because the differences were largely speculative and did not lead to many serious disagreements in practice. But divergent valuations of life itself can lead to sharply different consequences in the world of human relationships. These are not merely theoretical disputes for the consequences immediately spill over into practice, and, there is no way that the confrontation can be avoided once we recognize their intersection with the practical interpretation of rights. Dworkin articulates the prevailing inclination to avoid admitting the collision course by quarantining the disvaluation of human life entailed by abortion, in the hope that its plague will not infect the superstructure of preferred liberal rights. But it is a doomed exercise from the start, incapable of restoring the loss of humanity that has been admitted. Some sense of the scale of the loss hovers behind Dworkin's invocations of the sacredness of life, but he fails to rise to the occasion in his refusal to contemplate any connection between it and the determination of individual rights.

He would have had to ask the question of what effect the disregard of the sacredness of human life must have on the notion that human beings deserve to be treated with dignity and respect. Has there not been something lost that is bound to affect the depth of concern with which we view all other human beings? What kind of society can it be that accepts the callous disregard of the value of human beings in the earliest and most vulnerable stage of their lives? How can we afford to consider so lightly the destruction of the earliest actualization of all of the unique irreplaceable identity of a new human being? Has there not been an element of arbitrariness introduced into the process that threatens to expand and undermine all subsequent attempts to erect a foundation of value? If a criterion is drawn along one line and not another, what is to prevent the pressure that would induce us to place it elsewhere? Can there be any foundation to human value other than arbitrary administrative convenience?

The disturbing consequences of the decision to shortchange the rights of the unborn begin to make themselves felt across the whole moral landscape. Suppression of the rights of a few, especially when it is clothed with the respectability of law, cannot but render doubtful the whole foundation of rights for everyone else. What is it about human beings that makes them worthy of treatment with transcendent dignity and respect? If the grounds have shifted in one case, what is to prevent their dislocation in another? Even the whole tenor of the discussion whereby we enquire into whether the fetus or the comatose meet the criteria for personhood and therefore whether their rights can be abridged, smacks of a sense of godlike superiority to our own species and condition. It is as if we have imagined ourselves free from the finitude of birth and death to sit in judgment over them. They no longer represent the mysterious limits of our own existence, which we are obliged to respect and cannot expect to surmount through conceptualization. Now we have liberated ourselves from the constraints of the human perspective and can pronounce the definitive structure of our own origin and end. Of course, the success has all been imaginary. We have not managed to pinpoint the moment when we have begun to be no more than the moment when we have ceased to be.[17] Only the utilization of a certain definitional language has generated the illusion that such control is available to us. We have not succeeded in escaping the human condition.

The illusion of superiority, however, has powerful consequences because it cuts us off from the indispensable sense of direction in reality. In thinking that we are free to determine who is or who is not fully a member of the human species, entitled to all of the protections of human law, we feel that we have advanced into a new era of clarity about things. But that is a false confidence. If it is up to us to define membership in the human species, including even the strange notion of gradations of membership, then we soon realize that we have lost connection with any criteria simply given. All is now up for debate and determination. The shifting sands of opinion, prejudice, and interest will have their way, and we can never shake the sense that any drawing of the line, however plausibly argued, is at bottom something arbitrary. Thinking we have expanded our control of our own destinies, we have instead lost any landmarks by which to steer our course. In this state of disorientation we are at the mercy of all the forces that blow upon us.

We cannot declare fetal life to be relatively valueless without diminishing the value of all human life, or at least without suggesting that its value is something open to debate and determination. It is not necessary to insist on an inevitable slide down the "slippery slope" toward totalitarianism in order to recognize that the substance of respect for human dignity has been undermined from within. The right to equal concern is no longer rooted in the givenness of our humanity beyond the calculation of merit and qualifications; the link has been broken with the inexhaustible depth of transcendence from which the infinity of a human being is derived. Now we have been absorbed into the measured and calculated world of things. The putative expansion of our dignity and freedom extolled by our greater control over birth and death has turned out to be the cruelest of all deceptions. It has deprived us of the most central sense of the unconditioned worth of a human being that is the only purpose of self-determination. In attempting to step beyond the limits of what we can determine, deciding membership in the species, we have lost all that makes life worth living, the sense of human life as an end in itself.

By measuring human life in relation to some purpose or range of functions, however well intentioned such reflections may be, we cannot avoid its contraction to the mode of instrumentality. It is no longer human life itself that is the source of value, that in relation to which all other goods are measured. Rather, the order has been reversed, and we begin to measure life in relation to other goods. But what other goods? Good for whom? What is the function or purpose to be served? Who or what is the final end if it is not some human end? The vacuum opened up by the instrumentalization of human life consists in the impossibility of discovering any purpose to guide the instrumentality. No human purpose, whether the patient's own or someone else's, can represent the final end because we have already accepted the subordination of human life to some functional requirements. What we can never answer is the question of whose function is to be served if it is not the end of human ends in themselves. Even if we maintain that abortion or euthanasia are for the benefit of the patients themselves, we cannot really mean it since they will be no more. Their existence is to be subordinated to some other aspect of them. But then what is that aspect to serve? Not the welfare of their existence?

That is the darkness opened up by the admission of abortion or euthanasia in principle, and it is a sense of its shadow that is behind the uneasiness with the waste of human life perceived by Dworkin.[18] He may not have carried the meditation far enough but can discern the bleakness toward which it points. More important, by dwelling on it a little longer we begin to gain a sense of the growth of the soul that would enable us to decide it differently. We come to see that it is not merely a matter of finding a peaceful accommodation of a controverted moral issue, but of gaining a sense of the full dimensions of the reality at stake. The acceptance of our freedom to control the beginning and end of human life calls into question the whole notion that there is anything valuable about human beings at all that might not be drawn into the calculus of costs and benefits to themselves or others. In extending control over our destiny we have overstepped the limits and lost what makes life itself worth living. Who wants to live in a society that countenances the deliberate termination of human life, even of its most marginal members?

It is not merely a diffuse shame at the waste of human life, but a waste that effects a very real degradation of the value of the life that remains. The conflict is not in any sense an irritating sideline within the contemporary liberal polity but, as Dworkin indicates by his devotion of a book-length study to its contemplation, a central rupture that threatens through its expanding tangle to sap the inner substance of an order of liberal rights. Yet the argument I have developed is a meditation from within the incompletely articulated consensus of the liberal inspiration itself. It does not appeal to any explicitly religious authority or presuppositions. As a consequence, it shows the extent to which the resources for a very different resolution are present within the liberal framework and can indeed be heightened through the same reverence for the individual that has been historically differentiated within the liberal tradition. It does entail a deeper reflection and a willingness to undergo a sometimes painful growth of the soul to reach toward it. But the reality that sustains the meditative expansion is sufficiently present within the liberal experience that it can be trusted to disclose its powerful attraction as we allow ourselves to be drawn by it. The growth of the liberal soul can still sustain itself. That is the source of our confidence in the viability of a liberal public order, despite its manifest failures in the present time.

It is, after all, significant that the greatest deepening of American liberal democracy came in the context of the civil war and was given expression in the magisterial rhetoric of Abraham Lincoln. The slavery issue was surely one of the most divisive that any polity has had to face, precisely because it was so deeply entrenched in the economic and social patterns of life. What was significant about Lincoln's response to it was the extent to which he understood not only the human and social evil of the institution but also the degree to which it represented an inexorable challenge to the entire principle of free government. This was what set him on the path of opposition to its expansion, while at the same time struggling mightily to preserve and, when it had exploded, restore the national consensus on which the Union rested. Lincoln's approach was to remain scrupulously within the limits of the law and practicality, as he saw them, while working to build a powerful public sentiment of opposition to the practice. The secret of his rhetoric was to avoid invoking great philosophical or religious justifications, but instead to heighten and intensify the implications of the core principles of the Declaration of Independence on which the claim of the equal rights of Americans to rule themselves had been based. This is why the slavery issue reaches its culmination in Lincoln's Gettysburg formulation as the challenge "that this nation, under God, shall have a new birth of freedom—and that government of the people, by the people, for the people, shall not perish from the earth." Lincoln was, after Washington, the greatest American president because he breathed new life into the liberal democratic principles of the regime.[19]

Disclosure in Actualization

The prospects for a meditative expansion of the limits of the contemporary liberal ethos rest entirely on the recognition that the liberal public order is not a fixed quantity. If the shrill antagonism of political debate were all there is to the liberal construction, then we would indeed be in trouble. The jeremiads of those who can foresee nothing but the ever more precipitous descent into chaos would have uttered the last word. But, as we have seen, there is always the something more to a liberal order, and it is its presence that at least sustains the hope of a growth in moral responsibility. The strength and the frailty of the liberal construction has been its capacity to simultaneously evoke and conceal the source of its spiritual resonance. Its viability as an authoritative symbolism of order is heavily dependent on the realization of this philosophically incomplete status, an incompleteness that remains cognizant of that which is required to enlarge its foundations. More than any other order, a liberal order is peculiarly dependent on the recognition of the growth of the soul as preserving its tension.

Once the sense of a boundary of transcendence is lost, as, for example, in the most blasé proabortion position, we are in danger of losing touch with the sense of a human being as more than the sum of his parts. If we cross that divide of quantification, then we will have severed the connection with what underpins the liberal valuation of human dignity and rights. Once the notion of a cutoff point or limit is introduced, we begin to view human beings quite differently, as objects of measurement and functional analysis rather than as the inviolable ends in themselves that lie beyond all metrication. It has been the instinctive revulsion against this dehumanization that has prompted the resistance against abortion and caused the arousal of second thoughts among those willing to support it. Once the sanctity of life is suspended in one case, its imperative is to that extent diminished in all other cases. Even supporters of a right to abortion retain an uneasy conscience that is all the more evidenced by the elaborateness of the means enlisted to assuage it. Dworkin appeals to the freedom of conscience to choose our basic worldviews, but this is hardly more fundamental than the right to life itself. The merits of the argument are less significant than their background in the realization of the seriousness of the implications raised.

That germ of self-awareness can provide the means for the inexorable opening of the soul to the acknowledgment of the inviolability of all human beings. Much of the history of liberal societies has been the history of the impossibility of the denial of rights to some while guaranteeing them to others. The conflict involved is too sharp to be sustained because if some are excluded then it calls into question the validity of the basis for including others. No distinction between them seems capable of obliterating the fundamental identity of their common human nature. But it is not simply a question of consistency. The motive force for such reforms is the sense of the intolerableness of assigning a value or a limit to that which defies all quantification. Human life would lose all meaning if it were not rooted in the mysterious openness that is perpetually beyond all tangibility. We are constituted by the horizon of transcendence that surrounds our existence, and it is this that furnishes all the relish and vitality to human life. Even when we live toward the future, a false transcendence that will not be qualitatively different from the present, its appeal trades on the real sense of transcendence we continue to bear within us. There is no limit to the horizon constituting human existence, and it is this radical openness that renders the quantification of human life or liberty impossible.

The reformative expansion of the liberal ethos along such lines does not entail a departure from the parameters of liberal reflection. It does involve a heightening of awareness of the dimension of transcendence that is at stake, a growth of the soul toward the ultimate moral perspective within which to measure rightly how we should live. By dwelling on that without which life would not be worth living, we begin to live more deeply in attunement with it, and its light irradiates the conflicts and decisions that confront us. They begin to appear less problematic as we realize that we are not being pulled in different directions with the same force. Rather, some of the pulls are toward our immediate comfort or our intermediate convenience, but they are opposed by the imperious pull of what is right without which no other benefits become worth having. The orientation toward a good that transcends all utility comes into view as the defining reality for human life. It is this capacity that is the source of the dignity and respect owed to each human being. Themselves the assigners of utility, their own existence can never be measured in terms of utility no matter how elementary its condition may be.

It is not necessary to step outside a liberal vocabulary to evoke a sense of the transcendent finality of human existence. The fuller explication of that finality may lie in the area of religion, and a spiritual tradition is in some way essential to the preservation of such an understanding, but it is not strictly necessary from within the requirements of a liberal political order itself. That has succeeded by drawing into itself just enough of the substance of a Christian or spiritual faith to sustain the trust in the reality of an order in which human beings find their fulfillment beyond all the finite achievements and satisfactions of this world. Yet even without such an explication it is possible, as we have seen, to move toward such a sense of the unconditioned primacy of the person by meditatively unfolding the liberal impulse itself. The absorption of that transcendent inspiration into the liberal construction means that it remains there for its reevocation whenever there is a willingness to follow its intimations.

The separation from its religious underpinnings does not necessarily mean the erosion of liberal foundations. The same inspiration can continue and remain effective although its character has withdrawn into a sense of the implicit. This is how the liberal consensus has historically been fashioned, and it remains the secret of its stability. A price is indeed paid in terms of the philosophical incompleteness of the liberal construction, and there is an indisputable danger of instability that has reached crisis proportions within our own time. But there is no inherent necessity for the process of disintegration to continue to extremes. It is still possible for liberal polities to regather their forces in a renovation of the liberal public order. The liberal capacity for self-renewal is what has historically confounded its critics, and there is no reason why such a reevocation could not take place in our own time. Simply from within the resources of the liberal tradition, I have tried to show, it is possible to reach a more profoundly intuitive renovation of the liberal impulse.

The fragmentation of the more substantive spiritual traditions does generate a sense of irreversible decline and an almost irresistible tendency to extrapolate into a chaotic apocalypse. But the reality has been much less dramatic, and it is not entirely subsumable under the rubric of "muddling through." It is equally possible for the process of disintegration to be held at a certain level and even reversed somewhat, by the reintroduction of the earlier spiritual substance at a more intuitive level of discourse that nevertheless consolidates its influence and appeal. Simply because the philosophic and Christian symbolism is no longer publicly in evidence does not mean that it has ceased to have an effect. In many ways its effectiveness may be enhanced by the withdrawal to the level of intuitive consensus where its authority is accepted without question and its reach is limited to the essentials of the public order. One way of viewing the liberal construction is as a brilliant reevocation of the implicit substance of Christianity precisely at the point where its explicit authority was coming most forcefully under attack.

We might even go further along this line to suggest what has only rarely been recognized in discussions of liberal principles in the contemporary context: that the residually philosophic Christian substance of the liberal order has been more than a tactical retreat or strategic compromise. It is more properly understood as a process of refinement, a heightening of the Christian truth about man with specific illumination of its political implications. The liberal concentration on the dignity of each human being who must be regarded as a self-governing end in himself is recognized as a moral advance or clarification within the Christian context. That is the source of its authority within a civilization historically formed by Christianity and the continuing source of its authority within the more secular pluralist setting of our own time. The intuitive rightness of the liberal order is rendered transparent by the sharpness of the focus on the essential component of human dignity and the restriction of the elaboration to what is required to accord full political respect to what a human being is. All of the appeal of a liberal order is concentrated in that central complex of ideas and its effectiveness as a public symbolism is attributable in no small measure to the powerful resonance such a focus has been able to evoke.

We have seen in all the great exponents of the liberal tradition that it has been this preoccupation with liberty as imperative for the full acknowledgment of the status of a human being that has been the animating center of their thought. Locke regarded it as so fundamental that he considered the ruler who violated it to have ruptured the bond of common humanity; he had become a beast of prey who deserved to be hunted like an animal to its death. Rousseau and Kant found all the greatness of a human being to lie in the unutterable dignity of a being whose free self-responsibility was the source of the law by which he was governed. Tocqueville saw the capacity of human beings to govern themselves in freedom as the remaining aristocratic virtue that alone was capable of redeeming the conformist egalitarian tendencies of democracy. Dostoyevsky and some of our own contemporaries have confronted the question of whether the experiment in liberty is worth the price even if it does not seem to provide a reliable means of ensuring human happiness and contentment. The answer he gave was a resounding yes because the alternative would have been to accept the abolition of man, the loss of all that is essential to a truly human existence actualizing our capacity for understanding, responsibility, and love.

Even within the more restrained adumbrations of liberal order among the contemporary theorists, one is struck by the continuing confidence in the moral force and truth of its inspiration. Perhaps the moral substance is even more in evidence in such a setting where the absence of intellectual justification has been so patently in evidence. Rorty and the later Rawls, two of the representative cases, are convinced despite their confessed inability to defend it, that a liberal order corresponds to the most profoundly moral way to order a society in accordance with the dignity of human beings. Having learned from Nietzsche no longer to believe in truth, they are nevertheless believers in the liberal truth. It is eloquent testimony, if testimony were needed, of the capacity of the liberal order to absorb a whole transcendent perspective into itself so powerfully that the inspiration can survive and resonate even when it has become impossible to publicly uphold its content. The question, of course, is for how long this metaphysical high-wire act can be sustained. Perhaps not for much longer, but we really do not know. What is certain is that its success thus far, however problematic, is attributable to the powerful heightening of the philosophic Christian understanding of man whose concentration within the liberal construction endows it with the momentum of a moral advance.

The sense of constituting a moral advance is also what accounts for the sense of rivalry with Christianity that became quite overt in some of the Continental exponents of the liberal ideas. An anticlerical and even antireligious component remains a residue from the conflicts fought out among the militants on either side.[20] But it remains today little more than a trace since, in an increasingly secular society, antireligious sentiments are bound to appear obsolete if not downright quaint. Our concerns are more likely to be with the "naked public square" or the "habits of the heart" whose absence causes us to reflect on the ever more precarious intuitiveness of a liberal order utterly disconnected from the spiritual traditions that give it birth and sustained its growth. Indifference rather than antireligion is more likely to come to the fore in our reflections on the state of our liberal polity. All across the political spectrum we are confronted by a steady stream of commentary that is exercised by a concern about the moral and spiritual vacuum that seems to have invaded the liberal soul.

The sense of a moral advance, that the liberal order constitutes a differentiation of the dignity of human nature that supercedes all rivals, continues to be present but without the requisite background of a culture formed by philosophy and Christianity. Liberal principles are themselves the remaining residue of that religiously grounded culture. As a result, there is a certain brittleness in the way in which principles are asserted politically. We witness wild oscillations in the interpretation and prioritization of liberal rights, prompting many commentators to draw the parallel to civil war, and the propensity to regard rights claims as capable of standing apart from the concrete order of mutual responsibilities. For all the exemplary differentiation of human dignity within the liberal construction, we begin to see that it cannot stand alone. It represents a great historic advance in the definition of the political requirements for the recognition of what human beings are: that they cannot attain their full human status unless they are essentially self-governing in their public and private affairs. But this realization also cannot function utterly without reference to the transcendent imperative that sustains such a commitment in the face of manifest failures and dissatisfaction. Otherwise, what is to prevent us from abandoning the experiment in liberty when it no longer appears to deliver the promised results or stands in the way of our pursuit of happiness?

The great question is how such a transcendent foundation can be integrated into a public symbolism that eschews all reliance on foundations of any kind? That is the question that we have sought to answer through this study. It should by now be apparent how a tradition can form a presence even when it is not explicitly invoked. The liberal arrangement has been just such an absorption and a heightening of the transcendent substance of philosophy and Christianity. An understanding of the human condition and of the moral order that governs it can be presupposed as the silent background within which discussions of public and private good are carried on. The language of that public debate can be refined to appeal only to arguments that pertain to the exercise of rights, or to the common good defined in material or secular terms that are confined to human welfare within this life. It is an arrangement that works remarkably well, eliminating a whole range of difficult and unnecessary disputes from the public arena and permitting an impressive achievement of political tranquillity, so long as a sufficient consensus is maintained concerning ultimate justifications. No one should ask the kind of pointed questions Nietzsche raises concerning why human beings should be treated as unconditional ends in themselves.

When such questions are posed, as they are in the disconnected liberal chaos of our own day, they can be answered only by making philosophically explicit what had remained implicit in the liberal tradition. The depth of the spiritual crisis confronting modern civilization has prompted many of the most thoughtful contemporaries to focus largely on those fundamental questions of order. Especially those who witnessed the totalitarian convulsion firsthand—thinkers such as Voegelin, Strauss, Arendt, Maritain, and others—were impressed by the ultimate character of the political conflicts. They had become philosophical conflicts, and their resolution would have to reach to that level of reflection. The result is that a rich expansion of the philosophical horizons has indeed occurred, particularly through the retrieval of the perspective of the classical and Christian traditions and the concomitant relativization of the perspective of the modern world. We can now recognize that the assertions on which modernity is based are not in themselves ultimate and may represent a contraction of the human possibilities differentiated within the premodern forms. Such a critique is the apex of a broader self-questioning of modernity that has denominated our own era as a postmodern age.[21] The difficulty is that all of this philosophical expansion has occurred outside a liberal frame of reference and is incapable of enriching the public order until some convergence occurs between them. It is not enough to recognize the depth of the abyss that might engulf our fragile order or to have reached a personally compelling apprehension of a superior truth of order. No improvement can occur until the renovation of order can become publicly effective.

The great challenge is to find a means of bridging the gap between such personal growth of the soul and the common ethos. What makes the task so difficult is that it cannot entail any radical rejection of the liberal arrangement. We live in an irretrievably pluralist social context and while it is possible that we might return to a greater degree of cultural homogeneity, it is not at all probable. A way must be found of renewing and enlarging the public order from within that does not require us to jettison the liberal guarantee of autonomy or threaten those who might experience such a call to magnanimity as coercive. The public symbolism must remain intact, but its inner substance must undergo a spiritual enlargement. Somehow the expanded existential and philosophical horizons that have occurred through the catharsis of the modern world and the rediscovery of the depth of traditions must be infused into the liberal ethos without effecting a revolutionary change in the publicly authoritative form of order. What I am suggesting is a growth of the liberal soul.

It is only possible on the presupposition that the liberal construction is capable of enlargement still holds. The purpose of our meditative exploration of the limits of the liberal order both in the contemporary debate and in the historical tradition has been to demonstrate that it does contain such an amplitude of possibility. Liberal democracy is not a fixed quantity but an amazingly flexible and resilient set of arrangements that can draw on resources well below the surface precisely because it has rested on such silent depths for so long. It is an arrangement that has permitted the inner life of the great spiritual traditions, especially philosophy and Christianity, to continue as the wellspring of order because their withdrawal into privacy has preserved them from the ceaseless factional conflicts that would otherwise have exhausted their energies. We might read the liberal order, as we have suggested, as the form that the philosophic Christian understanding of man assumes when it is used to express the essentials of a just political order. That was clearly how the founders of our modern liberal democracies understood what they were doing, for they never countenanced the possibility that they were diverging from the common religious tradition of their society. Even the more militant antireligious brand of liberals conceived themselves as more faithful to the Christian heritage than their aristocratic opponents.

It is no more necessary today to make the connection with the spiritual traditions explicit than it was in the eighteenth century. Liberal self-understanding is capable of undergoing the kind of inner resuscitation that has always enabled it to overcome the crises confronting it. What is necessary is to recognize the capacity it still possesses for such a growth of the soul. Knowing that such a possibility exists and obtaining some sense of how it occurs is the key to a sustained effort to move the process forward. Too often those of the best intentions and best equipped to assist in this movement of enlargement of soul too-readily abandon the effort because they have concluded that it is utterly futile. Often it is enough to know that it is not impossible for the effort to be sustained. The spark that can leap from soul to soul is never amenable to our command or prediction, and, while the struggle may indeed appear as disproportional as the calf butting the oak, we may be as surprised as Solzhenitsyn to discover that the oak is indeed beginning to bend just a little.[22] Perhaps most contributive to our sanguinity about the outcome is that the liberal order itself is designed to remain susceptible of such inner enlargement.

It is an articulation of order that is to be characterized as minimal, remaining silent on most of the presuppositions that are required for the full actualization of that order. As a consequence, liberal democracy invites without compelling the process of discovery by which the depth on which its achievements rest is progressively made. It fits exactly Oakeshott's characterization of it as a practice in which the rules are no more than the minimum necessary to get the game started and prevent breakdowns from occurring at the first obstacle encountered. But the real learning of what it entails is practical. It is contained within the actual engagement of the creation and maintenance of a liberal polity, where the understanding of rights in concrete occurs and a mode of resolving conflicts between them must be worked out. The tradition of a liberal polity is the aggregation of such concrete practices, and the life of such a possibility consists of the effort to absorb the body of practical insights and follow out the intimations they contain for the changing circumstances in which we find ourselves. The utilization of a rhetoric of minimal order tends to create the impression that order is abstract or created through the invocation of abstract slogans, and this is the great danger of a liberal order—that it might become identified with its rhetoric. But the reverse side of that minimalism is that the misidentification is an elementary error and that little is needed to remind everyone of the incompleteness of a liberal bill of rights on its own.[23]

In this reliance on the emergence of the concrete knowledge of a practice, the liberal arrangement is in tune with the fundamental character of human existence that may be defined as the project of self-determination. Just as there is no preset pattern for human action or character, for it is always something freely chosen in the struggle between alternatives and forces, so the liberal arrangement appears to invest this intelligent openness with the appropriate significance. What is required of the public order is not a preconceived pattern to which human actions should conform, but the boundary conditions and rules that make it possible for us to assume the responsibility for our own lives. It is in this way that we slowly make our way toward the realization of our human stature. Freedom is the essential precondition for the growth of the person. Political order, therefore, must confine itself to the minimal regulations necessary to the emergence of self-responsibility in freedom. Politics, Oakeshott has reminded us, is more like the constitutive rules of a language or a game. It ought not to tell us what to do or what to say, but should provide the indispensable conditions of order that make it possible for us to freely choose what we are to say or do.

The nature of human beings is that they fully realize their nature only when they rise to the level of freely exercising responsibility for what they are to become. A liberal political order is the one most fully in accord with this insight. It not only permits the emergence of self-responsibility, which could be accomplished by allowing considerable space for private discretion, but also promotes such an emergence through the emphasis placed on self-government, especially the opportunity and obligation to participate in the political life of the community itself. At its best, the liberal construction evokes the realization that the highest purpose of human existence is served through the actualization of an order that has no purpose beyond itself than the full emergence of the practice of self-government. The exercise of free self-responsibility is an end in itself that surpasses any of the substantive purposes that might be adduced to the cooperative enterprises of human beings. Beyond any specific goals are the human beings that are enrolled in their pursuit, and it is their good that far outweighs the finite particular goods that might be proposed. The culminating expression of political order is that in which the human good as human is served, and that involves the unfolding of the specifically human capacity for free intelligent donation of self in responsibility and love.

The great lacuna in the liberal evocation is that the emphasis on the expansion of the realm of free self-determination conveys little of the sense of the great obligation and potential that underpins it. More often the protection from all but the minimal social and political constraints is experienced as a vacuity to be filled according to the whims and fancies of the moment. The freedom to "live as you like" (Aristotle *Politics* 1317b3) removes all authoritative pressures on the individual, and there is little to remind us of the high calling to self-responsibility that alone justifies the removal of so many of the formative influences of order. Left to themselves, individuals without the maturity or the virtues necessary to sustain the strenuous effort at self-government drift inexorably toward the most brutish forms of existence. Without any sure guideposts to pull them upward they sink to the lower levels of human attainment and eventually betray the validity of the faith in human nature that had inspired the experiment in liberty. All the great liberal theorists were concerned about the possibility that in freedom people might settle for a nasty, depraved existence, and there can be no doubt that this is the point of maximum vulnerability in the entire construction.

Is it possible to authoritatively communicate the great purpose of human freedom without prejudicing that freedom itself? This is another side of the problem of the incompleteness of the liberal formulation that is incapable of rendering a coherent account of its own foundations. Its focus on the primacy of the inviolability of freedom differentiated the indispensable condition for self-actualization, but it said nothing about the movement of self-actualization that was the source of the value of freedom. The guiding expectation was that the elevation of freedom to such priority would draw in its wake the aspiration to follow through on its fulfillment. The remaining background of philosophy and Christianity in modern society together with the vivifying emphasis on the centrality of individual responsibility would together be sufficient to ensure that the high calling of liberty would be adequately fulfilled. Inevitably, the passage of time and the press of history will take its toll on such noble aspirations, and it is perhaps unavoidable that the tension will be relaxed from time to time and stand in need of renewal. The great danger of our day is that we will mistake the relaxation of tension for the permanent condition of a liberal polity and not take the necessary steps to recall ourselves to the noble vocation of self-government.

Most striking among the contemporary liberal theorists surveyed in this study is that, irrespective of their political leanings, they betray not a hint of awareness of the inspirational dimension of their reflections. This is what causes the kind of instrumental superficiality, the suggestion that our problems can be solved through technical or rational means, in their writings. Even the best of them, like Oakeshott or Taylor, do not quite seem to grasp the importance of evoking that greatness of heart in their own meditations. All is cool and cerebral, as if the game is now over, and one is no longer sure even if they fully believe in their principles. By contrast there is a naïveté to the ruminations of Madison or Mill because they leave us in no doubt about the intensity with which the convictions are held. Their writings were not simply intended to communicate a particular line of argument; they also had the purpose of conveying some of the passion that was the principal means of their political effect.[24] In a construction with such limited possibility of expansive articulation, the liberal order relies more than most on the capacity to communicate the force of the powerful unspoken nobility of the responsibility of freedom.

The incompleteness of the philosophical elaboration must not be allowed to stand in the way of an evocation of the intuitive depths. To the extent that a liberal order lives on such subterranean impulses it is crucial that they be regularly actualized in life; otherwise they will atrophy like any other organic reality that is no longer engaged in its functions. Nor should the self-consciousness of the precarious intellectual rationale by which we are compelled to support them be used as an excuse for not bringing forth a forceful expression of our convictions. The entire argument we have traversed has had no other goal than to suggest that when we do confront seriously the convictions that are at the root of our liberal order, without fixating on the lack of intellectual coherence of the formulations in which they are conventionally articulated, we will begin to discover a deeper path whose intimations can eventually give shape to a far more expansive understanding. Beyond the justification of a liberal order derived from the presuppositions of everyman, we begin to discern the much greater cogency that it assumes for the concrete men and women whose own achievement of self-government has been the principal illumination of its meaning.

But it is then that the real miracle of actualization begins to occur. The evocation of the profound spiritual impulses that lie behind the liberal construction is itself a movement in political reality that in turn affects the way in which everything is perceived. Simply by virtue of bringing such inspiration more fully into consciousness it emerges more fully into reality with a power and presence of its own. The actualization of our deepest intimations is a process of enlarging their reality. As a consequence, they assume a dynamic of their own, in which the newly emergent reality begins to overshadow all of the hesitations that had preceded it. Not only do we begin to see things differently but the difficulties that had previously seemed so insuperable dissolve into insignificance as well. A revitalization of the liberal impulse reinforces the inspiration from which it springs and in turn feeds back upon itself to enhance its appeal and authority. Having evoked the nobility of freedom, an expansion of spiritual reality occurs that has greater sustainability because now the attraction of the exercise of responsibility has become more manifest to us. As in any performance, the most difficult steps are the first, but once set in motion the process calls forth unsuspected resonances that make its continuation more self-sustaining. The forces of the newly emergent reality reinforce the original appeal. A growth of the soul has taken place. That capacity for a qualitative change in the mode of experience is what is most often overlooked in the minimal rhetoric of liberal politics.

Yet it is by far the most common feature of what sustains and has ensured the durability of the liberal order. Unfortunately, both the abstraction of liberal formulations and the relative placidity of liberal society conspire to keep the depths of its inner life hidden from view. They are called forth and are very much manifest, however, when they are sensed to be under threat. This is why it has been moments of great national struggle that have constituted the "finest hour" and the point of heightened self-transparence for the liberal democracies. Our own era of deep self-searching and testing is in moral terms comparable, for we are again pushed to express and acknowledge what it is for which we stand and what is to constitute the meaning of our political life. Abortion is perhaps the most pivotal of a range of issues rattling our liberal self-confidence and requiring just such a pulling together of all of the reserves of courage and forthrightness that lie within us. The result, as we have seen on the small scale of our meditation above, invites a growth of the soul to the point that our capacity to see things rightly is enlarged beyond the comfortable limits with which we began.

The greatest surprise of all is that the process of meditative expansion eventually makes clear the impossibility of ever resolving the moral crises of our day within the parameters of the liberal agenda. Simply by following out the intimations of our liberal convictions we are pointed beyond the range of liberal formulations. The incompleteness of the liberal construction begins to be filled out by the emergence of our relationship to a reality that transcends all our political arrangements. It is perhaps the final irony to discover that the political construction designed to avoid the controversies entailed by the introduction of ultimate questions cannot survive unless it is somehow rooted in just such a relationship of transcendent proportions. But this is no longer the impossibly threatening imposition of religion or morality that can only horrify liberal sensitivities. Now it is a conclusion reached through strict fidelity to liberal principles when the profile of those principles has in turn been stretched to accommodate that recognition. Perhaps it might be called a post-liberal insight, but I would prefer to see it as most profoundly in tune with the deepest component of the liberal tradition.

We are back at the religiously grounded liberal order that prevailed up to the twentieth century, only now we have reached it by going through the abyss of a liberal politics shorn of all transcendent connections. In that sense, it is not the same as the Lockean conjunction of Christian liberal philosophy. It is the fruit of a struggle reached at the other side of despair, and, as such, it is attenuated and not by any means a securely and widely held conviction. Indeed, only a few have yet made the journey, and the present study is more of an invitation than a description. But it is an insight that can be reached from within the liberal framework, if I have made the case, only because it is already deeply buried within its inspiration. The process of discovering this transcendent openness on which the vitality of a liberal polity so crucially depends is not a wholly intellectual exercise. It involves an enlargement of our liberal horizons that is tantamount to the growth of the soul.

A growth of the soul is indispensable because we are dealing with an exploration of reality that comes into view only to the extent that we have been able to participate in it. The incomplete character of our existence means not only that we are free to determine the character we are to become, but also that our perspective on reality is crucially dependent on the direction we choose to unfold. There are none for whom the intimation of a transcendent openness, however the ultimate end of the aspiration is conceived, is completely absent. But there is a continuum within which that awareness can be actualized, and it is considerably deepened and enhanced in those who have undertaken the existential opening to its order. Without that effort to actualize the pull of transcendence, there is much less of the reality to apprehend. This is, of course, the source of the uncertainties from which spiritual controversies arise, and the liberal accommodation of tolerance does not in any way remove the conditions under which the struggle for order takes place.

All that we can do is take note of the dynamics of experience that render the uncertainties more manageable. Through the growth of the soul the uncertainty is considerably reduced as the transcendent pull manifests its preeminent reality within us. Once we have begun to allow its imperious pull to take hold of us, the uncertainties and vacillations dissolve away into insignificance. We realize that the measure by which we are drawn is of a rightness that outweighs the loss of everything else in existence. That impulse is still visible even in the diminished and modest liberal reflection of Rawls and Rorty as they assert the imperative of respecting the exigencies of right, a right whose truth and reality calls us inexorably beyond the controversies of the good. What they do not do is advert to the structure of their own experience; they neglect the illumination of reality contained within their own participation in the transcendent. In this they overlook or even deny the wellspring that alone sustains a liberal public order. For it is the capacity of the liberal symbolization to evoke the sense of participation in an order of rightness that transcends all considerations of pragmatic success or satisfaction that has been the principal means of its survival. At the level of argument nothing is added, but existentially everything has changed so that the previously unresonant rhetoric begins to sing with a power or a reality that carries us beyond our finite selves.[25]

Such a heightening of awareness of transcendence is, of course, not a permanent possession, and it is a great error to assume that it is ever achieved once and for all. It is something that must be won and rewon in the daily struggle to live our lives in attunement with the order that discloses itself through the process of attunement itself. One of the great mistakes of the liberal formulations has been to suggest that order consists of a relaxed and comfortable attainment, which can be repeated and sustained without arduous effort. On the contrary, the growth of the soul to the point where the founding impulse of a liberal democratic order becomes transparent is to be gained only as the fruit of struggle. There is no final resting place in which it becomes a possession amenable to our command and control. The attempt to reduce the inspiration to an item of convenience results in the deformation by which we are left with no more than the empty husk of abstract rights from which the substance has vanished. It is only if we make the truth of liberal reverence for the transcendent openness of human beings live again that its reality becomes accessible to us. The sustaining transcendent reality reveals itself only to those who are already willing to undergo the struggle to remain faithful to its commands.

Difficulties, uncertainties, and crises are in that sense not the worst fate to overtake us. Far worse is the cowardice or attachment to comfort that inclines us to settle them without a struggle. We are in danger of failing to grasp the enormous opportunity for growth that is presented by such controversy, so long as we are unwilling to follow it all the way without premature resolution. For it is when we begin to contemplate the extremes that lie before us that we begin to arouse the countermovement of resistance to self-destruction within us. In that movement the reality of good is called forth, if we respond to its pull and resist the fatality of evil, and it grows to a stature whose power we had hitherto not suspected was possible within us. The growth of the soul in response to the dehumanizing pressures that confront us is the means by which the strength of resistance to deformation is obtained. It is from that summit of actualization that the reality of transcendent good discloses itself to us as the presence drawing us from the beginning to the end.

At that moment we might glance back over our shoulder and see the generations that preceded us. We realize that the predecessors who created the liberal symbolization of order did so not in a moment of relaxed good humor but under the pressures and vicissitudes of recurrent periods of crisis in which all seemed to be on the verge of being lost. Liberal order is an achievement of justice that is snatched precariously from the jaws of a roaring chaos ever ready to overwhelm it. Franklin's remark after the Constitutional Convention that America now had "a republic if we can keep it," rings in our ears as the necessity of maintaining the struggle required of us to keep the experiment in liberty alive. When we raise our eyes even further over the historical horizon we realize that this is the condition that imposes itself on all human life. There has never been an age of security and quiet in which the necessity for struggle had been relieved. The great symbolizations of order, such as philosophy and Christianity, arose at points of crisis in which disintegration and corruption seemed about to engulf all. The truth of order is won only through the struggle with disorder. Conflict and suffering are not to be shunned but accepted as the path apparently fated for human beings to make their way slowly, fitfully and finally toward the order of right that endures. Even for the reticent and pampered liberal soul, struggle is the only means available for its growth. Death is finally the price at which we too obtain life.

Notes

Chapter 1: Crisis of Liberal Politics

1. Alasdair MacIntyre's *After Virtue* had the kind of broad public impact that it did because it was a forceful intellectual expression of a social situation that was becoming widely self-evident. He summarized the "catastrophe" that has overtaken modern civilization.

> The project of providing a rational vindication of morality had decisively failed; and from henceforward the morality of our predecessor culture—and subsequently of our own—lacked any public, shared rationale or justification. In a world of secular rationality religion could no longer provide such a shared background and foundation for moral discourse and action; and the failure of philosophy to provide what religion could no longer furnish was an important cause of philosophy losing its central cultural role and becoming a marginal, narrowly academic subject. (50)

A recent survey of the social fault lines is provided by James Davison Hunter in *Culture Wars: The Struggle to Define America.*

2. This is the title of a famous book by George Dangerfield, *The Strange Death of Liberal England, 1910–1914,* which recounts the collapse of the Liberal political party in England just before the Great War.

3. It is not at all comforting to discover that the most influential American jurist of the century had concluded that there was "no reason for attributing to man a significance different in kind from that which belongs to a baboon or to a grain of sand" (quoted in Walter Berns, *The First Amendment and the Future of American Democracy,* 162–63).

4. For an account of the way in which welfare-state liberalism is the outgrowth of the earlier laissez-faire liberalism, see the classic argument by L. T. Hobhouse in *Liberalism.* John Dewey represents a parallel call for the expansion of liberal formulations to include a more energetic role for government planning and intervention. See his *Individualism Old and New, Freedom and Culture,* and *Liberalism and Social Action.*

5. I am indebted to the work of several liberal critics of liberalism for this portrait, especially John Gray, *Liberalism* and *Liberalisms: Essays in Political Philosophy,* and William Galston, *Liberal Purposes: Goods, Virtues and Diversity in the Liberal State.*

6. T. S. Eliot, *The Idea of a Christian Society,* 65. A more philosophic elaboration of the same conclusion emerges in John Hallowell's *Decline of Liberalism As an Ideology,* although characteristically Hallowell is proposing the rejuvenation of liberal democracy ten years later in *The Moral Foundation of Democracy.*

7. See, for example, Jacques Maritain, *Man and the State;* Michael Polanyi, *The Logic of Liberty;* and Friedrich Hayek, *The Constitution of Liberty.*

8. Isaiah Berlin, *Four Essays on Liberty,* 172. Karl Popper, *The Open Society and Its Enemies.*

9. Other notable examples of liberal theorizing certainly include Joseph Raz, *The Morality of Freedom;* Richard E. Flathman, *The Philosophy and Politics of Freedom;* Bruce Ackerman, *Social Justice in the Liberal State;* Stephen Macedo, *Liberal Virtues;* and Galston, *Liberal Purposes;* a representative example of the high level of recent symposia on the character of liberal order is R. Bruce Douglas, Gerald M. Mara, and Henry S. Richardson, eds., *Liberalism and the Good.*

10. The thesis that liberal democracy represents the end point of political development in light of the disappearance of its last ideological rival has been developed by Francis Fukuyama in *The End of History and the Last Man.*

11. Western knowledge of the Nazi Holocaust, it has been established, was extensive, but it is only with the Stalinist holocaust that Western cooperation rose to the level of active participation. This was in the shameful forced repatriation of approximately two million Soviet citizens who were in the West after the conclusion of hostilities, as part of an agreement with Stalin. Those that did not commit suicide along the way were immediately dispatched to the Communist concentration camps.

12. The air of foreboding that hangs over modern civilization began to receive profound expression in the nineteenth century, especially with the pessimism of Schopenhauer and Nietzsche, as well as in the more historical reflections of Tocqueville, Burckhart, and Spengler. Even an American thinker, such as Orestes Brownson, could detect the connection between nihilism and totalitarianism then being forged. See Gregory Butler, *In Search of the American Spirit: The Political Thought of Orestes Brownson.* In our own century it has become commonplace to view the horror of the totalitarian convulsion through its relationship to the modern civilization that has produced it. See Hannah Arendt, *The Origins of Totalitarianism;* Eric Voegelin, *The New Science of Politics* and *From Enlightenment to Revolution;* Albert Camus, *The Rebel;* Alexander Solzhenitsyn, *The Gulag Archipelago.*

13. See Henri de Lubac, *The Drama of Atheist Humanism;* David Walsh, *After Ideology: Recovering the Spiritual Foundations of Freedom.*

14. The experience that transformed Dostoyevsky is recounted in *The Diary of a Writer,* 209–10. In *After Ideology,* I have tried to show how such experiences are the means by which large-scale shifts of moral orientation, a growth of the soul, actually occurs.

15. Michael Sandel, "The Procedural Republic and the Unencumbered Self" and *Liberalism and the Limits of Justice.*

16. Michael Sandel has expressed the problem with great clarity:

> If the good is nothing more than the indiscriminate satisfaction of arbitrarily-given preferences, regardless of worth, it is not difficult to imagine that the right (and for that matter a good many other sorts of claims) must outweigh it. But in fact the morally diminished status of the good must inevitably call into question the status of justice as well. For once it is conceded that our conceptions of the good are

morally arbitrary, it becomes difficult to see why the highest of all (social) virtues should be the one that enables us to pursue these arbitrary conceptions "as fully as circumstances permit" (*Liberalism and the Limits*, 168).

A similar identification of the ambiguity of Rawls was voiced by George Parkin Grant:

> One may be glad that Rawls has inherited the noble belief in political equality, and the belief that "the free and rational person" is "valuable" in a way quite different from members of other species. But in an era such as ours, we cannot help hoping that he will tell us why it is so. His writing is typical of much modern liberal thought in that the word "person" is brought in mysteriously (one might better say sentimentally) to cover up the inability to state clearly what it is about human beings which makes them worthy of high political respect. Where Kant is clear concerning this, Rawls is not. (*English-Speaking Justice*, 33)

17. Rawls is not of course alone in preferring such reticence. Bruce Ackerman is even stronger in endorsing liberal detachment:

> When you and I learn that we disagree about one or another dimension of the moral truth, we should not search for some common value that will trump this disagreement; nor should we try to translate it into some putatively neutral framework; nor should we seek to transcend it by talking about how some unearthly creature might resolve it. We should simply say *nothing at all* about this disagreement and put the moral ideals that divide us off the conversational agenda of the liberal state. ("Why Dialogue?")

18. Brigitte and Peter Berger have sought to uncover a middle ground of consensus in the abortion debate, but they readily acknowledge that the issue may be seen as outweighing the call for civil harmony: "In view of this perception of the issue by large numbers of Americans, the accusation by [the pro-choice side] that these people are engaged in 'single issue politics' missed the point entirely: Given this perception, what single issue could be more important than a million murders per year?" (*The War over the Family*, 67). The scale of the issue is perhaps best captured by the title of a popular treatment by John Powell, *Abortion: The Silent Holocaust.*

19. The contrast with Lincoln's assessment of the situation when he confronted the arguably more overt conflict regarding slavery is instructive. He recognized that the issue could be settled politically only if it was first settled philosophically. "Whenever this question [of slavery] shall be settled, it must be settled on some *philosophical basis.* No policy that does not rest upon some *philosophical public opinion* can be permanently maintained" (Roy B. Basler, ed., *The Collected Works of Abraham Lincoln,* 17).

20. On this background, see Harold Berman, *Law and Revolution: The Formation of the Western Legal Tradition;* James Stoner, *The Common Law and Liberal Theory.*

21. Richard Flathman, *Toward a Liberalism,* 203. It should be noted that Flathman does retain the possibility of asserting a pacifist defense for noncooperation, although it remains a highly "qualified" avenue of escape from liberal compulsion.

22. Richard Rorty proposes to discourage the raising of philosophical questions about the source of order as a necessity imposed by the irreducible pluralism of contemporary liberal societies.

> If one's moral identity consists in being a citizen of a liberal polity, then to encourage light-mindedness will serve one's moral purposes. Moral commitment, after all, does not require taking seriously all the matters that are, for moral reasons, taken

seriously by one's fellow citizens. It may require just the opposite. It may require trying to josh them out of the habit of taking those topics so seriously. There may be serious reasons for so joshing them. ("The Priority of Democracy to Philosophy," 272)

23. The same incredible sense of an impossible high-wire balancing act could be discerned in Rawls's earlier construction, as Michael Sandel perceptively discerned. Discussing the difference principle, Sandel observed that the assumption that all assets are at the disposition of society to redistribute "fairly" undermines the independence of the deontological self it was intended to protect.

> Either my prospects are left at the mercy of institutions established for "prior and independent social ends" . . . ends which may or may not coincide with my own, or I must count myself a member of a community defined in part by those ends, in which case I cease to be unencumbered by constitutive attachments. Either way, the difference principle contradicts the liberating aspiration of the deontological project. We cannot be persons for whom justice is primary and also be persons for whom the difference principle is a principle of justice. (*Liberalism and the Limits,* 178).

24. Compare this with Albert Camus's meditation on the existential discovery of an order of moral limits in the act of revolt against injustice

> What is a rebel? A man who says no, but whose refusal does not imply a renunciation. . . . He means, for example, that "this has been going on too long," "up to this point yes, beyond it no," "you are going too far," or, again, "there is a limit beyond which you shall not go." . . . Rebellion cannot exist without the feeling that, somewhere and somehow, one is right. . . . When he rebels, a man identifies himself with other men and so surpasses himself, and from this point of view human solidarity is metaphysical. (*The Rebel* 13, 17)

25. Ibid., 236.

Chapter 2: Enduring Moral Authority

1. The most notorious such expression was the article by Francis Fukuyama and the spectacular attention it received. Fukuyama, "The End of History?" *National Interest.* He gave a more considered elaboration in *The End of History and the Last Man.* Artistically, the exuberance is captured in the widely broadcast concert conducted by Leonard Bernstein at the collapsed Berlin Wall in 1989, where the "An die Freude" ("Ode to Joy") in the last movement of Beethoven's Ninth Symphony is transformed into "An die Freiheit."

2. Few books captured the renewed appreciation of the value and achievements of capitalist political economy as well as Michael Novak, *The Spirit of Democratic Capitalism.*

3. One thinks of the kind of critique of the West expressed most forcefully by Alexander Solzhenitsyn in his "Harvard Address" and other political commentaries of the mid-seventies. See his *A World Split Apart* and *Detente: Prospects for Democracy and Dictatorship.*

4. The problem of liberal neglect of proselytization or at least of disseminating a clear understanding of their own political order is a long-standing one. Hannah Arendt, among others, has pointed out the remarkable failure to communicate the nature of the American founding, beginning right after the founding itself. Indeed

it is still the case that much of even the liberal democratic world is ignorant of the genius of the American political tradition (*On Revolution,* 222).

5. This is seen most clearly in the critics of the liberal construction on the left and the right who turn out, on closer examination, to be really critics within the liberal framework. Writers on the right such as Russell Kirk in *The Conservative Mind: From Burke to Eliot* or John Courtney Murray in *We Hold These Truths: Catholic Reflections on the American Proposition* propose a conservative return of the liberal polity to the earlier sources of its inspiration. Michael Walzer, beginning from a more socialist inclination, argues in *Spheres of Justice* for greater fidelity to the liberal distinctions between the spheres of the public and the private as the way to block illegitimate power transactions within society. The inescapability of the liberal framework imposes itself on the critics most prepared to revise it.

6. For all the forcefulness of the critique of the liberal construction by advocates of the broader spiritual and moral traditions, there is little in the way of concrete efforts to envision an alternative. One would search in vain in the works of Strauss or Voegelin or the natural-law thinkers, such as John Courtney Murray or John Finnis, for anything approaching the idea of a new political form for the modern world. Even among those who focus most specifically on the moral dimension of the public order, the proposal is for a modification rather than a rejection of the liberal arrangements. See, for example, Patrick Devlin, *The Enforcement of Morals* and Robert P. George, *Making Men Moral: Civil Liberties and Public Morality.*

7. An interesting reflection on the way in which the U.S. Constitution points toward the "faith" on which it rests, as in the oaths of office or the Ninth Amendment reference to unenumerated rights, is contained in Sanford Levinson, *Constitutional Faith.* The precarious character of that faith at present is perhaps best indicated by the author's own avowal of relativism (61) and his failure to meditate on the nonrelative character of his own convictions.

8. It is intriguing to note that even the most severe of the deconstructionists, Jacques Derrida, seems to have veered toward something recognizably similar to this Aristotelian concrete sense of right. Derrida now conceives of justice as the unformulatable concrete sense of responsibility, of what each owes to the other, which is what provides the criterion of judging the adequacy or inadequacy of law. "Justice in itself, if such exists, outside or beyond law is not deconstructible. No more than deconstruction, if such a thing exists. Deconstruction is justice." He goes on to describe "the paradox that I'd like to submit for discussion is the following: it is this deconstructible structure of law *[droit],* or if you prefer of justice as *droit,* that also ensures the possibility of deconstruction." Justice itself is irreducible. "Deconstruction is possible," John Caputo comments on "the scandal" of these passages, "only insofar as justice is undeconstructible, for justice is what deconstruction aims at, what it is about, what it *is*" (quoted in "Hyperbolic Justice: Mythologizing Differently with Derrida and Levinas," 193). For the full essay, see Derrida, "Force of Law: The 'Mystical Foundations of Authority.' "

9. The most comprehensive account of Oakeshott to date within a comparative perspective is provided by Paul Franco, *The Political Philosophy of Michael Oakeshott.*

10. Discussing the problem of different perceptions of the good, Aristotle admits, "that in an unqualified sense and from the standpoint of truth the object of wish is the good, but that for each individual it is whatever seems good to him . . . Thus,

what is good and pleasant differs with different characteristics or conditions, and perhaps the chief distinction of a man of high moral standards is his ability to see the truth in each particular moral question, since he is, as it were, the standard and measure for such questions" (*Nicomachean Ethics* 1113a-b).

11. Political education, Michael Oakeshott constantly emphasizes, is practical and vocational. It is learned as any concrete body of practical knowledge is acquired, by doing or by working closely with those who know. Political education is primarily a matter of fitting into an ongoing tradition for, no matter how bad a shape the tradition may be in, it is never hopeless nor are there any other resources available. There is no free-standing science of politics separate from the various concrete political traditions. Even when society is afflicted by crisis there are "no resources outside the fragments, the vestiges, the relics of its own tradition of behavior which the crisis has left untouched. For even the help we may get from the traditions of another society (or from a tradition of a vaguer sort which is shared by a number of societies) is conditional upon our being able to assimilate them to our own arrangements and our own manner of attending to our arrangements" (*Rationalism and Politics,* 59).

12. Alexander Solzhenitsyn, ed., *From under the Rubble;* Leopold Labedz, ed., *Solzhenitsyn: A Documentary Record,* 375–79.

13. The program of the science of behavioral control is disclosed in the title of a book by its leading proponent, B. F. Skinner, *Beyond Freedom and Dignity.* The classic refutation had been formulated earlier by C. S. Lewis in *The Abolition of Man.* On the problematic relationship between technology and liberalism, see Jacques Ellul, *The Technological Society;* Martin Heidegger, *The Question Concerning Technology and Other Essays;* George Parkin Grant, *Technology and Justice;* and Barry Cooper, *Action into Nature.*

14. See Leon Kass, "The New Biology: What Price 'Relieving Man's Estate'?"; David Ehrenfeld, *The Arrogance of Humanism.*

15. "Indeed it has been observed correctly," Richard John Neuhaus argues, "that in the last two decades medical technology has been the salvation of ethics as a profession. Thousands of medical ethicists and bioethicists, as they are called, professionally guide the unthinkable on its passage through the debatable on its way to becoming the justifiable until it is finally established as the unexceptionable" ("The Return of Eugenics").

Chapter 3: Utopian Forgetfulness of Depth

1. Ludwig Wittgenstein, *Tractatus Logico-Philosophicus,* 3.

2. Washington had concluded his historically self-conscious "Farewell Address" in 1797 with the following penetrating observation: "And let us with caution indulge the supposition that morality can be maintained without religion. Whatever may be conceded to the influence of refined education on minds of peculiar structure, reason and experience both forbid us to expect that national morality can prevail in the exclusion of religious principle." This might even be considered the consensus of the American founding generation, despite the secular overtones of the political order they created and the noted detachment from conventional Christianity many of them evidenced. Predictably, John Adams declared in his first year as vice president: "We have no government armed with power capable of contending with human passions unbridled by morality and religion. Our constitution was made only for

a moral and a religious people. It is wholly inadequate for the government of any other" (quoted in Stanley Hauerwas, *A Community of Character*, 79).

But even Jefferson, who became notorious for his remark that "it does me no injury for my neighbor to say that there are twenty gods, or no God. It neither picks my pocket nor breaks my leg," could go on in the context of his most dread-filled reflections on the institution of slavery to ask: "Can the liberties of a nation be thought secure when we have removed their only firm basis, a conviction in the minds of the people that these liberties are of the gift of God?" *(Notes on the State of Virginia)*.

The young Alexander Hamilton too could inveigh against the alleged atheism of Hobbes with similar conviction: "Good and wise men, in all ages, have embraced a very dissimilar theory. They have supposed, that the deity, from the relation we stand in, to himself and to each other, has constituted an eternal and immutable law, which is, indispensably, obligatory upon all mankind, *prior to any human institution whatever*" (quoted in Hadley Arkes, *Beyond the Constitution*, 64).

3. Voegelin, "The End of Modernity," chap. 6 in *New Science of Politics;* and Eric Voegelin, "The Eclipse of Reality," in *What Is History and Other Late Unpublished Essays*, pp. 111–62. A more recent perspective is furnished by Vaclav Havel's brilliant analysis of the nature of an ideologically constructed reality in his essay "The Power of the Powerless." And Martin Mahlia details both the cumulative Soviet dislocation from reality and the ideological blinkers of Western social scientists attempting to understand it in *The Soviet Tragedy: A History of Socialism in Russia*.

4. There are few more powerful demonstrations of the intimacy of the connection than that provided in Dostoyevsky's novel *The Possessed*. It is an account of the revolutionary outburst fomented by a tiny cell of extremists but sustained by a much larger circle of liberal sympathizers who abdicate their responsibility for the consequences. The relationship is epitomized by that between the father, Stepan Verkhovensky, a leading liberal intellectual, and his son, Peter, the most merciless and fanatical of the revolutionaries (288).

5. Reflecting on the question of what is to prevent the majority, through the House of Representatives, from exercising its will without regard to the rights of the minority, Madison responds that such tendencies will be obstructed by "the genius of the whole system; the nature of just and constitutional laws; and, above all, the vigilant and manly spirit which actuates the people of America—a spirit which nourishes freedom, and in return is nourished by it" (*The Federalist Papers*, no. 57). On the other hand, Madison is even better known for the concern he lavished on the problem of factions in the new republic, a problem he defined as occurring when there are "a number of citizens, whether amounting to a majority or minority of the whole, who are united and actuated by some common impulse of passion, or of interest, adverse to the rights of other citizens, or to the permanent and aggregate interests of the community" (*Federalist Papers*, no. 10). See also the even better known discussion in *Federalist Papers*, no. 51.

6. See particularly the "Harvard Address," *A World Split Apart*.

7. Even insiders are having second thoughts about the irresistible liberal impulse, as they begin to weigh its tendency to override all values that do not reinforce or conform to it. Commenting on its tendency to undermine many traditionalist perspectives, William Galston provides the following metaphor: "Think of a society based on liberal public principles as a rapidly flowing river. A few vessels may be strong

enough to head upstream. Most, however, will be carried along by the current. But they can still choose where in the river to sail, and where along the shore to moor. The mistake is to think of the liberal polity either as a placid lake or as an irresistible undertow" (*Liberal Purposes*, 296). An extensive critique of the liberal proclivity to encourage the unrestrained assertion of rights is contained in Mary Ann Glendon, *Rights Talk: The Impoverishment of Political Discourse*.

8. The problem is well illustrated in the infamous "Baby M" case where the biological mother was unwilling to surrender her child in accordance with the terms of the surrogate motherhood contract. The New Jersey judge decided the case on exactly the same lines as any other breach of contract dispute, requiring compliance strictly to its terms. Legislatures have since moved to render such contracts unenforceable, but the case provided a chilling glimpse of judicial reductionism in action (In *Baby M*. 217 N.J. Super. 313; 525 A.2d 1128 [March 31, 1987]).

9. Jeremy Bentham, "Anarchical Fallacies: Being an Examination of the Declaration of Rights Issued during the French Revolution," 53.

10. Ibid., 147.

11. Edmund Burke, *Reflections on the Revolution in France*, 87–88.

12. It is interesting to note that Pope Leo XIII issued the same kind of warning at almost the same time in his 1888 encyclical on liberalism, *Libertas Praestantissimum;* the text is available in *The Church Speaks to the Modern World: The Social Teachings of Leo XIII*.

13. A similar objection to the brittleness of liberal rhetoric seems to be the essence of the communitarian critique.

> Liberalism teaches respect for the distance of self and ends, and when this distance is lost, we are submerged in a circumstance that ceases to be ours. But by seeking to secure this distance too completely, liberalism undermines its own insight. By putting the self beyond the reach of politics, it makes human agency an article of faith rather than an object of continuing attention and concern, a premise of politics rather than its precarious achievement. This misses the pathos of politics and also its most inspiring possibilities. It overlooks the danger that when politics goes badly, not only disappointments but also dislocations are likely to result. And it forgets the possibility that when politics goes well, we can know a good in common that we cannot know alone. (Sandel, *Liberalism and the Limits*, 183)

14. It is interesting to note the degree to which John Paul II has emphasized the constitutive role of truth in his most profoundly philosophical encyclical on the crisis of morality, which is appropriately titled *Splendor Veritatis*.

> To the affirmation that one has a duty to follow one's conscience is unduly added the affirmation that one's moral judgment is true merely by the fact that it has its origin in the conscience. But in this way the inescapable claims of truth disappear, yielding their place to a criterion of sincerity, authenticity and "being at peace with oneself," so much so that some have come to adopt a radically subjectivistic conception of moral judgment. (par. 32)

15. This is a point earlier developed by Wilmoore Kendall.

> The proposition that all opinions are equally—and hence infinitely—valuable, said to be the unavoidable inference from the proposition that all opinions are equal, is only one—and perhaps the less likely—of two possible inferences, the other being: all opinions are equally—and hence infinitely—*without* value, so what difference does it make if one, particularly one not our own, gets suppressed? This we may

fairly call the central paradox of the theory of freedom of speech. In order to practice tolerance on behalf of the pursuit of truth, you have first to value and believe in not merely the pursuit of truth but Truth itself, with all its accumulated riches to date. The all-questions-are-open-questions society cannot do that; it cannot, therefore, practice tolerance towards those who disagree with it. It must persecute—and so, on its very own showing, arrest the pursuit of truth. ("The 'Open Society' and Its Fallacies," reprinted in John Stuart Mill, *On Liberty*, 154–67).

16. MacIntyre quotes (*Whose Justice? Which Rationality?* 386) the following illuminating passage in which Roland Barthes rejects the possibility of a coherent, contextually relevant meaning to texts.

> That is not the case with a work *(oeuvre):* the work is without circumstance and it is indeed perhaps what defines it best: the work is not circumscribed, designated, protected, directed by any situation, no practical life is there to tell what meaning to give to it . . . in it ambiguity is wholly pure: however extended it may be, it possesses something of the brevity of the priestess of Apollo, sayings conforming to a first code (the priestess did not rave) and yet open to a number of meanings, for they were uttered outside every *situation*—except indeed the situation of ambiguity. . . ." (*Critique et Verité*, 56)

"This is a splendid description," MacIntyre goes on to observe, "of what traditional texts detached from the context of tradition must become, presented by Barthes as though it were an account of how necessarily texts always are" (*Whose Justice?* 386).

17. Charles Taylor has recently provided an excellent sketch of just such an approach, in which he sympathetically takes up such contemporary liberal preoccupations as respect for difference and multiculturalism, but points out that their realization depends on the presence of a common horizon of meaning.

> To come together on a mutual recognition of difference—that is, of the equal value of different identities—requires that we share more than a belief in this principle; we have to share also some standards of value on which the identities concerned check out as equal. There must be some substantive agreement on value, or else the formal principle of equality will be empty and a sham. We can pay lip-service to equal recognition, but we won't really share an understanding of equality unless we share something more. Recognizing difference, like self-choosing, requires a horizon of significance, in this case a shared one." (*The Ethics of Authenticity*, 52)

Chapter 4: Liberal Achievement of Order from Disorder

1. "Ever since its emergence as a definite strand of thought and practice in early modern Europe, liberalism has been preoccupied with an inquiry into its own foundations" (Gray, *Liberalism*, 45). See also Voegelin, "Liberalism and Its History."

2. Robert Bellah and his colleagues derived the title of their best-selling *Habits of the Heart: Individualism and Commitment in American Life* from Tocqueville, thereby indicating their continuity with his abiding concerns. For the seventeenth-century background in which those concerns first arose with the decline of the traditional ordering symbolisms, see John Redwood, *Reason, Ridicule and Religion*, and W. M. Spellman, *John Locke and the Problem of Depravity*.

3. Voegelin's abandonment of the project of writing a "History of Political Ideas" exemplifies this insight into the interdependence between theory and practice.

> Human society is not merely a fact, or an event, in the external world to be studied by an observer like a natural phenomenon. Though it has externality as one of its

important components, it is as a whole a little world, a cosmion, illuminated with meaning from within by the human beings who continuously create and bear it as the mode and condition of their self-realization. It is illuminated through an elaborate symbolism, in various degrees of compactness and differentiation—from rite, through myth, to theory—and this symbolism illuminates it with meaning in so far as the symbols make the internal structure of such a cosmion, the relations between its members and groups of members, as well as its existence as a whole, transparent for the mystery of human existence. The self-illumination of society through symbols is an integral part of social reality, and one may even say its essential part, for through such symbolization the members of a society experience it as more than an accident or a convenience; they experience it as of their human essence. . . . Hence, when political science begins, it does not begin with a *tabula rasa* on which it can inscribe its concepts; it will inevitably start from the rich body of self-interpretation of a society and proceed by critical clarification of socially pre-existent symbols. (*New Science of Politics,* 27–28)

Alasdair MacIntyre has grasped the same point within his own horizon of concerns. "There ought not to be two histories, one of political and moral action and one of political and moral theorizing, because there were not two pasts, one populated only by actions, the other only by theories. Every action is the bearer and expression of more or less theory-laden beliefs and concepts; every piece of theorizing and every expression of belief is a political and moral action" (*After Virtue,* 61).

Quentin Skinner and his school have done much to establish the importance of the relationship between ideas and their historical setting, but they have been unwilling to recognize the philosophical character of the relationship as a quest for truth. See the inconclusive character of the debate in James Tully, ed., *Meaning and Context: Quentin Skinner and His Critics.*

4. Jean Bodin, *Colloquium of the Seven about the Secrets of the Sublime.* On Bodin's mystical exploration of the truth behind all religions, see Paul Lawrence Rose, *Bodin and the Great God of Nature: The Moral and Religious Universe of a Judaizer.* Bodin's espousal of *politique* toleration is already well known from the advice he gives in the *République* (1583) against compelling citizens to accept a particular religion (see bk. 4, chap. 7).

5. The future that Hooker so clearly foresaw is sympathetically portrayed in Christopher Hill's *The World Turned Upside Down: Radical Ideas during the English Revolution.* The connection between Hooker's analyses and our own ideological age is highlighted in Voegelin's *New Science of Politics,* chapters 4 and 5.

6. This is an omission that was to prove fateful both for Protestant Christianity and for the political order it sought to sustain. John Henry Newman is among the most perceptive of those who had to struggle with the implications of liberal Protestant theology in the nineteenth century. He concluded that it was indeed the excessive reliance on the book alone that was responsible for its self-disintegration before the assaults of the scientific methodology. "A book, after all, cannot make a stand against the wild living intellect of man, and in this day it begins to testify, as regards its own structure and contents, to the power of that universal solvent, which is so successfully acting on religious establishments." It was this conclusion that persuaded Newman to abandon his lifelong Anglican commitment to take the difficult step toward Rome as the only church suited to the task of "smiting hard and throwing back the immense energy of the aggressive, capricious, untrustworthy intellect" (*Apologia Pro Vita Sua,* 188, 189).

7. This is the beginning of the process by which liberal political thought and practice gradually eviscerates all independent institutional carriers of moral and spiritual truth. It is a process that points toward the closure to transcendence that can eventually result in the elimination of the basis for the liberal order of rights itself. The end point is perhaps best embodied in the problematic reflected upon in Richard John Neuhaus's *The Naked Public Square* or in the surprise at the hostility of our contemporary liberal politics toward religion evinced by Stephen Carter in *The Culture of Disbelief: How American Law and Politics Trivialize Religious Devotion.* It does indeed appear that there is some necessity to the medieval recognition of the transpolitical institutional authority of the Church. See Murray, *We Hold These Truths.*

8. See, for example, the study of Stalin's activities along these lines by Robert Conquest in *Stalin: Breaker of Nations.*

9. The renewed attention to Hobbes in the twentieth century arises from the sense that he addressed the same radical political conflict that has been our own. This is particularly the case in the great ideological wars and convulsions that have dominated this century. It is therefore no accident that the leading political theorists of the past fifty years wrote extensively and admiringly of the theorist of the English civil war. See Leo Strauss, *The Political Philosophy of Hobbes* and his *Natural Right and History;* Michael Oakeshott, *Hobbes on Civil Association;* and Voegelin, *New Science of Politics.*

10. I am not inclined to accept the line of interpretation developed by Strauss that the early modern thinkers engaged in "a deliberate lowering of the ultimate goal . . . in order to increase the probability of its attainment" (*Natural Right and History,* 178). A more nuanced recent formulation of this approach is provided by Robert Kraynak's argument that Hobbes sought to make the fear of violent death a "natural" passion through "a process of enlightenment" concerning their allegedly higher ideals. It is indeed the case that Hobbes borrows "moral capital" from the tradition, but that does not necessarily indicate an intention of overthrowing it (*History and Modernity in the Thought of Thomas Hobbes,* 200). It is just as plausible to read the same texts as expressions of Hobbes's effort to win order from a more disordered and fractured social setting. I give more weight to the awareness of philosophy and Christianity, which the Straussian interpretation also acknowledges, in forming the self-conscious background for the early modern synthetic constructions.

11. It seems unnecessary to attribute any devious intention to the avowedly Christian anthropology of Hobbes. We may take it for what it is, an analysis of human nature as he experienced it, because that is the simplest explanation accounting for all the available texts and leaving no remainder unexplained. In the absence of any clear indication to conceal his intentions, we should not incline toward the more complicated hypothesis.

12. It is noteworthy that Hobbes's Christian setting is coming increasingly to be recognized and given its due in recent scholarship. See especially the fine study by Joshua Mitchell, *Not by Reason Alone: Religion, History and Identity in Early Modern Political Thought;* A. P. Martinich, *The Two Gods of "Leviathan": Thomas Hobbes on Religion and Politics;* and Eldon Eisenach, *Two Worlds of Liberalism: Religion and Politics in Hobbes, Locke and Mill.*

13. Norberto Bobbio, *Thomas Hobbes and the Natural Law Tradition.*

14. One of the "opinions" about justice recounted by Glaucon arises from the unwillingness of men to really be just.

What people say is that to do wrong is, in itself, a desirable thing; on the other hand, it is not at all desirable to suffer wrong, and the harm to the sufferer outweighs the advantage to the doer. Consequently, when men have had a taste of both, those who have not the power to seize the advantage and escape the harm decide that they would be better off if they made a compact neither to do wrong nor to suffer it. . . . So justice is accepted as a compromise, and valued, not as good in itself, but for lack of power to do wrong; no man worthy of the name, who had that power, would ever enter into such a compact with anyone; he would be mad if he did. (Plato *Republic* 359a-b)

The same note of disdain for the social contract basis of order is also present in Aristotle. "Otherwise, too, law becomes a mere covenant—or (in the phrase of the Sophist Lycophron) 'a guarantor of men's rights against one another'—instead of being, as it should be, a rule of life such as will make the members of a polis good and just" (*Politics* 1280a22-b32). Cicero too weighs in against the impossible notion that the commonwealth can be sustained on the basis of a social contract derived from the mutual distrust of men toward one another (*On the Commonwealth* 3.13).

15. This is a subject that preoccupied Hobbes for the remaining years of his long life. His *Behemoth or the Long Parliament,* completed in 1668 and published in 1682, is his brilliant analysis of the English civil war that he undertook because, as he explains in the dedication, there "can be nothing more instructive towards loyalty and justice than will be the memory, while it lasts, of that war." As Stephen Holmes suggests in his introduction (xlvii), Hobbes was not a legal positivist. The whole purpose of the meditation was to demonstrate the grounds of obligation of obedience to the sovereign. "They wanted not wit," Hobbes observes of the Parliament and the people, "but the knowledge of the causes and grounds upon which one person has a right to govern, and the rest an obligation to obey; which grounds are necessary to be taught the people, who without them cannot live long in peace amongst themselves" (*Behemoth,* 160). Hobbes's whole project may be seen as an effort to persuade men concerning their duty, which presupposes that they are capable of such a recognition and response (ibid., 39, 45, 62, 144).

16. Hobbes has been accused of transforming the classical and medieval understanding of "right by nature" into the modern conception of "natural rights," of equivocally exploiting the two meanings of right to endow the subjective assertion of rights with the moral authority of what is right. But whatever may have been the effect of his formulations, his intention seems to have been to distinguish between the two senses of "right." "For though they that speak of this subject, use to confound *Jus,* and *Lex, Right* and *Law;* yet they ought to be distinguished; because *Right,* consisteth in liberty to do, or to forbeare; Whereas *Law,* determineth, and bindeth to one of them: so that Law, and Right, differ as much, as Obligation, and Liberty; which in one and the same matter are inconsistent" (*Leviathan,* 189). Hobbes's purpose seems to have been to strengthen the obligatory force of the law of nature, by removing the sense of rightness from what is merely an exercise of liberty in judging measures necessary to preserve ourselves. His "rule of Reason, That every man ought to endeavour Peace, as farre as he has hope of obtaining it; and when he cannot obtain it, that he may seek, and use, all helps, and advantages of Warre," places obligation first. Right only comes into play when the conditions of obligation no longer hold.

17. An example of Hobbes's willingness to press the reading of Scripture in the direction he wishes it to go is his interpretation of the famous passage: "Thou art

Peter and on this rock I will build my church . . ." (Matt. 16:18). Hobbes insists that the "rock" refers back to Peter's confession, "Thou art Christ, the Son of the living God," since he did not in any way want to accept the most famous proof text of divine authorization of the priesthood and the independence of the church (*Leviathan*, 578).

18. The charge of promoting unlimited acquisition, most forcefully elaborated by C. B. MacPherson's portrayal of Locke in *The Political Theory of Possessive Individualism: Hobbes to Locke,* has been well answered by the recent study of James Tully, *A Discourse on Property: John Locke and His Adversaries.* Tully's identification of the medieval sources of Locke is confirmed by Janet Coleman, *"Dominium* in Thirteenth- and Fourteenth-Century Political Thought and Its Seventeenth-Century Heirs: John of Paris and Locke."

19. Richard Ashcraft, *Revolutionary Politics and Locke's Two Treatises of Government;* Peter Laslett, introduction to *John Locke: Two Treatises of Government;* Maurice Cranston, *John Locke: A Biography;* John Dunn, *The Political Thought of John Locke.*

20. This aspect of Locke's thought is searchingly explored in an apparently neglected monograph by Wilmoore Kendall, *John Locke and the Doctrine of Majority Rule.*

> For the writer who believes that there are objective moral standards and that the majority of each political society both accept and know how to apply these standards can say that what the majority wills is right without committing himself to the idea that what the minority wills is wrong *because* it is willed by a minority. He can, too, easily slip into the habit of asserting that what the majority wills is right without reminding his readers that he intends nothing more than a judgment regarding the moral capacity of majorities. . . . The individual can, in his view, covenant to obey the majority without subjecting himself to the absolute and arbitrary authority of other persons, since the judgments of the majority are those of reason and justice. In short, Locke's doctrine of majority-rule becomes a series of identical propositions the moment we attribute to it such a latent premise as the above, and, on any other premise, must be dismissed as highly extravagant ethical nonsense. (133–35)

I am indebted to Lee Cheek for calling this work to my attention.

21. "We have tried to show," Peter Laslett insists, "that the main theme of Locke's book was the development of the implications of this doctrine of natural political virtue, defined, checked and safeguarded by the concept of trust" (*John Locke,* 130). Laslett points out that Locke is careful to avoid the use of the word *contract* to define the character of the political order, preferring always to use the more general term *compact* with all its overtones of a community of mutual trust and fidelity (126).

22. Saint Thomas, who also recognizes the necessity of removing a tyrant, is more cautious concerning who should be entrusted with the task. "It would be dangerous for the community and its rulers if anybody by private initiative were to attempt to kill its public officers, even if they were tyrants. It is more often the case that evil persons expose themselves to such great dangers than do the good. . . . It seems then that actions should arise more from public authority against the brutality of tyrants than from anybody's private initiative" ("De Regimine Principium").

23. Ashcraft, who has completed the most thorough study of Locke's own revolutionary activities, emphasizes the extent to which they were indeed treasonable. It is equally astonishing to take the full measure of Locke's endorsement of revolutionary action by the lowest social classes, the rabble of tradesmen and mechanics, the "brisk boys of Wapping."

Locke's theory of resistance, to summarize the discussion, extends the meaning of "the people" to the lowest social classes, and at the same time, endows them with a moral responsibility that cannot be described in terms of a concretely designated political group. This, I have argued, reflects Locke's response to the particular ideological debate concerning revolution that prevailed during the period he was writing the *Second Treatise,* and it also reflected a defense of the kinds of individuals with whom Locke was himself associated in the Whig revolutionary movement, with respect to the latter's social composition and the nature of its political organization. (*Revolutionary Politics,* 311–12)

24. For some reflections on the complex and problematic relationship between Mill and liberalism, see Gertrude Himmelfarb, *On Liberty and Liberalism: The Case of John Stuart Mill,* and Maurice Cowling, *Mill and Liberalism.*

25. Mill's relationship to Tocqueville is surely deserving of more scholarly exploration than it has received. See the two introductions that Mill attached to the English edition of *Democracy in America.* Mill reveals himself to be a careful reader of Tocqueville, fully understanding his concerns and capable of appending his own correctives to them. Mill pointed out that it is the ascendancy of a large middle class, not simply the passion for equality, that is the cause of "the growing insignificance of individuals in comparison with the mass."

It is not because the individuals composing the mass are all equal, but because the mass itself has grown to so immense a size, that individuals are powerless in the face of it; and because the mass having, by mechanical improvements, become capable of acting simultaneously, can compel not merely any individual, but any number of individuals, to bend before it. The House of Lords is the richest and most powerful collection of persons in Europe, yet they not only could not prevent, but were themselves compelled to pass, the Reform Bill. (introduction to vol. 2, xlv)

26. "J.S. Mill's suggestion that governments devote themselves to optimizing the balance between leaving people's private lives alone and preventing suffering seems to me pretty much the last word" (Richard Rorty, *Contingency, Irony, and Solidarity,* 63).

27. An anonymous reviewer wrote in 1859:

Mr. Mill's essay regards "liberty" from first to last in its negative rather than its positive significance. But in that sense in which the very word "liberty" is apt to excite the deepest enthusiasm of which human nature is capable, it means a great deal more than the mere absence of restraints on the individual; it implies that fresh and unconstrained play of national character, that fullness of social life and vivacity of public energy, which it is one of the worst results of such constraint to subdue or extinguish. But any sympathy with a full social life or fresh popular impulses is exactly the element in which Mr. Mill's book is most deficient. The only liberty he would deny the nation is the liberty to be a nation. He distrusts social and political freedom. There is a depressed and melancholy air about his essay in treating of social and political organisms. He thinks strongly that individuals should be let alone, but virtually on condition that they shall not coalesce into a society and have a social or political life that may react strongly on the principles of individual action. . . . An aggregate of individually free minds, if they are to be held asunder from natural social combinations by the stiff framework of such a doctrine as Mr. Mill's, would not make in any true or deep sense a free society or a free nation. (Mill, *On Liberty,* 133)

28. See the interesting study by Alan Kahan, *Aristocratic Liberalism: The Social and Political Thought of Jacob Burckhardt, John Stuart Mill, and Alexis de Tocqueville.*

29. John Gray in a helpful note clarifies the nature of Mill's misinterpretation of Bentham along these more noble lines (*On Liberty and Other Essays,* 588 n. 201).

30. The following is surely a heartfelt expression of sentiment:

> It is not good for man to be kept perforce at all times in the presence of his species. A world from which solitude is extirpated, is a very poor ideal. Solitude, in the sense of being often alone, is essential to any depth of meditation or of character; and solitude in the presence of natural beauty and grandeur, is the cradle of thoughts and aspirations which are not only good for the individual, but which society could ill do without. Nor is there much satisfaction in contemplating the world with nothing left to the spontaneous activity of nature; with every rood of land brought into cultivation, which is capable of growing food for human beings; every flowery waste or natural pasture ploughed up, all quadrupeds or birds which are not domesticated for man's use exterminated as his rivals for food, every hedgerow or superfluous tree rooted out, and scarcely a place left where a wild shrub or flower could grow without being eradicated as a weed in the name of improved agriculture. If the earth must lose that great portion of its pleasantness which it owes to things that the unlimited increase of wealth and population would extirpate from it, for the mere purpose of enabling it to support a larger, but not a better or a happier population, I sincerely hope, for the sake of posterity, that they will be content to be stationary, long before necessity compels them to it. (Mills, *Principles of Political Economy,* 116)

Chapter 5: Struggle as Source of Liberal Richness

1. James Tyrrell in a note in his copy of the *Essay* (now in the British Museum). See John Locke, *The Reasonableness of Christianity* (1958), 9. Some sense of the community of fellow seekers of truth that Locke gathered around himself is to be obtained from a journal entry of 1675. There after reflecting on the degree to which men are inclined toward their views by their partisan attachments, and recognizing that there is no party that is instituted to take care of the truth, "she hath no sect," he describes their own deliberate efforts to search impartially for the truth. "These thoughts moved us to endeavour to associate ourselves with such as are lovers of truth and virtue, that we may encourage, assist, and support each other in the ways of them, and may possibly become some help in the preserving truth, religion, and virtue amongst us, whatever deluge of misery and mischief may overrun this part of the world" ("Philanthropy, or the Christian Philosophers," in *Political Writings of John Locke,* 232–34).

2. See, for example, Saint Thomas's response to the question, "Is the Natural Law the Same for All Men?"

> Consequently, we must say that the natural law as to general principles is the same for all both as to rectitude and as to knowledge. But as to certain matters of detail, which are conclusions, as it were, of those general principles, it is the same for all in the majority of cases both as to rectitude and as to knowledge, and yet, in some few cases, it may fail both as to rectitude by reason of certain obstacles (just as natures subject to generation and corruption fail in some few cases on account of some obstacle) and as to knowledge, since, in some, the reason is perverted by passion or evil habit or an evil disposition of nature; thus, formerly, theft, although it is expressly contrary to the natural law, was not considered wrong among the Germans, as Julius Caesar relates. (*Summa Theologiae* I-II, Q.94, a.4)

3. Locke's thinking on this subject clarifies as he deals with it in his later *A Paraphrase and Notes on the Epistles of St. Paul.* He considers Rom. 5:12 and notes that there is no fixed punishment attached to the law of nature until God reveals it as a positive law, made determinate through the assignation of a penalty (2:523–25).

4. There has been growing recognition in recent years of the importance of faith within Locke's construction of the world. As John Dunn observes:

> To set this out crudely, the Lockean social and political theory is to be seen as the elaboration of Calvinist social values, in the absence of a terrestrial focus of theological authority and in response to a series of particular challenges. The explanation of why it was Calvinist social values which Locke continued to expound is that he was brought up in a Calvinist family. And the reason why he *continued* to expound them, is that his own experience was too dominated by "uneasiness," too anxious, to make a self-confident naturalism a tolerable interpretation of the world. (*Political Thought*, 259).

James Tully concludes his excellent study of Locke's notion of property with the observation that "If there is one leitmotive which unites Locke's works it is surely a philosophy of religious praxis. . . . The fundamental and undifferentiated form of property is the natural right and duty to make use of the world to achieve God's purpose of preserving all his workmanship. A commonwealth which arranges men's action accordingly is the complementary kind of society" (*Discourse on Property*, 174–75). See also Richard Ashcraft, "Faith and Knowledge in Locke's Philosophy"; Dewey D. Wallace, "Socinianism, Justification by Faith, and the Sources of John Locke's 'The Reasonableness of Christianity' "; Spellman, *John Locke and the Problem;* and Mitchell, "Locke: The Dialectic of Clarification and the Politics of Reason," chap. 3 in *Not by Reason Alone;* Eldon Eisenach, pt. 2 of *Two Worlds of Liberalism.*

5. Spellman probably errs on the side of orthodoxy in emphasizing Locke's differences with deism, against which the *Reasonableness* had admittedly been written.

> The Deists, after all, tended to cheapen the significance of [Christ's coming, of his life and death]; John Locke and the men who met to discuss religion at Thomas Firmin's did just the opposite. As part of their undertaking, Locke and his associates laboured to fully illuminate the nature of the Fall. To mitigate its severity, they knew, meant to lessen the significance of Christ's sacrifice. The Deists, it can be said, willingly accepted that lessening; the Broad-Churchmen, John Locke included, adamantly refused to countenance the crucial diminution. (*John Locke and the Problem of Depravity*, 103)

A more recent study by John Marshall takes a more cautious line in insisting that the "evidence seems insufficient to this author to be certain with what kind of antitrinitarian view Locke ended his life; it is most important to emphasize with Wainwright that it was unequivocally an antitrinitarian view" (*John Locke: Resistance, Religion and Responsibility*, 427).

6. This faith in an essential Christianity that can readily be distinguished from the "indifferent" elements attached to it, this latitudinarian Christianity, seems to have characterized Locke's outlook from the beginning. It is a distinction that enabled him to argue in the early *Tracts on Government*, written between 1660 and 1662, for the magistrate's authority to enforce conformity in the external dimensions of religion. His interest seems to be directed against the extremism of the sectarian religious movements, the assertion of one right way of worshiping God, and its replacement with the idea of a common Christian truth that mandated a fundamental toleration

within this framework. By the time he came to write *An Essay Concerning Toleration* in 1667, he had already begun to see that there is no good reason to give the magistrate an excessive grant of authority in this area. The picture, however, is not that of a violent rupture in Locke's convictions on this matter; it is more a process of maturation and refinement of convictions that remained fundamentally constant. For a convenient source, see Locke's *Political Writings*.

7. He explicitly rejects the characterization of deism, as he explains the rigorously scriptural basis of his Christianity:

> But when I had gone through the whole and saw what a plain, simple, reasonable thing Chiristianity was, suited to all conditions and capacities, and in the morality of it now, with divine authority, established into a legible law so far surpassing all that philosophy and human reason had attained to or could possibly make effectual to all degrees of mankind, I was flattered to think it might be of some use in the world, especially to those who thought either that there was no need of revelation at all, or that the revelation of our Savior required the belief of such articles for salvation, which the settled notions and their way of reasoning in some, and want of understanding in others, made impossible to them. Upon these two topics the objections seemed to turn, which were with most assurance made by Deists against Christianity, but against Christianity misunderstood. It seemed to me that there needed no more to show them the weakness of their exceptions, but to lay plainly before them the doctrine of our Savior and his apostles, as delivered in the Scriptures, and not as taught by the several sects of Christians. (quoted in *Reasonableness* [1965], 199)

See also the remark from *A Third Letter for Toleration*, in *The Works of John Locke* (6:154), in which Locke rejects the formulation of creeds, asking " . . . are these creeds in the words of Scripture? . . . But if the creed to be imposed be not in the words of divine revelation, then is it in plainer, more intelligible expressions or not? If not plainer, what necessity of changing those which men inspired by the Holy Ghost made use of?" (quoted in *Reasonableness* [1965], 212).

8. Locke's theology in *Paraphrase and Notes* is considerably more nuanced and developed, but there are no radical changes of direction from *Reasonableness*. In the former he lays even greater stress on the primacy of revelation over reason; asserts that Christ died for men, although he still maintains that it was not a satisfaction for sin; proclaims more forcefully that righteousness is given in and by Christ; and acknowledges the spiritual presence of Christ in the sacrament of the Eucharist. "The total picture that emerges," concludes Arthur Wainwright in the introduction, "is not that of a thinker who had undergone a complete change of outlook; there is too much continuity with his previous writings for such a conclusion to be reached. But his mind was not in a state of rigidity. He was open to new ideas, and did not always endeavour to remain consistent with his previous thoughts. As his mind interacted with that of Paul, ideas emerged which were recognizably the product of the same Locke who was responsible for his earlier writings. But it was the same Locke at a different stage of his intellectual and spiritual pilgrimage" (1:59).

9. See, for example, Locke's assertion in "A Discourse of Miracles," written in 1702, that we can be confident that God would never allow his power to be eclipsed by another's miracle:

> For those supernatural signs being the only means God is conceived to have to satisfy men as rational creatures of the certainty of any thing he would reveal, as coming from himself, can never consent that it should be wrested out of his hands,

to serve the ends and establish the authority of an inferior agent that rivals him. His power being known to have no equal, always will, and always may be safely depended on, to shew its superiority in vindicating his authority, and maintaining every truth that he hath revealed." (*Reasonableness* [1958], 85)

The reliability of reason that judges the authenticity of miracles is itself grounded in faith in the Creator who would not deceive us. Faith is the foundation of reason for Locke, which is why he can assert so confidently that God would not perform a miracle to confirm something contrary to reason. Writing twenty years earlier in a passage called "Inspiration" in his journal, he concluded that "the miracles were to be judged by the doctrine, and not the doctrine by the miracles" (*Political Writings*, 240). This is the circularity of a reason that establishes the existence of God and employs the existence of God to validate the reliability of reason, as noted by Richard Ashcraft ("Faith and Knowledge in Locke's Philosophy," 205). It was not the problem for Locke that it is for contemporary commentators because reason and faith were continuous for him. Even James Tully, who is otherwise completely fair in acknowledging that for Locke "Scripture is the foundation of our moral reasoning," cannot find a more intelligible term for the circularity of faith and reason than the utterly opaque designation of *voluntarism*. Locke's faith is not arbitrarily willed but, rather, arises organically from a reason that knows its own incapacity to ground its presuppositions. See Tully, *An Approach to Political Philosophy: Locke in Contexts*, 227, 230.

10. It is difficult to square this passage and the many others we have quoted above with the view of Locke as a consistent subverter of Christian piety, presented in Thomas Pangle's *The Spirit of Modern Republicanism: The Moral Vision of the American Founders and the Philosophy of Locke*. It is significant that even Pangle moderates his criticism of Locke in a telling reflection toward the end of the book, although he ultimately backs away from revising the assessment of Locke that precedes it:

> Locke's failure to explain or do justice to his own political theory's dependence on moral devotion leaves us unsure of the firmness of Locke's grounds for rejecting the greatest alternative to his (and all other strict versions of) rationalism. One of the most powerful testimonies, perhaps the most powerful testimony, favoring the claims of revelation (or making plausible a quest for guidance from higher powers), is the human soul's awareness of and reverence for an otherwise inexplicable, self-forgetting dedication to justice and nobility. This purported awareness may not verify, but it powerfully evokes, the belief in or hope for transcendent support and grounding. Those who seek to show the limitations of strict rationalism are prone to contend that reason always finds itself at a loss to explain the key springs of moral action. Such action at its noblest, they argue, can only be understood—insofar as it can be understood—as inspired, or solicited, or in some way made possible and backed up, by a mysterious suprarational divine order. It would certainly seem that Locke has neither convincingly explained, nor explained away, nor even demonstrated his own escape from, experiences of self-transcendence, with their manifold implications and unanswered questions. (271)

11. It should be noted that it is also the bedrock on which the liberal democratic tradition rested in the centuries after Locke. Even his approach to Scripture was widely emulated in the eighteenth century, and his *Paraphrase and Notes* enjoyed considerable authority and influence. See Wainwright's introduction, 1:59–73.

12. The examples of Holbach, Helvétius, and Condorcet come to mind in their derivation of a sensationalist or materialist psychology from Locke and their develop-

ment of a strictly manipulative politics on the basis of this philosophical anthropology. See the extensive discussion in Eric Voegelin, *From Enlightenment to Revolution,* and in John Yolton, *Locke and French Materialism.*

13. The outstanding example of this deeply Christian extension of Locke is the great American theologian and leading figure of the Great Awakening, Jonathan Edwards. In his *Treatise on Religious Affections,* Edwards employs Lockean psychology to grapple with the most serious philosophical objections that can be posed against faith, especially the charge that our idea of God is nothing more than a projection or expression of our own longing.

> Some say that all love arises from self love; and that it is impossible in the nature of things, for any man to have any love to God, or any other being, but that love to himself must be the foundation of it. . . . But how came these things to be so agreeable to him, that he esteems it his highest happiness to glorify God, etc.? Is not this the fruit of love? A man must first love God, or have his heart united to him, before he will esteem God's good his own, and before he will desire the glorifying and enjoying of God as his happiness. . . . Something else, entirely distinct from self-love might be the cause of this, *viz.* A change made in the views of his mind, and relish of his heart; whereby he apprehends a beauty, glory, and supreme good, in God's nature, as it is in itself. (240–41)

Egotism can never be a sufficient explanation for faith because, even if we believe for selfish reasons, we still have the problem of explaining what it is about the divine that renders it attractive to us. Whence derives this taste or "relish" for religous affections? A good overview is available in Sang Hyun Lee, *The Philosophical Theology of Jonathan Edwards.* For a sample of the range of involvement between Christianity and liberal politics in eighteenth-century America, see Ellis Sandoz, ed., *Political Sermons of the American Founding, 1730–1805;* and for Locke's influence in general, see Steven M. Dworetz, *The Unvarnished Doctrine: Locke, Liberalism and the American Revolution.* Jonathan Clark in his recent masterful study of the intellectual and political forces within the Anglo-American context of the eighteenth century has made a persuasive case that the issues were framed in theological terms.

> 1776 was a "Lockeian moment" chiefly in the sense in which Locke himself had been an anti-Trinitarian, preoccupied by the political menace (as he saw it) of orthodox religion, firmly located within a denominational and theological context. The American Revolution opened a new era; but its origins had little to do with vision of a hitherto-unrealized future, much to do with ancient divisions and hatreds. The Revolution of 1776 was, therefore, not unique: like many of the crises which had convulsed the early-modern world, it still retained many of the characteristics of a war of religion. (*The Language of Liberty 1660–1832,* 45)

14. Leo Strauss, in chapter 6 of *Natural Right and History,* identifies Rousseau's significance this way as, along with Burke, representing the first self-consciousness of the crisis of modern natural right. The second wave of crisis Strauss suggests, it seems correctly, is our own awareness that begins with Nietzsche. This significance of Rousseau has something to do with the profusion of studies that have appeared of his thought in our own time. Especially useful are the magisterial biographies provided by Maurice Cranston, *Jean-Jacques: The Early Life and Work of Jean-Jacques Rousseau, 1712–1754* and *The Noble Savage: Jean-Jacques Rousseau, 1754–1762,* as well as the classic study by Jean Starobinski, *Jean-Jacques Rousseau: Transparency and Obstruction.*

15. The note of pessimism and foreboding is sounded in other remarkable ways in the Enlightenment, most strikingly in Voltaire's *Candide* with its relentless demonstration of the futility of reason, its obsessive concentration on pain and cruelty, and its final abdication of all rational schemes for human self-improvement to withdraw into "work in the garden."

16. There is an interesting parallel between Rousseau and David Hume, who also wrote an influential essay on the tendency of the arts and sciences to decline as well as progress: "Of the Rise and Progress of the Arts and Sciences," which was published in 1742. Hume parallels Rousseau primarily in the degree of radical insupportability he acknowledges in the conventional articulations of moral order. He is well known for his observation that "Reason is, and ought only to be, the slave of the passions, and can never pretend to any other office than to serve and obey them" (*Treatise of Human Nature*, bk. 2, pt. 3, sec. 3). What is less well recognized is that Hume's project was a recovery of the experiential sources of virtue similar to that undertaken by Rousseau. He even formulates it in language that echoes the latter, after noting the concrete flexibility of moral judgments in ordinary life. "No action can be either morally good or evil," he concludes, "unless there be some natural passion or motive to impel us to it, or deter us from it; and it is evident that the morality must be susceptible of all the same variations which are natural to the passion" (ibid., bk. 3, pt. 2, sec. 6). The contrast with Rousseau is that Hume carries little of the sense of impending crisis into this radical reflection, and therefore can assume the role of the conservative historian of tradition along with his inescapable skepticism.

17. Rousseau had earlier distinguished between these two passions, but in *Emile* he is often willing to see them as continuous.

> *Amour-propre* [vanity] and *Amour de soi-même* [self-love], two very different passions in their nature and their effects, must not be confused. Self-love is a natural sentiment which inclines every animal to attend to its self-preservation and which, guided in man by reason and modified by pity, produces humanity and virtue. Vanity is only a relative sentiment, factitious, and born in society, which inclines every individual to set greater store by himself than by anyone else, inspires men with all the evils they do one another, and is the genuine source of honor. (Rousseau's own note to *Second Discourse*, pt. 1, par. 35)

18. In a footnote to this passage, Rousseau demonstrates his prescience: "I hold it to be impossible that the great monarchies of Europe still have long to last. All have shined, and every state which shines is on the decline. I have reasons more particular than this maxim for my opinion, but it is unseasonable to tell them, and everyone sees them only too well" (*Emile*, 194 n).

19. Hume again provides an interesting benchmark as someone much less sympathetic to religion, a more avowed critic of "enthusiasm and superstition," yet still absorbed with the project of articulating a "natural religion." If we take the three principal speakers in his 1779 *Dialogues Concerning Natural Religion* as each speaking for Hume in one way or another, as he seems to suggest in commenting on the dialogue form, then it is surely significant that they converge in their fundamental aspiration for the "true philosophical religion." Atheism, despite the enthusiasm of Antony Flew and others, is nowhere in sight, and the *Dialogue* concludes with Philo forcefully affirming the longing of philosophical skepticism for revelation. See the excellent collection by Hume, edited by Flew, *David Hume: Writings on Religion*.

20. Joshua Mitchell's *Not by Reason Alone* (chap. 4 in particular) is one of the

few recent works that takes the character of Rousseau's piety seriously. Starobinski, who provides the most extensive discussion of Rousseau's mystical explorations, recognizes its filiation with Christianity and its departure from it. Commenting on Rousseau's method of confessional self-elaboration, Starobinski acknowledges that it essentially gives rise to

> a secular morality, but it cannot be understood without reference to a religious model. The act of the will whereby I seem to be what I am plays the role that is played in theology by Christ the mediator, who regenerates the soul of the believer. The difference is that according to Rousseau the act whereby I seem to be what I am in fact is an immediate one, which transforms me without requiring me to take any explicit action to change myself, and without requiring me to turn for assistance to any outside power or grace. (*Jean-Jacques Rousseau*, 63)

21. Jean Starobinski has provided the most profound analysis of the peculiarity of Rousseau's cast of mind, which does not so much deny the reality of evil as overlook the necessity of struggle against it. It is an orientation that is absorbed in the immediate emergence of virtue within the heart to such an extent that it can forget the mediated process from which it emerges. This has much to do with the failure of Rousseau's ideal community at Clarens, as developed in *La nouvelle Héloïse*, and his own final disconnection from the common social world in the later years of his life, especially as voiced in *The Reveries*. "Hence his task is not simply to overcome evil or to fight against the possibility of sin; to do so would be to admit that he was vulnerable to sin, that his innocence was at the mercy of an error or a weakness. Rather, his task is to ensure that, by his very nature, sin can never be laid at his door; it must always be something alien . . ." (*Jean-Jacques*, 248). The fate of Rousseau is powerful testament to the limits of the human quest for the immediate and transparent evocation of virtue and to the impossibility of leaping over the process of struggle by which virtue alone is precariously achieved and sustained.

22. For the background to Rousseau's conception of the general will, see Patrick Riley, *The General Will before Rousseau* and *Will and Political Legitimacy: A Critical Exposition of Social Contract Theory in Hobbes, Locke, Rousseau, Kant and Hegel.*

23. In the earlier *Discourse on Political Economy*, written as an article for the 1755 *Encyclopédie*, Rousseau explained:

> There is no reason to believe that a person can injure or cut off an arm without any sensation of pain being carried to his head, and it is no more believable that the general will would authorize any member of the state, whoever he might be, to harm or destroy another than that the fingers of a man in possession of his reason would go and put out his eyes. The safety of the individual is so closely bound up with the public confederation that, without the respect one owes to human weakness, this agreement would rightfully be dissolved if a single citizen who could have been helped perished inside the state, if a single one were wrongly kept in prison, or if a single court case were lost through an obvious injustice, for, once fundamental agreements are violated, it is no longer apparent what right or what interest could hold the people in the social union, unless it is restrained by force alone, which brings about the dissolution of the civil state. (*Rousseau's Political Writings*, 70)

24. The parallel with the American Founding Fathers, who were developing their ideas around the same time, can be explored in relation to Rousseau's venture into practical political advice on *The Government of Poland*. Here Rousseau proposes a federation of smaller republics as the means of balancing political strength with political freedom, thereby showing how the insights of the social contract might be

applied to the modern nation-state. He continues to underestimate the persistence of factions under the best constitutional arrangements, unlike the American framers. However, it should also be recalled that the American statesmen were convinced that they could avoid the development of regular political parties. In addition, Rousseau provides something like a constitutional protection for individuals and minorities in his insistence in *Government of Poland* that constitutional changes have unanimous support. "My reasoning here is this: it is contrary to the nature of the body politic for it to impose laws upon itself that it cannot repeal. But it is not contrary to nature, or to reason, for it to be unable to repeal those same laws except with the same solemn procedures that were used for their adoption. This is the one fetter the body politic can place upon itself as regards the future" (57).

25. Benjamin Constant was among the first to voice such objections to the general will. He understood Rousseau's intention of bringing all the members of the society to share the same condition, but he pointed out the deep practical limitations on such an arrangement. For

> as soon as the sovereign must make use of the power which he possesses, or in other words, as soon as it is necessary to proceed to the practical organization of authority, as the sovereign cannot exercise it himself, he must delegate it, and all those attributes disappear. Because the action performed in the name of all is necessarily, whether we like it or not, at the disposal of a single individual or of a few, it happens that, in giving oneself to all, one does not give oneself to nobody, on the contrary, one submits oneself to those who act in the name of all. Hence it follows that, by giving ourselves entirely, we do not enter a condition equal for all, because some derive exclusive advantage from the sacrifice of the rest. It is not true that nobody has an interest in making the conditions of the others more onerous, because there are associates who are above the common condition. (*Principles of Politics* [1815] in *Political Writings*, 177–78)

See also the criticisms developed by Jacob Talmon in *The Origins of Totalitarian Democracy*, Irving Babbit in *Rousseau and Romanticism*, and Claes Ryn in *Democracy and the Ethical Life*.

26. Evil appears as that force that can be turned toward good if we know how to take advantage of it.

> If, for example, they are trained early enough never to consider their own persons except in terms of their relations with the body of the state, and not to perceive of their own existence, so to speak, except as a part of that of the state, they may finally succeed in identifying themselves in some way with this greater whole, in feeling themselves members of the homeland, in loving it with that exquisite sentiment which every isolated man feels only for himself, in perpetually lifting up their souls toward this great objective, and thus in transforming into a sublime virtue that dangerous disposition from which all our vices arise. (*Discourse on Political Economy*, 73)

27. For Hegel's understanding of the state, see Shlomo Avineri, *Hegel's Theory of the Modern State;* Joachim Ritter, *Hegel and the French Revolution;* and Z. A. Pelczynski, introduction to *Hegel's Political Writings*.

28. The best overall survey of Hegel that locates his political thought in relation to his whole project remains, in my view, Charles Taylor's *Hegel*. Also useful are Steven B. Smith's *Hegel's Critique of Liberalism* and Lawrence Dickey's *Hegel: Religion, Economics and the Politics of Spirit, 1770–1807*. Alexandre Kojève's *Introduction à la lecture de Hegel* remains an indispensable guide.

29. Taylor does not make this mistake in his study of Hegel, for, he explains, the apparent unfairness in the Hegelian interpretation of Rousseau's "general will" as the will of all individuals, is quite intelligible if it is understood as the mere aggregation of *human* wills. The vacuity of the universal human will of Rousseau and Kant was to be replaced by the fullness of *Geist*, whose content is the Idea that produces a differentiated world out of itself. "What reason and freedom enjoin on man's will is to further and sustain that structure of things which so reveals itself to be the adequate expression of the Idea." In place of the paralysis or the factionalism of abstractly liberal states, Hegel sought an "articulated structure, involving different relationships of different 'estates' to political power, which is ultimately justified as a reflection of cosmic order" (Taylor, *Hegel*, 374, 451).

30. See especially the discussion of Christianity in Hegel, *Early Theological Writings,* and the two volumes of intellectual biography that have so far appeared from H. S. Harris: *Hegel's Development toward the Sunlight, 1770–1801* and *Hegel's Development: Night Thoughts.*

31. I have covered some of the controversy concerning Hegel's dialectical unification of the divine and human natures in "The Ambiguity of the Hegelian End of History," and his relationship to the German mystical tradition in "The Historical Dialectic of Spirit: Jacob Boehme's Influence on Hegel." See also Alexandre Kojève, *Introduction;* Eric Voegelin, "On Hegel—A Study in Sorcery," in *Published Essays,* ed. Ellis Sandoz; Barry Cooper, *The End of History: An Essay on Modern Hegelianism;* and Cyril O'Regan, *The Heterodox Hegel.*

32. That Hegel was no longer content with the traditional means of bridging the distance between man and God through prayer and meditation is evident in his characterization of such forms as expressions of an "unhappy consciousness." "Where the 'other' is sought, it cannot be found, for it is supposed to be just a beyond, something that can *not* be found" (*The Phenomenology of Spirit,* 478). By contrast he formulated his own goal as: "Absolute freedom of all spirits who bear the intellectual world in themselves, and cannot seek either God or immortality outside themselves" ("The 'Earliest System-Program of German Idealism,' " in H. S. Harris, *Hegel's Development toward the Sunlight,* 511).

33. Clearest evidence for the neglect of the liberal dimension of Hegel's thought is surely to be found in the streams of left- and right-wing Hegelians who developed its more radical implications. See the excellent survey by Karl Löwith, *From Hegel to Nietzsche.* Only in more recent times has Hegel begun to be viewed again as a brilliant exponent of the liberal constitutional tradition. See Charles Taylor, *Hegel;* and Z. A. Pelczynski, introduction to *Hegel's Political Writings;* and Z. A. Pelczynski, ed., *The State and Civil Society.*

34. The preeminent example of this attitude of expectation of revelation that yet shows itself not to seriously expect an irruption from the Beyond is Martin Heidegger. The mendacity of his waiting for the disclosure of Being is perhaps best exposed in the infamous interview Heidegger gave toward the end of his life (" 'Only a God Can Save Us': The *Spiegel* Interview [1966]"). See also Eric Voegelin, *Science, Politics and Gnosticism,* on Heidegger's "parousiasm" (44–49).

35. An extensive survey of his objections to Christianity is available in Mill's essay "The Utility of Religion" in *Collected Works,* 10:424–25.

36. Mill's reflections are, for example, in contrast to the more unreflectively optimistic orientation of John Dewey in his parallel meditation on the necessity for a "religious" core to a democratic order

Were men and women actuated throughout the length and breadth of human relations with the faith and ardor that have at times marked historic religions the consequences would be incalculable. . . . There is the technical skill with which to initiate a campaign for social health and sanity analogous to that made in behalf of physical public health. Human beings have impulses toward affection, compassion and justice, equality and freedom. It remains to weld all these things together. (*A Common Faith*, 80–81)

See also ibid., 87.

37. The profound contradiction between transcendent sentiments and the inability to acknowledge their meaning in traditionally religious terms was common in Mill's day and in our own. Thomas Huxley, explaining why he had given up a youth of immorality to reform, rejected the idea that it had anything to do with a future life. "No, I can tell you exactly what has been at work. Carlyle's *Sartor Resartus* led me to know that a deep sense of religion was compatible with the entire absence of theology. Secondly, science and her methods gave me a resting place independent of authority and tradition. Thirdly, love opened me up to a view of the sanctity of human nature and impressed me with a deep sense of responsibility." Bertrand Russell singles out the "universal, infinite and impartial" side of human nature:

Distant ages and remote regions of space are as real to it as what is present and near. In thought, it rises above the life of the senses, seeking always what is general and open to all men. In desire and will, it aims simply at the good, without regarding the good as mine or yours. In feeling, it gives love to all, not only to those who further the purposes of the self. Unlike the finite self, it is impartial; its impariality leads to truth in thought, justice in action, and universal love in feeling. (quoted in Charles Taylor, *Sources of the Self*, 405, 408)

Taylor's observation that such reflections indicate that "for the first time an alternative moral horizon was available to belief in God" should not be allowed to obscure the recognition that these were after all experiences of participation in transcendent being. They represent some of the most effective means available to modern human beings to put themselves in touch with the "really real," the *ens realissimum*.

38. It is significant that while Mill rejects God as immoral, he still remains close to the example of Christ. It is of course the figure of Christ as moral exemplar, but it carries overtones of the transcendent pull he exercises on the imagination of men.

For it is Christ, rather than God, whom Christianity has held up to believers as the pattern of perfection for humanity. It is the God incarnate, more than the God of the Jews or of Nature, who, being idealized, has taken so great and salutary a hold on the modern mind. And whatever else may be taken away from us by rational criticism, Christ is still left—a unique figure, not more unlike all his precursors than all his followers, even those who had the direct benefit of his personal teaching. (*Collected Works*, 10:487)

39. On Constant's understanding of the relationship between religion and politics, see Guy Dodge, *Benjamin Constant's Philosophy of Liberalism: A Study in Politics and Religion;* and Stephen Holmes, *Benjamin Constant and the Making of Modern Liberalism*.

40. See, for example, Novalis's essay, "Christendom or Europe"; Coleridge, *Church and State* in *Coleridge's Writings On Politics and Society*.

41. For a sense of what was involved in the movement of de-Christianization within the Revolution, see the selections in Paul H. Beik, ed., *The French Revolution*

(266–71, 299–312), which includes Robespierre's 1794 report on "Religious and Moral Ideas and Republican Principles."

42. Burke, of course, had earlier understood the "spirit of atheistical fanaticism that is inspired by a multitude of writings dispersed with incredible assiduity and expense, and by sermons delivered in all the streets and places of public resort in Paris" (*Reflections on the Revolution in France,* 176).

43. Tocqueville's own wrestling with faith was a complex affair whose most defining characteristic was his inability to settle the question in the negative, even if it could not always be resolved in the affirmative. It is well explored for its Pascalian resonances by Peter Lawler, *The Restless Mind: Alexis de Tocqueville on the Origin and Perpetuation of Human Liberty.* See also André Jardin, who concludes, in his *Tocqueville: A Biography,* after sifting all the available evidence, that the crisis of faith in his earlier years marked his spiritual outlook up to the end. Without affirming any deathbed conversion, Jardin is "inclined to think that he died in a feeling of communion with a religion that Abbé Lesueur had once taught him to love, without accepting its dogmas" (532). See also Beaumont's original account of Tocqueville's death (ibid., 529). A well-balanced discussion of Tocqueville's complex understanding of the relation between religion and politics in the modern world is provided by Doris S. Goldstein in *Trial of Faith: Religion and Politics in Tocqueville's Thought.*

44. Orestes Brownson is a contemporaneous American example. See Gregory Butler, *In Search of the American Spirit: The Political Thought of Orestes Brownson.* Twentieth-century examples include: Jacques Maritain, *Man and the State;* John Courtney Murray, *We Hold These Truths;* and Richard John Neuhaus, *The Catholic Moment: The Paradox of the Church in the Postmodern World.*

45. There are many passages in Tocqueville that evoke the chilling specter of Nietzsche's "last man," such as:

> It is believed by some that modern society will be always changing its aspect; for myself, I fear that it will ultimately be too invariably fixed in the same institutions, the same prejudices, the same manners, so that mankind will be stopped and circumscribed; that the mind will swing backwards and forwards forever without begetting fresh ideas; that man will waste his strength in bootless and solitary trifling, and, though in continual motion, that humanity will cease to advance. (*Democracy,* 2:277–78)

Chapter 6: Source of Liberal Appeal

1. Locke remains the paradigmatic example of the transparent incompleteness of the liberal construction. "Locke is, perhaps," Peter Laslett observes, "the least consistent of all the great philosophers, and pointing out the contradictions either within any of his works or between them is no difficult task. . . . Nevertheless it is of importance to see in Locke, the recognized point of departure for liberalism, the liberal dilemma already present, the dilemma of maintaining a political faith without subscribing to a total, holistic view of the world" (introduction to *Two Treatises,* 95–103).

2. The continuity of liberal political ideas from the medieval world has received increasing attention over the past two decades. Quentin Skinner provides the best summary in his masterful survey *The Foundations of Modern Political Thought.*

His first volume traces the reemergence of republican ideals of liberty and self-government through the Italian city-states from the twelfth century forward. Their position between the twin powers of pope and emperor provoked the articulation of the right of self-government as abiding in each community. The second strand of the liberal tradition, the defense of individual rights and the limitation of governmental power, is explored in Skinner's second volume. There he shows how the resistance against absolute government, which began among the sixteenth-century Calvinists and reached its height in the Whig revolution of the next century, drew its arguments from the Catholic revival of medieval constitutional ideas. Conciliarist and nominalist arguments, as well as Roman law contract theory, were resuscitated by such figures as Maier, Almain, Vitoria, Molina, Suarez, and Bellarmine in formulations that anticipated the classic seventeenth-century constructions. They included the conception of a state of nature in which each is an executioner of the law, as well as the social contract by which the prepolitical community becomes a civil society and the subjective assertion of individual rights. The striking conclusion toward which Skinner's innovative study points is that the founders of modern "liberal" politics derived their positions from the medieval struggle for balance between spiritual and temporal powers. "It is of course true that the men who argued in favor of revolution during this period tended to be Calvinists. But it is not true that in general that they made use of specifically Calvinist arguments. . . . So far from breaking away from the constraints of scholasticism to found a 'new politics,' we find the Huguenots largely adopting and consolidating a position which the more radical jurists and theologians had already espoused" (323). See also Richard Tuck, *Natural Rights Theories: Their Origin and Development.*

3. See Hans Georg Gadamer, *Truth and Method;* Voegelin, *In Search of Order,* vol. 5 of *Order and History.*

4. This point has been made in a nonpolitical critique by René Guenon in *The Reign of Quantity and the Signs of the Times.*

5. Locke has often been misunderstood as basing his case for toleration on the fallibility of human reason that, in religious matters, is incapable of arriving at definitive knowledge. This is an important misconception because it is often seen as a central presupposition of the whole liberal tradition, and its skeptical estimation of the capacity of human knowledge returns to subvert the very conviction on which the liberal order itself rests. I do not accept that fallibility is the central foundation of the liberal order, and it is clearly not the "principal consideration" for Locke. His observation that "in this great variety of ways that men follow, it is still doubted which is the right one," occurs within a context where he has just considered what divides denominations and concluded that "for the most part, they are such frivolous things as these that (without any prejudice to religion or the salvation of souls, if not accompanied with superstition or hypocrisy) might either be observed or omitted" (*A Letter Concerning Toleration,* 31). Locke's conviction is that there is a broad or latitudinarian interpretation of Christianity that no reasonable person can deny and that within that context the remaining differences are indeterminable and insignificant. This is evident from the penultimate paragraph of *A Letter Concerning Toleration:* "In a word, he that denies not anything that Holy Scriptures teach in express words, nor makes a separation upon occasion of anything that is not manifestly contained in the sacred text—however he may be nicknamed by any sect of Christians and declared by some or all of them to be utterly void of

true Christianity—yet in deed and in truth this man cannot be either a heretic or schismatic" (62).

6. Locke's identification of the drive for self-determination as the guiding principle is well detailed in Peter A. Schouls, *Reasoned Freedom: John Locke and the Enlightenment*. See also Nathan Tarcov, *Locke's Education for Liberty*.

7. It is of course worth noting that Locke countenanced slavery and felt it necessary to include a chapter on it in the *Second Treatise*. When he came to the discussion in principle he insisted on the incompatibility between free rational creatures and slavery. He was adamant that a man "not having the power of his own life, *cannot*, by compact, or his own consent, *enslave himself* to anyone." Slavery arises when an individual has forfeited his life through an act that deserves death but the other delays to take it and uses him in service.

This is not so enormously inconsistent with the direction of Locke's principles, although we would be less inclined to conclude that a criminal even under a capital sentence has forfeited all his rights as a human being and can be reduced to a sheer instrument. The death sentence is, after all, a sentence that still recognizes the responsibility of the criminal and is an attempt to treat him as a human being. The great inconsistency in Locke is in what he was willing to contemplate as an act of war justifying enslavement. He was willing to regard African slaves as all justifiably taken in war, and he recognized that every freeman "shall have absolute power and authority over his negro slaves" in his *Fundamental Constitutions of Carolina* (written for Shaftesbury and the other proprietors in 1669, par. 110). In addition, Locke encouraged the institution of "leet-men" as a hereditary condition that prevented men from departing from the estate without the lord's permission. This, as David Wooten remarks, was "serfdom by another name" (introduction to *Political Writings of John Locke,* 43).

8. Nowhere is the variability of Rousseau's spirituality more apparent than in that strange series of meditations he penned in the final years of his life, when he felt himself alone and rejected by the world. The sentiments span the range from almost Christian resignation to the ineluctable will of God, to the attainment of a stoic independence and indifference, to the barely concealed outbursts of resentment and hubris, to escape into the psychic disintegration of daydreaming.

> God is just; his will is that I should suffer, and he knows my innocence. That is what gives me confidence. My heart and my reason cry out that I shall not be disappointed. Let men and fate do their worst, we must learn to suffer in silence, everything will find its proper place in the end and sooner or later my turn will come. . . . What is the source of our happiness in such a state [floating in a boat or by the shore]? Nothing external to us, nothing apart from ourselves and our own existence; as long as this state lasts we are self-sufficient like God. The feeling of existence unmixed with any other emotion is in itself a precious feeling of peace and contentment. . . . The movement which does not come from outside us arises within us at such times. Our tranquillity is less complete, it is true, but it is also more agreeable when pleasant and insubstantial ideas barely touch the surface of the soul, so to speak, and do not stir its depths. One needs only enough of such ideas to allow one to be conscious of one's existence while forgetting all one's troubles. (*Reveries of the Solitary Walker,* 45, 89–90)

See also ibid., 104, 130.

9. One can sense the enlargement of Kant's own soul in his famous conclusion to the *Critique of Practical Reason*. "Two things fill the mind with ever new and

increasing admiration and awe, the oftener and the more steadily we reflect on them: the starry heavens above and the moral law within."

10. For an account of that conversation within German idealism, George Armstrong Kelly's *Idealism, Politics and History: Sources of Hegelian Thought* remains indispensable. "Viewed systematically, the politics of transcendental idealism . . . is in no sense a code of prudential political techniques dependent on a theory of human nature." Rather, it is

> part of a total project transcending the mere fact of politics. The Idea of the state participates, together with the Ideas of art, morality, religion and knowledge, in the comprehensive Idea which is the absolute reflection of all harmony. . . . [This] means that the purely political aspects of idealist philosphy cannot be interpreted *sui generis* without likely distortion. Abstracted from their architectural whole, certain political expressions of the Germans (indeed of Rousseau) turn out to be according to one's choice, liberal, reactionary, totalitarian, often quite maddening to the thoughtful empiricist. (293–94)

The idealists begin, not with a theory of human nature, but with a concept (freedom) "whose essence is its own supranatural *telos,*" which must overcome the impure human basis of political life. It is interesting that Kelly's last book, *Politics and Religious Consciousness in America,* provides a parallel reflection on the relation between liberal politics and Christianity on this side of the Atlantic.

11. This is the attainment of absolute knowledge at the culmination of *The Phenomenology of Spirit:* "What in religion was *content* or a form for presenting an *other,* is here the Self's own act; the Notion requires the *content* to be the *Self's* own *act.* For this Notion is, as we see, the knowledge of the Self's act within itself as all essentiality and all existence, the knowledge of this subject as substance and of the substance as this knowledge of its act" (485). The ambiguity of Hegel's construction of course consists precisely in his refusal to distinguish between this identity of self-consciousness of the human and divine and their identity of being. "God is God only so far as he knows himself: his self-knowledge is, further, a self-consciousness in man and man's knowledge *of* God, which proceed to man's self-knowledge *in* God" (*Philosophy of Mind,* par. 564).

12. Hegel's intention, announced in the preface to *The Phenomenology of Spirit,* to "bring philosophy closer to the form of Science, to the goal where it can lay aside the title 'love of knowing' and be *actual* knowing," turns out to spell the end of both philosophy and science. This is Alexandre Kojève's great insight into the meaning of the end of history as the end of all questioning.

13. Voegelin's last work pointed toward this positive significance of Hegel. "Hegel's deformation of certain structures of consciousness, however, must not obscure the fact that he acted in revolt against the even worse deformation of the same structures in the public unconscious that surrounded him socially. He could deform fundamental experiences only by first rediscovering them in opposition to symbols that had lost the experiential source of their meaning and, as a consequence, had become a dead body of ideas and opinions. Hence, the preceding enumeration should not be read as a critique of Hegel but, on the contrary, as an attempt to clarify and stress his achievement. His rediscovery of the experiential source of symbolization, as well as his identification of the fundamental problems in the structure of consciousness, is irreversible" (*Order and History,* 5:69–70).

14. The dangers became palpably clear to Tocqueville in the Revolution of 1848 where he recognized, despite the defeat of the socialist impulse at this time, its ultimate triumphal forward movement. The people, whose political power had been steadily growing for the past sixty years, were bound to consider

> that they might use their power to escape their poverty and inferiority. . . . And to speak specifically about property, which is, so to speak, the foundation of our social order, when all the privileges that cover and conceal the privilege of property had been abolished and property remained as the main obstacle to equality among men and seemed to be the only sign thereof, was it not inevitable, I do not say that it should be abolished in its turn, that at least the idea of abolishing it should strike minds that had no part in its enjoyment? (Tocqueville, *Recollections: The French Revolution of 1848*, 75–76)

15. Konstantin Mochulsky is among the few commentators who recognize this deep significance of Dostoyevsky's "Legend."

> The Inquisitor's monologue is a chef d'oeuvre of oratorical art: his deductions follow logically from the premises, his conclusions strike one as irrefutable; but his negative argumentation suddenly is transformed into a positive one; the accusator's speech becomes the greatest theodicy in world literature. The *Legend* culminates the work of Dostoevsky's whole life: his struggle for man. In it he discloses the religious foundations of the personality and the inseparability of faith in man from faith in God. With unheard-of force he affirms *freedom* as the image of god in man and shows the Antichrist principle of power and despotism. Without freedom, man is a beast, mankind—a herd; but freedom is supernatural and superrational; in the order of the natural world there is no freedom, there is only necessity. Freedom is a divine gift, the most precious property of man. Not by reason, nor by science, nor by the natural law can one prove it—it is rooted in God, is revealed in Christ. *Freedom is an act of faith*. Atheistic lovers of mankind reject God, in that evil exists in the world. But evil exists only because there is freedom. Under this false compassion for the sufferings of mankind is hidden a diabolic hatred of human freedom and the "image of God" in man. Here is why, beginning with love of mankind, it ends in despotism. . . . Never in all world literature has Christianity been advanced with such striking force as *the religion of spiritual freedom*. The Christ of Dostoevsky is not only the Savior and the Redeemer, but also the Sole Emancipator of man. (*Dostoevsky: His Life and Work*, 621–22)

See also Walsh, *After Ideology*, 174–84; and Ellis Sandoz, *Political Apocalypse: A Study of Dostoevsky's Grand Inquisitor.*

Chapter 7: Incompleteness of Liberal Order

1. Even within everyday politics we are repeatedly reminded of the impossibility of balancing the transfinite value of the person against the finite distribution of resources. It is a difficulty that becomes strikingly evident in the area of health care, and the effort to provide a comprehensive health system will forever remain befuddled until this philosophical collision is recognized. Perhaps the easiest way of illustrating it is in the joke about the man who brings his wife into the hospital and says, "Doctor, my wife's dying. Can you cure her? I'll pay anything within reason!" The point of course is that we cannot put a price on the life of a human being, and any attempt to solve the problem of limited resources must find a way through this. Pragmatic limitations must be imposed in such a way that they do nothing

to undermine the transcendent valuation of the person whose worth outweighs all social goods. It is an interesting unintended consequence of our achievement of near-comprehensive control of biology, that we are compelled to assume near-comprehensive responsibility. The direction to look for a resolution is surely in some surrender of the claim and aspiration of this totalistic technological aspiration, such as in a more humble acceptance of the limits of the human condition where we are not ultimately our own masters. For an interesting, although finally unsatisfactory, reflection on these problems, see Daniel Callahan, *Setting Limits: Medical Goals in an Aging Society.*

2. In answer to the question of whether Christ is the head of all men, Saint Thomas responds in the affirmative.

> Therefore we can say that in general throughout the history of the world, Christ is the head of all men but in different degrees. First and mainly he is the head of those who are united to him in heaven. Secondly he is head of those who are actually united with him in love. Thirdly, of those who are actually united with him in faith. But fourthly of those who are not yet actually united with him but will actually be so united according to the divine plan. Fifth, he is head of those who are potentially united with him but will never actually be so united—such as the people in this world who are not predestined. When they leave this world they cease entirely to be members of Christ since they are no longer potentially united with him. (*Summa Theologiae* III, Q.8, a.3)

Eric Voegelin has provided a contemporary formulation of this insight into the centrality of Christ by extending Plato's anthropological principle that "The polis is man written in larger letters," to "History is Christ written large" ("Immortality: Experience and Symbol," in *Published Essays,* ed. Ellis Sandoz, 78).

3. A luminous series of books by Peter Berger continues to make this point. See his *The Sacred Canopy, A Rumor of Angels,* and *A Far Glory: The Quest for Faith in an Age of Credulity.*

4. The issue has been well formulated by T. E. Jessup in his essay "The Scientific Understanding of Man."

> Knowing, the process that has to other events the unique relation of apprehending them, is above the causal order, in the sense that, although in it, it also knows it. Science as knowing transcends the scientific world; its claim to be true lifts it above the type of order its content depicts. Deny the claim and the content is worthless; admit the claim and the content is set in a larger context. Science can explain things naturally, but never itself. It cannot be true in a purely scientific world. (quoted in John Hallowell, *The Moral Foundations of Democracy,* 40)

A comical illustration of this confusion is provided in one of the letters of Charles Darwin in which he confesses his "innermost conviction" that "the universe is not the result of chance. But then with me the horrid doubt always arises whether convictions of man's mind which has developed from the mind of the animals, are of any value or at all trustworthy. Would anyone trust in the conviction of a monkey's mind, if there are any convictions in such a mind?" (letter of July 3, 1881, quoted in Francis Darwin, ed., *The Life and Letters of Charles Darwin,* 68).

5. The two most significant statements are John XXIII's *Mater et Magistra,* published in 1961, and the Second Vatican Council's 1965 *Declaration on Religious Liberty.* Most prominent in preparing this shift were undoubtedly the works of Jacques Maritain and John Courtney Murray who, in the preceding decades, had emphasized

the mutual compatability between Christianity and constitutional democracy. Not only did they maintain Christianity as the essential foundation for a democratic order, but they also asserted the Christian character of the liberal democratic construction. One of the most striking statements in Maritain's *Man and the State* concerns the American Constitution, which, he asserts, "can be described as an outstanding lay Christian document tinged with the philosophy of the day" (183). See also Murray, *We Hold These Truths: Catholic Reflections on the American Proposition*. For the opposing view that insists on the degree to which liberal democratic society fails to live up to its Christian aspirations, see Reinhold Niebuhr, *Moral Man and Immoral Society*, and an updated version in Glenn Tinder, *The Political Meaning of Christianity*.

6. It is surely unease with this inexorable political logic that is behind the popularity of Stephen Carter's *The Culture of Disbelief: How American Law and Politics Trivialize Religious Devotion*. A more considered perception of the problem is provided by Richard J. Neuhaus, *The Naked Public Square*.

> The result of subordinating free exercise to no establishment—of interpreting the separation of church and state to mean the separation of religion from public life—is to turn religion's constitutional privilege into a constitutional impediment. The result of that, in turn, has been an unnatural constriction of the democratic process by excluding from court and legislature the religiously grounded beliefs of the American people. . . . When the ultimacies, including religious ultimacies, to which the people subscribe are excluded from the public order, the state cannot resist the tempatation to get into the business of what Cassirer calls mystery and magic. This is not simply because the modern state is ambitious and possessed of the lust for power, although such dynamics should not be underestimated. It is more importantly because someone must articulate in public the meanings by which the society is given a sense of moral legitimacy and purpose. (Neuhaus, *America Against Itself: Moral Vision and the Public Order*, 45–46)

7. Mark Twain captured that supreme self-restraint in observing that it is "by the goodness of God that in our country we have those three unspeakably precious things: freedom of speech, freedom of conscience, and the prudence never to practice either of them" (*Following the Equator*, quoted in Joseph R. Conlin, *The Morrow Book of Quotations in American History*, 294).

8. A brilliant portrayal of the radical indefinability of the individual human being is furnished by Dostoyevsky's "Underground Man," a character with few moral resources except his passionate revulsion against all mathematizing attempts to categorize him *(Letters from the Underworld)*.

9. It is interesting to observe as deep and as reflective an individual as Vaclav Havel working out this central philosophical problem in the context of his prison meditations on human existence.

> I would say that the meaning of any phenomenon lies in its being anchored in something outside itself . . . . If, however, we fall to doubting, then calling in doubt these "signifying circumstances" must sooner or later lead to questioning the meaning of "life itself," that is, the meaning of the very circumstances that impart meaning. The answer, of course, cannot logically be sought "inside" the entities whose meaning we seek, that is, in the world of those relative and ephemeral contexts, but only inside "life itself": in the context of the absolute, against the absolute horizon. . . . The hidden backbone and the deepest source of everything that has meaning is always—whether we realize it or not—this "anchoredness in the absolute." (*Letters to Olga*, 242–43)

10. This is the central problem with which Eric Voegelin is engaged throughout his work. For his final reflections on it, see *In Search of Order* (vol. 5 of *Order and History*) in which he explores the transcendent ground of immanent symbols in Hesiod, Plato, and Hegel. Hesiod is illustrative of the earliest awareness of the difficulty that transcendent Being cannot be assigned any immanent symbolization without eroding its transcendent character.

> In his compact language of the myth, Hesiod expresses his insight into Remembrance as the reflective distance to the existentially ordering event in the metaxy [in-between of existence]. The reflectively distancing Mnemosyne is the dimension of consciousness in which the presence of the Beyond, experienced as the ordering force in the event, gains the reality of its Parousia in the language of the gods. The "existence" of the gods is the presence of the divine Beyond in the language symbols that express its moving Parousia in the experience of the not-experientiable ordering force in the existential event. With Hesiod, we are touching the limits of symbolization in the language of the gods: there are no gods without a Beyond of the gods. (72)

Derrida appears to have arrived belatedly at this same recognition in his "Force of Law: The 'Mystical Foundation of Authority,' " 919–1045.

11. Graham Walker has developed the Augustinian character of this transcendent foundation of constitutional order in his excellent study, *The Moral Foundations of Constitutional Thought*. He shows how the transcendent intimations of Augustinian thought can provide the indispensable context for liberal constitutional practice, although he does not explain how the latter might reach toward that enlarged spiritual perspective. The same parallel between Augustine and the liberal tradition has also been noted by the Augustinian scholar R. A. Markus, in his *Saeculum: History and Society in the Theology of St. Augustine* (especially appendix C).

12. Martin Buber is of course the proximate source for the distinction between "I-Thou" and "I-It" relationships, personal and instrumental modes of relating to the world and other persons. It is a fascinating point from which to begin reflection on the problem, although one should be cautious about accepting the conceptual distinction as definitive in life. They are pure types that may never actually coincide with the concrete richness of experience in which, for example, we rarely relate to another person in exclusively instrumental terms. See Buber's *I and Thou* and *Between Man and Man*.

13. The locus classicus for this conception of the analogy of Being is Saint Thomas Aquinas, *Summa Theologiae* I, Q.13, especially a.5, "Whether What is Said of God and of Creatures Is Univocally Predicated of Them?"

14. Derrida's deconstructionism and Rorty's pragmatism are only the latest in a line of philosophical reflection (which includes the whole analytic tradition) that fails to recognize the impossibility of breaking the link between language and reality. Simply because reality cannot be isolated apart from language, they have mistakenly concluded that language can be treated independently of its link to reality. The crucial realization is that language and reality are indissolubly linked through experience. It is the complex of consciousness-language-reality that is the constant. As Voegelin has explained:

> There is indeed no beginning to be found in this or that part of the complex; the beginning will reveal itself only if the paradox is taken seriously as the something that constitutes the complex as a whole. This complex, however, as the expansion

of equivocations shows, includes language and truth, together with consciousness and reality. There is no autonomous, nonparadoxic language, ready to be used by man as a system of signs when he wants to refer to the paradoxic structures of reality and consciousness. Words and their meanings are just as much a part of the reality to which they refer as the being things are partners in the comprehending reality; language participates in the paradox of a quest that lets reality become luminous for its truth by pursuing truth as a thing intended. This paradoxic structure of language has caused certain questions, controversies, and terminological difficulties to become constants in the philosopher's discourse since antiquity without approaching satisfactory conclusions. (*Order and History*, 5:16–17)

15. Contrary to the conservative critique of Locke and the liberal thinkers as subverters of the philosophic-revelatory tradition, they might more correctly be viewed as sustainers of the tradition through the evocation of precisely what remains viable within it. What appears from one perspective to constitute the impoverishment of a tradition, turns out from another viewpoint to be the most effective means of its preservation. This is the nuance that is most often missed in Strauss, MacIntyre, and others, although this does not preclude the conservative critics also being right on the inability of the liberal center to ultimately avoid a further dissolution.

16. Richard Ashcraft has made a very strong case for reading the *Second Treatise* as, despite its reputation as a justification for the Glorious Revolution, an aggrieved expression of a minority perspective on the constitutional deliberations that now felt itself excluded from the debate ("A Radical Manifesto, chap. 11 of *Revolutionary Politics and Locke's Two Treatises*).

17. This is the insight of Dostoyevsky whose analysis of the logic of the modern revolutionary movement attains a clarity even greater than that of Nietzsche. Where Nietzsche sees only the will to power as the motive force behind the schemes of humanitarian emancipation, Dostoyevsky perceives the tragic course of their development from idealism to an absolute morality that no longer recognizes limits. It is well explored in *Crime and Punishment* as Raskolnikov moves from utilitarian reflections to the assertion of his power as a "Napoleonic" individual, free to commit murder. The same theme is explored in the other great novels, especially through Ivan and the Inquisitor in the *Brothers Karamazov*. A twentieth-century reflection on it is provided by that exemplary philosophical meditation, Albert Camus's *The Rebel*, which exactly captures the sense of moving into a realm beyond good and evil. "The rebels, who have decided to gain their ends through violence and murder, have in vain replaced, in order to preserve the hope of existing, 'We are' by the 'We shall be' " (282).

18. See, for example, the opening reflections in Voegelin's *In Search of Order* (vol. 5 of *Order and History*), which make clear that there is no absolute starting point for philosophical reflection that is, therefore, compelled to recognize that reality is not simply an object for consciousness but "the something in which consciousness occurs as an event of participation between partners in the community of being" (15).

19. The continuing vitality, if not the resurgence, of religion at the close of the twentieth century is sufficiently well remarked to require no further comment. For a recent provocative account, see Gilles Kepel's *The Revenge of God: The Resurgence of Islam, Christianity and Judaism in the Modern World*. Less dramatically evident, but of no less significance, is the breadth and depth of scholarly recovery of the great spiritual traditions that has occurred in this century. When MacIntyre or Voegelin or Strauss or Gilson call attention to the robust character of premodern traditions,

often in contrast to the superficiality of our own conception of order, it must never be forgotten that they too are part of the modern world. Their own achievements give the lie to the claim that modern human beings are incapable of absorbing the wisdom of a Plato or Saint Thomas. If one, for example, contrasts the understanding of classical or medieval philosophy that has prevailed since the the sixteenth century, one will be inclined to conclude that we are living in the midst of one of the great periods of traditional understanding. Did Kant or Hegel evidence any genuine appreciation for the dialogues of Plato? When one adds to this such publishing ventures as the *Classics of Christian Spirituality* (published by Paulist Press) or the vast appreciation of the non-Western spiritual forms, it is difficult to resist the conclusion that we are in the midst of a veritable profusion of spiritual riches. Their impact is still relatively confined, but it is hard to imagine that it will forever remain so restricted.

20. The philosopher, in Strauss's view, is "ultimately compelled to transcend not merely the dimension of common opinion, of political opinion, but the dimension of political life as such; for he is led to realize that the ultimate aim of political life cannot be reached by political life, but only by a life devoted to contemplation, to philosophy" (*What Is Political Philosophy?* 91). Voegelin, more expansively, explains that philosophy has two functions for Plato.

> It is first, and most importantly, an act of salvation for himself and others, in that the evocation of right order and its reconstitution in his own soul becomes the substantive center of a new community which, by its existence, relieves the pressure of the surrounding corrupt society. Under this aspect Plato is the founder of the community of philosophers that lives through the ages. Philosophy is, second, an act of judgment—we remember the messenger to mankind sent from Hades by the Judges. Since the order of the soul is recaptured through resistance to the surrounding disorder, the pairs of concepts which illuminate the act of resistance develop into the criteria (in the pregnant sense of instruments or standards of judgment) of social order and disorder. Under this second aspect Plato is the founder of poltical science. (*Order and History,* 3:68–69)

See also MacIntyre, *Three Rival Versions,* 82–83.

21. The "Letters to a German Friend" (1943–1944) are available in Albert Camus, *Resistance, Rebellion, and Death,* 3–32.

22. Solzhenitsyn, *The Gulag Archipelago,* 1:559.

23. See, for example, Viktor Frankl, *Man's Search For Meaning;* Etty Hillesum, *An Interrupted Life: The Diaries of Etty Hillesum, 1941–1943;* Walter J. Ciszek, *He Leadeth Me;* Natan Sharansky, *Fear No Evil;* Irina Ratushinskaya, *Grey Is the Color of Hope;* Armando Valladares, *Against All Hope;* Nien Cheng, *Life and Death in Shanghai;* and Vaclav Havel, *Open Letter: Selected Writings, 1965–1990* and *Letters to Olga.*

24. George Parkin Grant lucidly contrasts the difference between the premodern and modern approaches to justice. "The view of traditional philosophy and religion is that justice is the overiding order which we do not measure and define, but in terms of which we are measured and defined. The view of modern thought is that justice is a way which we choose in freedom, both individually and publicly, once we have taken our fate into our own hands, and know that we are responsible for what happens" (*English-Speaking Justice,* 74).

25. Taylor seems to have a more profound appreciation of the Platonic movement toward transcendence. "For the right order in us is to be ruled by reason, which cannot come about unless reason reaches its full realization which is in the perception

of the Good; and at the same time, the perception of the Good is what makes us truly virtuous" (*Sources,* 122). Beyond this mere acknowledgment, however, Taylor seems unwilling to go; it figures not at all in his own wrestling with the structure of order within the modern self. Strauss, too, provides only a perfunctory reflection on this most central topic of the *Republic,* unable or unwilling to grapple with its inner substance. See, for example, the inconclusive puzzling about "whether the highest as Plato understands it is still properly called an idea" (*The City and Man,* 119). In contrast stands not only Voegelin's more profoundly existential and philosophical reading but also a line of great classical scholars that includes Paul Friedländer, Kurt Hildebrandt, and Werner Jaeger. The latter, for example, sees the full significance of the Ascent toward the Good.

> To replace the gods and heroes of legend, who were the models of areté in human form set up by the paideia of earlier Greece in the works of the great poets, Plato's new philosophical paideia in *The Republic* sets up divine Good as the perfect paradeigma. And thus the great saying in *Theatetus,* that the philosopher's life according to areté is "assimilation to God," becomes the noblest expression of Plato's paideia; and the connexion between the Idea of Good and the education of the philosopher in which it is to be "the greatest subject" is made perfectly plain. If God is by nature good, if in fact he is Good itself, then the highest areté attainable by man is a process of coming to resemble God. (*Paideia,* 287)

26. Charles Taylor has raised the crucial question in regard to Berlin's affirmation of negative freedom as the only one to be considered: "Once we see that we make distinctions of degree and significance in freedoms depending on the significance of the purpose fettered/enabled, how can we deny that it makes a difference to the degree of freedom not only whether one of my basic purposes is frustrated by my own desires but also whether I have grievously misidentified this purpose?" ("What's Wrong with Negative Liberty," in Taylor's *Philosophy and the Human Sciences: Philosophical Papers,* 228).

27. See, for example, Amitai Etzioni, *The Spirit of Community: Rights, Responsibilities and the Communitarian Agenda,* and Daniel Bell, *Communitarianism and Its Critics.*

28. Marx appended the following paragraph to the preface of his doctoral dissertation. "Philosophy does not make a secret of it. The confession of Prometheus: 'In one word, I hate all the gods,' is its very own confession, its own sentence against all heavenly and earthly gods who refuse to recognize human self-consciousness as the supreme divinity. And none shall be held beside it" (Karl Marx and Friedrich Engels, *Werke* Supp. Vol., pt. 1 [Berlin: Dietz, 1973], 262). As Marx explains, "for socialist man the *entire so-called history of the world* is nothing but the begetting of man through human labour . . . he has the visible, irrefutable proof of his *birth* through himself" (*Marx-Engels Reader,* ed. Robert Tucker [New York: Norton, 1978], 92). Similarly, Nietzsche's Zarathustra at a culminating moment declares his intention to "reveal my heart to you entirely, my friends: *if* there were gods, how could I endure not being a god!" (*Thus Spoke Zarathustra,* 86). In general, see Walsh, *After Ideology,* chap. 3.

29. Toward the end of *A Theory of Justice,* Rawls considers the traditional unification of goods in the highest good, God. The problem he encounters is that "if God is conceived (as surely he must be) as a moral being, then the end of serving him above all else is left unspecified to the extent that the divine intentions are

not clear from revelation, or evident from natural reason." And while Rawls seems to distinguish service of God from the pursuit of any immanent objective good as the highest, he nevertheless concludes with a blanket condemnation of all notions of a single highest good. "Human good is heterogeneous because the aims of the self are heteroegeneous. Although to subordinate all our aims to one end does not strictly speaking violate the principles of rational choice (not the counting principles anyway), it still strikes us as irrational, or more likely as mad. The self is disfigured and put in the service of one of its ends for the sake of the system" (554). What is clear is that the opening of the soul toward God plays no role in the illumination of our moral existence.

30. Voegelin, commenting on the Decalogue of Moses, observes: "The commands are not general rules of conduct but the substance of divine order to be absorbed by the souls of those who listen to the call. . . . It is framed by the firm blocks of the first and tenth commandments with their injunctions against the antitheistic rebellion of pride and the antihuman rebellion of envy. Between the two protective dams, in the middle, can move the order of the people through the rhythm of time" (*Order and History*, 1:426–27). Aristotle's *Ethics* displays a similar structure.

> The passages concerning the *spoudaios* (mature man) show very clearly that, for Aristotle, what is right by nature cannot become a set of eternal, immutable propositions, for the truth of a concrete action cannot be determined by its subsumption under a general principle but only by asking the *spoudaios*. Appeal is made, therefore, not from the action to an immutably correct principle but to the existentially right order of man. The criterion of rightly ordered human existence, however, is the permeability for the movement of being, i.e., the openness of man for the divine; the openness in its turn is not a proposition about something given but an event, and ethics is, therefore, not a body of propositions but an event of being that provides the word for a statement about itself. (Voegelin, *Anamnesis*, 65)

31. This is the whole point of Aristotle's meditation on the good for man as that which is "final and self-sufficient," that for the sake of which everything else is done. By contrast, the Spartans in their concentration on the intermediate good of military prowess and political power failed to reach the human good. "Today the Spartans have lost their empire," he observes in a poignant passage, "and we can all see for ourselves that they were not a happy community and their legislator was not right. It is indeed a strange result of his labours; here is a people which has stuck to his laws and never been hindered in carrying them out, and yet it has lost all that makes life worth living" (*Politics* 1333b18).

32. This insight is not by any means confined to the Christian horizon, for the divine forebearance is a theme in all the world religions, and the divine suffering of evil is compactly present within them. The "Songs of the Suffering Servant" of Isaiah have a generality that renders them universally compelling; their meaning is not confined to their prefiguration of the redemptive fulfillment of Christ.

Chapter 8: Meditative Expansion of Limits

1. "Natural desire cannot be empty, since *nature does nothing in vain*. But nature's desire would be empty if it could never be fulfilled. Therefore man's natural desire can be fulfilled. But not in this life, as we have shown. Therefore it must be fulfilled

after this life. Therefore man's ultimate happiness is after this life" (*Summa Contra Gentiles,* chap. 48).

2. The pattern is remarkable as one traces the numbers of contemporary commentators who have made the transition from *liberal* to *conservative,* as those terms are used in current political parlance. Perhaps the innermost circle is occupied by those individuals named *neoconservatives* to emphasize the recency of their embrace of conservative principles. This is a large and distinguished group that includes such luminaries as Irving Kristol, Norman Podhoretz, Michael Novak, Richard Neuhaus, George Gilder, William Bennet, Mary Ann Glendon, and many others. A second concentric circle is formed of even more recent arrivals at conservative conclusions that stress the more communal aspects of that tradition and are generally identified by their self-designation as "communitarians." This includes such chief promulgators as Amitai Etzioni, William Galston, Michael Sandel, Robert Bellah, and even Charles Taylor. The outermost circle contains those self-doubting liberals who might be denominated as *neoliberal* and are perhaps best represented by the successful blend of spiritual and liberal rhetoric in the Clinton administration. A particularly fine example of it is the speech delivered by Hillary Clinton in a more reflective mood at the University of Texas. She invited her audience to

> take a step back and ask ourselves, why is it in a country as economically wealthy as we are despite our economic problems, in a country that is the longest surviving democracy, there is this undercurrent of discontent—this sense that somehow economic growth and prosperity, political democracy and freedom are not enough— that we lack at some core level meaning in our individual lives and meaning collectively—that sense that our lives are part of some greater effort, that we are connected to one another, that community means that we have a place where we belong no matter who we are. And it isn't very far below the surface because we can see popping through the surface the signs of alienation and despair and hopelessness that are all too common and cannot be ignored. . . . And yet, it is not just the most violent and the most alienated that we can look to. The discontent of which I speak is broader than that, deeper than that. We are, I think, in a crisis of meaning. ("Remarks of the First Lady at Liz Carpenter's Lectureship Series," University of Texas, April 7, 1993)

3. To take one example, it is instructive to follow the progressive evisceration of the free-exercise clause of the First Amendment as it is cumulatively subordinated to the nonestablishment clause, to produce the amazing welter of confusion in the judicial treatment of religious practice and expression in the United States. See the survey in Terry Eastland, *Religious Liberty in the Supreme Court: Cases that Define the Debate over Church and State.*

4. Eldon Eisenach in *The Two Worlds of Liberalism* has fairly uncovered the peculiar inner tensions within the great liberal thinkers, a tension that he considers sufficient to describe as the experience of living in two worlds. The one is the well-known liberal picture of a society of rational "possessive individualists"; the other is the world of lawful oberservance of duties to one another and to God. It is as clearly exemplified, Eisenach finds, in the two halves of the *Leviathan* as anywhere. But what is striking is the degree to which the tension remains unproblematic within the liberal tradition almost up to the present. Perhaps no example is as telling as that of David Hume, whose radical philosophical skepticism was combined with a strongly conservative political orientation, apparently without provoking any noticeable dissociation. It is

a tradition that well illustrates Cardinal Newman's maxim: "A thousand difficulties do not make a doubt."

5. It should of course go without saying that there is nothing exclusivist about this understanding of the maximal degree of differentiation achieved within Christianity. The same themes are more or less compactly present within all the world religions and, for this reason, can provide the spiritual underpinning for the emergence of an order of liberal human rights. The degree to which such spiritual undergirding is available outside of the Christian orbit is one of the great empirical questions of contemporary politics and political science. Without prejudging the outcome of that experiment, we can observe that the most fundamental support is already available in any society imbued with a spiritual tradition. That is, that the moral order of existence does not depend on the purely human choice of values but is itself a mode of participation and submission to the order of transcendent being. From there it is not a great step to the notion of the individual who transcends the order of society and is therefore endowed with inalienable rights. This central idea is shared by all the world religions, as Karl Jaspers has shown in pointing to the discovery of universal humanity in his so called "axis-time," between 800 and 200 B.C. There is, for example, the remarkable contemporaneity of Heraclitus and Parmenides in Greece, Isaiah in Israel, Confucius and Lao-tse in China, the Buddha in India, and Zoroaster in Persia around 600 B.C. (Jaspers, *The Origin and Goal of History*). However, the capacity of the various traditions to differentiate the consequences of the transcendent constitution of humanity admits of a wide amplitude. This is why, as Lucian Pye has shown, it has been difficult for liberal democratic practices to go beyond the traditional paternalist forms of Asian societies (*Asian Power and Politics: The Cultural Dimensions of Authority*). However, the presence of even the more compact awareness of participation in transcendent order is an indispensable condition for the specific form that the liberal democractic tradition has assumed in those countries. It would be a mistake to assume that the only viable form of liberal democracy is the Anglo-American model.

6. See, for example, Stanley Hauerwas, *A Community of Character.*

7. C. S. Lewis, *That Hideous Strength*. An interesting contrast are the many accounts of the "Velvet Revolutions" of Eastern Europe by which communism simply fell apart. See, for example, George Weigel, *The Final Revolution: The Resistance of the Church and the Collapse of Communism;* and Barbara von der Heydt, *Candles behind the Wall.*

8. Who could not be impressed by the resolve of the old Russian woman who had hidden the metropolitan of the Orthodox church in his escape, but refused to yield the names of any of her collaborators to the torturers. "There is nothing you can do with me even if you cut me into pieces. After all, you are afraid of your bosses, and you are afraid of each other, and you are even afraid of killing me. . . . But I am not afraid of anything. I would be glad to be judged by God right this minute" (Solzhenitsyn, *Gulag Archipelago*, 1:131). Or there is the equally amazing account of the young girl, Etty Hillesum, who eventually grew spiritually to the point that she chose to go to the camps in order to live out her fidelity to her fellow Jews (*An Interrupted Life*).

9. Viktor Frankl, *Man's Search for Meaning*, 124.

10. One is often reminded of the distance the liberal tradition has to go to reach this realization, through the inability of the most perceptive critics to recognize it.

John Gray, to cite another example of a philosophically astute contemporary, whose self-critique of the liberal dead end is almost unmatched, cannot yet bring himself to consider seriously an alternative that would reach beyond dogmas to their source. He is even able to acknowledge "the mystical and religious context of Aristotelian, Thomist, and Lockean thought" as the crucial missing element, but does nothing to undertake its recovery himself (*Liberalism*, 261). Indeed, in his few remarks on the great tradition Gray demonstrates a shocking insensitivity to the inner character of classical philosophy. "In his response to the germs of modern liberalism present in the teachings of the Sophists, Plato elaborated one of the most systematic and powerful attacks on the idea of human freedom to be found in intellectual history" (ibid., 3).

11. Francis Canavan expressed this view succinctly when he noted that

> it is doubtful whether the typical response of the liberal pluralist society is any longer adequate, that is, to take the dangerously controversial matters out of politics and relegate them to the consciences of individuals. For this way of eliminating controversy in fact does much more. Intentionally or not, it contributes to a reshaping of basic social institutions and a revision of the moral beliefs of multitudes of individuals beyond those directly concerned. It turns into a process by which one ethos, with its reflection in law and public policy, is replaced by another. Liberal pluralism then becomes a sort of confidence game in which, in the guise of showing respect for individual rights, we are in reality asked to consent to a new kind of society based on a new set of beliefs and values. ("The Dilemma of Liberal Pluralism," 15)

12. The experience of Ireland is instructive because it arises within a much more homogeneous society than that of most of the world. Yet even passage of a right-to-life amendment appended to the Irish Constitution in 1983 could not prevent the abortion controversy from erupting into the judicial process. A rather unique case involving the travel of a rape victim to England to procure an abortion presented the opportunity for the Irish Supreme Court to interpret the amendment as tolerating abortion. A second amendment was required in 1992 to reiterate the intention of the earlier pro-life amendment, but this was now mixed with the ambiguous recognition of the right to travel to secure abortion services and access to abortion information. It is an interesting demonstration of the capacity for political and constitutional victories to evaporate in the absence of real social agreement and consensus.

13. One thinks of the horrendous social pressures marshaled by government in enforcing China's "one child" policy, although population control advocates elsewhere also always seem to have to remind themselves to avoid coercive means. It is a reminder that would hardly seem to be necessary if the temptation were not so perennial.

14. The debate surrounding the point at which the fetus becomes a person, which is the central pivot of *Roe v. Wade* since persons are constitutionally protected, seems irretrievably entangled in a category mistake. It is as if we are requiring the fetus to demonstrate to our satisfaction that it possesses the qualities of consciousness, self-concept, ability to communicate, and so on that we consider central to the constitution of a person. But we never require such a demonstration from one another. We begin with the presumption that the other is a person, that he or she is "other" and are already related to them. We know one another intersubjectively. It is impossible for a person to demonstrate to another that he is a person in any kind of definitive objective way.

15. The most notorious example is Michael Tooley, *Abortion and Infanticide*.

16. This is the issue that sparked the inconclusive efforts of the Reagan administration to extend the protections of federal civil-rights statutes to newborns with handicaps. It is noteworthy that the Indiana court that provoked the controversy had ruled, on the basis of *Roe v. Wade,* that the newborn Down's syndrome child who suffered from an intestinal blockage requiring surgery, could not be considered a person entitled to the full range of constitutional and legal protections. This was the famous "Baby Doe" case that began in 1982. For an intriguing overview of the tangled controversy, see Hadley Arkes, "Neonates and Reprobates," chap. 9 in *Beyond the Constitution*.

17. See, for example, the provocative reflections of Hans Jonas, "Against the Stream: Comments on the Definition and Redefinition of Death," in his *Philosophical Essays: From Ancient Creed to Technological Man*.

18. A contrasting meditation is provided by Mother Teresa who also laments the waste of life in abortion but connects it directly with the epidemic of violence that arises from the same degradation of human life and respect. In a Washington prayer breakfast, attended by President and Mrs. Clinton as well as by members of the cabinet, she delivered a homily that was unique in the utter simplicity of the connection she identified. In a city plagued with violence, Mother Teresa seemed almost alone in recognizing the line of responsibility. "[I]f we accept that a mother can kill even her own child, how can we tell other people not to kill one another? . . . By abortion, the mother does not learn to love, but kills even her own child to solve her problems. And, by abortion, the father is told that he does not have to take any responsibility at all for the child he has brought into the world. That father is likely to put other women into the same trouble. So abortion just leads to more abortion. Any country that accepts abortion is not teaching its people to love, but to use any violence to get what they want. This is why the greatest destroyer of love and peace is abortion" (*Crisis* [March 1994], 18).

19. A recent anthology with excellent commentaries is *Lincoln on Democracy,* ed. Mario Cuomo and Harold Holzer. For an intriguing reflection on the abortion controversy in relation to the Lincoln example, see George McKenna, "On Abortion: A Lincolnian Position."

20. The distinct lack of sensitivity to the spiritual dimensions of existence, still discernable in contemporary liberals, has a long historical lineage. It is exemplified by Guido de Ruggiero in his classic study titled *The History of European Liberalism*.

> But at bottom there is a permanent reason for this opposition, independent of all transitory facts, in the authoritarian structure of the Church, as claiming to be invested with power from above; in its doctrine of sin, redemption, and grace, implying the fallen character of human liberty and reason, and the need of external aid; and in the function which it claims, of a supernatural mediator between man and God: whereas Liberalism assumes that, without any intermediary and by his own unaided efforts, man is fully able to realize all the values of the spiritual life. (399–400)

His discussion of Leo XIII's encyclical, *Libertas Praestantissimum,* is a good example of the inability of liberals to understand what is at issue in the traditional critiques. Ruggiero is tone-deaf to Leo XIII's assertion of the need for a spiritual substance to sustain the order of individual freedom, or his warning of the dangerous unraveling tendencies as men are left entirely to decide for themselves without any authoritative exemplars. This is of course the perennial blindspot that prevents liberals from recognizing the extent to which liberalism teaches relativism. A more updated version of the anti-Christian inspiration of liberal political order is provided by Pierre Manent in *An Intellectual History of Liberalism*.

21. No more powerful expression of the self-questioning of modernity can be conceived than the necessity that has been provoked of mounting a defense of modernity. See Hans Blumenberg, *The Legitimacy of the Modern Age*.

22. Solzhenitsyn, *The Oak and the Calf*. Solzhenitsyn's work may be seen in part as a long argument with Tolstoy, asserting that it is indeed individuals who make history and that their responsibility is decisive within it.

23. A useful exercise is simply to read the opinion of the United States Supreme Court in the 1944 case *Korematsu v. U.S.* This was the case that tested the constitutionality of the World War II internment of Americans of Japanese descent in camps througout the Midwest. Justice Jackson, in his dissent, pointed out that the actions of the president and the military flew in the face of everything contained in the constitutional protection of individuals. But the Court had concluded that they were not going to stand in the way of the executive determination of the requirements for national security. What makes the case shocking in retrospect, an unease that is now only beginning to be assuaged through the award of monetary compensation, is the extent of the incarceration involved, the utter absence of any imputation of guilt, the degree to which a racially identifiable group rather than any other descendents of hostile nations were singled out, and the almost complete absence of any further discussion once a summary decision had been reached. Jackson explained in his clearheaded dissent

> I should hold that a civil court cannot be made to enforce an order which violates constitutional limitations even if it is a reasonable exercise of military authority. The courts can exercise only the judicial power, can apply only law, and must abide by the Constitution, or they cease to be civil courts and become instruments of military policy. . . . I would not lead people to rely on this Court for a review that seems to me wholly delusive. The military reasonableness of these orders can only be determined by military superiors. If the people ever let command of the war power fall into irresponsible and unscrupulous hands, the courts wield no power equal to its restraint. The chief restraint upon those who command the physical forces of the country, in the future as in the past, must be their responsibility to the political judgments of their contemporaries and to the moral judgments of history.

It is an illustration, if any were needed, of the character of bills of rights as "parchment barriers" in the absence of the profound inner convictions needed to animate them. Mary Ann Glendon has called attention to the need to preserve this inner substance of agreement from the erosion of simplistic "rights talk" that

> risks undermining the very conditions necessary for preservation of the principal value it thrusts to the foreground: personal freedom. By infiltrating the more carefully nuanced languages that many Americans still speak in their kitchens, neighborhoods, workplaces, religious communities, and union halls, it corrodes the fabric of beliefs, attitudes, and habits upon which life, liberty, property, and all other individual and social goods ultimately depend. (*Rights Talk: The Impoverishment of Political Discourse*, 15)

24. It is worth wondering whether this situation has something to do with the separation of theory and practice, reflection and action today. We live in a society where there is generally no theory from actors and no action from theorists.

25. The American transcendentalists Emerson, Thoreau, and Whitman have in their own way made that journey. George Kateb observes of them in his *The Inner Ocean: Individualism and Democratic Culture,*

> I find that the theory of democratic individuality, like some other individualisms, cultivates a sense of individual infinitude; that is, a sense of one's inner ocean, of everybody's inexhaustible internal turbulent richness and unused powers. . . . Beyond the experience at even the extraordinary level lies a rare moment, mood, or episode of transcendence. This highest level is contemplative and consequently only impersonal: an evanescent loss of the sense of one's unique self in favor of everything outside it. (34)

The limited character of their impact on the American political tradition, however, arises from the divergence of their spirituality from the traditional Christian understanding still effective within American society. The transcendentalists are the preeminent example of the necessity of concrete religious traditions to act as a guide and restraint on the more visionary Prometheanism and the blindness of self-made mystical experiences.

Bibliography

Primary Sources

Arendt, Hannah. *The Human Condition*. Chicago: University of Chicago Press, 1958.

———. *On Revolution*. New York: Viking, 1963.

———. *The Origins of Totalitarianism*. Rev. ed. New York: Harcourt Brace Jovanovich, 1968.

Berlin, Isaiah. *Four Essays on Liberty*. New York: Oxford University Press, 1969.

Camus, Albert. *The Rebel*. Trans. Anthony Bower. New York: Vintage, 1956.

———. *Resistance, Rebellion, and Death*. Trans. Justin O'Brien. New York: Vintage, 1974.

Coleridge, Samuel. *On Politics and Society*. Vol. 1 of *Coleridge's Writings*, ed. John Morrow. Princeton: Princeton University Press, 1991.

Constant, Benjamin. *Political Writings*. Trans. and ed. Biancamaria Fontana. New York: Cambridge University Press, 1988.

Dostoyevsky, Fyodor. *The Brothers Karamazov*. Trans. Constance Garnett. New York: Modern Library, 1950.

———. *The Diary of a Writer*. Trans. Boris Brasol. Santa Barbara: Peregrine Smith, 1979.

———. *Letters from the Underworld*. Trans. C. J. Hogarth. New York: Everyman, 1968.

———. *The Possessed*. Trans. Andrew MacAndrew. New York: Signet, 1962.

Dworkin, Ronald. *Law's Empire*. Cambridge: Harvard University Press, 1986.

———. *Life's Dominion: An Argument about Abortion, Euthanasia and Individual Freedom*. New York: Knopf, 1993.

————. *Taking Rights Seriously.* Cambridge: Harvard University Press, 1977.

Galston, William. *Liberal Purposes: Goods, Virtues and Diversity in the Liberal State.* New York: Cambridge University Press, 1991.

Gewirth, Alan. *Reason and Morality.* Chicago: University of Chicago Press, 1978.

Gray, John. *Liberalism.* Minneapolis: University of Minnesota Press, 1986.

————. *Liberalisms: Essays in Political Philosophy.* New York: Routledge, 1989.

Hayek, Friedrich. *The Constitution of Liberty.* Chicago: University of Chicago Press, 1960.

Hegel, Georg Wilhelm Friedrich. *Hegel Early Theological Writings.* Trans. T. M. Knox. Philadelphia: University of Pennsylvania Press, 1971.

————. *Phenomenology of Spirit.* Trans. A. V. Miller. New York: Oxford University Press, 1977.

————. *Philosophy of Mind.* Trans. William Wallace. Oxford: Clarendon Press, 1971.

————. *Philosophy of Right.* Trans. T. M. Knox. New York: Oxford University Press, 1967.

————. *Sämtliche Werke. Jubiliaumausgabe.* Ed. Hermann Glockner. Stuttgart: Frommann, 1927–1930.

Hobbes, Thomas. *Behemoth or the Long Parliament.* Ed. Stephen Holmes. Chicago: University of Chicago Press, 1990.

————. *The English Works of Thomas Hobbes.* Ed. William Molesworth. 11 vols. London: Bohn, 1839–1845.

————. *Leviathan.* Ed. C. B. Macpherson. Harmondsworth: Penguin, 1968.

————. *Man and Citizen (De Homine and De Cive).* Ed. Bernard Gert. Indianapolis: Hackett, 1991.

Hooker, Richard. *Of the Laws of Ecclesiastical Polity.* Ed. Arthur Stephen McGrade. New York: Cambridge University Press, 1989.

Kant, Immanuel. *Critique of Practical Reason.* Trans. Lewis W. Beck. New York: Liberal Arts, 1956.

————. *Groundwork of the Metaphysic of Morals.* Trans. H. J. Paton. London: Hutchinson, 1948.

————. *Political Writings.* Ed. Hans Reiss and trans. H. B. Nisbet. New York: Cambridge University Press, 1970.

————. *Werke.* Ed. Wilhelm Weischedel. Wiesbaden: Insel, 1956–1964.

Lewis, C. S. *The Abolition of Man.* London: MacMillan, 1947.

————. *That Hideous Strength.* 1946. Reprint, New York: Macmillian, 1986.

Locke, John. *An Essay Concerning Human Understanding.* Ed. P. H. Nidditch. Oxford: Clarendon Press, 1979.

————. *Essays on the Law of Nature*. Ed. W. von Leyden. Oxford: Clarendon Press, 1954.

————. *John Locke: Two Treatises of Government*. Ed. Peter Laslett. New York: Cambridge University Press, 1963.

————. *A Letter Concerning Toleration*. Indianapolis: Bobbs-Merrill, 1955.

————. *A Paraphrase and Notes on the Epistles of St. Paul*. Ed. Arthur Wainwright. 2 vols. Oxford: Clarendon Press, 1987.

————. *Political Writings of John Locke*. Ed. David Wooten. New York: Mentor, 1993.

————. *The Reasonableness of Christianity*. Ed. and abridged by I. T. Ramsey. Stanford: Stanford University Press, 1958.

————. *The Reasonableness of Christianity*. Ed. George W. Ewing. Washington: Regnery, 1965.

————. *Some Thoughts Concerning Education*. Ed. John W. Yolton and Jean S. Yolton. Oxford: Clarendon Press, 1989.

————. *The Works of John Locke*. 10 vols. London: Thomas Tegg, 1823.

MacIntyre, Alasdair. *After Virtue*. 2d ed. Notre Dame: University of Notre Dame Press, 1984.

————. *Three Rival Versions of Moral Inquiry*. Notre Dame: University of Notre Dame Press, 1990.

————. *Whose Justice? Which Rationality?* Notre Dame: University of Notre Dame Press, 1988.

Madison, James, Alexander Hamilton, and John Jay. *The Federalist Papers*. New York: Mentor, 1961.

Maritain, Jacques. *Christianity and Democracy and the Rights of Man and Natural Law*. Trans. Doris Anson. San Francisco: Ignatius Press, 1986.

————. *Man and the State*. Chicago: University of Chicago Press, 1951.

————. *The Person and the Common Good*. Trans. John J. Fitzgerald. Notre Dame: University of Notre Dame Press, 1966.

Mill, John Stuart. *Autobiography*. Ed. John M. Robson. New York: Penguin, 1989.

————. *Essays on Ethics, Religion and Society*. Vol. 10 of *Collected Works of John Stuart Mill*, ed. J. M. Robson. Toronto: University of Toronto Press, 1969.

————. Introduction to *Democracy in America,* by Alexis de Tocqueville. New York: Schocken, 1961.

————. *The Logic of the Moral Sciences*. London: Duckworth, 1987.

————. *On Liberty*. Ed. David Spitz. Norton Critical Edition. New York: Norton, 1975.

———. *On Liberty and Other Essays.* Ed. John Gray. New York: Oxford University Press, 1991.

———. *Principles of Political Economy.* Ed. Donald Winch. Bks. 4 and 5. London: Penguin, 1970.

———. *Theism.* Ed. Richard Taylor. Indianapolis: Bobbs-Merrill, 1957.

Montesquieu, Charles de Secondat. *The Spirit of the Laws.* Trans. and ed. Anne M. Cohler, Basia C. Miller, and Harold S. Stone. New York: Cambridge University Press, 1989.

Nietzsche, Friedrich. *The Gay Science.* Trans. Walter Kaufmann. New York: Vintage, 1974.

———. *Thus Spoke Zarathustra.* Trans. Walter Kaufmann. New York: Penguin, 1978.

———. *Twilight of the Idols.* In *The Portable Nietzsche.* Trans. and ed. Walter Kaufmann. New York: Viking, 1968.

———. *The Will to Power.* Trans. Walter Kaufmann. New York: Vintage, 1967.

Nozick, Robert. *Anarchy, State and Utopia.* New York: Basic, 1974.

———. *The Examined Life.* New York: Simon and Schuster, 1989.

Oakeshott, Michael. *Experience and Its Modes.* New York: Cambridge University Press, 1986.

———. *Hobbes on Civil Association.* Berkeley and Los Angeles: University of California Press, 1975.

———. *On Human Conduct.* Oxford: Clarendon Press, 1975.

———. *Rationalism and Politics.* Rev. ed. Indianapolis: Liberty Press, 1991.

Rawls, John. "Justice as Fairness: Political Not Metaphysical." *Philosophy and Public Affairs* 14 (1985): 223–51.

———. *Political Liberalism.* New York: Columbia University Press, 1993.

———. *A Theory of Justice.* Cambridge: Harvard University Press, 1971.

Rorty, Richard. *Consequences of Pragmatism.* Minneapolis: University of Minnesota Press, 1982.

———. *Contingency, Irony, and Solidarity.* New York: Cambridge University Press, 1989.

———. "The Priority of Democracy to Philosophy." In *The Virginia Statute for Religious Freedom,* ed. Merrill Peterson and Robert C. Vaughan, 257–82. New York: Cambridge University Press, 1988.

Rousseau, Jean-Jacques. *Emile.* Trans. Allan Bloom. New York: Basic, 1979.

———. *The First Discourse.* Ed. and trans. Victor Gourevitch. New York: Harper, 1990.

——. *The Government of Poland.* Trans. Wilmoore Kendall. Indianapolis: Hackett, 1985.

——. *Oeuvres complètes.* 4 vols. Bibliotheque de la Pléiade. Paris: Gallimard, 1959–1964.

——. *Reveries of the Solitary Walker.* Trans. Peter France. New York: Penguin, 1979.

——. *Rousseau's Political Writings.* Ed. Alan Ritter. New York: Norton, 1988.

——. *The Second Discourse.* Ed. and trans. Victor Gourevitch. New York: Harper, 1990.

Stout, Jeffrey. *Ethics after Babel.* Boston: Beacon, 1988.

Strauss, Leo. *The City and Man.* Reprint, Chicago: University of Chicago Press, 1964.

Taylor, Charles. *The Ethics of Authenticity.* Cambridge: Harvard University Press, 1992.

——. *Hegel.* New York: Cambridge University Press, 1975.

——. *Philosophy and the Human Sciences: Philosophical Papers.* Vol. 2. New York: Cambridge University Press, 1985.

——. *Sources of the Self.* Cambridge: Harvard University Press, 1989.

Tocqueville, Alexis de. *De la démocratie en Amérique.* Historical-critical edition revised and augmented by Eduardo Nolla. 2 vols. Paris: Vrin, 1990.

——. *Democracy in America.* Trans. Henry Reeve. Revised and corrected by Francis Bowen and Phillips Bradley. 2 vols. New York: Vintage, 1956, 1958.

——. *Oeuvres, papiers et correspondence.* Ed. J.-P. Mayer. 18 vols. Paris: Gallimard, 1951–1986.

——. *The Old Regime and the French Revolution.* Trans. Stuart Gilbert. Garden City, N.Y.: Doubleday, 1955.

——. *Recollections: The French Revolution of 1848.* Ed. J. P. Mayer and A. P. Kerr. Trans. George Lawrence. New Brunswick, N.J.: Transaction, 1987.

Voegelin, Eric. *Anamnesis.* Trans. Gerhart Niemayer. Notre Dame: University of Notre Dame Press, 1978.

——. *From Enlightenment to Revolution.* Ed. John Hallowell. Durham: Duke University Press, 1975.

——. "Liberalism and Its History." *Review of Politics* 37 (1974): 504–20.

——. *The New Science of Politics.* Chicago: University of Chicago Press, 1952.

————. *Order and History*. Vols. 1, 2, and 5. Baton Rouge: Louisiana State University Press, 1956, 1957, 1987.

————. *Published Essays*. Ed. Ellis Sandoz. Baton Rouge: Louisiana State University Press, 1990.

————. *Science, Politics and Gnosticism*. Chicago: Regnery, 1968.

————. *What Is History and Other Late Unpublished Essays*. Ed. Thomas Hollweck and Paul Caringella. Baton Rouge: Louisiana State University Press, 1990.

Secondary Sources

Ackerman, Bruce. *Social Justice in the Liberal State*. New Haven: Yale University Press, 1981.

————. "Why Dialogue?" *Journal of Philosophy* 86:1 (1989): 16.

Arkes, Hadley. *Beyond the Constitution*. Princeton: Princeton University Press, 1990.

Ashcraft, Richard. "Faith and Knowledge in Locke's Philosophy." In *John Locke: Problems and Perspectives,* ed. John W. Yolton. Cambridge: Cambridge University Press, 1969.

————. *Revolutionary Politics and Locke's Two Treatises of Government*. Princeton: Princeton University Press, 1986.

Avineri, Shlomo. *Hegel's Theory of the Modern State*. New York: Cambridge University Press, 1972.

Babbit, Irving. *Rousseau and Romanticism*. Cleveland: Meridian, 1964.

Barthes, Roland. *Critique et Verité*. Paris: Editions du Seuil, 1966.

Basler, Roy B., ed. *The Collected Works of Abraham Lincoln*. Vol. 4. New Brunswick, N.J.: Rutgers University Press, 1953.

Beik, Paul H., ed. *The French Revolution*. New York: Walker, 1978.

Bell, Daniel. *Communitarianism and Its Critics*. New York: Oxford University Press, 1993.

Bellah, Robert, et al. *Habits of the Heart: Individualism and Commitment in American Life*. New York: Harper, 1985.

Bentham, Jeremy. "Anarchical Fallacies: Being an Examination of the Declaration of Rights Issued during the French Revolution." In *Nonsense upon Stilts,* ed. Jeremy Waldron, 46–76. New York: Methuen, 1987.

Berger, Brigitte, and Peter Berger. *The War over the Family*. Garden City, N.Y.: Doubleday, 1983.

Berger, Peter. *A Far Glory: The Quest for Faith in an Age of Credulity*. New York: Doubleday, 1992.

————. *A Rumor of Angels*. Garden City, N.Y.: Doubleday, 1969.

————. *A Sacred Canopy*. Garden City, N.Y.: Doubleday, 1967.

Berman, Harold. *Law and Revolution: The Formation of the Western Legal Tradition*. Cambridge: Harvard University Press, 1983.

Berns, Walter. *The First Amendment and the Future of American Democracy*. Chicago: Gateway, 1985.

Blumenberg, Hans. *The Legitimacy of the Modern Age*. Trans. Robert Wallace. Cambridge: Massachusetts Institute of Technology, 1983.

Bobbio, Norberto. *Thomas Hobbes and the Natural Law Tradition*. Trans. Daniela Gobetti. Chicago: University of Chicago Press, 1993.

Bodin, Jean. *Colloquium of the Seven about the Secrets of the Sublime*. Trans. M. L. D. Kuntz. Princeton: Princeton University Press, 1975.

Buber, Martin. *Between Man and Man*. Trans. R. G. Smith. London: Collins, 1947.

————. *I and Thou*. Edinburgh: Clark, 1923.

Burke, Edmund. *Reflections on the Revolution in France*. Indianapolis: Bobbs-Merrill, 1955.

Butler, Gregory. *In Search of the American Spirit: The Political Thought of Orestes Brownson*. Carbondale: Southern Illinois University Press, 1992.

Callahan, Daniel. *Setting Limits: Medical Goals in an Aging Society*. New York: Simon and Schuster, 1984.

Canavan, Francis. "The Dilemma of Liberal Pluralism." *Human Life Review* 5 (1979): 5–16.

Caputo, John. "Hyperbolic Justice: Mythologizing Differently with Derrida and Levinas." In *Demythologizing Heidegger*, 186–231. Bloomington: Indiana University Press, 1993.

Carter, Stephen. *The Culture of Disbelief: How American Law and Politics Trivialize Religious Devotion*. New York: Basic, 1993.

Cheng, Nien. *Life and Death in Shanghai*. New York: Grove Press, 1987.

The Church Speaks to the Modern World: The Social Teachings of Leo XIII. Ed. Etienne Gilson. Garden City, N.Y.: Doubleday, 1954.

Ciszek, Walter J. *He Leadeth Me*. Garden City, N.Y.: Doubleday, 1973.

Clark, Jonathan. *The Language of Liberty, 1660–1832*. New York: Cambridge University Press, 1994.

Coleman, Janet. "*Dominium* in Thirteenth- and Fourteenth-Century Political Thought and Its Seventeenth-Century Heirs: John of Paris and Locke." *Political Studies* 33 (1985): 73–100.

Conlin, Joseph R. *The Morrow Book of Quotations in American History*. New York: McMorrow, 1984.

Conquest, Robert. *Stalin: Breaker of Nations*. New York: Viking, 1991.

Cooper, Barry. *Action into Nature*. Notre Dame: University of Notre Dame Press, 1992.

————. *The End of History: An Essay on Modern Hegelianism*. Toronto: University of Toronto Press, 1984.

Cowling, Maurice. *Mill and Liberalism*. 2d ed. New York: Cambridge University Press, 1990.

Cranston, Maurice. *Jean-Jacques: The Early Life and Work of Jean-Jacques Rousseau, 1712–1754.* Chicago: University of Chicago Press, 1983.

———. *John Locke: A Biography*. New York: Oxford University Press, 1985.

———. *The Noble Savage: Jean-Jacques Rousseau, 1754–1762*. Chicago: University of Chicago Press, 1991.

Cuomo, Mario, and Harold Holzer, eds. *Lincoln on Democracy*. New York: Harper Collins, 1990.

Dangerfield, George. *The Strange Death of Liberal England, 1910–1914.* 1935. Reprint, New York: Perigree, 1980.

Darwin, Francis, ed. *The Life and Letters of Charles Darwin*. New York: Appleton, 1896.

Derrida, Jacques. "Force of Law: The 'Mystical Foundations of Authority.' " *Cardozo Law Review* 11 (1990): 919–1045.

Devlin, Patrick. *The Enforcement of Morals*. New York: Oxford University Press, 1965.

Dewey, John. *A Common Faith*. New Haven: Yale University Press, 1934.

———. *Freedom and Culture*. 1939. Reprint, New York: Capricorn, 1963.

———. *Individualism Old and New*. 1929. Reprint, New York: Capricorn, 1962.

———. *Liberalism and Social Action*. 1935. Reprint, New York: Capricorn, 1963.

Dickey, Lawrence. *Hegel: Religion, Economics and the Politics of Spirit, 1770–1807*. New York: Cambridge University Press, 1987.

Dodge, Guy. *Benjamin Constant's Philosophy of Liberalism: A Study in Politics and Religion*. Chapel Hill: University of North Carolina Press, 1980.

Douglas, R. Bruce, Gerald M. Mara, and Henry S. Richardson, eds. *Liberalism and the Good*. New York: Routledge, 1990.

Dunn, John. *The Political Thought of John Locke*. Cambridge: Cambridge University Press, 1969.

Dworetz, Steven M. *The Unvarnished Doctrine: Locke, Liberalism and the American Revolution*. Durham: Duke University Press, 1990.

Eastland, Terry. *Religious Liberty in the Supreme Court: Cases That Define the Debate over Church and State*. Washington, D.C.: Ethics and Public Policy Center, 1993.

Edwards, Jonathan. *A Treatise Concerning Religious Affections*. Ed. John E. Smith. Vol. 1 of *The Works of Jonathan Edwards*. New Haven: Yale University Press, 1959.

Ehrenfeld, David. *The Arrogance of Humanism*. New York: Oxford University Press, 1978.

Eisenach, Eldon. *Two Worlds of Liberalism: Religion and Politics in Hobbes, Locke and Mill.* Chicago: University of Chicago Press, 1981.

Eliot, T. S. *The Idea of a Christian Society.* New York: Harcourt, Brace, 1940.

Ellul, Jacques. *The Technological Society.* Trans. John Wilkinson. 1954. Reprint, New York: Vintage, 1964.

Etzioni, Amitai. *The Spirit of Community: Rights, Responsibilities and the Communitarian Agenda.* New York: Crown, 1993.

Flatham, Richard E. *The Philosophy and Politics of Freedom.* Chicago: University of Chicago Press, 1987.

———. *Toward a Liberalism.* Ithaca: Cornell University Press, 1989.

Franco, Paul. *The Political Philosophy of Michael Oakeshott.* New Haven: Yale University Press, 1990.

Frankl, Viktor. *Man's Search for Meaning.* Trans. Ilse Lasch. New York: Washington Square, 1983.

Fukuyama, Francis. "The End of History?" *National Interest* 16 (summer 1989): 3–18.

———. *The End of History and the Last Man.* New York: Free Press, 1992.

Gadamer, Hans Georg. *Truth and Method.* Trans. Joel Weinsheimer and David G. Marshall. 2d rev. ed. New York: Crossroad, 1989.

George, Robert P. *Making Men Moral: Civil Liberties and Public Morality.* New York: Oxford University Press, 1993.

Glendon, Mary Ann. *Rights Talk: The Impoverishment of Political Discourse.* New York: Free Press, 1991.

Goldstein, Doris S. *Trial of Faith: Religion and Politics in Tocqueville's Thought.* New York: Elsevier, 1975.

Grant, George Parkin. *English-Speaking Justice.* 1974. Reprint, Notre Dame: University of Notre Dame Press, 1985.

———. *Technology and Justice.* Notre Dame: Univeristy of Notre Dame Press, 1986.

Guenon, René. *The Reign of Quantity and the Signs of the Times.* Baltimore: Penguin, 1972.

Hallowell, John. *Decline of Liberalism as an Ideology.* Berkeley and Los Angeles: University of California Press. 1943.

———. *The Moral Foundation of Democracy.* Chicago: University of Chicago Press, 1954.

Harris, H. S. *Hegel's Development: Night Thoughts.* Oxford: Clarendon Press, 1983.

———. *Hegel's Development toward the Sunlight, 1770–1801.* Oxford: Clarendon Press, 1973.

Hauerwas, Stanley. *A Community of Character.* Notre Dame: University of Notre Dame Press, 1981.

Havel, Vaclav. *Letters to Olga.* Trans. Paul Wilson. London: Faber, 1988.

——. "The Power of the Powerless." In *Open Letters: Selected Writings, 1965–1990,* ed. Paul Wilson, 125–214. New York: Vintage, 1992.

Heidegger, Martin. " 'Only a God Can Save Us': The *Spiegel* Interview (1966)." In *Heidegger: The Man and the Thinker,* ed. Thomas Sheehan, 45–67. Chicago: Precedent, 1981.

——. *The Question Concerning Technology and Other Essays.* Trans. William Lovitt. New York: Harper and Row, 1977.

Hill, Christopher. *The World Turned Upside Down: Radical Ideas during the English Revolution.* Harmondsworth: Penguin, 1975.

Hillesum, Etty. *An Interrupted Life.* New York: Pantheon Books, 1983.

Himmelfarb, Gertrude. *On Liberty and Liberalism: The Case of John Stuart Mill.* New York: Knopf, 1974.

Hobhouse, L. T. *Liberalism.* 1911. Reprint, New York: Oxford University Press, 1964.

Holmes, Stephen. *Benjamin Constant and the Making of Modern Liberalism.* New Haven: Yale University Press, 1984.

Hume, David. *David Hume: Writings on Religion.* Ed. Antony Flew. La Salle, Ill.: Open Court, 1992.

——. "Of the Rise and Progress of the Arts and Sciences." in *Essays Moral, Political and Literary,* ed. Eugene Miller, 111–37. Indianapolis: Liberty Press, 1987.

——. *A Treatise of Human Nature.* 2 vols. New York: Dutton, 1968.

Hunter, James Davidson. *Culture Wars: The Struggle to Define America.* New York: Basic, 1991.

Jaeger, Werner. *Paideia.* Trans. Gilbert Highet. Vol. 2. New York: Oxford University Press, 1943.

Jardin, André. *Tocqueville: A Biography.* Trans. L. Davis with H. Hemenway. New York: Farrar, Strauss and Giroux, 1988.

Jaspers, Karl. *The Origin and Goal of History.* Trans. Michael Bullock. London: Routledge and Kegan Paul, 1953.

Jefferson, Thomas. *Notes on the State of Virginia.* Chaps. 17 and 18. 1787.

Jonas, Hans. "Against the Stream: Comments on the Definition and Redefinition of Death." In his *Philosophical Essays: From Ancient Creed to Technological Man,* 132–40. Englewood Cliffs, N.J.: Prentice Hall, 1974.

Kahan, Alan. *Aristocratic Liberalism: The Social and Political Thought of Jacob Burckhardt, John Stuart Mill, and Alexis de Tocqueville.* New York: Oxford University Press, 1992.

Kass, Leon. "The New Biology: What Price 'Relieving Man's Estate'?" In *Toward a More Natural Science.* New York: Macmillan, 1984.

Kateb, George. *The Inner Ocean: Individualism and Democratic Culture.* Ithaca: Cornell University Press, 1992.

Kelly, George Armstrong. *Idealism, Politics and History: Sources of Hegelian Thought.* London: Cambridge University Press, 1969.

————. *Politics and Religious Consciousness in America.* New Brunswick, N.J.: Transaction, 1984.

Kendall, Wilmoor. *John Locke and the Doctrine of Majority Rule.* Urbana: University of Illinois Press, 1965.

————. "The 'Open Society' and Its Fallacies." *American Political Science Review* 54 (1960): 972–79.

Kepel, Gilles. *The Revenge of God: The Resurgence of Islam, Christianity and Judaism in the Modern World.* University Park: Pennsylvania State University Press, 1993.

Kirk, Russell. *The Conservative Mind: From Burke to Eliot.* 1953. Reprint, Chicago: Regnery, 1978.

Kojève, Alexandre. *Introduction à la lecture de Hegel.* Paris: Gallimard, 1947.

Kraynak, Robert. *History and Modernity in the Thought of Thomas Hobbes.* Ithaca: Cornell University Press, 1990.

Labedz, Leopold, ed. *Solzhenitsyn: A Documentary Record.* Harmondsworth: Penguin, 1974.

Laslett, Peter. Introduction to *John Locke: Two Treatises of Government.* Cambridge: Cambridge University Press, 1988.

Lawler, Peter. *The Restless Mind: Alexis de Tocqueville on the Origin and Perpetuation of Human Liberty.* Lanham, Md.: Rowman and Littlefield, 1993.

Lee, Sang Hyun. *The Philosophical Theology of Jonathan Edwards.* Princeton: Princeton University Press, 1988.

Levinson, Sanford. *Constitutional Faith.* Princeton: Princeton University Press, 1988.

Löwith, Karl. *From Hegel to Nietzsche.* Trans. David E. Green. Garden City, N.Y.: Doubleday, 1967.

Lubac, Henri de. *The Drama of Atheist Humanism.* Trans. Edith M. Riley. New York: New American Library, 1950.

Macedo, Stephen. *Liberal Virtues.* Oxford: Clarendon Press, 1990.

MacPherson, C. B. *The Political Theory of Possessive Individualism: Hobbes to Locke.* Oxford: Clarendon Press, 1962.

Mahlia, Martin. *The Soviet Tragedy: A History of Socialism in Russia.* New York: Free Press, 1994.

Manent, Pierre. *An Intellectual History of Liberalism.* Trans. Rebecca Balinski. Princeton: Princeton University Press, 1994.

Markus, R. A. *Saeculum: History and Society in the Theology of St. Augustine.* New York: Cambridge University Press, 1970.

Marshall, John. *John Locke: Resistance, Religion and Responsibility.* New York: Cambridge University Press, 1994.

Martinich, A. P. *The Two Gods of "Leviathan": Thomas Hobbes on Religion and Politics.* New York: Cambridge University Press, 1992.

Marx, Karl. *Marx-Engels Reader.* Ed. Robert Tucker. New York: Norton, 1978.

McKenna, George. "On Abortion: A Lincolnian Position." *Atlantic Monthly* 276 (September 1995): 51–68.

Mitchell, Joshua. *Not by Reason Alone: Religion, History and Identity in Early Modern Political Thought.* Chicago: University of Chicago Press, 1993.

Mochulsky, Konstantin. *Dostoevsky: His Life and Work.* Trans. Michael Minihan. Princeton: Princeton University Press, 1967.

Murray, John Courtney. *We Hold These Truths: Catholic Reflections on the American Proposition.* 1960. Reprint, Garden City, N.Y.: Doubleday, 1964.

Neuhaus, Richard John. *America against Itself: Moral Vision and the Public Order.* Notre Dame: University of Notre Dame Press, 1992.

———. *The Catholic Moment: The Paradox of the Church in the Postmodern World.* San Francisco: Harper and Row, 1987.

———. *The Naked Public Square.* Grand Rapids: Eerdmans, 1984.

———. "The Return of Eugenics." *Commentary* 85 (1988): 15–26.

Newman, John Henry. *Apologia Pro Vita Sua.* Ed. David J. DeLaura. New York: Norton, 1968.

Niebuhr, Reinhold. *Moral Man and Immoral Society.* New York: Scribner's, 1932.

Novak, Michael. *The Spirit of Democratic Capitalism.* New York: Simon and Schuster, 1982.

Novalis. "Christendom or Europe." In *Hymns to the Night and Other Selected Writings,* trans. Charles E. Passage. Indianapolis: Bobbs-Merrill, 1960.

O'Regan, Cyril. *The Heterodox Hegel.* Albany: State University of New York Press, 1994.

Pangle, Thomas. *The Spirit of Modern Republicanism: The Moral Vision of the American Founders and the Philosophy of Locke.* Chicago: University of Chicago Press, 1988.

Pelczynski, Z. A. Introduction to *Hegel's Political Writings.* Oxford: Clarendon Press, 1964.

———, ed. *The State and Civil Society.* New York: Cambridge University Press, 1984.

Polanyi, Michael. *The Logic of Liberty.* Chicago: University of Chicago Press, 1951.

Popper, Karl. *The Open Society and Its Enemies.* 2 vols. London: Routledge and Kegan Paul, 1972.

Powell, John. *Abortion: The Silent Holocaust.* Allen, Tex.: Argus, 1981.

Pye, Lucian. *Asian Power and Politics: The Cultural Dimensions of Authority.* Cambridge: Harvard University Press, 1985.

Ratushinskaya, Irina. *Grey Is the Color of Hope.* Trans. Alyona Kojevnikov. New York: Knopf, 1988.

Raz, Joseph. *The Morality of Freedom.* Oxford: Clarendon Press, 1986.

Redwood, John. *Reason, Ridicule and Religion.* London: Thames and Hudson, 1976.

Riley, Patrick. *The General Will before Rousseau.* Princeton: Princeton University Press, 1986.

————. *Will and Political Legitimacy: A Critical Exposition of Social Contract Theory in Hobbes, Lock, Rousseau, Kant and Hegel.* Princeton: Princeton University Press, 1982.

Ritter, Joachim. *Hegel and the French Revolution.* Trans. R. Winfield. Cambridge: Massachusetts Institute of Technology Press, 1982.

Rose, Paul Lawrence. *Bodin and the Great God of Nature: The Moral and Religious Universe of a Judaizer.* Geneva: Droz, 1980.

Ruggiero, Guido de. *The History of European Liberalism.* Trans. R. G. Collingwood. London: Oxford University Press, 1927.

Ryn, Claes. *Democracy and the Ethical Life.* Washington: Catholic University of America Press, 1989.

Sandel, Michael. *Democracy's Discontent: America in Search of a Public Philosophy.* New York: Free Press, 1996.

————. *Liberalism and the Limits of Justice.* New York: Cambridge University Press, 1982.

————. "The Procedural Republic and the Unencumbered Self." *Political Theory* 12 (1984).

Sandoz, Ellis. *A Government of Laws.* Baton Rouge: Louisiana State University Press, 1990.

————. *Political Apocalypse: A Study of Dostoevsky's Grand Inquisitor.* Baton Rouge: Louisiana State University Press, 1971.

————, ed. *Political Sermons of the American Founding, 1730–1805.* 2 vols. Indianapolis: Liberty Press, 1990.

Schouls, Peter A. *Reasoned Freedom: John Locke and the Enlightenment.* Ithaca: Cornell University Press, 1992.

Sharansky, Natan. *Fear No Evil.* Trans. Stefani Hoffman. New York: Random House, 1988.

Skinner, B. F. *Beyond Freedom and Dignity.* New York: Knopf, 1971.

Skinner, Quentin. *The Foundations of Modern Political Thought.* 2 vols. Cambridge: Cambridge University Press, 1978.

————. *Reason and Rhetoric in the Philosophy of Hobbes.* New York: Cambridge University Press, 1996.

Smith, Steven B. *Hegel's Critique of Liberalism*. Chicago: University of Chicago Press, 1989.

Solzhenitsyn, Alexander. *Detente: Prospects for Democracy and Dictatorship*. New Brunswick, N.J.: Transaction, 1980.

———. *The Gulag Archipelago*. Trans. Thomas Whitney. 3 vols. New York: Harper and Row, 1974–1978.

———. *The Oak and the Calf*. Trans. Harry Willets. New York: Harper and Row, 1979.

———. *A World Split Apart*. Trans. I. I. Alberti. New York: Harper and Row, 1978.

———, ed. *From under the Rubble*. Chicago: Regnery Gateway, 1981.

Spellman, W. M. *John Locke and the Problem of Depravity*. Oxford: Clarendon Press, 1988.

Starobinski, Jean. *Jean-Jacques Rousseau: Transparency and Obstruction*. Trans. Arthur Goldhammer. Chicago: University of Chicago Press, 1988.

Stoner, James. *The Common Law and Liberal Theory*. Lawrence: University of Kansas Press, 1992.

Strauss, Leo. *Natural Right and History*. Chicago: University of Chicago Press, 1953.

———. *The Political Philosophy of Hobbes*. Trans. Elsa Sinclair. Oxford: Clarendon Press, 1936.

———. *What is Political Philosophy?* Reprint, Chicago: University of Chicago Press, 1959.

Talmon, Jacob. *The Origins of Totalitarian Democracy*. New York: Norton, 1970.

Tarcov, Nathan. *Locke's Education for Liberty*. Chicago: University of Chicago Press, 1984.

Thomas Aquinas, Saint. Selections from the *Summa Theologiae* and *De Regimine Principium*. In *Saint Thomas Aquinas on Law, Morality and Politics*, ed. William Baumgarth and Richard Regan, 263–71. Indianapolis: Hackett, 1988.

Tinder, Glenn. *The Political Meaning of Christianity*. San Francisco: Harper Collins, 1990.

Tooley, Michael. *Abortion and Infanticide*. New York: Oxford University Press, 1983.

Tuck, Richard. *Natural Rights Theories: Their Origin and Development*. New York: Cambridge University Press, 1979.

Tully, James. *An Approach to Political Philosophy: Locke in Contexts*. New York: Cambridge University Press, 1993.

———. *A Discourse on Property: John Locke and His Adversaries*. Cambridge: Cambridge University Press, 1980.

————, ed. *Meaning and Context: Quentin Skinner and His Critics.* Princeton: Princeton University Press, 1988.

Valladares, Armando. *Against All Hope.* Trans. Andrew Hurley. New York: Ballantine, 1986.

von der Heydt, Barbara. *Candles behind the Wall.* Grand Rapids: Eerdmans, 1993.

Walker, Graham. *The Moral Foundations of Constitutional Thought.* Princeton: Princeton University Press, 1990.

Wallace, Dewey D. "Socinianism, Justification by Faith, and the Sources of John Locke's 'The Reasonableness of Christianity.'" *Journal of the History of Ideas* (1984): 49–66.

Walsh, David. *After Ideology: Recovering the Spiritual Foundations of Freedom.* San Francisco: Harper Collins, 1990.

————. "The Ambiguity of the Hegelian End of History." In *After History: Frances Fukuyama and His Critics,* ed. Timothy Burns, 171–95. Lanham, Md.: Rowman, Allen and Littlefield, 1994.

————. "The Historical Dialectic of Spirit: Jacob Boehme's Influence on Hegel." In *History and System: Hegel's Philosophy of History,* ed. Robert Perkins, 15–35. Albany: State University of New York Press, 1984.

Walzer, Michael. *Spheres of Justice.* New York: Basic, 1983.

Weigel, George. *The Final Revolution: The Resistance of the Church and the Collapse of Communism.* New York: Oxford University Press, 1992.

Wittgenstein, Ludwig. *Tractatus Logio-Philosophicus.* Trans. D. F. Pears and B. F. McGuiness. London: Routledge and Kegan Paul, 1961.

Yolton, John. *Locke and French Materialism.* Oxford: Clarendon Press, 1991.

Index